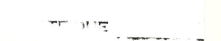

SMITHSONIAN INSTITUTION

BUREAU OF AMERICAN ETHNOLOGY

BULLETIN 183

SENECA THANKSGIVING RITUALS

By WALLACE L. CHAFE

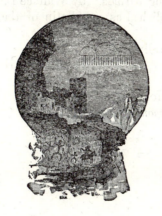

UNITED STATES

GOVERNMENT PRINTING OFFICE

WASHINGTON : 1961

For sale by the Superintendent of Documents, U.S. Government Printing Office
Washington 25, D.C. - Price $2.25 (cloth)

LETTER OF TRANSMITTAL

Smithsonian Institution,
Bureau of American Ethnology,
Washington, D.C., December 28, 1960.

Sir: I have the honor to transmit herewith a manuscript entitled "Seneca Thanksgiving Rituals," by Wallace L. Chafe, and to recommend that it be published as a bulletin of the Bureau of American Ethnology.

Very respectfully yours,

Frank H. H. Roberts, Jr.,
Director.

Dr. Leonard Carmichael,
Secretary, Smithsonian Institution.

II

CONTENTS

III

CONTENTS

iii

SENECA THANKSGIVING RITUALS

By Wallace L. Chafe

INTRODUCTION

Presented in this work are two ceremonial texts in the Seneca language with translations and grammatical commentary. Transcriptions of songs that are performed in conjunction with one of the texts are also given. The title of a work is rarely an adequate description of its contents, and all three words of the present title call for elaboration here.

The word 'Seneca' is at once too narrow and too broad. The longhouse or Handsome Lake religion which these texts represent is followed by Seneca and other Iroquois groups on half a dozen reservations in New York State and Ontario, so that general Iroquois ceremonialism is reflected here to a large degree. On the other hand, local differentiation has been recognized as a phenomenon of peculiar interest to students of contemporary Iroquois culture (Fenton, 1951, pp. 3 ff.), and from that point of view it is significant that the texts are from the Tonawanda Reservation Seneca, the principal source of Lewis Henry Morgan's material, whose present-day ceremonies are outlined in Fenton (1941).

The word 'thanksgiving' seems no worse a choice than any other and has been used by most previous writers. When confronted with the Seneca words involved, some speakers balk at any attempt to give an English equivalent. Others translate, to some extent according to context, as 'thank, be thankful or grateful to or for, rejoice in, bless, greet'. The trouble is that the Seneca concept is broader than that expressed by any simple English term, and covers not only the conventionalized amenities of both thanking and greeting, but also a more general feeling of happiness over the existence of something or someone. One result is that the English distinction between 'give thanks to' and 'give thanks for' has no relevance.

Finally, the word 'ritual' is used here as a technical term to mean 'component of a ceremony'. If a Seneca ceremony is delimited as any formal gathering that includes activities aimed at communication with the supernatural, any ceremony can be said to consist of several rituals. Rituals can be classified as speeches, dances (songs), games, etc. Lists of Iroquois ceremonies and rituals can be found in Morgan (1901), Fenton (1936, 1941), and Speck (1949). There are three Seneca rituals directed in whole or in part at thanksgiving that are very similar in content, although one is a speech, one a combination of speech and dance, and one a speech accompanied by the burning of tobacco. It is the first two of these that are presented in detail here.

The first is called in Seneca the *kanɔ́:nyɔk*, morphologically an imperative: 'let it be used for thanksgiving!' But the word is used nominally in syntax and can be translated 'thanks' or 'thanksgiving'. I shall use the English equivalent 'Thanksgiving Speech'. This is the most ubiquitous of all Seneca rituals, for it opens and closes nearly every ceremony. The only exceptions are the Funeral Ceremony and the *ʔohki:we:h* 'Dance for the Dead', where its omission is sometimes explained by saying that "it wouldn't make sense to give thanks" in matters concerning death. A myth of its origin can be found in Hewitt (1928, pp. 568–570), and a charter for its performance is given in the *káiwi:yo:h*, the 'Good Message' of Handsome Lake: "It is said that when these rites are performed one person is to be selected to offer thanks to the Creator" (Parker, 1913, p. 51). The speaker stands to recite in front of his seat. The speech consumes from 15 to 25 minutes, depending partly on the speed of the speaker and partly on whether he "gets everything in." Speakers are sometimes criticized for leaving something out or for adding extraneous material. A short version, in which a number of the sections of the complete speech are lumped together in one, is frequently given and is common particularly at the end of a ceremony.

The name of the second ritual, the *konéoɔʔ*, cannot be satisfactorily analyzed on the basis of Seneca alone. Evidence from other Iroquois languages suggests that the meaning at one stage was 'they are covered with hide'.[1] The same stem with a masculine prefix, *honéoɔʔ*, refers to a man who does the chores for the *ʔohki:we:h* ceremony.[2] Perhaps the best English equivalent is 'Thanksgiving Dance'.[3] This ritual is one of the *ke:i niyóiwa:ke:h*, the 'Four Rituals' which were singled out in the Good Message as being of

---

[1] Speck (1949, p. 138) translates the cognate Cayuga name 'covered with skin'. The term has been taken to refer to the drum which is used (Fenton, 1947, p. 6), although the feminine prefix, translatable as 'they', might suggest that it referred to the dancers, perhaps to their feet.

[2] Cf. Fenton and Kurath, 1951, p. 143. The corresponding masculine nonsingular is *honɛ́neoɔʔ*, showing that the stem contains the reflexive -(ɛ)-, which has a zero allomorph with the singular objective prefix.

[3] Parker (1913, p. 41) calls it 'Harvest Dance', a term which is used by others for one of the calendrical ceremonies. Speck says 'Skin Dance'. Fenton uses the term Thanksgiving Dance, but also sometimes 'Drum Dance'. On the reservations the Seneca word is generally interpolated into English, but I have also heard 'Worship Dance' (at Cattaraugus).

transcendent importance: "Four words [4] the Creator has given for
bringing happiness. They are amusements devised in the heaven
world, the Osto'wägo'wa, Gonē'owoⁿ, Adoⁿ'weⁿ and Ganäwĕⁿ'gowa"
(Parker, 1913, pp. 40–41; see also Fenton, 1936, p. 16). The Thanksgiving Dance is performed twice during the year, during the two
calendrical ceremonies which include all of the Four Rituals. One of
these is the New Year's or Midwinter Ceremony, in January or February, when the Thanksgiving Dance takes place on the fifth day
at Tonawanda, the seventh at Cattaraugus, and the eighth at Allegany. The other is the Green Corn Ceremony, in late August or
early September, when it is held on the first day at Tonawanda and
Cattaraugus, but the third day at Allegany.

The Thanksgiving Dance, described in Speck (1949, pp.138–141) for
the Sour Springs Cayuga, and in Fenton (1947, pp. 6–10) for the
Seneca, is performed by a speaker, two singers, and a varying number
of dancers from the assembled crowd. The singers sit facing each
other, straddling a bench placed lengthwise in the center of the longhouse floor. This is the position of the singers during the Feather
Dance also (Kurath, 1951, pp. 125–126), but while in the latter both
singers have turtle rattles which they pound on the bench, in the
Thanksgiving Dance the lead singer uses a water drum and the other
singer a horn rattle (Conklin and Sturtevant, 1953, pp. 274–283).
As in the Feather Dance, some of the performers wear costumes of
a generalized "Indian" type. The ritual has three major parts. It
begins with a group of songs, after which the speaker takes his place,
standing next to the singers, and begins the second part, an alternation of spoken intervals with monotone songs led by the speaker.
This middle part is called the ʔahtahkwayétahkwaʔ, lit. 'used for put-
ting down a shoe', probably with reference to the special dance step
that occurs here. The third and final part is another, shorter group
of songs, usually or always repetitions of songs from the first group.

A representative performance of the Thanksgiving Dance took
place on the Tonawanda Reservation on February 6, 1960. The
morning of that day began with a recital of the Thanksgiving Speech
in the longhouse, after which those present, principally Faith Keepers
(Fenton, 1936, p. 6) and Chiefs, moved to the old cookhouse,[5] where
the Tobacco Invocation (discussed further below) was recited. Personal Chants were then performed by five of the men present, after
which everyone moved back to the longhouse, where a number of
others had already gathered. The speaker next burned tobacco in

---

[4] The noun root in niyóiwa:kɛ:h in some contexts means 'word'. Here it is equivalent to what I am calling
'ritual'. The other three are the ʔostówæʔko:wa:h 'Feather Dance', ʔatɔ:weʔ 'Personal Chant', and kanɛ:-
hwéʔko:wa:h 'Bowl, Dish, or Peach Stone Game', also called kajéʔkekha:ʔ ('characterized by a bowl'),
kayɛ:taʔ ('game'), or kayɛtowa:neh ('great game').

[5] A new cookhouse has been built at Tonawanda for the serving of meals, but the old building is still
used for ceremonial purposes.

the stove at the east or men's end of the longhouse, telling the Creator that the time had come for the Four Rituals which he had requested people to perform for him. Then came the Feather Dance, which was followed almost immediately by the announcement of the Thanksgiving Dance.

The morning's rituals so far had consumed slightly more than 2 hours, with approximately 20 minutes for the Thanksgiving Speech, 1 hour for the Tobacco Invocation, 10 minutes for the Personal Chants, 5 minutes for the tobacco burning in the longhouse, and 15 minutes for the Feather Dance. The time unaccounted for was occupied by announcements, changes of location, and brief pauses between rituals. The total number of Seneca in the longhouse at this point was about 70.

At 10:40 a.m. the two singers took their places for the Thanksgiving Dance, the speaker stood beside them and uttered a whoop characteristic of this ritual, and the singing began. The opening group of songs occupied 15 minutes and included 35 songs. Eight costumed men left their seats during the fifth song, walked counterclockwise in a line around the singers' bench, and with the sixth song began dancing. Here they were joined by three costumed women who moved in a second counterclockwise circle inside the men's, performing a different step. This gross pattern of movement is identical with that of the Feather Dance. The dance steps, too, are similar or the same, although performed in the Thanksgiving Dance with less gesticulation and abandon. The costumed dancers were gradually joined by a total of eight uncostumed men and six uncostumed women. All of the uncostumed men returned to their seats before the end of this group of songs.

At 10:55 a.m. the speaker, who had been dancing last in the line of costumed men, moved to a position next to and south of the center of the singers' bench, facing north; he remained on this side of the bench throughout the spoken portion of the ritual. At the end of the last song he leaned over between the singers and sang loudly *wíh yá* . . ., his voice descending in pitch and increasing in glottalization during the final sustained vowel. He then intoned alone on a single pitch *nya:wɛh nya:wɛh nya:wɛh* ('thank you'). This was taken up and repeated several times by the singers, while the speaker turned and danced to the east end of the bench, faced about and danced to the west end, and finally returned to the midpoint, where at the end of a repeated phrase he again interrupted the singers with *wíh yá* . . . .

The first spoken interval now began. The dancers resumed dancing whenever there was a period of singing, but during the spoken intervals they simply walked slowly in the same counterclockwise direction. The dance step during the intervals of monotone singing here was distinct from that which accompanied the initial and final group of songs. The first spoken interval was punctuated at several points by a single beat of the drum. At its conclusion the speaker changed from a speaking to a singing voice for the linguistically meaningless syllables *kwá: híh*, and introduced the second interval of monotone singing. On this occasion the syllables of the second interval were the meaningless *wihiyah yowihiyah*. Others which occurred during subsequent intervals were *yowihiyah yowihiyah yowihiyah, yowihih yowihih*, and *to:kɛs neˀho watókothaˀ konéhoɔˀ*, the last meaning 'truly the Thanksgiving Dance is being performed', but with the form *konéhoɔˀ* that, intriguingly, looks like a survival of an earlier stage of the word *konéoɔˀ*. It is said that there is no fixed order for these monotone phrases; that the speaker intones the first one that comes into his head, although he tries to avoid immediate repetition of any particular one. The speaker observed privately that his mind was always occupied during these intervals with the content of the following speech.

At the end of the last spoken section, which ended only a minute or two before noon (Morgan, 1901, vol. 1, p. 184), the speaker uttered the conventional Seneca conclusion *tá: neˀhoh* 'that is it', and resumed his place at the end of the costumed dancers for the last group of songs, which were eight in number and consumed 5 minutes. Some uncostumed dancers joined the others during these songs, and the total number of women dancers, some accompanied by children, surpassed that in the first song group. All of the songs were repetitions from the first group, in the same order but with many omissions.

The morning concluded with announcements by several different individuals, including one by the principal speaker to the effect that the Bowl Game and Personal Chants would be performed on the following morning, and there was a shorter version of the Thanksgiving Speech, the whole consuming about another half hour.

The third ritual whose content is similar to that of the Thanksgiving Speech and Thanksgiving Dance is the speech accompanied by the burning of tobacco, called by Fenton (1936, pp. 13, 16) the Tobacco Invocation. Seneca terms for it are less standardized than those for the first two rituals, but it may be called either *hatíyeˀkɔ:- thwas* 'they are burning tobacco', *kayéˀkɔthwe:ˀ* 'tobacco burning', or *kajíyɔthwɛ:ˀ* 'dog burning'. The last name accords with the observations of early writers that this speech was an accompaniment to the burning of the white dog, a ritual now long extinct. The Tobacco Invocation is performed on the fifth day of the New Year's Ceremony at Tonawanda, on the sixth day at Cattaraugus, and on the eighth day at Allegany (but see Fenton, 1936, pp. 11 f.). At Allegany it is also part of the third day of the Green Corn Ceremony, but is absent from that ceremony on the other two Seneca reservations in New York. In a variant form it is also a component of nearly all medicine society ceremonies (e.g., Fenton, 1953, pp. 145–148).

A fourth place where a similar content appears is in the Good Message, during the first day of the recitation. As Handsome Lake lies ill, he observes the things around him and is thankful for them. This passage is abbreviated in Parker (1913, p. 22). In the current version of the Good Message more than half a dozen items for which Handsome Lake expresses gratitude are taken up, but the list still does not compare in extent with that found in the three rituals just described (see below).

Both texts presented here are based on tape recordings made in August 1959. The speaker for both was Chief Corbett Sundown. The singers for the Thanksgiving Dance were Chief Ellsworth George and Delahanty George. For the two singers to be brothers, as in this case, deviates from the ideal pattern according to which they should belong to opposite moieties. The recording of both rituals was done in a private home, and thus in an artificial situation. Notations of the syllables used in the songs, originally written down by the late Simeon Skye, were used as a memory aid by Ellsworth George, the lead singer. The initial song group of the recording contains 43 songs, as compared with the 35 of the longhouse performance described above, where George was again the lead singer.

The Thanksgiving Speech consists of 16 sections which are clearly distinguishable by their content and, in the longhouse, by the utterance at the end of each of *nyóh*, expressing assent, from the men and a few old women. Each section is focused on a particular natural or supernatural item of the environment. Each item has a fixed place in the sequence, which, according to Sundown, corresponds to an order observable in nature and represents the sequence of creation. The rationale of this order is stated in the Good Message: "Now when thanks are rendered begin with the things upon the ground and thank upward to the things in the new world above" (Parker, 1913, p. 51). The sequence followed by Sundown is as follows:

1. The people
2. The earth
3. The plants
4. The water
5. The trees
6. The animals
7. The birds
8. The Sisters (corn, beans and squash)
9. The wind
10. The Thunderers
11. The sun
12. The moon
13. The stars
14. The Four Beings (messengers to Handsome Lake)
15. Handsome Lake
16. The Creator

There is some evidence that speakers are aware of a division between the first eight items, which are terrestrial, and the last eight, which are celestial, as well as of a split in the latter group between the first five items, which are tangible, and the last three, which are intangible. For one thing, the summarization that takes place in the shorter version of the Thanksgiving Speech usually follows these divisions. Some stylistic evidence is noted on page 148.

Except for some deviation in the first section, all of the items are treated in accordance with a fixed pattern. Each section opens with a statement that the Creator decided on, or ordained, the existence of the item. The purpose that the item serves, the manner in which it benefits mankind, is then explained in terms of an assignment given to it by the Creator. There follows a statement that the item is still present and carrying out its assignment. Finally those present are asked to concentrate on thankfulness for it.

The first section is concerned with the people; more specifically, with the members of the community participating in the ceremony. This section forms a kind of introduction to the rest of the speech, establishing the expression of gratitude itself as something ordained by the Creator. The Four Beings, referred to here as the 'Sky Dwellers', are said to have directed that men should have love for each other. There is the observation that the first thing people do whenever they meet is to greet each other, the relevance being in the Seneca equating of greeting with thanksgiving noted above. The responsibility of the Creator for the health of the community is mentioned, and the people are enjoined to be thankful that they are present and in good health.

The subject of the second section is the earth, which serves both as a support for people's feet and as a source of food. Here, and again in the sections dealing with the Sisters, the Thunderers, the sun, and the moon, the Creator is said to have prescribed a set phrase, beginning with a kinship term, that people are to use in referring to the item. The earth is to be called 'our mother, the support for our feet'.

The third and fifth sections are the longest, because of the inclusion of subsections, in the one dealing with the strawberry, in the other, with the maple. The third section begins with the plants. The Seneca term covers all relatively small uncultivated plants, roughly those smaller than bushes. The only function ascribed to them is medicinal. It is said that they all have names, a statement that is repeated for the birds and the stars.[6] Turning to the strawberry, he speaker notes its ceremonial importance as a reminder of the

---

[6] A great number of the Seneca names have actually passed out of use, making this statement to an extent anachronistic.

Creator (Parker, 1913, p. 25). Here there is again a prescription of terminology, but this time of a different nature: two terms are given, one of which is for celestial use and the other for use by mankind. Not present in Parker, but contained in the Seneca version of the Good Message commonly heard today are several other pairs of this type. Among them are (with the celestial form given first): *tekaʔnikɜ́ete:nyɔs kaʔnikɜ́ehtɔ́ʔthaʔ* 'it changes the mind, it blots out the mind' vs. *ʔo:ne:kaʔ* 'drink' (both terms for 'whiskey'); *koyaʔtahtɜ́ʔɔh koʔníkɔɛʔ* 'their minds are lost' vs. *kotkɔʔ* 'they are witches' (for 'witchcraft'); *kawɛnɔhtáshæʔ* 'loss of reputation' vs. *yenɜehtayɛte:ih* 'they know how to attract' (for 'love potions'); *yewiyæhtɜ́ʔthaʔ* 'they destroy their offspring' vs. *yɔtwi:nyaʔs* 'they cut off their offspring' (for 'sterilization').

The fourth section deals with the water, whose function is mentioned only in a general way as being the satisfaction of the people. Its importance is underlined by the observation that the first thing people do upon arising in the morning is to fetch water.

In the fifth section attention is first given to the trees and forests in general, which are said to have a dual function: as medicines and as heating fuel. One tree, the maple, is then focused upon. It provides sugar, the speaker observes, "for those who take notice of it." Like the strawberry it has a particular ceremony devoted to it.

Game animals, classified as small and large, are the subject of the sixth section. They serve, first, to provide amusement for the warriors (young men), and second, to yield food for everyone. Reference is made to a tradition that the large animals all became extinct after the advent of the white man, but were later resupplied in smaller numbers by the Creator.

The seventh section turns to the birds, which are said to be a kind of animal. Their functions are also two: to provide food, and to lift the minds of men with their beautiful voices. Again there is a classification into small and large, and the migration of the small birds is mentioned.

The corn, beans, and squash are not mentioned by name in the eighth section, but are subsumed under the term 'the Sisters, our sustenance' (or 'our life supporters'; e.g., Fenton, 1936, p. 17). Their function is to contribute to people's contentment and to strengthen people's breath, breath being thought of as a basic manifestation of life. They are said to have been included in the ritual since the time when the Good Message arrived.

The wind is the subject of the ninth section, and it too is said to strengthen the breath. A revolving object of some sort, covered by a veil, is described as the source of the wind (Parker,

1913, p. 67). The Four Beings predicted that one day it would revolve too fast and cause great destruction, but to date destructive winds have always bypassed the reservations, another cause for thanksgiving.

The tenth section deals with the Thunderers, who are to be called 'our grandparents, hiʔnoʔ, the Thunderers', who live in the West and are responsible for bringing water. There is a concern that they, too, should always maintain a moderate strength. The name hiʔnoʔ is considered by the present speaker to refer to the several Thunderers collectively. In the tradition described by Morgan (1901, vol. 1, pp. 149–151) he is a single spirit.

The eleventh section takes up the sun. Seneca has a single noun root for both 'sun' and 'moon', and the distinction is made when necessary by adding words meaning 'diurnal' or 'nocturnal'. The sun is to be called 'our elder brother, the sun', and his task is to provide light and heat. The heat is said to contribute to the growth of plants. The sun is described as attached or stuck onto the sky, although there is an apparent contradiction between this and the observation that he moves across the earth, always going in the same direction.

The moon, in the twelfth section, is 'our grandmother, the moon', and she appears when the earth is dark and people are at rest. Her responsibilities are three. She provides light so that people can find their way about during the night, she furnishes a means of measuring time, and she is responsible for the birth of children.

The stars, the subject of the thirteenth section, indicate directions for people who are traveling at night, and are also responsible for moisture falling on the earth during that period.

The Four Beings (called 'messengers' by Parker, 'angels' by Speck) are the subject of the fourteenth section. They are described as the protectors of mankind, for it is their duty, first, to come to people's aid in the accidental mishaps that are bound to occur; second, to keep in check the wind, the Thunderers, the sun, and the moon, who might otherwise bring destruction. Sundown explains that these last are referred to as the 'Four Groups', because, while three of them are single individuals, the Thunderers constitute a group and bring the total to more than four individuals.

The fifteenth section discusses Handsome Lake. His illness is described in wording like that of the Good Message. There is reference to his repentance of his past life, his realization that there must be a Creator, and his feeling of gratitude for the Creator's works (cf. Parker, 1913, pp. 21–22). The Creator, observing the lack of morality on the earth and impressed by the behavior of Handsome

Lake, sent the Four Beings to him with a message of guidance for the future. Handsome Lake's subsequent preaching and death are alluded to.

In the sixteenth and final section the Creator himself is the subject. He is said to be continually observant of what people do, and to have ordained the giving of thanks, which, he directed, should conclude with him.

The Thanksgiving Speech regularly ends with a short epilogue in which the speaker tells that he has done his best to recite the speech in the way that he learned it.

The spoken portion of the Thanksgiving Dance contains the same sequence, except that the order of the Four Beings and Handsome Lake is reversed; i.e., Handsome Lake comes before the other. Moreover, there are six additional items. Four of them come between the second and third items of the Thanksgiving Speech, and reflect a fourfold division of the community by status. Numbered as they occur, they are:

3. The Chiefs
4. The Faith Keepers
5. Those with no assigned responsibility
6. The children

The fifth addition deals with the Four Rituals, and occurs immediately after the children in the ritual as it is given at Tonawanda during the Midwinter Ceremony, but between the Sisters and the wind in the version presented here, the order followed in the Green Corn Ceremony. The last addition occupies the very final position, after the Creator, and is devoted to the two singers. Besides giving thanks for each item, as in the Thanksgiving Speech, the speaker of the Thanksgiving Dance adds a request that the item will continue for another year. Speakers at Cattaraugus request that it continue indefinitely, but at Tonawanda this is considered unwarranted, since each performance of the ritual constitutes a renewal of the request.

The function of the Chiefs is, in general, to look after the security and well-being of the people. In religious matters they make themselves available to the Faith Keepers to help in conducting the ceremonies, specifically by doing the speaking.

The Faith Keepers are explicitly the helpers of the Creator. They set the time for the ceremonies and see that these are carried out properly. They are said to be all of equal rank. Tonawanda Seneca are critical of the fact that at Cattaraugus and Allegany certain Faith Keepers are of higher rank than the rest (the 'Head Ones'; Fenton, 1936, p. 7). There is a statement that those with no assigned responsibility should consent to what the Faith Keepers say.

This third group is not disparaged. It is referred to as "those with no assigned responsibility" only as "a way of speaking," and these people are said to be as willing as the others to help with the ceremonies. Specifically mentioned as belonging under this heading are the warriors and the women.

The children are still "taking their places on the earth," running and crawling about. The earth is said to be strong because of them, in reference to the Creator's particular sympathy for children (Parker, 1913, p. 33 fn.), which is believed to have kept him from ever being willing to destroy the earth.

The Four Rituals are said to have been left by the Creator to serve as a means by which people are able to manifest their gratitude.

In the last section the speaker states his own happiness at having been able to express the gratitude of the people. He then turns his attention to the singers, noting that the Creator gave different people talents for learning different things. (It is not unusual for accomplished speakers to consider themselves bad singers, and vice versa.) He thanks the singers for having cooperated with the Faith Keepers, and encourages them to repeat their performance at a future ceremony. Finally, he leaves up to them the number of songs they will sing in the final group.

The Tobacco Invocation contains the same sequence as the Thanksgiving Dance, without of course the section for the singers and with the earth mentioned between the children and the plants, except that the sequence is recited first in reverse order and then repeated in the normal order. During the first sequence the burning of the tobacco is accompanied by an expression of thanksgiving; during the second sequence, by a request that the item will continue for another year. In other respects there is little difference in the spoken content of the two rituals. The final sentences of the section dealing with the wind as it occurs in both the first and second sequences of the Tobacco Invocation are given on pages 140–141.

No two performances of a ritual are identical. At any one stage of history three classes of variations can be distinguished: (1) those which appear in different performances by the same individual, (2) those which appear in performances by different individuals of the same community (or longhouse), and (3) those which appear in performances of different communities. In addition there are modifications of a ritual associated with its occurrence in different ceremonies, one example of this type being the varying position of the section dealing with the Four Rituals in the Thanksgiving Dance. Historical records also provide evidence of variations through time. A complete study of Iroquois ritualism would have to take into account a number of performances related in these various ways,[7] and only then could statements regarding the significance of variations be made with some confidence. Whether there is reason to divide the third type listed above along lines that would coincide with linguistic or geographic groupings is not now clear. With regard to the extent of variations, the evidence that is available supports the obvious hypothesis that variations of the first type are the least extensive, those of the third type, the most.

With no attempt at complete coverage, but simply to illustrate the nature of the variations that are likely to occur within one section of the Thanksgiving Speech, excerpts from two other performances are given on pages 140–145. Each is the section dealing with the wind. The excerpt on pages 140–143 is made from another recording made by Corbett Sundown (Tonawanda Reservation, 1959 c).[8] On pages 142–145 is an excerpt from a recording by the late Solon Jones (Cattaraugus Reservation, 1956). Thus with relation to the full version given in this work these two illustrate respectively variations of the first and third types.

Sundown's two versions are relatively very similar, perhaps the more so because of the fact that they were recorded on the same day and in the same place. The sequence of ideas is the same, and the only differences seem to be in the choice and arrangement of words.

Jones's version, on the other hand, is markedly different. Most obviously, it is shorter. Aside from the terseness of the sentences, the sequence in which the ideas are presented is not the same. Nevertheless, most of the ideas as well as the words which express them are also contained in Sundown's speech, and this small amount of material gives us no firm basis for separating local from individual differences.

Apart from types of variation found within the individual sections of a speech, it is possible to observe variations in the organization of the entire speech, principally in the inventory and order of the items mentioned. In this respect the two Thanksgiving Speeches of Sundown are identical. The speech of Jones, however, allots a separate section to the strawberry, but includes the birds in the section on the animals. There is no section dealing with the Sisters. The order of the third through seventh items is: water, the strawberry, plants, animals, trees. Handsome Lake precedes the Four Beings.

Beside variations in different performances of the same ritual, it is also possible to compare similar components in different rituals. The justification for pairing the Thanksgiving Speech and the Thanksgiving Dance in this work was, in fact, the occurrence in both of the

---

[7] Cf. in this connection Fenton, 1953.
[8] See the list of recorded versions that follows the Bibliography, pp. 301–302.

thanksgiving sequence in similar although not identical form. I shall end this introduction with a few remarks based on a comparison of all the versions of the thanksgiving rituals listed on pages 301–302. The features compared will be those of inventory and order, which, being the easiest to observe, have been the features most satisfactorily recorded in the past.

As far as inventory is concerned, Sundown includes in his speeches all the items that are widespread in other versions. Frequently, however, separate sections are devoted to the strawberry and the maple. The only item of his which is of relatively infrequent occurrence is the birds. Items not included by him which appear in one or more of the other versions are grass, tobacco, the raspberry, the sunflower, corn, bushes, fruit trees, nut trees, the hickory, fish, fire, clouds, cold (chiefly a supplication that it not become excessive), and the honɔtsinɔhkɛ*, a word that now refers to the holders of charms, but according to Morgan (1901, vol. 1, p. 212) "included the whole spiritual world."

Possibly there is significance in the fact that the two items necessarily associated with the Handsome Lake religion, the Four Beings and Handsome Lake himself, do not occur in four out of five of the earliest recorded versions: from 1900 and before, only in Cattaraugus Reservation, 1896. They are present in all later versions. It is suggestive although by no means conclusive evidence that the sequence occurred first without the Handsome Lake items and continued thus through most of the 19th century, and further that the inclusion of these items spread from Cattaraugus, or perhaps from the longhouses of the Seneca Nation (Cattaraugus and Allegany).

The order of the items is consistent in moving from things terrestrial to things celestial. After the people, the earth is always mentioned first, then come the plants, (bushes), and trees, consistently in that order. The animals (and birds) come next. The water is found in various positions between these first items. The wind, always, and the Thunderers, usually, precede the sun, moon, and stars, but the Thunderers and stars are sometimes juxtaposed (presumably because of their water-bringing function). The position of Handsome Lake and the Four Beings varies, but the Creator is consistently last unless there is an added section for the singers of the Thanksgiving Dance.

The texts are presented with Seneca and English on facing pages. The translation is a "free" one. So much has been said concerning the problems of translators that I shall make no other apology than to observe that Seneca and English are probably as unlike as two languages can be. While no interlinear translation is given, a word for word and even a morpheme for morpheme translation is accessible through the grammatical commentary. The sentences are numbered in parentheses for reference there, and to facilitate comparison between the Seneca and the translation.

Although this is primarily a volume of linguistic texts, it has seemed worthwhile to include the Thanksgiving Dance music, transcribed by one who has had some musical training but is by no means a professional musicologist. It is remarkable how well the music can be accommodated by the traditional Western notation system. But while this is consistently true of the sections sung by the chorus (the two singers, often joined by the speaker), it is frequently not true of the opening of each song, where the solo lead singer makes abundant use of tonal and rhythmic deviations that I have not attempted to record. I have noticed this peculiarity in a good deal of Iroquois music. Regarding unconventional usages in the notation: bar lines are used to indicate phrases sung in one breath, and in the drum part staccato notes indicate that the drum is struck very lightly.

The printed page can only suggest the beauty of these rituals in actual performance, and can convey little of the satisfaction and security found in them by those who have grown up with them as part of the annual round. They are emotional experiences as deeply felt and devoutly regarded as the religious expressions of any people. They should be approached with the reverence and respect that is always due traditions by which men are profoundly moved.

TEXTS

1. The People

(1) ta onɛ tíh, nikɛtyohkó?tɛ:h, wa?ɔkwayá?taye:íh.   (2) ta:ne?ho
wai niotiye:éh, hatiɔyá?ke:onó?, ne? wai n ɔkhí:owí:h, ?ɛyɔkwayɛ:-
tá?k, ne kanoɔhkwá?shæ?, ne yɔ́ɛja?kéh, teyɔkwatawɛnyé:h.   (3) ta:
ne? wai ?ɛtyotyéɛhtɔ́:ɔk, n ɛyakoya?tayéihsé?, ne yɔ́ɛja?kéh, ne
?ɛtyɔtawɛ:nyé:?, ne ?ɔ:kwéh.   (4) ta:ne?ho wai nityóhsá:?, teyɔ́kwe?-
ta:ké:h, tɛ:yatate:ké?, ne? tyotyéɛhtɔ́h, hotí:wa:yé?, wáonɔ?e:-
shá?, skɛ:nó?, yɛnɔ́htɔnyɔ́h.   (5) ne? wai ne tɛ:yatahnɔ́:nyɔ́:?, ta:
nɛ:wáih, hɛ:ni:wá?hɔté?, ne hiyá?tí:h, honóti:wa:té?.   (6) ta:ne?ho
wai nioye:éh, hotye:nó?kta?ɔ he tyɔhé?, hawɛ:?ɔ́h, ne? ɛyakaɔ?es-
háhsé?, hekáya?tí:h, ne ?ɔ:kwéh, ne yɔ́ɛja?kéh, teyakotawɛnyé:h.
(7) ta:nɛ:ké:h, nityɔ́kwe?ta:ké:h, wa?ɔkwayá?taye:íh, ?ɔkwaiwáyɛ-
stɔ́ waih, ?ɛyɔkwatɔ?esé:ɔk.   (8) ne?ho kho niyó?té:h, ne kanɔ-
takwéhtá:?, hɛ?ɛ tɔ?ɔ́kwa:ɔkéh, nɛ: ne kano:ɔ́?, ki?shɛh, nɔ:yotyé:-
ɔk.   (9) ta: ne?ho nɛ: niyó?té:h, kakéɔta:tyé?, koyá?to:ækhɔ́?,
?onɔhsotaiyɔ́:?, ta: ne? kwa: ne ha:hɔ? wai næ:h, kaiwayétahkɔ́h,
n o:tyɛ:nó?kta?ɔ́h.   (10) ta: ne?ho wai ni:ká:?, nɛ: ?aɔ?e:sát, n
ɛyɔkyɔ?éshahsé:k, ne? nɔ?ké:?, ?ɔkwaya?takɔhsóhtɔ:ɔtyé?, nɛ: he
káiwaya:sóh, n i? ɛtwí?, skɛ:nɔ? twɛnɔ́htɔnyɔ́h.   (11) ta: ne? ti n
ɛswe:hé:k, ?i? kɛ nɛ: tayakwatye:ét, ?o?tyakwatáhnɔ:ɔnyɔ́:?, ta:
ne?ho wai nɛyó?tɛ:ɔ́k, n ɔkwa?nikɔ́ɛ?.

16

1. The People

(1) And now, we are gathered in a group. (2) And this is what the Sky Dwellers [9] did: they told us that we should always have love, we who move about on the earth. (3) And this will always be first when people come to gather, the people who move about on the earth. (4) It is the way it begins when two people meet: they first have the obligation to be grateful that they are happy.[10] (5) They greet [11] each other, and after that they take up the matter with which just they two are concerned. (6) And this is what Our Creator [12] did: he decided, "The people moving about on the earth will simply [13] come to express their gratitude." (7) And that is the obligation of those of us who are gathered: that we continue to be grateful. (8) This, too, is the way things are: we have not heard of any unfortunate occurrence that there might be [14] in the community. (9) And the way things are, there are people lying here and there, held down by illness; and even that, certainly, is the responsibility of the Creator.[15] (10) And therefore let there be gratitude; we are always going to be grateful, we who remain, we who can claim to be happy. (11) And give it your thought: the first thing for us to do is to be thankful for each other. And our minds will continue to be so.

---

[9] The Four Beings (p. 9).
[10] Lit. 'that they are thinking well', with reference to both mental and physical health.
[11] Or 'are thankful for'; see p. 1.
[12] Lit. 'he fashioned our lives'.
[13] I.e., it is all that will be required of them.
[14] More lit., 'that a difficult thing might accidentally occur', a euphemism for death.
[15] I.e., it is for him to decide whether or not they will recover.

2. The Earth

(12) ta: nɛ: wai nyo:ye:éh, hotyɛ:nóʔktaʔɔ he tyɔhéʔ, hawe:ʔóh,
ʔɛkɔɛja:tá:t, neʔho tɛyɔtawɛ:nyé:ʔ, ne ʔɔ:kwéh. (13) neʔho ti kho
nɛ: wa:séʔ, tɛyakotáʔɔ:ɔtyéʔ, ne ʔɔ:kwéh hé:ɔwe :yóɛja:té:k.
(14) ta: neʔ ti ne kanɔ:kshǽʔ, n o:ne ne ʔɛyɔthyonyá:néʔ, ʔɛyóɛ-
ja:té:k, neʔ ti n ɛ:nɔtɔ́:ɔk, ʔakhínoʔɛ tɛyɔkwɛ:hsiʔtakɛʔsǽhkóh.
(15) ta: neʔ wai ne tkaye:íʔ, ʔɔkwatyǽ:ʔtahkóh, haʔtewɛ:níshæké:h,
haʔtéwahsɔtaké:h, neʔho tɛyɔkwatawenyé:h, hé:ɔwé yɔɛjatéʔ. (16)
neʔho kho tɛyɔkwahkwéɔtyéʔ, nɛ: ne skɛ:nóʔ, ʔi:kɛ: twɛnóhtɔnyóh,
hé:ɔwe yɔɛjatéʔ. (17) ta: neʔho wai ni:káʔ, ʔáɔʔe:sát, ʔitwe:
ʔóiwakwe:kóh, koiwayéistóh, nɛ: ʔethínoʔɛ tɛyɔkwɛ:hsiʔtakɛʔsǽhkóh,
he niyóiwáʔ, shakoiótasʔóh, ta: ʔɛswe:hé:k, ti waʔakwatyɛ:nɔ:níʔ,
ʔo:nɛ: néʔ, ʔoʔtyakwanɔ:nyó:ʔ, tɛyɔkwɛ:hsiʔtakɛʔsǽhkóh, ta: neʔho
wai nɛyóʔte:ók, n ɔkwaʔnikóɛʔ.

3. The Plants

(18) ta one wai né:h, nyo:ye:éh, hotyɛ:nóʔktaʔóh. (19) tkaye:iʔ
wai hawe:ʔóh, neʔ ti néh, hé:ɔwe :yóɛja:té:k, neʔ n ɛyotʔeohtɔní:ak.
(20) neʔ ne tkaye:íʔ, kakwe:kóh, ʔɛyótihsenɔye:tó:k, he ni:yó:h,
ʔɛyotʔeohtɔní:ak, ʔeyóɛja:té:k. (21) neʔ ne kato:ké:h, he niyó:-
waʔkéh, ʔo:nɛ tɛwenɔɛjotkáʔwahsé:k, ʔa:hóʔ, ti ʔɛwɔtotyáhsé:k.
(22) neʔ ti nɛ:kɛ́:h, ʔonɔhkwaʔshǽʔshɔʔóh, ʔo:nɔtɔʔseʔɔ́:ɔk, ne ʔɔ:-
kwéh, ne yóɛjaʔkéh, ʔoʔtyɔtawɛ:nyéʔ, neʔho waih, nioʔnikɔɛwéʔɔh.
(23) ta: neʔ wai ne tkaye:íʔ, nɛ: he niyótoʔkta:tyéʔ, ʔɔkwatyǽ-
ʔtahkóh. (24) nɛ: ʔonɔhkwaʔshǽʔshɔʔóh, háɔnya:nóʔ, n o:tyɛ:-
nóʔktaʔóh. (25) há:we:ʔóh, neʔho nɛyóʔtɛ:ók, tɛyakohkwéɔtyéʔ,
ʔeyóɛja:té:k, ʔewɔtihsí:æʔk, ʔonɔhkwaʔshǽʔshɔʔóh. (26) ta: neʔ

2. The Earth

(12) And now this is what Our Creator did: he decided, "I shall establish the earth, on which the people will move about. (13) The new people, too, will be taking their places on the earth. (14) And there will be a relationship when they want to refer to the earth: they will always say 'our mother, who supports our feet'." (15) And it is true: we are using it every day and every night; we are moving about on the earth. (16) And we are also obtaining [16] from the earth the things that bring us happiness. (17) And therefore let there be gratitude, for we believe that she has indeed done all that she was obligated to do, the responsibility that he assigned her, our mother, who supports our feet. And give it your thought, that we may do it properly: we now give thanks for that which supports our feet. And our minds will continue to be so.

3. The Plants

(18) And now this is what the Creator did. (19) He decided, "There will be plants growing on the earth. (20) Indeed, all of them will have names, as many plants as will be growing on the earth. (21) At a certain time they will emerge from the earth and mature of their own accord. (22) They will be available in abundance as medicines to the people moving about on the earth." That is what he intended. (23) And it is true: we have been using them up to the present time, (24) the medicines which the Creator made. (25) He decided that it would be thus: that people would be obtaining them from the earth, where the medicines would be distributed.

---

[16] Lit. 'lifting'.

wai ne?ho nioye:éh, hotyɛ:nó?kta?óh, hawe:?óh, ?ɛyakóæ?sé?, ti

ne kanó:kte:shæ?, ne yóɛja?kéh, teyakotawɛnyé:h, ta: ne? wai n

ɛkayɛ:tá?k, n ɛyakoyá?take:há?. (27) ta: ne? wai néh, ha?teyonóh-

kwa?shæ:ké:h, hotká?wéh, hé:ɔwe yɔɛjaté?, ne ?ɛyɔkwaya?takeha-

shǽ?kɛ:ók. (28) ta: ne?ho kho nyo:ye:éh, hotyɛ:nó?kta?óh. (29)

ne: he niyó?té:h, ?ot?éohtɔ:ní:h, hé:ɔwe yɔɛjaté?, ne? wai ne hawe:-

?óh, ?ɛka?eohtatóke:ók, kato:ke: he niyó:wa?kéh, ?ɛwɔ:yaníyɔthá:k.

(30) ne? ti ne?ho ?etkháwihták, ?ɛyɔkashǽ:?sé:k, ne ?ɔ:kwéh, ne yóɛ-

ja?kéh, ?ɔ?tyɔtawɛ:nyé:?. (31) ne? ti kɛs n ɛyɔtɔ?éshɛnyó:?, n o:n

ɛyótkathó?, ?ɛwó:yaniyɔ:té?, niyɔɛjáke:yá:t. (32) ta: ne? wai ne

hatiɔyá?ke:onó?, ne? nɛ: hotíyastóh, ne shés?á:h. (33) ta: ne yóɛ-

ja?ké teyɔkwatawɛnyé:h, ne? wai n í?, ne?h o:néh, ne? n i? ne jistɔ-

tá?shǽ?, ?etwáyasthá:k. (34) ta: tkaye:í?, wai ?etwátkathó?, na?te-

tyo?táié:h, teyɔæwe:nyé:h, he yɔɛjaté?, tkaye:í?, ?ɔ?wá:yaniyɔ:té?,

nɛ: jistɔtá?shǽ?. (35) ta: ne? kho ne tkaye:í?, ?etwatyǽ:?ták, hetwá:-

nekɔ:nét, he nyo:ye:éh, hawe:?óh, ne?ho kɛs ?ɛyekɔ:ták, he koya?ta-

yéisthá?, tɛyénɔ:ɔnyó:?, ha?teyɔkwé?také:h, he ni:yɔ: koya?takóh-

sothá?, tɛyɔtɛnó:nyó:?, n o:n ɛyótkathó?, ?ɔ?wá:yaniyɔ:té?, ne?ho

wai nyo:ye:éh. (36) ta: tkaye:í?, wai ?o?káiwaye:íh, he nɔ?wé:?,

tetyo?táiɛs?óh, he yɔɛjaté?, ne? n o?titwaténɔ:ɔnyó:?, ?óiwakwe:kóh.

(37) ta: ne? ti nɛ:kɛ: n ɛswe:hé:k, ska:t kɛ wa?akwayé:?, ?ɔkwa?-

nikóɛ?, nɛ: ne ?o?tyakwanó:nyó:?, he ni:yɔ: ?ot?éohtɔ:ní:h, ?ɔk-

wánɔhkwa:?shǽ?, ta: ne?ho wai neyó?tɛ:ók, n ɔkwa?nikóɛ?.

4. The Water

(38) ta: ne?ho nioye:éh, hotyɛ:nó?kta?ɔ hé tyɔhe?, hawe?ó wai

ne? n ɛyo:nekítkɛshó:k, ti hé:ɔw ɛyóɛja:té:k. (39) ne? ti kho n

(26) And this what the Creator did: he decided, "Illness will overtake the people moving about on the earth, and these will always be there for their assistance." (27) And he left on the earth all the different medicines to assist us in the future. (28) And this too, the Creator did. (29) With regard to the plants growing on the earth he decided, "There will be a certain plant on which berries will always hang at a certain time. (30) I shall then cause them to remember me, the people moving about on the earth. (31) They will always express their gratitude when they see the berries hanging above the earth." (32) And the Sky Dwellers called them *shês?a:h.*[17] (33) But we who move about on the earth shall always call them *jistɔtá?shæ?.*[18] (34) And it is true: we see them when the wind becomes warm again on the earth; the strawberries are indeed hanging there. (35) And it is also true that we use them, that we drink the berry water.[19] For this is what he did: he decided, "They will always bring them to their meeting place and give thanks, all the people, as many as remain. They will be thankful when they see the berries hanging." That is what he did. (36) And it is true: it comes to pass. When in the course of things it becomes warm again on the earth, we are thankful for everything. (37) And give it your thought, that with one mind [20] we may give thanks for all the plants, our medicines. And our minds will continue to be so.

4. The Water

(38) And this is what the Creator did: he decided, "There will be springs on the earth. (39) And there will be brooks [21] on the earth

---

[17] A term reserved for the ceremonially important wild strawberry. See pp. 7-8.
[18] The generic word for strawberry, wild or cultivated, lit. 'embers attached to it'.
[19] The ceremonial mixture of strawberries and water.
[20] Lit. 'we establish our minds as one'.
[21] Lit. 'veins, arteries'.

ɛyojinɔ́:yaʔtɛɔnyɔ́:k, nɛ: hɛ́:ɔwe yɔéjatéʔ, ʔɛyotihahtɛtyɔ́kwa:ɔ́k,
 neʔ kho ne yɔejakɔ:shɔ́ʔ, nɛyoæhtɔ́:ɔk. (40) ta: neʔ kho ne ʔɛká:-
nekɛɔnyɔ́:k, ʔɛka:nekowanɛ́ʔsé:k, neʔ ti tɛwɔtiyenɔwɔ́ʔkhɔ́:k, he
nɔʔkeyɛnɔ́ʔtɛʔhɛ́ʔt, ʔoʔkɔ́eja:tá:t, tkaye:iʔ ɛyotisháteʔsé:k. (41) ta:
neʔ ne tkaye:íʔ, ʔo:nekasé:ʔ, nɛ: ʔíʔ, ʔɔkwátɔʔse:ʔɔ́h, ne yɔ́ejaʔkéh,
teyɔkwatawɛnyé:h, kho he ni:yɔ́:h, hotkáʔwɛ́ n ɔkwaʔnikɔiyɔ́s-
tahkɔ́h, tkaye:iʔ háeʔkwa ʔo:nekasé:ʔ, honɔ́tɔʔse:ʔɔ́h. (42) ta: neʔ
wai ne tkaye:íʔ, he niyɔ́toʔkta:tyéʔ, ʔɔkwatyéæʔtahkɔ́h. (43) neʔ
wai tyotyéɛhtɔ ʔɛtwatyǽ:ʔták, n o:nɛ wa:sé:ʔ, ʔɛtwatyaʔtákeskɔ́ʔ,
n o:nɛ wa:sé:ʔ, tɛjawetɔ:tíʔ, neʔ tyotyéɛhtɔ́h, n o:nekanɔ́s, ʔɛtwaty-
yǽ:ʔták. (44) ta: tkaye:íʔ, wai ʔáɔʔe:sát. (45) ʔoiwayeiʔɔ́:tyéʔs,
he nyo:ʔnikɔewéʔɔh, hotyɛ:nɔ́ʔktaʔɔ hé tyɔheʔ. (46) ta: ʔɛswe:-
hɛ́:k, ti waʔakwatyɛ:nɔ:níʔ, ʔo:nɛ: néʔ, ʔoʔtyakwanɔ́:nyɔ́:ʔ, nɛ:
ʔo:nékitkɛ:shɔ́ʔ, ʔojinɔ:yáʔtɛɔnyɔ́ʔ, ʔotíhahtɛtyɔkwéh, nɛ: kho ka:-
nekɛɔnyɔ́ʔ, ka:nekowa:nɛ́s, ta: neʔho wai nɛyɔ́ʔtɛ:ɔ́k, n ɔkwaʔnikɔ́eʔ.

5. The Trees

(47) ta onɛ wai nɛ: nioye:ɛ́h, hotyɛ:nɔ́ʔktaʔɔ́h. (48) neʔ wai ne
hawe:ʔɔ́h, neʔ ti néh, hɛ́:ɔwe :yɔ́eja:té:k, neʔ ne tkaye:íʔ, ʔɛyote-
hatɔní:ak. (49) neʔ wai ne tkaye:íʔ, neʔ n ɛyotehatɔní:ak, ne
ʔɛyakoyaʔtakehashǽʔkɛ:ɔ́k, ne ʔo:kwéh, ne yɔ́ejaʔkéh, ʔoʔtyɔta-
wɛ:nyéʔ. (50) neʔ wai ne tkaye:íʔ, hawe:ʔɔ́ kato:ké: shɔ: nɛyɔ-
nishɛ́ʔse:k, tɛkæ:wɛ:nyéʔ, nɛyoʔtáiɛhsé:k, ta: kato:kɛ: háeʔkwa
nikáiwí:s, neʔ nɛ: n ɛkánɔʔnɔ́s. (51) ta: neʔ wai nɛ́:h, ʔɛyotehatɔ-
ní:ak, hɛ́:ɔw ɛyɔ́eja:té:k, neʔ nɛ: ne tkaye:íʔ, ne ʔo:tiyaʔtataiaʔ-
tahkɔ́:ɔk, neʔho wai nioʔnikɔewéʔɔh, n o:tyɛ:nɔ́ʔktaʔɔ́h. (52) ta:
tkaye:iʔ wai nɛ́:h, he niyɔ́toʔkta:tyéʔ, toʔoiwánɔʔko:wás, tohka:ʔa

as well; rivers will flow, and will pass by under the earth. (40) And there will also be ponds [22] and lakes.[23] They will work hand in hand, the way I fashion them on the earth. And moisture will continue to fall." (41) And it is true: fresh water is available in abundance to us who move about on the earth. And, in fact, to all those things which he provided for our contentment, fresh water is abundantly available too. (42) And it is true: we have been using it up to the present time. (43) It is the first thing we use when we arise each new time. When the new day dawns again, the first thing we use is water. (44) And let there indeed be gratitude. (45) It is coming to pass as Our Creator intended. (46) And give it your thought, that we may do it properly: we now give thanks for the springs, the brooks, the flowing rivers, and the ponds and lakes. And our minds will continue to be so.

5. The Trees

(47) And now this is what the Creator did. (48) He decided, "There will be forests growing on the earth. (49) Indeed, the growing forests will be of assistance to the people moving about on the earth." (50) He decided, "There will always be a certain period when the wind will become warm, and a certain length of time, also, when it will become cold. (51) And the forests growing on the earth will provide heat for them." That is what the Creator intended. (52) And it is true: it continues unchanged up to the present time. A few of us [24]

---

[22] Lit 'waters on it'.
[23] Lit. 'large waters'.
[24] Thus the recording. The speaker considered this a slip of the tongue, and would rather have said simply 'we'

neʔ nɛ:kɛ́:h, ʔɔkwayaʔtataiáʔtahkóh, ʔotéhatɔ:ní:h, hɛ́:ɔwe yɔɛjatéʔ.
   4   2   4   2   2   3 31

(53) ta: neʔho kho nyo:ye:ɛ́h, neʔ haeʔkwa ne ʔonɔhkwaʔshǽʔshɔʔóh,
                              4   2   4

háɔnya:nó?, ʔothɔtɔ:ní:h, hɛ́:ɔwé yɔɛjatéʔ. (54) hawe:ʔóh, háeʔkwa
 2   4   2   2   3   31   2   4   2

ʔɛkakwe:níʔ, ʔonɔhkwaʔshǽʔshɔʔɔ ʔɛyakotɔʔseʔó:ok, ne ʔɔ:kwéh, ne
     4   2   4   2   4   2

yóɛjaʔkéh, ʔoʔtyɔtawɛ:nyé:ʔ. (55) ta: neʔho kwa: kho nyo:ye:ɛ́h,
   4   2   3 31

nɛ: ne hawe:ʔóh, ne ʔaeʔ n ɛkɛɔtatoké:ɔk, neʔho nɛ:kɛ́:h, ʔɛtkháwih-
 2   4   4   2   2

ták, neʔ nɛ: ʔɛyakoshǽ:ʔséʔ, ʔiʔ eyɔkashǽ:ʔséʔ, ne teyakotawɛnyé:h.
 4   2   2   3   31

(56) nɛ:kɛ: ʔɛwotí:otɔnyó:k, ne wahtáʔ, hɛ́:ɔw ɛyóɛja:té:k, neʔ nɛ:
      2   4   2   4   2   4   2

ʔɛtka:nekáiʔsé:k, n ɛyowæno:ék. (57) neʔ ti kɛs n o:né tɛtyoʔtáiɛ́h,
        4   2   3   31   2   4   2

he yɔɛjatéʔ, ta one ʔɛtka:nekáiʔt, neʔ ti n ó:nɔʔe:sháʔ, skɛ:nó?,
 2   4   2   2   2   4

henénɔhtɔ:nyóh, ʔo:ne ʔáeʔ, nɛ:ta hɔsáka:éʔ, nɛ:kɛ: néh, tkaye:íʔ,
         4   2   4   2   4   2   2   4

teshátisnyé:ʔ, watí:otɔnyóʔ, ne wahtáʔ. (58) ta: neʔ nɛ: niyók-
 2   4   2   4   31   2

weʔta:kɛ́:h, hoti:wastéistóh, toʔoiwánɔʔko:wás, henóhke:otháʔ,
 4   4   4   2   4   2   4

tkaye:íʔ, wá:tihsenɔ:níʔ, ʔowæ:nó?, hawe:ʔóh, ʔɛyakotɔʔseʔó:ɔk, ne
 2   4   4   2   4   4   2

ʔɔ:kwéh, ne yóɛjaʔkéh, teyakotawɛnyé:h. (59) ta: tkaye:íʔ, toʔoi-
     4   2   4   2   3   31   4   2

wánɔʔko:wás, niyótoʔkta:tyéʔ, ʔahs ɔkwatyéæʔtahkóh. (60) ta:
        4   4   2   2   4   3   31   2

neʔho ʔáeʔ, ni:káʔ:ʔ, ʔáɔʔe:sát, ʔahsɔ ʔóiwakwe:kóh, ʔohte:tyó:h, he
    4   2   4   2   4   4   2   4   2

nioiwíhsaʔóh, hotyɛ:nóʔktaʔóh. (61) ta: n ɛswe:hé:k, ti waʔakwa-
        4   2   4   3   31   2   4   2

tyɛ:nɔ:níʔ, ʔo:nɛ: néʔ, ʔoʔtyakwanó:nyó:ʔ, ʔotéhatɔ:ní:h, hɛ́:ɔwe
      4   2   4   2

yɔɛjatéʔ, ta: neʔho wai neyóʔtɛ:ók, n ɔkwaʔnikóɛʔ.
 4   2   4   2   41

6. The Animals

(62) ta onɛ wai nyo:ye:ɛ́h, hotyɛ:nóʔktaʔɔ he tyɔhéʔ, hawe:ʔóh,
     2   4   2   4   2   2

neʔ ti ne tkaye:íʔ, ʔɛkyáʔtata:thó:ʔ, kanyo:ʔ ɛkatakhenɔtyéʔsé:k, h
 2   4   2   4   3   4

ɛyóɛja:té:k. (63) neʔ wai ne tkaye:íʔ, neʔ nɛkɛ́:h, to:nɛʔnikɔɛ-
 2   4   31   2   4   2   4   2

wɛnyáʔtó:ɔk, nɛ: ne wa:tóh, hotiskɛʔékehtóh, hotiyaʔtá:ni:yóh.
       4   4   2   4   2   4   3   31

(64) hawe:ʔóh, neʔ næ: hakókɛ:yataní:h, hotiskɛʔékehtóh, hotiyaʔ-
    2   4   2   4   2   4   2

are using them for heat, the forests growing on the earth. (53) And this also he did: he made them medicines as well, the trees growing on the earth. (54) He decided, "They can also be available as medicines to the people moving about on the earth." (55) And he even did this as well: he decided, "Again, there will be a certain tree which I shall cause to remind the people moving about to think of me. (56) The maples will stand on the earth, and the sweet liquid will drip from them.[25] (57) Each time when the earth becomes warm, then the sap will flow and they will be grateful for their happiness. When the time arrives again, they will attend to the maples standing there." (58) And for those people who take notice of it, it continues unchanged: they do indeed tap them and store the sugar. For he decided that it would be available in abundance to the people moving about on the earth. (59) And it is true: it continues unchanged up to the present time; we are still using it. (60) And therefore again let there be gratitude that it all still continues as the Creator planned it. (61) And give it your thought, that we may do it properly: we now give thanks for the forests growing on the earth. And our minds will continue to be so.

6. The Animals

(62) And now this is what Our Creator did: he decided, "I shall now establish various animals to run about on the earth. (63) Indeed, they will always be a source of amusement for those who are called warriors, whose bodies are strong." (64) He decided to provide the warriors, whose bodies are strong, with the animals running

---

[25] Lit. 'the liquid will drip, it will always be sweet'.

tá:ni:yóh$_{4\;2}$, nɛ: ne kanyó:ʔ$_{4}$, katákhenɔ:tyéʔs$_{4\;2}$, neʔ tɛ:nɛʔnikɔɛwen-
yáʔthá:k$_{21}$. (65) ta: neʔ ti ne ʔaténɔʔshǽʔ$_{4\;2}$, ti yakotɔʔseʔɔ́:ɔk$_{4\;2}$, ne
ʔɔ:kwéh$_{4\;2}$, ne yóɛjaʔkéh$_{4\;2\;3}$, teyakotawenyé:h$_{31}$. (66) ta onɛ he niyó-$_{2}$
toʔkta:tyéʔ$_{4}$, tkaye:iʔ$_{2}$ tetwáka:néʔ$_{4}$, nikanyoʔtáʔsʔá:h$_{2}$, hatítak-
henɔtyéʔs$_{4\;2}$, niyotehátoʔkta:tyéʔs$_{4\;2}$, neʔho kho né:h$_{4}$, kahatakɔ́:shɔʔ$_{2\;1}$.
(67) ta: kwa: nɛ:ké:h$_{2}$, he niyótoʔkta:tyéʔ$_{4\;2}$, ʔo:nɛ tejitwaká:néʔ$_{4\;2'}$,
kanyóʔtowa:nɛ́s$_{2}$, henɔtkɛʔɔ́:neʔs$_{4\;2\;41\;1}$. (68) tkaye:iʔ$_{2}$ wai ne to:kwa
nɔʔyóshǽké:ʔ$_{4\;2}$, n o:nɛ hɛʔɛ teʔjitwakéh$_{4\;2}$, ne kanyóʔtowá:nɛs$_{4\;42\;1}$. (69) ta$_{2}$
onɛ kwa: nɛ: niyótoʔkta:tyéʔs$_{4\;2}$, ʔo:nɛ tejitwaká:néʔ$_{4\;2}$, kanyóʔto-$_{4\;2}$
wa:nɛ́s$_{4\;2}$, katákhenɔ:tyéʔs$_{4\;2}$, ʔaténɔʔshǽ$_{4\;2}$, tkaye:íʔ$_{4\;2}$, jɔkwátɔʔsé:h$_{4\;2}$, nɛ:
niyótoʔktá:tye?$_{4\;3\;42\;1}$. (70) ta: ʔɔkwatyǽ:ʔtahkɔ́ waih$_{4}$, he nioʔnikɔɛwéʔɔh$_{4\;2}$,
hotyɛ:nóʔktaʔɔ hé tyɔhe?$_{2\;4\;2\;1}$. (71) ta: neʔho wai ni:ká:ʔ$_{2}$, ʔáɔʔe:sát, he$_{4\;2}$
nioʔnikɔɛwéʔɔh, tkaye:íʔ$_{4}$, ʔahsɔ ʔóiwakwe:kɔ́h$_{2\;4}$, ʔohtɛ:tyɔ́:h$_{4\;2}$, ta:$_{4\;2}$
ʔɛswe:hé:k, ti waʔakwatyɛ:nɔ:níʔ$_{4\;2}$, ʔo:nɛ: neʔ oʔtyakwanɔ́:nyɔ́:ʔ$_{4}$,
nɛ:kɛ: kanyó:ʔ$_{2}$, katákhenɔ:tyéʔs$_{4}$, ta: neʔho wai neyóʔtɛ:ɔ́k$_{4\;2}$, n
ɔkwaʔnikɔ́ɛ?$_{2\;41}$.

7. The Birds

(72) ta: neʔho nioye:éh$_{2}$, hotyɛ:nóʔktaʔɔ hé tyɔhe?$_{4\;2\;1}$. (73) hawe:ʔɔ́$_{2\;4}$
waih, neʔ ne tkaye:íʔ$_{2\;2}$, ʔɛkyáʔtata:thɔ́:ʔ$_{4\;2}$, tɛyonɔteʔsætɛsyɔtyéʔsé:k$_{4\;2}$,
niyɔɛjáke:yá:t$_{2}$, neyótoʔktáʔk$_{4\;2\;3\;31}$. (74) ta: neʔ hǽ:ʔkwa ne kanyó:ʔ$_{2\;4}$,
ʔɛɔtiyásɔ:ɔ́k$_{23\;31}$. (75) neʔ ne niyɔɛjáke:yá:t$_{2}$, neyóhsawáʔk, nitkáshatɔ:-
tyéʔs, neyótoʔktáʔk$_{4\;2\;3\;2\;31}$. (76) ta: neʔ ne tkaye:íʔ$_{2}$, háeʔkwa kakwe:kɔ́h$_{4\;2\;4}$,
hotíhsenɔyɛ:tɔ́ʔ$_{2}$, nɛ: ne jiʔtɛʔɔshɔ́ʔɔh$_{4\;2}$, teyonɔteʔsætɛsyɔtyéʔs$_{4\;3\;31}$. (77) ta:$_{2}$
neʔ kwa: né:h$_{4}$, nya:tijiʔtaʔsʔá:h$_{2}$, neʔ wai nɛ: ne hawe:ʔɔ́h$_{4\;2}$, neʔ nɛ:
ne tkaye:íʔ$_{4}$, kato:kɛ: he neyónishéʔt$_{2}$, neʔho to:nɔtawenyé:ak$_{4\;2}$, ta onɛ$_{2}$
ʔɛshɛnɔtká:ɛkɔ́ʔ$_{4\;2}$, hé:kwa: tyone:nɔ́ʔ$_{4\;2\;3\;31}$, heshɛ:né:ʔ$_{}$. (78) ta: neʔ ne$_{2}$

about, to be a source of amusement for them. (65) "And they will be available as food to the people moving about on the earth." (66) And up to the present time we have indeed seen the small animals running about along the edges of the forests, and within the forests as well. (67) And at the present time we even catch glimpses of the large animals again.[26] (68) There were in fact a number of years during which we no longer saw the large animals. (69) But now at the present time we again see the large animals running about, and at the present time they are actually available to us again as food. (70) And we are using them as Our Creator intended. (71) And therefore let there be gratitude that it all does still continue as he intended. And give it your thought, that we may do it properly: we now give thanks for the animals running about. And our minds will continue to be so.

7. The Birds

(72) And this is what Our Creator did. (73) He decided, "I shall establish various creatures that will spread their wings from just above the earth to as far upward as they can go. (74) And they too will be called animals. (75) They will begin just above the earth, and will go all the way into the clouds. (76) And they too all have names, the birds with outspread wings." (77) And with respect to the small birds he decided, "There will be a certain period when they will stir, and they will turn back, going back to where it is warm.

---

[26] Lit. 'we see them again . . . they appear momentarily'. See p. 8.

tɛtyoʔtáiéh, he yɔejatéʔ, ta on ɛshatiyáʔtaʔti:héʔt, neʔ n a:ʔtewa-
tiwenɔ:ké:h, ʔɛswenɔtíʔstáɛʔ, watiwɛni:yóʔs. (79) ta: neʔ wai tɛk-
áhkwáʔt, hotiʔnikóɛʔ, he ni:yó:h, hotiyaʔtakɔhsótháʔ, ʔo:nɛ né
:shatiyáʔtaʔti:héʔt, nikajiʔtáʔsʔá:h. (80) tá:neʔho kwa:nyo:ye:éh,
háeʔkwa n aténɔʔshǽʔ, ʔɔkwátɔʔse:ʔóh, nɛ: teyonɔteʔsætésyɔtyéʔs,
jiʔtɛʔɔshóʔɔh. (81) tkaye:iʔ háeʔkwa ʔɔkwatyǽ:ʔtahkóh, nɛ: jiʔtɛʔ-
ɔshóʔɔ teyonɔteʔsætésyɔtyéʔs, ʔaténɔʔshǽʔ, ʔɔkwátɔʔse:ʔóh. (82) ta:
ʔitwe: kwa: háeʔkwa kakwe:kóh, háeʔkwa hoti:wayéistóh, he niyóiwáʔ, hoti:wayetáhkóh. (83) kakwe:kó wai ʔoʔkíʔ, hotíhsenɔye:tóʔ,
he nɔ:tiyáʔtoʔtéʔ. (84) ta: neʔ ti nɛ :swe:hé:k, waʔakwatye:nɔ:níʔ,
ʔo:nɛ: néʔ, ʔoʔtyakwanó:nyó:ʔ, jiʔtɛʔɔshóʔɔ teyonɔteʔsætésyɔtyéʔs,
ta: neʔho wai nɛyóʔtɛ:ók, n ɔkwaʔnikóɛʔ.

8. The "Sisters"

(85) ta onɛ wai nyo:ye:éh, hotyɛ:nóʔktaʔɔ he tyɔhéʔ. (86) neʔ wai
ne tkaye:íʔ, ʔo:nɛ ʔi:e hé:ɔwe yɔejatéʔ, neʔ ne tkaye:íʔ, ʔɛka:tkáʔ,
ta onéh, honɔ:hóʔ, to:nɔtáteʔnya:ɛ́ʔ, ne ʔɔ:kwéh, teyakotawɛnyé:h.
(87) neʔ ti ne yɔejakó:h, ʔɛɔtiyéʔ:ɔk, ʔa:hóʔ, ʔɛwɔtotyáhséʔ:k, neʔho
to:tihkwéɔtyéʔ, ne skɛ:nóʔ, ʔɛ:nɛnɔhtɔnyó:ɔk. (88) ta: wai néʔ:h,
he niyótoʔkta:tyéʔ, tkaye:iʔ tetwáka:néʔ:ʔ. (89) ʔo:nɛ teyonɔɛ-
jotkáʔwéh, ʔo:nɛ néʔ, tetwáka:néʔ:ʔ, ʔɛyɔkwaʔnikóiyosták, ʔo:nɛ
tɔta:wéʔ, tɛskate:níʔ, teyoæwɛ:nyéʔ:h. (90) ta: neʔ wai ʔɔkyɔishæ:-
niyéhkóh. (91) ta: neʔ wai n o:néh, tsaʔka:yóʔ, kaʔníkɔ:iyó:h, neʔ
wai ne ʔɔkwatokéhséʔ:ʔ, ʔo:nɛ háeʔkwa ʔɛkæ:tyéʔséʔ:k, ʔotí:wahtɛ:-
tyóʔ:h, ke:i niyóiwa:kéʔ:h. (92) neʔ wai ne ʔonɔtóisyɔhkóh, neʔ kho
nɛ: tɛwɛnɔtéʔ:nɔtǽʔk, nɛ: héʔ:ɔwéh, neʔ tewátiʔnyáʔ:ʔ, haʔtewɛ:nís-
hǽké:h. (93) ta:neʔ o:néʔwaih, ʔo:néh, neʔho niyo:wéʔ, kanɔ:kshǽʔ,

(78) And it will become warm again on the earth, and they will return. With all their voices they will sing once more their beautiful songs. (79) And it will lift the minds of all who remain when the small birds return." (80) And he arranged as well that they are available to us as food, the birds with outspread wings. (81) It is true: we are using them too, the birds with outspread wings. They are available to us as food. (82) And we believe that they too are all carrying out their responsibility. (83) They all, as I said, have names, according to their type. (84) And give it your thought, that we may do it properly: we now give thanks for the birds with outspread wings. And our minds will continue to be so.

8. The "Sisters"

(85) And now this is what Our Creator did. (86) It was indeed at this time that he thought, "I shall leave them on the earth, and the people moving about will then take care of themselves. (87) People will put them in the earth, they will mature of their own accord, people will harvest them and be happy." (88) And up to the present time we have indeed seen them. (89) When they emerge from the earth we see them. They bring us contentment. They come again with the change of the wind.[27] (90) And they strengthen our breath. (91) And when the Good Message came we were advised that they too should always be included in the ceremonies, in the Four Rituals.[28] (92) Those who take care of them every day asked, too, that they be sisters. (93) And at that time there arose a relationship between them: we shall say "the Sisters, our sustenance" when we want to

---

[27] I.e., not a change in direction, but from cold to warm.
[28] I.e., this should be one of the items for which thanks is expressed. The Four Rituals (pp. 2-3) are here synonymous with longhouse ceremonialism.

ʔotóʔɔh, he watíyaʔta:téʔ, neʔ nɛ: nɛtwátó:ɔk, tewɛnɔté:nɔ:té:ʔ,
tyɔhéhkɔh, n o:nɛ neʔho ʔɛtwathyonyá:néʔ. (94) ta: neʔ wai ne
tkaye:íʔ, ʔɔkwaʔnikó:iyó:h, nɛ:kɛ: niyótoʔkta:tyéʔ, tetwáka:né:ʔ,
ʔotɔ:ní:h. (95) ta: ʔɛswe:hé:k, ti waʔakwatyɛ:nɔ:níʔ, ʔo:nɛ: ne
ʔoʔtyakwanó:nyó:ʔ, nɔʔtewɛnɔtɛ:nɔ:té:ʔ, ʔakyóhehkóh, ta: neʔho
wai neyóʔtɛ:ók, n ɔkwaʔnikóɛʔ.

9. The Wind

(96) ta onɛ wai nyo:ye:éh, hotyɛ:nóʔktaʔɔ he tyɔhéʔ, hawe:óhʔ,
ʔo:nɛ tíh, neʔ ne hɛʔɛ taʔakakwe:níʔ, neʔhó shɔ: nɔ:yoʔté:ɔk. (97)
ta: neʔ wai néh, hawe:ʔóh, neʔ ti né tkaye:íʔ. (98) neʔ ne haʔte-
kakó:t, tɛyoæwenyé:ak, ta: neʔ ti ʔeotiyaʔta:níyó:ɔk, ne ʔɔ:kwéh,
ʔoʔthɛnɔtawɛnyé:ʔ, ʔoʔkhéyatkáʔ, hé:ɔwe ʔoʔkóɛja:tá:t. (99) ta:
neʔ wai ne hosyɔ:ní:h, ʔotáʔeoóh, hekæ:hkwéʔskwá:h, nɔʔwɔ:tíh,
neʔ ne skenóʔɔ: nityoye:éh, ʔotkahatóʔ:h. (100) neʔ wai nɛ:ké:h,
neʔho tyotatɔ:ní:h, tɛyoæwe:nyé:h, ta onɛ skɛ:nóʔ twɛnóhtɔnyóh,
tkaye:iʔ ɔkyɔishæ:ni:yóh, he yóɛjaʔkéh, tɛyɔkwatawɛnyé:h. (101)
neʔho shɔ: kho nitka:téʔ, tɛyoæwe:nyé:h, n ɔkwaʔnikɔiyóstahkóh,
skɛ:nɔʔ i:ké:h, twɛnóhtɔnyóh. (102) ta: neʔ kwa: n ɔkhí:owí:h,
wai ne hatiɔyáʔke:onóʔ, neʔ wai ne ho:né:h, neʔ ne ʔakwé:h, ʔɛyót-
kathóʔ, ne shenɔ:kshóʔ. (103) nɛ: ne ʔo:ɛtóʔ:h, ʔoʔwé:nishætenyɔ:-
tyéʔ, neʔ kiʔshéh, neʔho nɛya:wéh, n ɛtyakwɛʔnéoʔktéʔ heyó:éh,
ʔɔkwatkáɛóʔ. (104) neʔ kiʔshɛ neyóʔhastéh, ʔɛwótkaha:tóh, neʔ wai
ne ʔakwé:h, neʔ ne ka:ɛkwáh, n a:ʔtɛkakɛ:séʔ:, hé:ɔwe yɔɛjatéʔ.
(105) neyóʔhasté kiʔshɛ tɛkæ:wɛ:nyéʔ:, neʔ wai n akwé:h, ʔɛyako-
tówehták, ne ʔɔ:kwéh, tɛyakotawɛnyé:h, neʔho waih, nyo:tiye:éh.

refer to them. (94) And it is true: we are content up to the present time, for we see them growing. (95) And give it your thought, that we may do it properly: we now give thanks for the Sisters, our sustenance. And our minds will continue to be so.

9. *The Wind*

(96) And now this is what Our Creator did: he decided, "Now it can't always be just this way." [29] (97) And this, in fact, is what he decided. (98) "There must be wind, and it will strengthen [30] the people moving about whom I left on the earth. (99) And in the west he made the thing that is covered by a veil; slowly it moves and revolves. (100) There the wind is formed, and we are happy. It indeed strengthens our breath, for us who move about on the earth. (101) And the wind is just the strength for us to be content with it and be happy. (102) But the Sky Dwellers told us: they said, "We believe that your kinsmen [31] will see (103) that in future days it may happen that it will be beyond our control. It is the most important thing for us to watch. (104) It may become strong in its revolving, and we believe that it will scrape off everything on the earth. (105) The wind may become strong, we believe, and bring harm to the people moving about." That is what they said. (106)

---

[29] I.e., there is something missing.
[30] By providing them with air to breathe.
[31] Meaning here 'your descendants'.

(106) ta: nɛ: niyóto'kta:tyé', ne tkaye:í', 'ɛtwaiwakwáihsí', ne'ho
   2   4   2   4   2   4   2

niya:wɛ́s, 'o'kaiwáhtɔ́'t, hɛ́:ɔwe nɛ:kɛ́:h, hoti'nikɔ́:iyó:h, 'o'kai-
  4   2   4   2   4   2

wáhtɔ́'t, kɛs 'o'kakwe:ní', ne' wa'ó'hastéh, 'o'tkæ:wɛ:nyé:'.
   4   2   2   3   21

(107) ta: ne' kwa: n í', n ɔkwa'nikɔiyóstahkɔ́ shɔ:h, he niyó'hasté',
   2   4   2   2

teyoæwɛ:nyé:h, skɛ:nɔ́' twenɔ́htɔnyɔ́h.   (108) ta: 'ɛswe:hɛ́:k, ti
   2   4   2   4   2   3   21   2   4   2

wa'akwatyɛ:nɔ:ní', 'o'tyakwanɔ́:nyɔ́:', 'otá'eoɔ tyotatɔ:ní:h, te-
   4   2   4   2   4   2

yoæwɛ:nyé:h, ta: ne'ho wai nɛyó'tɛ:ɔ́k, n ɔkwa'nikɔ́ɛ'.
   4   2   4   2   41

10. The Thunderers

(109) ta onɛ nyo:ye:ɛ́h, hotyɛ:nɔ́'kta'ɔ he tyɔhé', hawe:'ɔ́h,
   2   4   2   4   2

'ewɔkatɛhɔ'shɛ:tá'k, hekæ:hkwɛ́'skwá:h, nɔ'wɔ:tíh, ne'ho næ:h,
   2   4   4   2   3

'ethéni'tyɔ:tá'k. (110) ne'ho ti næ: ne'ho 'ethɛnehtáhkwá:k, tɛ:-
  2 3   21   2   4   2

nɔtawenyé:', he nikáshatɔ:tyé's, ne' ti næ: né', 'o:nekasé:', 'ɛɔ-
   4   2   4   2   4   2   2

tíawi'sé:k. (111) ne' nɛ: néh, 'éɔtiɛtosæ:hsé:k, he ni:yɔ: hotkɑ́?-
   21   2   4   2   4   2
wɛ́h, 'a:hɔ́', watɔ:níh, hɛ́:ɔwé yɔɛjaté'. (112) ta: ne' kwa: néh,
  4   2 3   2   4   2   3   21   2   4

hawe:'ɔ́h, kanɔ:kshǽ', ti n o:nɛ ne 'ɛyɔthyonyá:né', ne' ti nɛ:
  2   4   2   4   2   4   2

nɛ:nɔtɔ́:ɔk, ne' n ethíhsɔ́:t, hi'nɔ́', hatiwɛnotatyé's, ne'hó waih,
   4   2   4   2   4   2   3   2

nɛɔtiye:hɑ́:k. (113) ta: ne' wai néh, hekæ:hkwɛ́'skwá:h, heakɔyát-
  3   31   2   4   2

ka'wɛ́h, ne'ho 'ethɛnehtáhkwá:k. (114) ta: ne' ne tkaye:í', ne'ho
   4   2   4   41   2   4   2

nɛyó'hastɛ́:k, n ɛyako'nikɔiyostáhkɔ́:ɔk, ne 'ɔ:kwéh, n o:nɔ́te'shǽ',
   4   2   4   2

teyakotawenyé:h. (115) ta: hoti:wayéistɔ́h, he niyokɛhísɔ:ɔtyé',
   2   3   21   2   4   2   4

ne'ho to:nɔtawenye:nikáshatɔ:tyé's, 'o:nekasé:', honɔ́nya:nɔ:tyé's,
   2   4   2   4   2   4

nɛ: 'otíhahtɛtyɔkwéh, nɛ: kho ka:nekɛɔnyɔ́', ka:nekowa:nɛ́s. (116)
   2   4   2   4   2   3   21

ta: 'ɛswe:hɛ́:k, ti wa'akwatyɛ:nɔ:ní', 'o:nɛ: né', 'o'tyethinɔ́:nyɔ́:',
   2   4   2   4   2   4   2

nɛ: 'ethíhsɔ́:t, hi'nɔ́', hatiwɛnotatyé's, ta: ne'ho wai nɛyó'tɛ:ɔ́k,
   2   4   2   4   2   3   2

n ɔkwa'nikɔ́ɛ'.
   2   41

And indeed up to the present time we can attest to it: the way it occurs, it destroys their homes.[32] From time to time it is destructive, for the wind can become strong. (107) But as for us, we are content, for no matter how strong the wind has been we have been happy. (108) And give it your thought, that we may do it properly: we give thanks for the thing that is covered by a veil, where the wind is formed. And our minds will continue to be so.

10. The Thunderers

(109) And now this is what Our Creator did: he decided, "I shall have helpers who will live in the west. (110) They will come from that direction and will move about among the clouds, carrying fresh water." (111) They will sprinkle all the gardens which he provided, which grow of their own accord on the earth. (112) And he decided, "There will be a relationship when people want to refer to them: they will say 'our grandparents, *hiⁱnoⁱ*, the Thunderers'.[33] That is what they will do." (113) And he left them in the west; they will always come from that direction. (114) And truly they will always be of such a strength that the people, their grandchildren, who move about will be content with them. (115) And they are performing their obligation, moving about all through the summer among the clouds, making fresh water, rivers, ponds, and lakes. (116) And give it your thought, that we may do it properly: we now give thanks for them, our grandparents, *hiⁱnoⁱ*, the Thunderers. And our minds will continue to be so.

---

[32] Lit. 'where they are content', referring to the homes of white men in the surrounding area. See p. 9.
[33] Lit. 'they are speaking out', or 'spreading the word'.

11. The Sun

(117) ta onɛ wai nyo:ye:ɛ́h, hotyɛ:nóʔktaʔɔ he tyɔhéʔ, neʔ wai ne
hawe:ʔóh, ʔɛkéɔya:téːk, ne hetkɛh, naʔakonóʔɛːtíh, ne ʔɔːkwéh,
ʔoʔtyɔtawɛːnyéː. (118) neʔ wai néh, haʔtekakóːt, ne ʔɛwɔkaté-
hɔʔshɛːtáʔk, háeʔkwa he ʔɛkéɔyaːtéːk. (119) ta: neʔ wai ne tkayeːíʔ,
howɔióʔtasʔóh, hotǽʔnetaːktóh, héːɔwe kéɔyatéʔ. (120) neʔ nɛ:
neʔho to:tawényeːák, tɔɛjíyaʔkthá:k, kato:kɛ: he:kwáːh, nɛ-
the:tháːk, he:kwá: kho hɛːetháːk. (121) ta: neʔ kwa: ne kanɔːkshǽʔ,
háeʔkwa nyoːyeːɛ n oːné ne ʔɛtwathyonyáːnéʔ, neʔ nɛ: netwátóːɔk,
ʔeteːkhaːʔ shetwáhjiʔ kǽːhkwáːʔ. (122) ta: tkayeːiʔ hoiwayéistóh,
neʔho :tǽʔnetaːktóh, héːɔwe kéɔyatéʔ, teyohathétsiːyóːh, ta onɛ
skɛːnóʔ, twenóhtɔnyóh. (123) ta: neʔ wai n itwéːh, ʔóiwakweːkóh,
háeʔkwa hoiwayéistóh, tkayeːíʔ, ʔonɔtɔhóhtɛtyóːh, he niːyɔ: hotkáʔ-
wéh, ʔaːhóʔ, watɔːníh, hɔwɔiwakéistaníːh, neʔ nɛ: ʔɛɔʔtáiaʔtháːk,
héːɔwe :yóejaːtéːk, ta onɛ skɛːnóʔ, ʔɛwenɔtóhohteːtíʔ, he niːy
oːtkáʔwéh, ʔaːhóʔ, watɔːníh. (124) ta: ʔitwéː waih, hoiwayéistóh,
he niyótoʔktaːtyéʔ, he niyóiwáʔ, hɔwɔióʔtasʔóh. (125) ta: neʔ ti n
ɛswe:héːk, waʔakwatyɛːnɔːníʔ, nɛː ne ʔɛtsakwanóːnyóːʔ, ʔeteːkhaːʔ
shakwáhjiʔ kǽːhkwáːʔ, ta: neʔho wai nɛyóʔtɛːók, n ɔkwaʔnikóɛʔ.

12. The Moon

(126) ta onɛ wai nyoːyeːɛ́h, hotyɛːnóʔktaʔɔ he tyɔhéʔ, haweːʔó
wai katoːkɛ: tí shoː he nɛyónishéʔt, ʔoːnɛ nɛːkéːh, ʔɛwɔtéɔnostháːk,
ʔɛyóejaːtéːk. (127) katoːkɛ: kho nɛyónishéʔt, ʔɛwéːnishǽtenyóːk.
(128) ta: neʔ wai ne tkayeːíʔ, taːkaːnǽhjiːwéh, kotatyaʔtakehá:nóʔ,
ne ʔɔːkwéh, teyakotawɛnyéːh. (129) ta: neʔ wai ne haweːʔóh, neʔ
ti ne ʔɛyɔtóisheːók, haʔtɛskayétaʔséʔ, ti he yeyáʔtayetatyéʔ, ʔɛyɔ-

11. The Sun

(117) And now this is what Our Creator did: he decided, "There will be a sky above the heads of the people moving about. (118) I must have a helper in the sky as well." (119) And indeed he assigned him to be attached [34] to the sky. (120) There he will move about, and will cross the earth. He will always come from a certain direction, and will always go in a certain direction. (121) And he also prescribed a relationship when we want to refer to it: we shall say "our elder brother, the sun." (122) And it is true: he is carrying out his responsibility, attached there to the sky; there is beautiful daylight, and we are happy. (123) And we believe that he too has done all that he was obligated to do; everything that he [35] left to grow of its own accord is flourishing. He gave him the added responsibility of making it warm on the earth, so that everything he left to grow of its own accord would flourish. (124) And we believe that he is performing his obligation up to the present time, the assignment he was given. (125) And give it your thought, that we may do it properly: we give thanks for him, our elder brother, the sun. And our minds will continue to be so.

12. The Moon

(126) And now this is what Our Creator did: he decided, "There will be a certain period when the earth will be in shadow, (127) as well as a certain period when it will be day." (128) And indeed he saw well that the people moving about were taking care of themselves. (129) And he decided, "They will rest. They will lay down their bodies and

---

[34] In the sense of 'stuck or glued on.'
[35] The Creator.

tóishé:ɔk, he nɛ:wě:ʔ, ʔɛwɔtéɔnosthá:k, neʔho wai nyo:ʔnikɔɛwéʔɔh.
3   4   2   4   2   4   2   4 1

(130) ta: neʔ kwa: kiʔshɛ neʔho nɛya:wéh, ne káɛtiʔkwa niyo:wéʔ,
          2   4   2   4

ʔɛtyakohsótaʔís.   (131) ta: neʔ kwa: ne thika:téʔ, ʔɛwɔkatého ʔs-
2   3 21   2   4   2

he:táʔk, ʔɛkǽ:hkwá:aʔk, hé:ɔw ɛkéɔya:té:k.   (132) neʔ nɛ: nɛ:no-
    4   2   4   2   4 3 21   2

tó:ɔk, ʔethíhso:t sɔekha:ʔ kǽ:hkwá:ʔ, neʔho nɛɔtiye:há:k, ne
4   2   4   2   4   2

ʔɛkakwe:níʔ, haʔtɛyakoshɛtáʔɔ:ɔkʔáh, tɛyakohatheʔtó:ɔk.   (133) ta:
      4   2   4   4   4 1   2

tkaye:íʔ, wai ne ʔɔkwatɛnɔʔkæ:htashétahkóh, he nɛyɔkwatkɛis-
4   2   4   2

tó:tyéʔ, ne yóɛjaʔkéh, tɛyɔkwatawenyé:h.   (134) neʔ wai nɛ: néh,
4 2   4 2   3 21   2   4

hawe:ʔóh, tɛkatenyóhsé:k, ti he niyóʔté:h, ʔotæ:hkwáhtɛ:tyó:h,
2   4   2   4   2

ʔɛwɔtɛ:níʔtoʔkthá:k, hotíyastóh.   (135) ta: tkaye:iʔ wai nɛ:ké:h,
2   4   2 3 21   2   4

ne ʔahs ɔkwatɛnɔʔkæ:htashétahkóh, he niyótoʔkta:tyéʔ, niyóʔté:h,
2   4   2   4   2 4

ʔɔkwatkéistɔ:ɔtyéʔ, ne yóɛjaʔkéh, tɛyɔkwatawenyé:h.   (136) ta:
2   4 2   4 2   3 21   2

ʔitwe: kwa: neʔho háeʔkwa tɛyawehtó:tyéʔ, toʔoiwánɔʔko:wás,
                                  4   2

to:titáʔɔ:ɔtyéʔ, saʔ nienɔhóʔsʔáh, hé:ɔwe yɔɛjatéʔ, watíyaʔta:téʔ,
2   4   2   4   2   4   2

ʔethínoʔɛ neʔho tɛyawehtó:tyéʔ.   (137) ta: neʔho wai ni:ká:ʔ,
2   41 31   2

ʔitwe: ʔóiwakwe:kóh, koiwayéistóh, he niyóiwáʔ, shakoiwakéistaní:h.
2   4   2   4   2   4   2   3 21

(138) ta onɛ ʔɛswe:hé:k, ti waʔakwatyɛ:nɔ:níʔ, ʔo:nɛ: néʔ, ʔoʔtyet-
      2   4   2   4   2

hinó:nyó:ʔ, nɛ: ʔethíhso:t sɔekha:ʔ kǽ:hkwá:ʔ, ta: neʔho wai
4   2   4   2

nɛyóʔtɛ:ók, n ɔkwaʔnikóɛʔ.
4   41

13. The Stars

(139) ta onɛ wai nyo:ye:éh, hotyɛ:nóʔktaʔɔ hé tyɔhéʔ.   (140)
      2   4   2   4   2 21

hawe:ʔó wai neʔ wai ne tkaye:íʔ, háeʔkwa ʔɛkajihsɔʔtahsí:æʔk,
2   4   2   4

hé:ɔw ɛkéɔya:té:k, he nɛ:wéʔ, ʔɛwɔtéɔnosthá:k.   (141) ta: neʔ
2   4   2   4   2 3   31

háeʔkwa ne kato:kɛ: naʔáhtɛʔéh, hakɔióTasʔóh, he neʔho nɛyóʔtɛ:ɔk.
4   2   4   2   4   1

(142) hawe:ʔó wai kakwe:kɔ háeʔkwa ʔɛyótihsɛnɔye:táʔk, he ni:yó:h,
2   4 2   42   4   2 4

ʔojistanóhkwéɔʔ, hé:ɔwe kéɔyatéʔ.   (143) ta: neʔ kho ne tkaye:íʔ,
2   4   2   3 21   2   4

rest while it is in shadow." That is what he intended. (130) "And perhaps it will happen that somewhere at a distance [36] they will run into darkness. (131) And I shall have another helper, another orb in the sky. (132) People will say 'our grandmother, the moon'. That is how they will do it. It can be a sort of guide for their steps, providing them with light." (133) And indeed it is a measure for us as we go along, we who move about on the earth. (134) He decided, "The moon will change its form as it goes." They have called it "phases." [37] (135) And it is true: it is still a measure for us up to the present time, the way it is as we go along, we who move about on the earth. (136) And we believe that they come from there too, that it continues unchanged: the little ones taking their places on the earth.[38] They are here and they come from our mothers. (137) And therefore we believe that she has done all that she was obligated to do, the assignment she was given. (138) And now give it your thought, that we may do it properly: we now give thanks for her, our grandmother, the moon. And our minds will continue to be so.

13. The Stars

(139) And now this is what Our Creator did. (140) He decided, "There will also be stars arrayed in the sky while it is dark." (141) And he assigned to them certain things as well, the way it would continue to be. (142) He decided, "They too will all have names, all the stars in the sky. (143) And they too, in fact, will be indicators, to

---

[36] I.e., from home.
[37] Lit., 'the moons always come to an end.'
[38] I.e., the cycle of reproduction is determined by the moon.

háeˀkwa ˀɛkaiwayéɔnya:nɔ́:k, n ɛyakotɛnɔˀkæ:htashɛtáhkɔ:ɔ́k, ne

ˀɔ:kwéh, teyakotawɛnyé:h, neˀho kiˀshɛ nɛya:wéh, n ɛyakohsɔ́taˀís,

nɛ: ˀatháinɔˀkéh, nɛ: koyǽ:ˀtɔ́h, ne ˀɔ:kwéh, teyakotawɛnyé:h.

(144) ta: neˀ wai tkaye:íˀ, ˀɛyɔtkɔskáhatéˀ, ˀojistanóhkwéɔˀ, ta: neˀ

wai ˀɛyakoyaˀtatókɛsták, tkaye:íˀ, neˀh ɛjɔ́tkɔ:ták, hɛ:ɔwé:kwa:

né:h, tetyakoˀníkɔhka:nyéh.   (145) ta: nɛ: niyótoˀkta:tyéˀ, neˀ

háeˀkwa hati:wayɛtáhkóh.   (146) nɛ: he nɛ:wé:ˀ, ˀotɛɔnóstɔ́h, ne

ˀéɔtisha:tét, he ni:yɔ: hotkáˀwe ˀa:hɔ́ˀ, watɔ:níh, hɛ́:ɔwe yɔejatéˀ.

(147) ta: tkaye:íˀ, ˀoti:nekáhsɔnyéˀs, he niwáhsɔ:tí:s, he ni:y

o:tkáˀwe ˀa:hɔ́ˀ, watɔ:níh, neˀ neˀho teyawehtɔ́:tyéˀ, nɛ: h ojih-

sɔˀtáhsi:áˀ, hɛ́:ɔwe kéɔyatéˀ.   (148) ta: neˀ wai n itwé:h, hoti:wa-

yéistɔ́h, háeˀkwa niyóiwáˀ, hati:wayɛtáhkóh, ta: ˀɛswe:hé:k, waˀak-

watyɛ:nɔ:níˀ, ˀo:nɛ: néˀ, ˀoˀtyethinɔ́:nyɔ́:ˀ, ˀojihsɔˀtáhsi:áˀ, hɛ́:ɔwe

kɛɔyatéˀ, ta: neˀho wai neyóˀtɛ:ɔ́k, n ɔkwaˀnikɔ́ɛˀ.

14. The Four Beings

(149) ta onɛ wai hotyɛ:nóˀktaˀɔ he tyɔhéˀ, hawe:ˀɔ́h, neˀ ti ne

ˀewɔkatéhɔˀshɛ:táˀk, ne ke:i niyɔ́kweˀta:ké:h, neˀ tɛshakonéˀ-

nyatɔ́:ˀ, ne ˀɔ:kwéh, ne yɔ́ejaˀkéh, ˀoˀtyɔtawɛ:nyéˀ:ˀ.   (150) tkáye:iˀ

wai ta:ka:nǽhji:wéh, hɛˀɛ taˀáyoska:sthéˀt, hotiyaˀtóskaˀáh, tao-

nɔtawényé:ak.   (151) neˀ wai ne tkaye:íˀ, haˀte:yɔ́:h, niyotye:éh,

he yɔejata:tyéˀ, neˀho ˀɛthɛnɔtawɛnyéˀ:ˀ.   (152) neˀ ne næ: shɔ:

ka:téˀ, ˀɛyakotye:ɔ́ˀ ne ˀɔ:kwéh, ne yɔ́ejaˀkéh, teyakotawɛnyéˀ:h.

(153) neˀ n ɛyakotí:watye:ɔ́ˀ, ne ˀɔ:kwe teyakotawɛnyéˀ:h, ne

yɔ́ejaˀkéh, n ɛthɛneˀnéoˀktéˀ.   (154) ta: tkaye:íˀ, kho twaiwak-

wáihsɔ́s, ne yɔ́ejaˀkéh, teyɔkwatawɛnyéˀ:h, neˀho nɛya:wéh, nɛ:

ˀɛyakotí:watye:ɔ́ˀ, n ɛthɛneˀnéoˀktéˀ, niyóˀtɛ: teyɔkwatawɛnyéˀ:h,

be used for measuring by the people moving about. If it happens that they run into darkness on their journey, they will use them, the people moving about. (144) And indeed they will lift their faces to the stars and will be set straight. They will head back directly toward their home." [39] (145) And up to the present time they have had an added responsibility. (146) While it is dark they will cause moisture to fall on everything that he left to grow of its own accord on the earth. (147) And truly they enjoy water throughout the night, everything that he left to grow of its own accord. It comes from the stars arrayed in the sky. (148) And we believe that they are performing their obligation, the responsibility that they too have. And give it your thought, that we may do it properly: we now give thanks for them, the stars arrayed in the sky. And our minds will continue to be so.

14. The Four Beings

(149) And now Our Creator decided, "I shall have the Four Beings as helpers to protect the people moving about on the earth." (150) Indeed, he saw well that it was not possible for them alone, that they could not continue to move about alone. (151) It was true: all sorts of things were going on on the earth where they would move about. (152) It was inevitable that the people moving about on the earth would have accidents. (153) The people moving about on the earth would have accidental things happen to them that would be beyond their control. (154) And indeed we too can attest to it, we who move about on the earth: it will happen that people are involved in accidents that are beyond their control. It is the way with us who move about

---

[39] Lit. 'where it bites their mind,' possibly referring to homesickness.

he yɔejaté?. (155) ta: ne? kho ne tkaye:í?, háe?kwa ne? hati:wa-
yɛtáhkɔ́h, ?ɛɔwɛnɔ́tkaɛɔ́?, hotého?shé?, ?i:kɛ: wa:tɔ́h, ke:i niké-
tyohkwá:ke:h. (156) nɛ: tɛɔtisnyé:k, hɛ́:ɔwe yɔejaté?, shɔkwátka?-
wéh, n ɛyɔkwa?nikɔiyostáhkɔ́:ɔk. (157) ta: ?itwe: háe?kwa hoti:wa-
yéistɔ́h, he niyóiwá?, hoti:wayɛtáhkɔ́h, nɛ: wa:tɔ́h, ke:i nyɛ:nɔtí:h,
teyɔkhiyé?nyatɔ́?. (158) ta: ne?ho wai ni:ká:?, ?áɔ?e:sát, ?itwe:
skɛ:nɔ? twɛnɔ́htɔnyɔ́ ?ɛswe:hé:k, ska:t wa?akwayɛ:? n ɔkwa?nikɔ́ɛ?,
?o:nɛ: né?, ?o?tyethinɔ́:nyɔ́:?, nɛ: hotéhɔ?shé?, ke:i nyɛ:nɔtí:h,
teyɔkhiyé?nyatɔ́?, ta: ne?ho wai nɛyó?tɛ:ɔ́k, n ɔkwa?nikɔ́ɛ?.

15. Handsome Lake

(159) ta onɛ wai nɛ: nyo:ye:éh, hotyɛ:nɔ́?kta?ɔ hé tyɔhe?. (160)
tkaye:i? wai hawe:?ɔ́h, ne? ti néh, ha?tekakɔ́:t, ne?ho nɛya:wéh, he
nio?nikɔ́?té:h. (161) ne? wai ne tkaye:í?, nɛ: sha?ka:t teyɔkwa-
tawɛnyé:nɔ́?, hɛ́:ɔwe yɔejaté?. (162) ne? wai n onɔ́hsotaiyɔ́:?,
waoye:nɔ́:?, tkaye:í?, wáonɔktanɛ:tá:k. (163) ne? wai ne ?o?yɔ́s-
hæké:?, ta:ɛ?tákwɛhtá:?. (164) ta: ne?ho wai niyó?té:h, nɛ ha?te-
kakɔ́:t, ta:tɛnɔ́:nyɔ́:?, wahsɔtate:nyɔ́?, wɛ:níshæte:nyɔ́?, kho ?i:éh,
ha?tekakɔ:t sɔ:ká:?, hayá?taté?, hosyɔ:ní:h, he ni:yɔ́:h, hotkáthwɛ:-
ɔtyé?. (165) ta: ne?ho kho nɛ:ké:h, tetháehá?, ne? ne kakwe:kɔ́h,
shatathewáthá?, he ni:yɔ́:h, ?i:é ne? hoyé?hihsé?s, yɔ́ɛja?kéh, to:-
tawɛ:nyé:h. (166) ta: ne? kwa: ne tkaye:í?, ha?tewɛ:níshæké:h,
to:tɛnɔ́:nyɔ́?, ti?kwa na?áhtɛ?ɛ wa:sé:?, wá:tkathó?. (167) ta onɛ
wai nɛ:ké:h, ne?ho nɔ?ɔ:wéh, n o:tyɛ:nɔ́?kta?ɔ ta:ka:næhji:wéh,
sɛ?ɛ tkaye:í?, he niyakotye:ɛ ne ?ɔ:kwéh, ne yɔ́ɛja?kéh. (168) ne?
n a:yé:?, hɛ?ɛ te?kátka?ho te?skayɛtáhkɔ́h, ne koɔ?níkɔ́ɛ?, ne teyako-

on the earth.   (155) And indeed they also have the added responsibility of keeping watch over those of his helpers called the Four Groups.[40]   (156) They will continue to look after us whom he left on the earth, and will bring us contentment.   (157) And we believe that they too are performing their obligation, the assignment they were given, those who are called the Four Beings, our protectors. (158) And therefore let there be gratitude, for we believe that we are happy.   Give it your thought, that with one mind we may now give thanks for his helpers, the Four Beings, our protectors.   And our minds will continue to be so.

15. Handsome Lake

(159) And now this is what Our Creator did.   (160) He did indeed decide it, and it must happen according to his will.   (161) Indeed he [41] was among us who moved about on the earth.   (162) Illness took hold of him, and he was confined to bed.   (163) For a number of years he lay helpless.   (164) And the way things were, he had to be thankful during the nights and the days, and he thought that there must be someone there who made all the things that he was seeing.[42] (165) And thereupon he repented everything, all the things he thought he had done wrong when he moved about on the earth.   (166) And indeed he was thankful each day for each new thing that he saw. (167) And now it happened that the Creator saw well how the people on the earth were acting.   (168) It seemed that nowhere was there any longer any guidance for the minds of those who moved about.

---

[40] See p. 9.

[41] The reference shifts here to Handsome Lake, who is not regarded as an incarnation of the Creator as the translation might be taken to imply.

[42] The wording here is reminiscent of the Good Message.

tawɛnyé:h. (169) ta onɛ ti nɛ́:h, ne?ho nɔ?ɔ:wɛ́h, thakɔyatényehtɔ́h,
hotéhɔ?shɛ́?, ne? hɔwɔwɛnɛ:?ɔ́h, shetwakowa:nɛ́ twatɔ́:k, kanyotai-
yɔ́?, tsa?tɔ́:tawɛnyé:h. (170) ne? wai howɔiwakéistaní:h, ne? nɛ:kɛ́:h
?ɛtsɔ́kwa:owí?, nejakwayé:ɔk, n o:ɛtɔ́:kwá:h. (171) ta: ne? wai ne
?o?yóshæ̃ké:?, ne? hothyówi:atyé?, he nya:wɛnɔ́?té:h, hotyɛ:nɔ́?k-
ta?ɔ́h. (172) ta: ne?ho wai niyɔ́?tɛ:ɔtyé?, he niyo:wɛ́?, ha?tɔsa:-
yoskwéhtá:at, ne? wai nɛ:kɛ́:h, hoɔyakɛ́?tɔ:ɔtyé?s. (173) ta: ne?
wai ne tkaye:í?, ?áɔ?e:sát, ne? ne ka:ɛkwa nikɛɔtyé?, ?o:nɛ nɛ:kɛ́:h,
tkaye:i? sayɔ́kwathɔ:téh, he nya:wɛnɔ́?té:h, n o:tyɛ:nɔ́?kta?ɔ́h.
(174) ta: ne? wai ne?ho ni:ká:?, ?áɔ?e:sát, ?ahsɔ ?ohte:tyɔ́:h, nioiwíhsa?ɔ́h. (175) ta: ?ɛswe:he:k ti wa?akwatyɛ:nɔ:ní?, nɛ: ne ?o?t-
sakwanɔ́:nyɔ́:?, nɛ: kanyotaiyɔ́?, ?akwátɔ́:k, ta: ne?ho wai nɛyɔ́?-
tɛ:ɔ́k, n ɔkwa?nikɔ́ɛ?.

16. The Creator

(176) ta onɛ wai nyo:ye:éh, hotyɛ:nɔ́?kta?ɔ hé tyɔhe?. (177) tka-
ye:i? wai hawɛ:?ɔ́h, hetkɛ n í?, nɔ?kéɔya:tíh, hɛskí?tyɔ:tá?k, ne?ho
ti hejáko?kthá:k, ne tɛyɔtenɔ́:nyɔ́:?, ne yɔ́ɛja?kéh. (178) ne? shɔ:
hekáya?tí:h, ?ɛyakoyɛ:tá?k, n atɔ́?eshɔ:nyɔ́k, he ni:yɔ́:h, ?ɛyakot-
káthwɛ:ɔtyé?, he nɔ?keyɛno?tɛ?hé?t, ?o?kɔ́ɛja:tá:t, kho he ni:yɔ́:h,
?ɛyakotkáthwɛ:ɔtyé?, ?ɛyotɔníatyé?, ne?ho wai nio?nikɔɛwé?ɔh.
(179) ?ɛyakoyɛ:tá?k, ti ne kanoɔhkwá?shæ̃?, ne yɔ́ɛja?kéh, n ɔ:kwéh,
?o?tyɔtawɛ:nyé:?, tɛyɔtɛnɔ:nyɔ́:ɔk, ti hekáya?tí:h. (180) ne?ho
?ɛyɔ́hsahá:k, hé:ɔw ɛyɔ́ɛja:té:k, tayɛnɔ́:nyɔ́:ɔk, he ni:yɔ: kotkáth-
wa?ɔ́h. (181) ne?ho hetkɛ hɛyéahsé:k, ne?ho hejáko?kthá:k, hɛskí?-
tyɔ:tá?k. (182) ?ɛwɔkathɔtehjí:wɛ:ɔ́k, ti ne ?ɛyeiwa:notátyɛ?sé:k,
ne ?o:kwéh, ne teyakotawɛnyé:h. (183) ne? kho ne tkaye:í?, tɛkhe-

(169) And now it happened that he sent his helpers to speak to our great one, whom we used to call Handsome Lake, when he moved about. (170) They gave him the responsibility to tell us what we should do in the future. (171) And for a number of years he told about the words of the Creator. (172) And the way things went, he labored until he collapsed. (173) And let there indeed be gratitude that from time to time now we again hear the words of the Creator. (174) And therefore let there be gratitude that it is still continuing as he planned it. (175) And give it your thought, that we may do it properly: we give thanks for him, whom we called Handsome Lake. And our minds will continue to be so.

16. The Creator

(176) And now this is what Our Creator did. (177) He decided, "I myself shall continue to dwell above the sky, and that is where those on the earth will end their thanksgiving. (178) They will simply continue to have gratitude for everything they see that I created on the earth, and for everything they see that is growing." That is what he intended. (179) "The people moving about on the earth will have love; they will simply be thankful. (180) They will begin on the earth, giving thanks for all they see. (181) They will carry it upward, ending where I dwell. (182) I shall always be listening carefully to what they are saying, the people who move about. (183) And indeed I shall always be watching carefully what

ka:næhji:wέ:ɔk, he neyakotyέ:ɔk, ne ʔɔ:kwέh, ne yɔ́eja ʔkέh. (184)
4 2   4   2   4 2 3   21

ta: neʔho wai nε: niyóto ʔkta:tyέʔ, neʔ wai ne ʔitwέ:h, tkaye:íʔ,
2   4 2   4   2 4

skε:nɔʔ twenóhtɔnyɔ́h, nityɔ́kweʔta:kέ:h. (185) ta: neʔho kho
2   4 2 3   21   2

ni:ká:ʔ, ne ʔáɔʔe:sát, he káiwaya:sɔ́h, ʔetwiʔ skε:nɔʔ twenóhtɔnyɔ́h.
4 2   3 2   4 2   3 21

(186) ta: ʔeswe:hέ:k, ti ʔo:nε kε ska:t waʔakwayέ:ʔ, n ɔkwaʔnikɔ́eʔ,
      2   4 2   4   2   4

ʔo:nε: néʔ, ʔoʔtsakwanó:nyɔ́:ʔ, n o:tyε:nɔ́ʔktaʔɔ he ʔakyɔ:hέʔ, ta:
2 4 2   4   2   4 2

neʔho wai neyɔ́ʔtε:ɔ́k, n ɔkwaʔnikɔ́eʔ.
    4   2   41

Epilogue

(187) ta: neʔho n íʔ nε:kε:h, niwátkwenyɔs, nε: hέ nyo:tiye:éh,
      2   4 3 23   2 3   2   3 4 3 4 2 3

hone:ʔɔ́h, ʔεkayέ:táʔk, ʔo:εtɔ́:h, kaiwatέhkɔh, hotíyastɔ́h, ʔeyakaɔʔ-
3 2 3   3 2 31 2   3 2 3   3   2 3 2   2 4 2 3   2

esháhseʔ, ne ʔeyakoyaʔtayέihséʔ, n o:εtɔ́:kwa:h, ta: neʔho ti n íʔ
4 2   2   41 31   2   4   2   3 2   4

shɔ:h, niwátkwenyɔs, neʔho n íʔ shɔ: niwakeyέʔheʔɔh, nε: ʔɔ́:εtɔ:h,
2   2 4   2   2   4 3   4 2   3 3 2

kaiwatέhkɔh. (188) tá: neʔhoh.
3 2 3   1   3   1

they do, the people on the earth." (184) And up to the present time, indeed, we people believe that we are happy. (185) And therefore let there also be gratitude that we can claim to be happy. (186) And give it your thought, that with one mind we may now give thanks for him, Our Creator. And our minds will continue to be so.

Epilogue

(187) And that is all that I myself am able to do. What they [43] did was to decide that a ritual of gratitude, as they called it, would always be observed in the future, when in the future people would gather. And that is all that I myself am able to do; that is all that I learned of the ritual which begins the ceremony. (188) That is it.

---

[43] The Four Beings.

THANKSGIVING DANCE

PART ONE: INITIAL SONG GROUP

Song I

(Whoop) yo we he _____ yo he

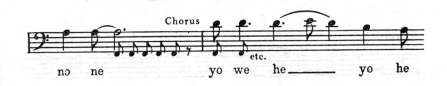

nɔ ne   yo we he _____ yo he

nɔ ne _ yo we he _ yo he nɔ ne _

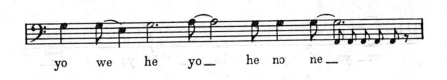

yo we he yo _ he nɔ ne _

we he ɔe ya ha   ka yo we ho

he nɔ ne yo we _ he _ yo he nɔ ne _

47

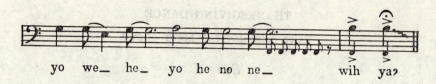

yo we___ he___ yo he no ne___ wih yaꞋ

Song II

Solo

(Whoop) we___ ya wi___ ye he

Chorus

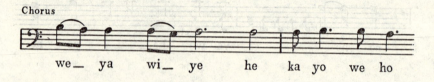

we___ ya wi___ ye he ka yo we ho

ya neꞋ___ nɔ ha wi ye he nɔ

we___ ya wi ye he____ ka yo we ho___

ya neꞋ nɔ ha wi ye he nɔ we___ ya wi___ ye he

ka yo we ho ya neꞋ___ nɔ ha wi ye

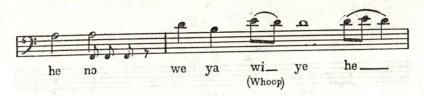

he　nɔ　　we ya wi　ye　he____
(Whoop)

ka yo　we　ho__　ya neʔ　nɔ　ha wi ye　he nɔ

we__ ya　wi__ ye　he____　ka yo　we　ho__

ya neʔ　nɔ　ha wi　ye　he　nɔ

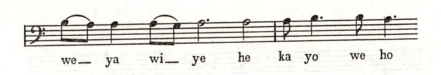

we__ ya　wi__ ye　he　ka yo　we ho

ya　neʔ__　nɔ　ha wi ye　wih　yaʔ

Song III

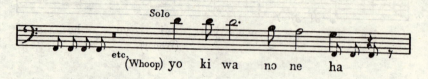

Solo

(Whoop) yo ki wa nɔ ne ha

etc.

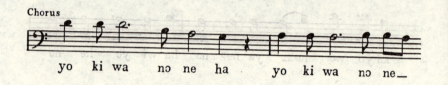

Chorus

yo ki wa nɔ ne ha   yo ki wa nɔ ne—

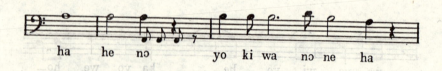

ha he nɔ   yo ki wa nɔ ne ha

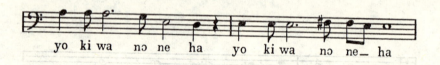

yo ki wa nɔ ne ha   yo ki wa nɔ ne— ha

he nɔ   yo ki wa nɔ ne ha   yo ki wa

accel.   ♩=192

nɔ ne ha he nɔ   yo ki wa nɔ ne ha

yo ki wa nɔ ne— ha   wih yaʔ

Song IV

♩=144 Solo

etc.

wi yo ya ne nɔ

Chorus

wi yo ya ne nɔ wi yo ya ṅe — nɔ

he nɔ wi yo ya ne nɔ wi yo ya— ne nɔ

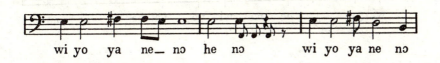

wi yo ya ne— nɔ he nɔ wi yo ya ne nɔ

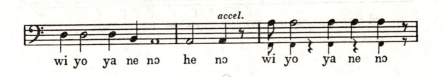

accel.

wi yo ya ne nɔ he nɔ wi yo ya ne nɔ

wi yo ya ne nɔ wih yaʔ

Song V

wi yo ya ne nɔ   wi yo ya ne nɔ

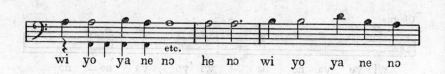

wi yo ya ne nɔ he nɔ wi yo ya ne nɔ

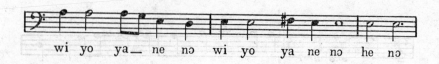

wi yo ya_ ne nɔ wi yo ya ne nɔ he nɔ

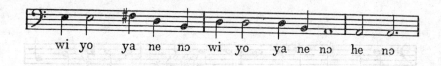

wi yo ya ne nɔ wi yo ya ne nɔ he nɔ

wi yo ya ne nɔ wi yo ya ne nɔ wih yaʔ

Song VI

wi yo ya ne nɔ   wi yo ya ne nɔ

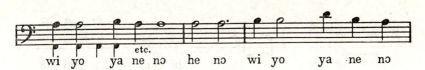

wi yo ya ne nɔ he nɔ wi yo ya ne nɔ

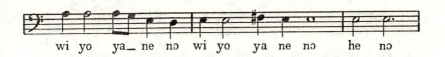

wi yo ya ne nɔ wi yo ya ne nɔ he nɔ

wi yo ya ne nɔ wi yo ya ne nɔ wih yaʔ

Song VII

Solo

ha yo we ha yo we ha yo we

Chorus

nɔ ta we he nɔ ha yo we ha yo we ha yo

we nɔ ta we he nɔ ha yo we ha yo we

ha yo we   nɔ ta we   he nɔ   ha yo we

ha yo we   ha yo we   nɔ ta we   wih yaʔ

Song VIII

Solo

ka nɔ to we   nɔ to we   he nɔ

Chorus

ka nɔ to we   nɔ to we   etc.   he nɔ

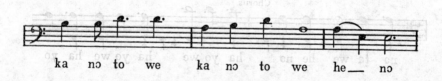

ka nɔ to we   ka nɔ to we   he__ nɔ

ka nɔ to__ we   nɔ to we   he nɔ

ka nɔ to— we nɔ to we wih yaɁ

Song IX

Solo

ka nɔ to we ka nɔ to we

Chorus

ka nɔ to we ka nɔ to we— nɔ to we he— nɔ

ka nɔ to we ka nɔ to we— nɔ to we he— nɔ

ka nɔ to wĕ ka nɔ to we— nɔ to we wih yaɁ

Song X

Solo

he ka nɔ ta we he

Chorus

he ka nɔ ta we he yoh hah heh

etc.

ka nɔ ta we he he ka nɔ ta we he

yoh hah heh ka nɔ ta we he he ka nɔ ta

we he yoh hah heh ka nɔ ta we wih yaʔ

Song XI

Solo

yoh hah heh ka nɔ ta we

Chorus

yoh hah heh ka nɔ ta we ka nɔ ta we
etc.

yoh hah heh   ka nɔ ta we   ka nɔ ta we

yoh hah heh   ka nɔ ta we   ka nɔ ta we

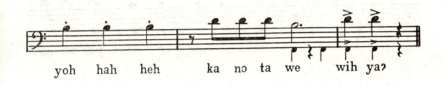

yoh hah heh   ka nɔ ta we   wih ya?

Song XII

Solo   Chorus

yoh hah heh   ha wi? yæ?   yoh hah heh

ha wi? yæ?   yo ha wi? yæ?   yoh hah heh

ha wi? yæ?   yo ha wi? yæ? yoh hah heh   ha wi? yæ?

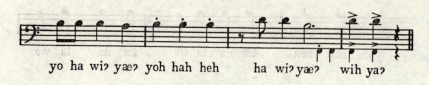

yo ha wiꜣ yaeꜣ yoh hah heh   ha wiꜣ yaeꜣ   wih yaꜣ

Song XIII

yo wa ne   no＿＿ haꜣ he no   yo wa ne

no＿＿ haꜣ he no   ha no to we ha wi ye   ꜣe

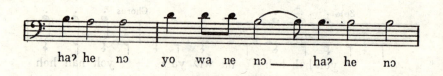

haꜣ he no   yo wa ne no＿＿ haꜣ he   no

ha no to we ha wi ye   ꜣe haꜣ he   no

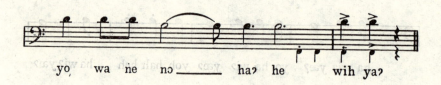

yo, wa ne no＿＿ haꜣ he   wih yaꜣ

Song XIV

ya we? ho ya ne ha ya we ho ya ne

ya we? ho ya ne ha ya we ho ya ne

ya we? ho ya ne ha ya we ho ya ne ya we? ho ya ne

ka nɔ to ?o we ka nɔ to we wih ya?

Song XV

yo he nɔh ti ya we

yo he nɔh ti ya we yo he nɔh ti ya we

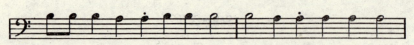

ha ya we he nɔh ti ya we   yo he nɔh ti ya we

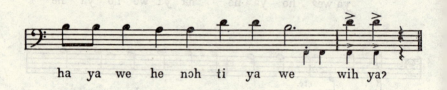

ha ya we he nɔh ti ya we   wih yaʔ

Song XVI

Solo

yo wi hi ya ya

Chorus

yo wi hi ya ya   yo wi hi ya ⎯

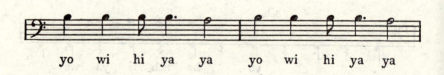

yo wi hi ya ya   yo wi hi ya ya

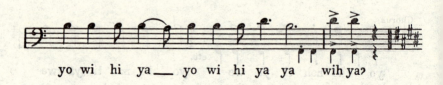

yo wi hi ya ⎯ yo wi hi ya ya   wih yaʔ

Song XVII

Solo
ka yo wa ne noh   ka yo wa ne noh

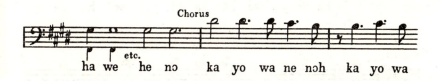

Chorus
ha we he no   ka yo wa ne noh   ka yo wa

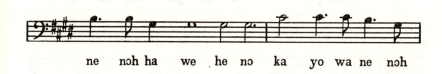

ne noh ha   we   he no   ka   yo wa ne   noh

ka   yo   wa ne noh   ka yo wa ne noh

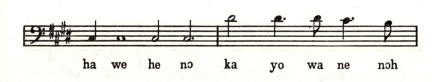

ha   we   he no   ka   yo   wa   ne   noh

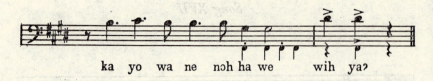

ka yo wa ne nɔh ha we   wih ya?

Song XVIII

Solo

ka ni ya we ha ka ni ya   we ha ne

Chorus

ka ni ya we ha ka ni   ya   we ha   ne

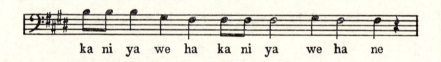

ka ni ya   we ha ka ni ya   we ha   ne

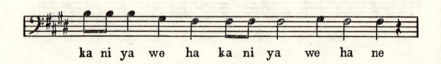

ka ni ya   we   ha ka ni ya   we   ha   ne

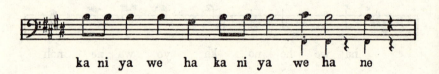

ka ni ya   we   ha ka ni ya   we   ha   ne

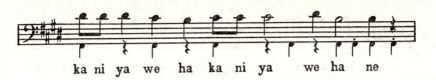

ka ni ya we ha ka ni ya we ha ne

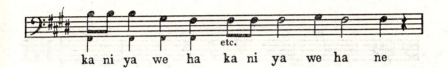

ka ni ya we ha ka ni ya we ha ne

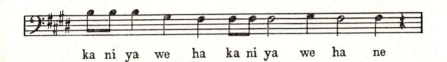

ka ni ya we ha ka ni ya we ha ne

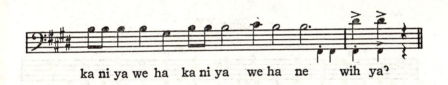

ka ni ya we ha ka ni ya we ha ne wih ya'

Song XIX

ha wi ye ha wi yæ'

ha wi ye ha wi yæ' hae' hɛ' he___ ha wi ye

ha wi ye ha wi yæ' ha wi ye___ ha wi yæ'

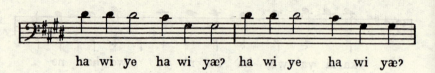

ha wi ye   ha wi yæ?   ha wi ye   ha wi yæ?

hae? hε?   he_____   ha wi ye   wih ya?

Song XX

Solo

Chorus

etc.

ha wi ye   he? nɔh   ha wi ye   he? nɔh

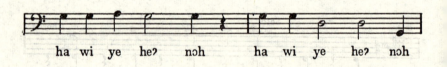

ha wi ye   he?   nɔh   ha wi ye   he?   nɔh

ha wi ye   he?   nɔh   ha   wi   ye   he?   nɔh

ha wi ye   he?   nɔ   we ya wi ye   wih ya?

Song XXI

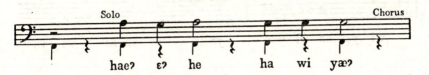

hae? ɛ? he ha wi yæ?

hae? ɛ? he ha wi yæ? yo ha wi yæh

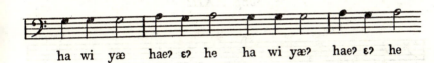

ha wi yæ hae? ɛ? he ha wi yæ? hae? ɛ? he

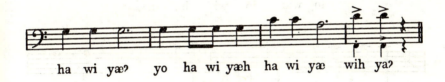

ha wi yæ? yo ha wi yæh ha wi yæ wih ya?

Song XXII

ya he ya ho ?o wi ye ha

wi yæ ya he ya ho ?o wi ye ha wi yæ?

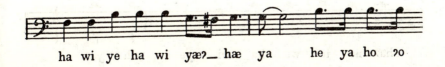

ha wi ye ha wi yæ?— hæ ya he ya ho ?o

wi ye ha wi yæ   ya   he ya ho ɂo wi ye

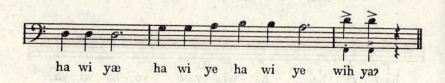

ha wi yæ   ha wi ye ha wi ye   wih yaɂ

Song XXIII

to wis   to wiɂ ha ne

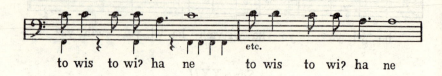

to wis to wiɂ ha ne   to wis   to wiɂ ha ne

to wis to wiɂ ha ne   haɂ nɔ to we ha wi ye

to wis   to wiɂ ha ne to wis   to wiɂ ha   ne

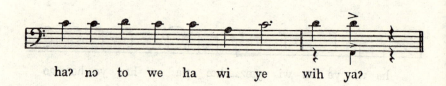

haɂ nɔ to we ha wi ye   wih yaɂ

Song XXIV

ka nɔ to ya neʔ

wi kʼa nɛ to yaʔ ha ne   ka nɔ to

ya neʔ   wi ka nɛ to yaʔ ha ne

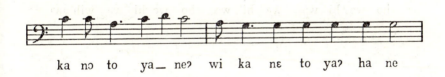

ka nɔ to ya_ neʔ wi ka nɛ to yaʔ ha ne

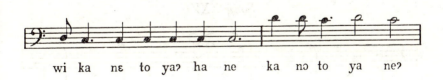

wi ka nɛ to yaʔ ha ne   ka nɔ to ya neʔ

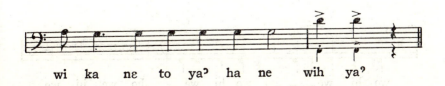

wi ka nɛ to yaʔ ha ne   wih yaʔ

Song XXV

we hi we ho

we hi we ___ we hi we ho we hi we ___

ho we hi we   we hi we ho we hi we

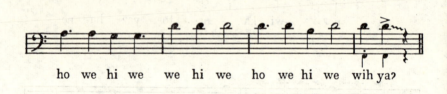

ho we hi we   we hi we ho we hi we wih ya?

Song XXVI

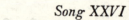

we hi we ___ ho we hi we

we hi we ___ ho we hi we ___ ho we hi we

we hi we ___ ho we hi we ___ ho we hi we

we hi we   we hi we ___ ho we hi we ___

ho we hi we ___   ho we hi we we hi we

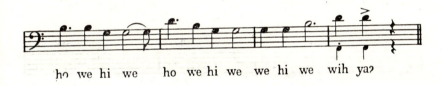

hɔ we hi we   ho we hi we we hi we wih yaʔ

Song XXVII

Identical with Song XXVI except for syllables wehiwe howehiyaʔ

Song XXVIII

Solo   Chorus

wi ___ yo ha he   nɔ

wi __ yo ha he nɔ   we __ yo ha he ___ nɔ

wi   yo   ha   he   nɔ   we   yo   ha   he   nɔ

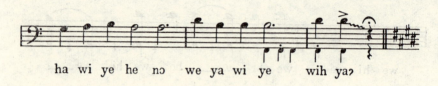

ha   wi   ye   he   nɔ   we   ya   wi   ye   wih   yaʔ

Song XXIX

Solo

(Whoop) we   ya   wi   ye   ha   wi   ye

Chorus

ha   wi   ye   we   ya   wi   ye

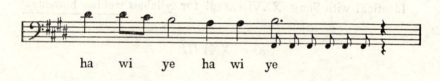

ha   wi   ye   ha   wi   ye

he   yo   ha   he   nɔ   ha   wi   ye   he   nɔ

we   ya   wi   ye   wih   yaʔ

Song XXX

(Whoop) we ya wi yo he

ʔe ya we he yæ ha wi yæ we ya wi yo

he ʔe ya we he yæ ha wi yæ haeʔ he ya

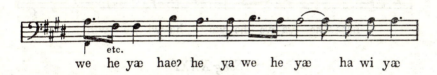

etc.

we he yæ haeʔ he ya we he yæ ha wi yæ

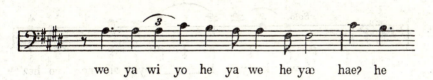

we ya wi yo he ya we he yæ haeʔ he

ya we he yæ haeʔ he ya we he yæ___

ha wi yæ we ya wi yo he ʔe ya we he

yæ ha wi yæ hae? he ya we he yæ

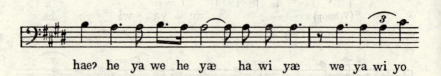

hae? he ya we he yæ ha wi yæ we ya wi yo

he ya we he yæ hae? he ya we he yæ

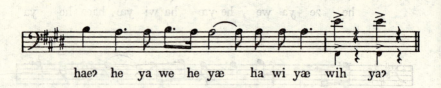

hae? he ya we he yæ ha wi yæ wih ya?

Song XXXI

wi ka yo he_____ yo ?i ne yo hɛ?

wi ka yo he yo ?i ne yo hɛ? wa tɔ ne

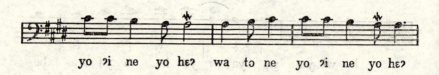

yo ?i ne yo hɛ? wa tɔ ne yo ?i ne yo hɛ?

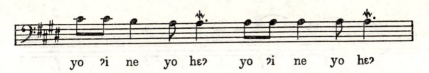

yo ʔi ne yo hɛʔ yo ʔi ne yo hɛʔ

yo ʔi ne yo hɛʔ yo ʔi ne yo hɛʔ

wi ka yo he___ yo ʔi ne yo hɛʔ wa to ne

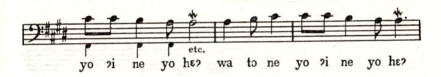

yo ʔi ne yo hɛʔ wa to ne yo ʔi ne yo hɛʔ

yo ʔi ne yo hɛʔ yo ʔi ne yo hɛʔ yo ʔi ne

yo hɛʔ yo ʔi ne yo hɛʔ wih heh

Song XXXII

wi ka yo he___ yo ʔi ne yo hɛʔ

wi ka yo he___ yo ʔi ne yo heʔ ha yo weh

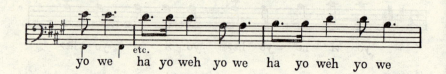

yo we ha yo weh yo we ha yo weh yo we

yo ʔi ne yo heʔ yo ʔi ne yo heʔ yo ʔi ne

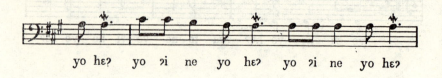

yo heʔ yo ʔi ne yo heʔ yo ʔi ne yo heʔ

wi ka yo he___ yo ʔi ne yo heʔ ha yo weh

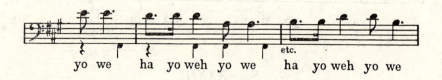

yo we ha yo weh yo we ha yo weh yo we

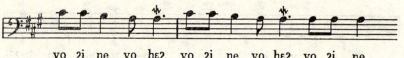

yo ʔi ne yo heʔ yo ʔi ne yo heʔ yo ʔi ne

yo hεʔ   yo ʔi ne   yo hεʔ   yo ʔi ne   yo hεʔ wih heh

Song XXXIII

Solo

ha ni   kɔ to

Chorus

we ya ne nɔ   ha ni kɔ to   we ya ne   nɔ

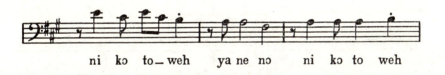

ni kɔ to—weh   ya ne nɔ   ni kɔ to weh

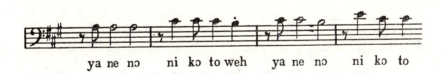

ya ne nɔ   ni kɔ to weh   ya ne nɔ   ni kɔ to

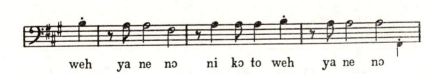

weh   ya ne nɔ   ni kɔ to weh   ya ne nɔ

ha ni kɔ to we ya ne   nɔ   ni kɔ to— weh

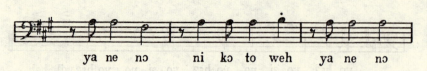

ya ne nɔ   ni kɔ to weh   ya ne nɔ

ni kɔ to weh   ya ne nɔ   ni kɔ to weh

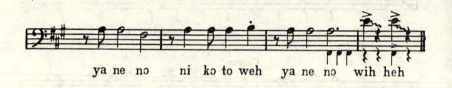

ya ne nɔ   ni kɔ to weh   ya ne nɔ   wih heh

Song XXXIV

Solo

ha ni kɔ to he   ya ne nɔ

Chorus

ha ni   kɔ to he   ya ne nɔ   ha ni   kɔ to

etc.

he   ya ne nɔ   ha ni kɔ to he   ya ne nɔ

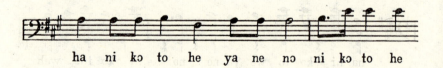

ha ni kɔ to he   ya ne nɔ   ni kɔ to he

ya ne nɔ   ni kɔ to he ya ne nɔ ha ni kɔ

to hǝ ya ne nɔ   ha ni kɔ to he ya ne nɔ

ni kɔ to he ya ne nɔ   ni kɔ to he ya ne. nɔ

ha ni kɔ to   he ya ne nɔ ha ni kɔ to he

etc.

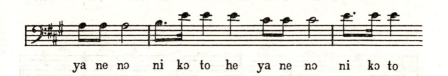

ya ne nɔ   ni kɔ to he ya ne nɔ   ni kɔ to

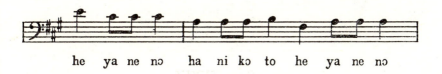

he ya ne nɔ   ha ni kɔ to he ya ne nɔ

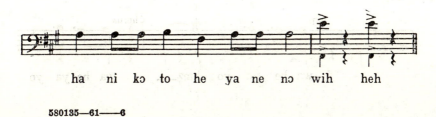

ha ni kɔ to   he ya ne nɔ wih   heh

Song XXXV

Solo

hae? heh   hae? ɛ? heh wa he   ya yo hæ?

Chorus

hae? heh   hae? ɛ? heh wa he   ya yo hæ?
etc.

wa he ya yo hæ?   hae? ɛ? heh   hae? ɛ? heh wa he

ya yo hæ? wa he ya yo hæ?   hae? heh   hae? ɛ? heh

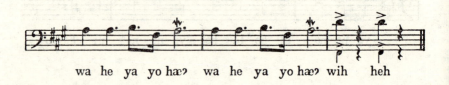

wa he ya yo hæ? wa he ya yo hæ? wih   heh

Song XXXVI

Solo   Chorus

wa he ya yo hæ?____   wa he ya yo

hæʔ___   haeʔ εʔ heh   haeʔ εʔ heh wa he

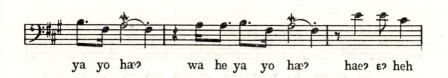

ya yo hæʔ   wa he ya yo hæʔ   haeʔ εʔ heh

hæʔ   εʔ heh   wa he ya yo hæʔ___

wa he ya yo hæʔ   wih heh

Song XXXVII

Solo

ya ho nε ne he nε ne

Chorus

ya ho nε ne hε nε ne   ho nε ne he nε neh

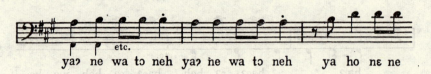

ya? ne wa to neh ya? ne wa to neh   ya ho nɛ ne

he nɛ ne ho nɛ ne he nɛ neh ya? ne wa to neh

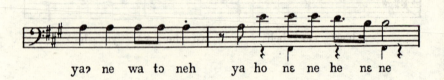

ya? ne wa to neh   ya ho nɛ ne he nɛ ne

ho nɛ ne he nɛ neh ya? ne wa to neh

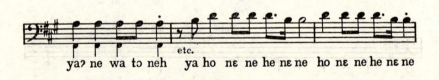

ya? ne wa to neh   ya ho nɛ ne he nɛ ne ho nɛ ne he nɛ ne

ya? ne wa to neh ya? ne wa to neh wih heh

Song XXXVIII

ya ne? he ya? ?o nɛ ne he he ya

ya ne? he ya? ?o nɛ ne he he ya

ya ne? he ya? ?o nɛ ne he he ya ya ne? he ya?

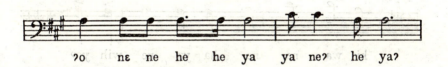

?o nɛ ne he he ya ya ne? he ya?

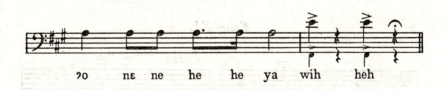

?o nɛ ne he he ya wih heh

Song XXXIX

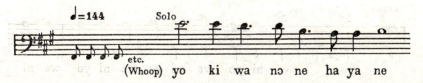

(Whoop) yo ki wa nɔ ne ha ya ne

Chorus

he   ɔ   yo ki wa nɔ ne ha ya ne he

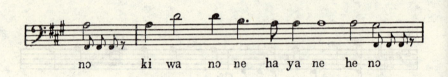

ɔ   ki wa   nɔ ne ha ya ne he nɔ

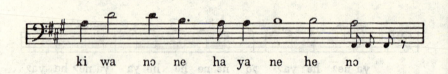

ki wa   nɔ ne   ha ya   ne he   nɔ

ki wa nɔ   neʔ   ha ya   ne wih yaʔ

Song XL

(Whoop)   yo wɛ ni yo

Chorus

yo   wɛ ni yo wɛ ni yo wɛ ni yo wɛ ni

yo wɛ ni yo   wɛ ni yo   yo ha ne nɔ ɔɔ we___

wa tɔ neɁ ho nɔ   Ɂɔ we he yæ we he yæ

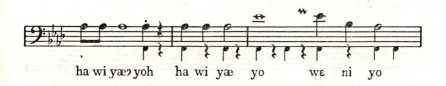

ha wi yæɁ yoh   ha wi yæ yo   wɛ ni yo

yo   wɛ ni yo wɛ ni yo wɛ ni yo wɛ ni yo

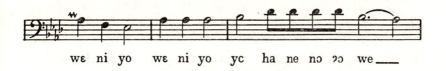

wɛ ni yo   wɛ ni yo   yc ha ne nɔ Ɂɔ we___

wa tɔ neɁ ho nɔ   Ɂɔ we he yæ we he yæ

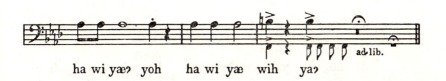

ha wi yæɁ yoh   ha wi yæ wih   yaɁ

Song XLI

Solo

yo   ʔo wi yo we he yæ

Chorus

yo   ʔo wi yo we he yæ   etc.

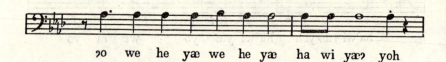

ʔo we he yæ we he yæ ha wi yæʔ yoh

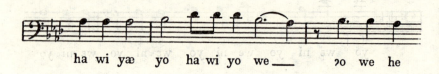

ha wi yæ yo ha wi yo we____ ʔo we he

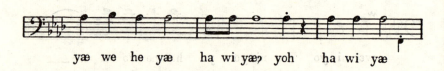

yæ we he yæ ha wi yæʔ yoh ha wi yæ

yo   ʔo wi yo we he yæ yo   ʔo wi

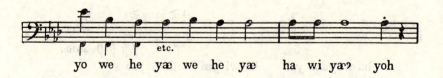

etc.

yo we he yæ we he yæ ha wi yæʔ yoh

ha wi yæ yo ha wi yo we ___ ɔo we he yæ

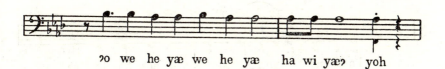

ɔo we he yæ we he yæ ha wi yæɔ yoh

ha wi yæ wih yaɔ   ad lib.

Song XLII

Solo

yo ___ ɔo

Chorus

wa tɔ neɔ ho tɔ ne yo ___ ɔo wa tɔ neɔ

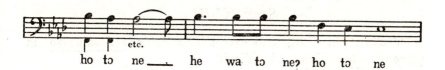

etc.

ho tɔ ne ___ he wa tɔ neɔ ho tɔ ne

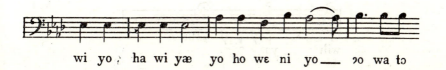

wi yo ; ha wi yæ yo ho wɛ ni yo ___ ɔo wa tɔ

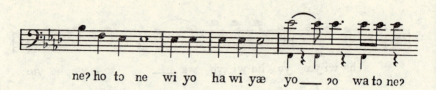

neˀ ho tɔ ne   wi yo   ha wi yæ   yo——ˀo wa tɔ neˀ

ho tɔ ne   yo——ˀo wa tɔ neˀ ho tɔ   ne——   etc.

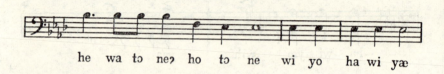

he wa tɔ neˀ ho tɔ ne   wi yo   ha wi yæ

yo ho wɛ ni yo——ˀo   wa tɔ neˀ ho tɔ ne

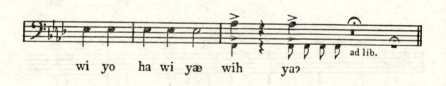

wi yo   ha wi yæ wih   yaˀ   ad lib.

Song XLIII

Identical with Song XLII except for syllables tsɔkwahɛniyo in place of yohowɛniyo, and ending:

wih   yaˀ   ad lib.

THANKSGIVING DANCE

PART TWO: ʔAHTAHKWAYɛTAHKWAʔ

♩=224

Solo

nya wɛh   nya wɛh   nya   wɛh

Chorus

nya wɛh   nya wɛh   nya   wɛh

Chorus repeat ad lib. to ending:

Solo   Chorus

wih   yaʔ   ad lib.

1. The People

(189) ta onɛ tíh, kaiwayétahkóh, ʔoʔwá:tóʔ, ʔiʔ hɔkatóisyɔhkwa:-
    2   4 2   4 2 3   2 41 3 2

ní:h, nɛ:ne wá:tóh, honɛ:ʔséshɛʔ, honóti:ót. (190) hone:ʔɔ ti neʔhóh,
  4   2 31 3 2   4 2 2 3 31   2   4

hɛkayakéhták, n e:yakwawɛnɔkwé:kóh, hé:ɔwé kyaʔtá:téʔ, neʔho wái
 2   4   31 2 3   4   41 2 2   4

nɛ:kéːh, niyáwɛʔóh, hotiʔnikóɛʔ. (191) ta:neʔ tí shó:h, ne katanité:-
 2 3   2 4 2 3   2   41   3 5 34 3   41

sthá ʔ, neʔhó kiʔshɛ nɛyá:wéh, ne ʔɛyɔkwáiwéʔs, h e:yawé:nó:h, ta:
 2   2 3   4 41 2   2   3 41 2   4 41 23 2

sɛːnɔ ti ʔáeswé:h, kwaʔ thá:ayé:ʔ, tkaye:íʔ swayéte:íh, sɛhke thi-
 4 41 2   4   4 1 2   4   2   2 3   2

yótɔʔóh, he tewakyaʔtowehtó:tyéʔs, we:níshæté:nyɔʔ. [Drum beat]
 4 2 3   2   3 2   41 2   2   4 41

(192) ta:néʔ shɔ:néh, ʔɛswáʔhɔtéʔ, ne tyɔ:kwá kiʔshéh, neʔho neyɔk-
    2 4   2 4   2 4 2 3   2 3   4 1 2   2

wayáʔtawéh, ʔɛtyonó:óʔ, heyóti:wí:nó:h, tkaye:íʔ, swáiwayɛte:íh.
 4 1 2   3 312   2 4 42 3   2 3   41

(193) ta:neʔ ti nɛ:kéːh, takatyéɛhták, wa:iʔ ɛkátó:isyók, ná:kɛ:ók,
    3   5   3   52 3   4 2   4   2 3

heʔɛ kwistɛʔ toʔóʔtéːh, swaʔníkɔɛʔ. (194) ta:hawe:ʔó waih, hotyɛ:-
 3   2   4 23   2 4 1   4   5 3   3

nóʔktaʔɔ hé tyɔhéʔ, neʔ nɛ:tɛyɔtawé:nyé:ʔ, hé:ɔw ɛyóejá:te:k. (195)
 5   2 3 4   41 2   3 2   4 41

ta:neʔ wai ne tkaye:íʔ, ó:kwéh, shɔkyó:ní:h, shɔkwátkáʔwéh, neʔhó
 4   5 52   3   2 42 4   3   4   2 3 4

yɔejatéʔ, teyɔkwatawɛnyé:h. (196) ta:káiwaya:só wái nó:h, skɛ:nóʔ,
 2 3   3 4   41   4   5 53 4   2 3

wɛ:níshætéʔ, nɛ:kɛ:né:wáʔ, teyohathétsi:yó:h, neʔho teyɔkwatawɛ-
 2 5 2   3 2 42 3   2   4 2 3   3   4

nyé:h. (197) ta:tkaye:iʔ kho neʔho niyóʔtéːh, he kanɔtakwéhtá:ʔ,
 41   4   5 23   4   5 2

heʔɛ toʔókwá:ɔkéh, nɛ:ne kano:óʔ kiʔshéh, nɔ:yotyé:ɔk. (198) ta:
 3   4   2 3   3   4 2   3   2   4 1   4

haʔtekakó:t kakwé:kóh, skɛ:nóʔ twɛnóhtɔnyóh, he nityókweʔtá:kéːh,
 5   52 3   1 3   2 3 1 2   2 3   31 2

waʔɔkwayáʔtaye:íh. (199) neʔ wai ne tkaye:íʔ, kakwé:kóh, twayɛté:-
 2   3   31   4   5   4 41   2 3   4

íh. (200) neʔ wai ne teyɔkwaté:nishæyɛtóʔ shó:h, ne yóejáʔkéh,
 41   4   5   2   2 3   4 2

teyɔkwatawɛnyé:h. (201) ta:neʔ wai ne tkaye:íʔ ʔáɔʔe:sát, nɛ:ta
 2 3   31   4   5   5 2   3   3

niyókweʔtá:kéːh, n ahs ɔkwayaʔtakɔsóthá ʔ, ʔo:nɛ ʔáeʔ, hɔsétwá:ahóʔ,
 4   41 2   2 3   4 3   12 3   23   2 4 1 2

nyóiwá:óʔ n o:tyɛ:nóʔktaʔɔ hé tyɔheʔ. (202) neʔ wai ne ke:i niyói-
 4   412   3 2   4 1

wa:kéːh, hotkáʔwéh, ne ʔɛyakoti:wahtɛtyaʔtó:ɔk, né ʔó:kwéh, ne
 5   5 51 2   3   4 412 3 31 2 2

yóejaʔkéh. (203) neʔ wai ne hawe:ʔó neʔ tí shó:h, hekáyaʔtíːh, neʔ
 3   31   5   23   3 4   2   3

1. *The People*

(189) And now it becomes my responsibility; those who are called cousins, the Faith Keepers, have requested it of me. (190) They decided that all our words would issue from me.[44] That was their intention. (191) And now I simply ask forgiveness if it should perhaps happen that we inadvertently drop some of the ritual as it proceeds; do not think, "He does it intentionally." Indeed you know that my thoughts are not normal these days.[45] (192) And you will just fill it in, if we happen to miss the way it goes, for indeed you are familiar with it. (193) And I have begun this way; I thought I would make this request, in order that you not be disturbed by anything.[46] (194) And Our Creator decided, "They will move about on the earth." (195) And indeed he made us, the people, and left us here on the earth to move about. (196) And we can at least claim to be happy today, this beautiful day, where we are moving about. (197) And in fact this, too, is the way things are in the community; we have not heard of any unfortunate occurrence. (198) And we must all be happy, the whole group that has gathered. (199) Indeed we all know (200) that the days are numbered for us who move about on the earth. (201) And let there indeed be gratitude that we people still remain another year, as Our Creator arranged the sequence of ceremonies.[47] (202) He provided the Four Rituals for the people on the earth to continue. (203) He decided, "They will simply give

---

[44] Lit. '(from) where I am in place'.
[45] The speaker had recently been under some personal stress, and might not otherwise have included this.
[46] Lit. 'that your minds wouldn't be so (because of) anything'.
[47] The cycle of annual ceremonies being equated with the passage of another year.

ne tɛyɔtɛnɔːnyɔ́ːɔk, n ɛyakotkáthwɛ́ːɔtyé?, he nɔ?keyɛnɔ?tɜ?hɛ́?t
?o?kɔ́ɛjáːtáːt, ne?hó waih, nio?nikɔɛwɛ́?ɔh. (204) taː hone:?ɔ́ tíh,
ne?ho hɛkayakɛ́hták, he kya?táːté?, nɛː ne ?atɔ́?eshɔːnyɔ́k, nɛː kho
?atɔisyɔ́hkwá?shǽ?, ne katóːkɛ́ːh, nɔːyo?téːɔk. (205) taː ?ɛswe:hɛ́ːk
tíh, ?i? kɛnɛ́ːkɛ́ːh, niyɔ́kwe?táːkɛ́ːh, tyɔkwáːyɔ́ːh. (206) káiwayaːsɔ́
wai ?ɔ́?kí?, skɛːnɔ́? twɛnɔ́htɔnyɔ́h. (207) taː ?ɛswe:hɛ́ːk tíh, ?i?
wa?akwatyɛ́ːnɔ́ːní?, tayakwatyɛ́ːɛ́t, ?o?tyakwatáhnɔ́ːnyɔ́ː?, taːne?hó
wáih, nɛyɔ́?tɛːɔ́k, n ɔkwa?nikɔ́ɛ?. [Drum beat]

Solo

yo wi hi ya   yo wi hi ya yo wi hi yah

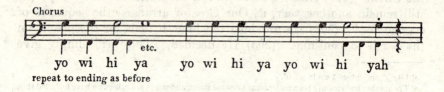

Chorus

yo wi hi ya   yo wi hi ya yo wi hi yah

repeat to ending as before

2. The Earth

(208) ta onɛ nɛːkɛː nityɔ́kwe?taːkɛ́ːh, ?oːnɛ wa?ɔkwayá?tayeːɪh.
(209) ne? wai ne haweː?ɔ́h, n oːtyeːnɔ́?ktaʔɔ he tyɔhɛ́?, ne? ne
?eyɔ́ɛjaːtéːk, ne?ho tɛyɔtawɛːnyɛ́ː?, ne ?ɔːkwɛ́h. (210) ne?ho ti kho
nɛːkɛː waːsɛ́ː?, teyakotá?ɔːɔtyé?, ?eyɔ́ɛjaːtéːk. (211) taː ne? wai
ne haweː?ɔ́h, ne? ti ne kanɔːkshǽ?, he nɛyɔ́?tɜːɔ́k, n oːnɛ ne?ho
?eyɔthyonyáːnɛ́?. (212) ne? wai ne haweː?ɔ́h, ne? ti nɛː ?eyɔ́tɔ́ːɔk,
ne? n akhínoʔɛ teyɔkwɛːhsi?takɛ?sǽhkɔ n oːnɛ ne?ho ?eyɔthyonyáː-
nɛ́?, ne?ho wai nio?nikɔɛwɛ́?ɔ́h. (213) taː tkayeːi? wai ?ɔkwɛ́ːnishǽː-

thanks as they see how I created the earth." That is what he intended. (204) And now they decided that it would issue from me, the gratitude and also the hope that it will continue in the same manner. (205) And give it now your thought, as many of us as have entered. (206) We can claim, as I said, to be happy. (207) And give it now your thought, that we may do it properly: we first give thanks for each other. And our minds will continue to be so.

2. The Earth

(208) And now we people have gathered. (209) Our Creator decided, "There will be the earth, and people will move about on it. (210) The new people, too, will be taking their places on the earth." (211) And he decided, "It will be in the nature of a relationship when they want to refer to it." (212) He decided, "They will say 'our mother, who supports our feet' when they want to refer to it." That is what he intended. (213) And indeed today we make use of it,

té?, ne? etwatyǽ:?ták, ne?ho :?titwatawenyé:?, hé:owe háoejatatóh.
4   2   4   2   4   2   4   2   3   31

(214) ne? ne tkaye:í?, ?etwatyǽ:?ták, he nioiwíhsa?óh, hawe:?o
2   4   2   4   2   4   2

teyakotawenyé:ák, h eyóeja:té:k.   (215) ta: ne? wai ne tkaye:í?,
4   2 3   31   2   4

?itwe: koiwayéistóh, he niyóiwá?, shakoióstas?óh.   (216) ne? wai næ:
2   4   2   4   2   3   31   2

ne ?óiwaké:h, hoiwakháhsokwéh, ne? yeiwayétahkóh, ne? ne:ké:h,
4   2   4   2   4

teyókhisnyé?, ne yóeja?kéh, teyokwatawenyé:h.   (217) ta: ne?ho
2   4   2 3   31   2

kwa: niyóto?kta:tyé?,ne:ke: né:wa?,ne kaya:sóh, ?okwa?nikó:iyó:h,
4   2   4   2   2   2   4

to?oiwáno?ko:wás.   (218) ta: ne? ti n eswe:hé:k, ne? ke ne wa?ak-
2   3   31   2   4   2

watye:no:ní?, ?o:ne: né?, ?o?tyethinó:nyó:?, ne ?akhíno?e teyokwe:-
4   2   4   2   4   2

hsi?take?sæhkóh. [Drum beat]   (219) ta: ne: ne? kho ne: ne?ho
3   31   2

totétwae? n eswe:he:k wa?akwatye:no:ní?, ke wa?akwatóisyók, ne:
4   2   4   2

ne kato:ké:h, he no:yo?té:ok,ne: ne ska:t heská:hó?, [sung] kwá:híh.
4   2   4   2   4   2

[Song: *nya:weh* etc., as on p. 87]

3. The Chiefs

(220) ta one ne:ké:h, nityókwe?ta:ké:h, ?o:ne ?okwaya?tayéi?óh.
2   4   2   4   2   3   31

(221) ne? wai ne hawe:?óh, n o:tye:nó?kta?o he tyohé?.   (222) ne?
2   4   2   31   2

wai hekáya?tí:h, n eyoto?eshonyó:ok, ne yóeja?kéh, teyakotawényé:h.
4   2   4   2   3   21

(223) ta: ne? wai ne hawe:?óh, ne? ti ne ?eotiyá?taté:k, ne: ne wa:-
2   4   2

tóh, hone:?séshé?, hatikowa:nés.   (224) ne? ti næ: ?ekaiwayetáh-
4   2   4   31   2

kó:ok, ne téotisnyé:k, ne: ne koshenonyáshǽ?, ne yóeja?kéh, teya-
4   2   4   2   4   2   3

kotawenyé:h.   (225) ne? háe?kwa kaiwayétahkóh, n o:ti:we?noní:ak,
31   2   4   2

n o:ti?nikóe?, n o:nítyohkwá?.   (226) ne? ti næ: heyáoska:áh, tha-
2   4   2 3   31   2   4   2

koyawí:h, ne ka?níko:iyó:h.   (227) ne? næ: teoti?nyæ:hkó:ok, ne
4   2   3   31   2   4   2

ske:no ?i:ké:h, ?a:yenohtonyó:ok, n o:nítyohkwá?, ne?ho wai ne:-
4   2   4   2   4   2

ké:h, nyo:ye:éh.   (228) ta: wai to?oiwáno?ko:wás, ne: niyóto?kta:-
4   2 3   31   2   4   2

tyé?, to?oiwáno?ko:wás, hatíhsi:á?, ne: ne wa:tóh, hone:?séshé?, hati-
4   2   4   2   4   2   3

kowa:nés.   (229) ne?ho ne tkaye:í?, ne?ho nyo:tiye:éh, he niyóiwá?,
2 1   2   2   4   2   4

we move about there still, where he established the earth. (214) Indeed we make use of it as he planned, for he decided, "They will move about on the earth." (215) And indeed we believe that she has carried out the responsibility that he assigned her. (216) For in fact he divided up all the responsibilities; her responsibility is to look after us who move about on the earth. (217) And right up to the present day we can claim to be satisfied; it continues unchanged. (218) And now give it your thought, that we may do it properly: we now give thanks for her, our mother, who supports our feet. (219) And we say it here again. Give it your thought, that we may do it properly: we ask that it will continue in the same manner for another year.

3. The Chiefs

(220) And now we people have gathered. (221) This is what Our Creator decided: (222) "They will simply continue to be grateful, those who move about on the earth." (223) And he decided, "The moiety partners who are called Chiefs will be present. (224) They will be responsible for looking after the security of those who move about on the earth. (225) And it will also be their responsibility to roll into one the minds of the people." (226) All that he gave them was good.[48] (227) "They will continue to look after the happiness of the people." That is what he did. (228) And it continues unchanged up to the present. It continues unchanged. They are standing there, the moiety partners who are called Chiefs. (229)

---

[48] I.e. their ceremonial speeches contain only good.

hati:wayɛtáhkóh.   (230) neʔ wai ne tyáwɛʔóh, neʔ tá:tiʔnyá:ʔ, ne
2 3   3 1   2   4 2   4   2

skɛ:nɔ ʔi:kɛ: ʔa:yɛnóhtɔnyó:ɔk, yekɛhjishóʔɔh, nɛ:kho yeksáʔshóʔɔh,
     4   2   4   2   4

ʔahsɔ tayékɔhsɔtatyéʔ.   (231) ta: nɛ: neʔ kho tkaye:íʔ, neʔ to:-
2   3   3 1   2   4 2

nɔtíʔstyaʔkóh, ne ʔɛyakoyáʔtaye:íh, kaetiʔkwá:ɔwéh.   (232) neʔ ne
4 2   4 2   2 3   3 1   2

hotí:weʔnɔ:ní:h, he nyo:tikwe:nyó:h, ne koʔníkɔɛʔ n o:nítyohkwáʔ.
     4   2   4   2   3   31

(233) neʔ hotíkeɔtatyéʔs, nɛ:kɛ: neskɛ:nóʔ, ʔi:kɛ:h, ʔa:yɛnɔhtɔnyó:-
     2   4   2   4   2 3   3

ɔk.   (234) ta: neʔ wai ne hawe:ʔóh, hotyɛ:nóʔktaʔóh.   (235) neʔ ti
1   2   4   2 3   21   2

næ: nɛ:kéh, ʔɛkaiwayɛtáhkó:ɔk, tɛɔtiyenɔwóʔkhó:k, ne wa:tóh,
     4   2   4   2   4   2

hone:ʔséshéʔ, honóti:ót.   (236) neʔ ti neʔho nɛ:kéh, ʔéɔta:ayéʔ,
2   4   2 3   31   2   4   2   4

ne hotí:ɔt, teʔétiʔkwa naʔáhteʔɛ nioʔnikóʔté:h, h ɛ:níʔtyóʔ, n a:ti-
2   4   2   4   2   4   2

kowa:nés.   (237) neʔ ti kaiwayétahkɔ nɛ: kɛtyóhkwáɛh, ʔó:thǽ:k,
3   21   2   4   2   4

n a:kowanéh.   (238) ta: tkaye:iʔ wai twayete:íh, toʔoiwánɔʔko:-
2 3   21   2   4   2

wás, neʔho niyóʔté:h, ʔotí:wahtɛ:tyó:h.   (239) neʔ óiwakwe:kóh,
4 2   4   2 3   31   2   4

hotitakwáihsó:h, n a:tikowa:nés, he niyóʔtɛ: ʔohtɛ:tyó:h, ke:i ni-
2   4   2   4   2   4   2

yóiwa:kéh.   (240) ta: neʔ wai ne tkaye:íʔ, toʔoiwánɔʔko:wás, ʔói-
3   31   2   4   2   4   2

wakwe:k ohtɛ:tyɔ:h, nioʔnikɔwéʔóh.   (241) ta: nya:wɛ ti ʔahsɔ
     2   3 31   2

tkaye:íʔ, hotiyaʔtakɔhsótháʔ, nɛ: ne wa:tóh, hatikowa:nés.   [Drum
4 2   4   2   4 2   3   21

beat]   (242) ta: neʔ ti ne waʔakwatɔisyók.   (243) nɛ: ne kato:kɛ:
     2   3   21   2

he nɔ:yoʔté:ɔk, ʔaotiyaʔtakɔhsóthá:k, nɛ: ne ska:t hɛská:hóʔ, [sung]
     4   2   4   2   3

kwá: híh.
2

Solo

wi   hi   yah   yo   wi   hi   yah

Chorus

etc.

wi   hi   yah   yo   wi   hi   yah

repeat to ending as before

They have indeed carried out their responsibility. (230) At all times they look after the happiness of the old people as well as of the children, of those yet unborn. (231) And indeed they also do the talking wherever people gather. (232) They roll into one, as far as they are able, the minds of the people. (233) They keep providing for their happiness. (234) And this is what the Creator decided: (235) "It will continue to be their responsibility to help the moiety partners who are called Faith Keepers. (236) The Faith Keeper will whisper to them whatever is on his mind. The Chiefs are there. (237) It will be the Chief's responsibility to speak in public." (238) And indeed we know that the form of the ceremonies continues unchanged. (239) The Chiefs keep the whole thing straight, as the Four Rituals are performed. (240) And indeed it continues unchanged; the whole things goes as he intended it. (241) And now indeed again there is thanks for those who are called Chiefs who remain. (242) And now we ask this: (243) that it will continue in the same manner; that they might still remain for another year.

4. The Faith Keepers

(244) ta₂ onε wai né:h, tayɔkwawεnitké?ɔ:ɔtyé?, ?atɔ?eshɔ:nyɔ́k,
wai hekáya?tí:h, ?ɔkwatyǽ:?tahkɔ́h.　(245) ta₂ onε wai nε: nio?-
nikɔεwé?ɔ́h, n o:tyε:nɔ́?kta?ɔ n o:nε tsa:yεnε:tá?t, hé:ɔwe yɔεjaté?.

(246) ta: ne? wai ne hawe:?ɔ́h, ne? ti n εwɔkatέhɔ?she:tá?k, tíh.

(247) nε: ne ?ɔ:kwéh, tsa?ka:t teyakotawεnyé:h, hé:ɔwe yɔεjaté?.

(248) ne? ti næ: ?εkaiwayεtáhkɔ́:k, ?εɔti:wakéskwahsé:k, ne ke:i
niyɔ́iwa:ké:h, ?o?katati:waké:ɔs, ne?ho wai nio?nikɔεwé?ɔ́h.　(249)
ta:ne? wai nε: néh, honε:?séshé?, honɔ́ti:ɔ́t, twa:tɔ́h.　(250) ne? wai
ne to?oiwánɔ?ko:wás, nε:kε: ne?ho hatíhsi:á?, hotá?εnɔ:té?, n
o:tyε:nɔ́?kta?ɔ́h.　(251) ne? ne tkaye:í?, taoti:wayeistɔ́:tyé?, hɔ́sa-
kaiwaehsɔ́:né?, wa:εné:?, ?o:nε ho?tkayéih.　(252) ta onε wai nε:
wa:ti:wakéskɔ́?, tε?éti?kwa na?áhtε?éh, honɔtwεníhsa?ɔ́h, ?o:nε:
né?, tetkáiwayεɔní:h.　(253) ta: tkaye:í?, wai taoti:wakéskwε:ɔtyé?,
nε: ne wa:tɔ́h, honɔ́ti:ɔ́t.　(254) ne? wai háe?kwa ne?ho nikaye:éh,
ne? ne tsa?tetkáεɔ:té?, nε: ne wa:tɔ́h, honε:?séshé?, honɔ́ti:ɔ́t?
(255) ta: ne? wai nε: ne tεkawεnɔ?tihé?sé?, ?otyæ:?táhkɔ n o:nε:?-
séshé?, honɔ́ti:ɔ́t, ne?ho kεtyɔ́hkwani:yɔ́:t, nε: ne wa:tɔ́h, ta?ákwistε?
te?kaiɔ́tahkɔ́h.　(256) ne? ska:t ha?ta:tiyenɔ́wɔ?khɔ́?, n o:nε tεɔ-
tiyá?to:wé:t, he:ne: ?o:nε ho?ká:e?, nyɔ́iwa:ɔ́?, n o:tyε:nɔ́?kta?ɔ́h.
(257) ta: ne? wai ne tkaye:í?, ne?ho niyɔ́?té:h, tayohtεtyɔ́:tyé?.
(258) ne? ne taoti:wayeistɔ́:tyé?, he niyɔ́iwá?, hati:wayεtáhkɔ́h.
(259) nε: he niyɔ́to?kta:tyé?, ne?ho háe?kwa hati:wayεtáhkɔ́h.
(260) ta: ne?ho wai ni:ká:?, ?áɔ?e:sát, ?ahsɔ to?oiwánɔ?ko:was
?ohtε:tyɔ: he nioiwíhsa?ɔ́h.　(261) ta: tε:nɔtέnɔ:ɔnyɔ́h, ti n e:két-

4. The Faith Keepers

(244) And now we are expressing our gratitude; that is all we can do.   (245) And now this is what the Creator intended, when he finished the creation of the earth.   (246) He decided, "I shall have helpers (247) who will be persons among those who move about on the earth.   (248) It will be their responsibility to get up the ceremonies, the Four Rituals, the ceremonies I laid down for myself." That is what he intended.   (249) And these are the moiety partners who are called Faith Keepers.   (250) It continues unchanged, they are standing there by the pole set up for the Creator.[49]   (251) Indeed, they are carrying out their responsibility.   When the ceremonies are due, they decide that it is the proper time.   (252) And then they get up whatever ceremony it is, announcing that a ceremony is indicated.   (253) And indeed, those who are called Faith Keepers have been getting up the ceremonies.   (254) It must also be so: the trees are of equal height [50] among the moiety partners who are called Faith Keepers.   (255) And there will be consent shown toward the Faith Keepers by those dependent on them, those who are called the ones with no assigned responsibility.   (256) They all work together as one when they deliberate.   They decided when the time comes, according to the way the Creator arranged the sequence of ceremonies. (257) And it is true: this is the manner in which it continues to operate. (258) They are carrying out the responsibility that was assigned to them.   (259) Up to the present time, too, this is their responsibility. (260) And therefore let there be gratitude that it still continues unchanged, operating as he planned it.   (261) And the entire group is

---

[49] Reference is to the support for the kettle containing soup prepared by the Faith Keepers (Fenton, 1936, p. 7).
[50] I.e., there is no difference in rank.   See p. 10.

yohkwakwe:kóh. (262) nɛ: he niyókweʔta:kе: koyaʔtakóhsothá?,
$_3$ $_{21}$ $_2$ $_4$

toʔoiwánɔʔko:wás, ʔahsɔ neʔho hatíhsi:á?, hotáʔɛnɔ:té?, nɛ: wa:tɔ
$_2$ $_4$ $_2$ $_4$ $_2$ $_4$ $_2$

honɛ:ʔséshé?, honóti:ót. [Drum beat] (263) ta: neʔ ti shɔ: ne
$_2$ $_3$ $_{21}$ $_2$

waʔakwatóisyók. (264) nɛ:kɛ: ne kato:kɛ: he nɔ:yoʔté:ɔk, nɛ: ne
$_3$ $_{31}$ $_2$ $_4$ $_2$

ska:t hɛská:hó?, he nɛyónishéʔt, [sung] kwá:híh.
$_4$ $_2$ $_4$ $_2$ $_{31}$

[Song: *yowihiyah* etc., as on p. 90]

5. *Those with No Assigned Responsibility*

(265) ta onɛ wai tayɔkwawenitkéʔɔ:ɔtyé, ʔatóʔeshɔ:nyók, hekáya-
$_2$ $_4$ $_2$ $_4$ $_2$

ʔtí:h, ʔɔkwatyǽ:ʔtahkóh. (266) ta onɛ wai hawe:ʔóh, n o:tyɛ:-
$_3$ $_2$ $_4$ $_3$ $_{31}$ $_2$ $_3$ $_2$

nóʔktaʔɔ he tyɔhé?. (267) neʔ ti háeʔkwa n ɛkhéyatká?, nɛ: ne
$_3$ $_{31}$ $_2$ $_4$ $_2$

wa:tóh, ʔahsɔ taʔákwistɛ? teʔkaiótahkóh, to:nɔtawenyé:h. (268)
$_4$ $_2$ $_4$ $_2$ $_3$ $_{31}$

hé:ɔwe yɔejaté?, neʔho shɔkwátkaʔwéh, teyɔkwatawenyé:h. (269) ta:
$_2$ $_4$ $_2$ $_4$ $_2$ $_3$ $_{31}$ $_2$

tkaye:i? wai tsaʔtetwayɛte:íh, skɛ:nɔ? shɔ: nǽ:h, he neʔho nika-
$_4$ $_2$ $_4$ $_2$ $_4$ $_2$ $_3$

wenóʔté:h. (270) neʔ wai nɛ: ne ska:t haʔtetwayenɔwóʔkhó?, nɛ: ne
$_{31}$ $_2$ $_4$ $_2$

wa:tóh, taʔákwistɛ? teʔkaiótahkóh, tiʔkwa naʔáhtɛʔɛ heyoti:wáh-
$_4$ $_2$ $_4$ $_2$ $_3$

tɛtyó:h. (271) ta: neʔ kwa: ne tkaye:í?, kɛtyóhkota:tyéʔs, háeʔkwa
$_{31}$ $_2$ $_4$ $_2$ $_4$ $_2$

toʔoiwánɔʔko:wás. (272) nɛ: ne wa:tɔ ʔahsɔ taʔákwistɛ? teʔkaió-
$_3$ $_{21}$ $_2$

tahkóh, n o:tiskɛʔékehtóh, nɛ: kho ʔonóthɔwi:séh. (273) ta: neʔ
$_4$ $_2$ $_4$ $_2$ $_3$ $_{21}$ $_2$

kwa: ne tkaye:í?, ʔitwe: háeʔkwa tkaye:í?, ʔóiwakwe:k ohtɛ:tyó:h.
$_4$ $_2$ $_4$ $_2$ $_3$ $_{21}$

(274) nɛ: he nioiwíhsaʔóh, n o:tyɛ:nóʔktaʔóh. (275) ta: nya:wɛ
$_2$ $_4$ $_3$ $_{21}$ $_2$

ti ʔahsɔ tkaye:í?, hotiyaʔtakɔhsótha? toʔoiwánɔʔko:wás, nɛ: wa:tɔ
$_4$ $_2$ $_3$ $_2$

thankful, (262) as many people as remain. It continues unchanged. The moiety partners who are called Faith Keepers are still standing there at the pole set up for him. (263) And now we ask only this: (264) that it will continue in the same manner for the period of another year.

5. Those with No Assigned Responsibility

(265) And now we are expressing our gratitude; that is all we can do. (266) And now this is what Our Creator decided. (267) "I shall also leave those who are called the ones with no assigned responsibility to move about (268) on the earth." There he left us and we are moving about. (269) And indeed we are all well aware that it is only a way of speaking. (270) We all lend a hand, those of us who are called the ones with no assigned responsibility, doing whatever things are necessary each time there is a ceremony. (271) And it is true: this group is still present; it, too, continues unchanged, (272) those who are called the ones with no assigned responsibility: the warriors, and also the women. (273) And indeed we believe that all of it, too, is continuing (274) as the Creator planned it. (275) And now indeed again there is thanks for the ones who remain of those who are called the ones who still are without any assigned responsi-

ʔahsɔ taʔákwistéʔ, teʔkaiɔ́tahkɔ́h. [Drum beat] (276) ta: neʔ ti
4 2 3 31 2
hekáyaʔti: ne tɔtayakwáɛʔ, neʔ ne waʔakwatɔ́isyɔ́k, ne kato:ké:h,
4 2 4 2 4
he nɔ:yoʔté:ɔk, ne ska:t hɛská:hóʔ, he nɛyɔ́nisheʔt, [sung] kwá: hih.
2 4 2 4 2 3 2 2 31

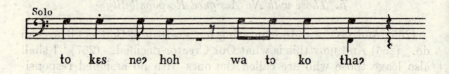

Solo

to kɛs neʔ hoh wa to ko thaʔ

Chorus

ko ne ho ɔʔ to kɛs neʔ hoh
repeat to ending as before
etc.

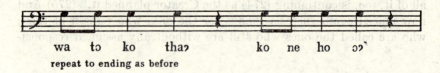

wa to ko thaʔ ko ne ho ɔʔ
repeat to ending as before

6. The Children

(277) ta: tayɔkwawɛnitkéʔɔ:ɔtyéʔ, wai hekáyaʔtí:h, ʔatɔ́ʔeshɔ:-
2 4 2 3 2 3
nyɔ́k. (278) nɛ́: he nioʔnikɔɛwéʔɔh, n o:tyɛ:nɔ́ʔktaʔɔ he tyɔhéʔ.
21 2 4 2 3 31
(279) neʔ wai ne hawe:ʔɔ́h, neʔ ti ne hatiksaʔshɔ́ʔɔh, ʔɛɔtitakhenɔ́-
2 2 4 2
tyeʔsé:k, tetwayaʔtókɛshɔ́ʔ. (280) neʔ ti ne ʔɛyɔtaʔkɛiʔsenɔtyéʔ-
4 2 3 41 2
sé:k, tetwayaʔtókɛshɔ́ʔ. (281) ta: neʔ wai ne tkaye:íʔ, toʔoiwá-
4 2 31 2 4 2 3
nɔʔko:wás. (282) nɛ: he niyótoʔkta:tyéʔ, teyethiká:néː?, ʔɔkwá-
31 2 4 2 4 2
ksaʔtáʔ, hatítakhenɔtyéʔs, tetwayaʔtókɛshɔ́ʔ. (283) neʔ ne tka:-
4 2 2 31 2
ye:íʔ, yɔtaʔkéiʔsenɔ:tyéʔs. (284) ta: ʔoiwayeiʔɔ́:tyéʔs, wai he nyo:-
4 2 3 21 2 4 2
ʔnikɔɛwéʔɔh, hotyɛ:nɔ́ʔktaʔɔh, hawe:ʔɔ wa:sé:ʔ, ti teyakotáʔɔ:-
4 2 4 2 4 2
ɔtyéʔ, ne ʔɔ:kwéh, ʔɛyɔ́ɛja:té:k. [Drum beat] (285) ta: neʔho wai
4 2 4 2 3 31 2
niyóʔté:h, neʔ o:níyehkɔ́h. (286) nɛ: teyɔkwe:hsiʔtakɛʔsǽhkɔ ʔethí-
4 2 3 31 2

bility. (276) And we simply say it here again: we ask that it may continue in the same manner for the period of another year.

6. *The Children*

(277) And we are expressing our gratitude; that is all we can do. (278) This is what Our Creator intended. (279) He decided that children would be running about among us. (280) They will be crawling about among us. (281) And it is true: it continues unchanged. (282) Up to the present time we have seen them, our children running about among us. (283) They are indeed crawling about. (284) And it is coming to pass as the Creator intended, for he decided that new persons would be taking their places on the earth. (285) And because of it she is strong, (286) our mother, the

noʔɛ he yɔejateʔ.   (287) nɛ: he toʔoiwánɔʔko:wás, to:titáʔɔ:ɔtyéʔ,
  3 31   2   4 2   4
saʔ nienɔhóʔsʔáh.   (288) ta: neʔho wai ni:ká:ʔ, ʔáɔʔe:sát.   (289) he
 2 3   31   2   4   3   31   2
ʔahsɔ ʔethiyatkáthwe:ɔtyéʔ, wa:se:ʔ hotíyɔ:ɔtyéʔ, saʔ nienɔhóʔsʔáh.
              4   2   4 2   4 2 3   31
(290) ta: neʔ ti ne tɛ:nɔténɔ:ɔnyóh.   (291) he toʔoiwánɔʔko:wás,
       2   3   21   2
teyakhiká:néʔ:ʔ, n ɔkwáksaʔtáʔ, hatítakhenɔtyéʔs, hɛnɔtaʔkéiʔsenɔ:-
 2   4   2   4 2
tyéʔs, teyakwayáʔtoke:shóʔ.   [Drum beat]   (292) ta: neʔ ti shɔ: ne
 4   2   3   21   2
waʔakwatóisyók.   (293) neʔ kɛ nɛ:kɛ: ne kato:ké:h, he nɔyoʔtéʔɔk,
 3   31   2   4   4
nɛ: ne ska:t hɛská:hóʔ, he nɛyónishéʔt, [sung] kwá: híh.
 2   4 2 3 2   2 31

[Song: *nya:wɛh* etc., as on p. 87]

7. The Plants

(294) ta: tɛ:nɔténɔ:ɔnyóh, ti n e:kétyohkwakwe:kóh.   (295) wai
       2   4 2   31   2
nɛ:kɛ: he niyáweʔóh, ne saʔníkóeʔ.   (296) neʔ wai ne seʔóh, neʔ ti n
          4   3 31   2   4   2
ɛyóeja:té:k, ʔehtáʔké:kwá:h, nɔʔkéɔya:tíh.   (297) neʔho ti tɛyɔ-
   4   2   3   31   2
tawe:nyéʔ:ʔ, ne ʔɔ:kwéh, ʔɛkhéyatkáʔ.   (298) ta: neʔ wai ne seʔóh,
   4   2 4   2 3 31   2
neʔ n ɛki:wakháhsɔ:kóʔ, he nɛyóʔte:ók, ʔeyohtetyó:ɔk, ʔeyóeja:té:k.
 2   4   2   4   4   2 3 31
(299) ta: neʔ wai ne seʔóh, neʔ ti ne tkaye:íʔ, ʔɛyotʔeohtɔní:ak,
       2   4   2   4 2
héː:ɔw ɛyóeja:té:k, kato:kɛ: he niyó:waʔkéh, ʔa:hóʔ, tɛwenɔejot-
 2   4   4   2 4 2
káʔwahsé:k.   (300) neʔ ti ne kakwe:kóh, ʔeyótihsɛnɔye:tóː:k, he
 3   31   2   4   2
ni:yɔ: ʔɛyotʔeohtɔní:ák.   (301) neʔ wai n o:nɛ tɛtyoʔtáiéh, teyoæ-
   3   31   2
we:nyé:h, he yɔejateʔ.   (302) ta: neʔ a:hóʔ, ti ʔewɔtotyáhsé:k,
 4   2 3   31   2   4
neʔho wai nisaʔnikɔewéʔóh.   (303) ta: neʔ wai kho ne seʔóh, neʔ ti
 2 3   31   2   4   2
ne kakwe:kóh, ʔeyótihsɛnɔye:tóː:k.   (304) wai næ: he nisaye:éh,
    4   2 3   31   2   4
tkaye:iʔ ɛyakóæʔséʔ, kanó:kte:shǽʔ, teyakotawenyé:h, ne yóejaʔkéh.
 2   4 2   4   2   4   2 3   31
(305) neʔ wai ne tkaye:íʔ, satkáʔwéh, héː:ɔwe yɔejatéʔ, neʔ ɛyakoyaʔ-
       2   4 2   3 2   4 2
takehashǽʔkɛ:ók.   (306) ta: neʔ wai n onɔhkwaʔshǽʔshɔʔɔ nɛ:kɛ:
 3   31   2

earth, who supports our feet.[51] (287) It continues unchanged: the little children are taking their places. (288) Therefore let there be gratitude (289) that we are still seeing them, the new ones coming along, the little children. (290) And now they are thankful (291) that it continues unchanged, that we see our children running and crawling about among us. (292) And now we ask only (293) that it may continue in the same manner for the period of another year.

7. The Plants

(294) And the entire group is thankful. (295) This is what you intended.[52] (296) You decided, "The earth will be there, below the sky. (297) There I shall leave the people who will move about." (298) And this is what you decided: "I shall divide up their responsibilities; that is the way things will function on the earth." (299) And this is what you decided: "There will be plants growing on the earth. At a certain time they will emerge from the earth of their own accord. (300) All of them will have names, as many plants as will be growing on the earth. (301) It will be when the wind becomes warm again on the earth. (302) And they will mature of their own accord." That is what you intended. (303) And this also is what you decided: "All of them will have names." (304) This is what you said: "Illness will overtake the people moving about on the earth." (305) And indeed you left something on the earth to assist them. (306) And the medicines are distributed on the earth, the

---

[51] See p. 11.

[52] From this point on the Creator is addressed in the second person. There appears to be no consistency or special significance in the shift.

watíhsi:á?, hé:ɔwe yɔejaté?, ?ot?éohtɔ:ní:h. (307) se?ɔ wai né?,

?eyakoya?takehashǽ?kɛ:ɔ́k, n o:ɛtɔ́:kwá:h, ho?wé:nishætenyɔ:tyé?.

(308) ta: ne?ho kho nisaye:éh, ne? ne ka?éohtato:kɛ: ne? sæ:kwéh.

(309) ne? wai nɛ: ne se?ɔ́h, ne? ti ne?ho ?ɛtkháwihták. (310) ne?

wai nɛ: ?ɛkakwe:ní?, ne ?eyɔkáshǽ:?sé?, ne ?ɔ:kwéh, ne yɔ́eja?kéh,

teyakotawɛnyé:h. (311) nɛ:kɛ: he nɔ?ɔ:wéh, n e:káya?ti o?ka:tká?,

n ɛyɔtɔ?eshɔnyɔ́:ɔk ne ?ɔ:kwéh, ne yɔ́eja?kéh. (312) ne? ti n o:nɛ

?eyɔ́tkathó?, ?ewɔ́:yaniyɔ:té?, niyɔejáke:yá:t. (313) ne? wai ne

se?ɔ́h, ?i? tɛyɔkasha:a?t ne ?ɔ:kwéh, teyakotawɛnyé:h. (314) ne?

wai nɛ: ne hatiɔyá?ke:onɔ́?, nɛ: ne shés?á:h, hotíyastɔ́h. (315) ta:

?ɔkhí:owí:h, wai ne yɔ́eja?kéh, teyɔkwatawɛnyé:h. (316) ne? ti

ne jistɔtá?shǽ?, ?eyakwatɔ́:ɔ́k. (317) ta: ?o?káiwaye:íh, wai tsɔ-

sayo?táiéh, teyoæwe:nyé:h. (318) ne? ne tkaye:í?, wa?ákwatka:thó?,

?o?wá:yaniyɔ:té?, niyɔejáke:ya:t shés?a: jistɔtá?shǽ?. (319) ta:

ne? wai nɛ: he niyáwɛ?ɔ́h, sa?níkɔ́e?. (320) ne? ti kɛs nɛ:ké:h,

?eyé:ék. (321) ne? ne?h ɛyekɔ:ták, hé:ɔwe koya?tayéisthá?. (322)

ne? ti nɛ:kɛ: ne ska:t ?ɛtyewɛni:tké?t, tɛyɔtɛnɔ́:nyɔ́:k, ne?ho wai

niyawɛ?ɔ ne sa?níkɔ́e?. [Drum beat] (323) ta: ne? wai ne wa:tí:wa-

ye:ís, n o:nɛ tsáɛnɔtka:thó?, ?o?wá:yaniyɔ:té?, shés?a: jistɔtá?shǽ?.

(324) ne? ne wa?akoyá?taye:íh, hɛ:ɔw ɔkwaya?tayéisthá?. (325) ne?

wai ne ska:t kakwe:kɔ tayewɛni:tké?t, he ni:yɔ: koya?takɔ́hsothá?.

(326) ne? ne tkaye:í?, ?o?tyesanɔ́:nyɔ́:?, ne skɛ:nɔ? yɛnɔ́htɔnyɔ́h,

?o:nɛ ?ae? sayɔ́tkathó?, nɛ: he nisáiwa:ɔ́?. (327) ta: wai nɛ: niyóto?-

kta:tyé?, to?oiwánɔ?ko:wás, ?óiwakwe:k ohtɛ:tyɔ́:h, he nisa?ni-

kɔewɛ́?ɔ́h. (328) ta: tɛ:nɔtɛnɔ:ɔnyɔ́h, ti hekáya?tí:h. (329) ta

growing plants. (307) You decided, "It will be of assistance to them in future days." (308) And this also is what you did: you chose a particular plant. (309) You decided, "I shall make it so (310) that it will be possible for them to remember me, the people moving about on the earth. (311) It will happen so that I simply provide for the people on the earth to show their gratitude. (312) It will be when they see the berries hanging above the earth." (313) This is what you decided: "The people moving about will remember me." (314) The Sky Dwellers call it *shés?a:h*. (315) But they told us who move about on the earth (316) to say *jistotá?shæ?*. (317) And it comes to pass, when the wind again becomes warm. (318) We see them indeed, the berries hanging above the earth, the *shés?a:h, jistotá?shæ?*. (319) And it is the way you intended it. (320) Each time they will gather them. (321) They will bring them to their meeting place. (322) There they will unite their voices in thanksgiving. That is what you intended. (323) And they do as they should when they see the berries hanging, the *shés?a:h, jistotá?shæ?*. (324) They gather at our meeting place. (325) They all unite their voices, as many people as remain. (326) Indeed they thank you, for they are happy to see it again, in accordance with the way you arranged the sequence of ceremonies. (327) And up to the present time it continues unchanged. It all continues to function as he intended. (328) And they simply are thankful. (329) And now they simply say it

oneε ti ne? hekáya?tí:h, tota:tíε?. (330) ne? ne wa?akwatóisyók,
ＮΕ: ne kato:kε: he no:yo?té:ok, nε: ne ska:t hεská:hó?, he nεyónis-
hé?t, [sung] kwá: híh.

[Song: *wihiyah yowihiyah* etc., as on p. 94]

8. The Water

(331) ta: tε:noténo:onyóh, ti n e:kεtyohkwakwe:kóh. (332) wai
né:h, he nisaye:éh, hé:owe yoεjaté?. (333) ne? wai ne se?óh, ne?
ne tkaye:í?, hé:ow εyóεja:té:k, ne? n εyo:nekítkeshó:k. (334) ne?
ti kho nε: n εyojinó:ya?tεonyó:k, n εyotihahtεtyókwa:ók. (335) ne?
kho kye: nε: ne yoεjako:shó?, nεyoæhtó:ók. (336) ne? ti kho nε:kε:
n εká:nekεonyó:k, n εka:nekowané?sé:k. (337) ne? ti ?ae? nε:
tεwotiyenowó?khó:k, he no?keyεnó?tε?hé?t, ?o?kóεja:tá:t, ne?ho wai
nisa?nikoεwé?óh. (338) ta: ne? wai ne tkaye:í?, nε: he niyóto?kta:-
tyé?. (339) nε: se?óh, he nεyo:nekítkeshó:k, heyóεja:té:k, ?εya-
koya?takehashæ?kε:ók, ne? n o:kwéh, ?o?tyotawε:nyé:?. (340) ne?
wai ne to?oiwáno?ko:wás, kotyæ:?táhko ne ?o:kwéh, teyakotawε-
nyé:h. (341) ne? wai ne wa:sé:?, ?εyotya?tákeskó?, ?o:nε tosaya-
wεto:tí?. (342) ne? tyotyéεhtóh, ne? n o:nekanós, ne? εyotyæ:?ták.
(343) ta: wai to?oiwáno?ko:wás, nε: ?otí:wahte:tyo: he nisa?nikoεwé-
?óh. (344) ta: ne?ho wai ni:ká:?, ?áo?e:sát. (345) nε: he se?óh,
ne? ti tεwotiyenowó?khó:k, he no?keyεnó?tε?hé?t, ?o?kóεja:tá:t.
(346) ne? ti ?εyohiyostahkó:ok, ta onε skε:nó?, ?εwεnotóhohte:tí?,
he ni:y o:?ka:tká?, hé:owe yoεjaté?, ne? o?khéya?takwεni:yós, ne
?o:kwéh, ?o?tyotawε:nyé:?. (347) nε: heyo:tó?k, kanyo:? katákhe-
no:tyé?s, satká?wε hé:owe yoεjaté?, ne? hae?kwa ?onotyæ:?tahkóh.

here again. (330) They ask that it will continue in the same manner for the period of another year.

8. The Water

(331) And the entire group is thankful. (332) This is what you did on the earth. (333) You decided, "There will be springs on the earth. (334) And there will be brooks and flowing rivers. (335) And some will pass by under the earth. (336) And there will be ponds and lakes. (337) They too will work hand in hand, the way I fashion them on the earth." That is what you intended. (338) And it is true: it continues up to the present time. (339) You decided, "There will be springs on the earth to assist the people moving about." (340) It continues unchanged: the people moving about are using it. (341) They arise each new time at daybreak, (342) and the first thing they will use is water. (343) And it continues unchanged: it is functioning as you intended it. (344) Therefore let there be gratitude. (345) You decided, "They will work hand in hand, the way I fashion them on the earth. (346) It will be good for them, and they will flourish, all the things that I left on the earth. I did it for the benefit of the people moving about." (347) Moreover, the animals running about, that you left on the earth, make use of it too. (348) And we

(348) ta: ˀakwe: ti ˀoiwakwe:kóh, ˀahsɔ toˀoiwánɔˀko:wás, ˀotí:-
wahtɛ:tyóˑh, ta: nya:wɛ ti ˀahsɔ tkaye:iˀ óiwakwe:kɔ ˀohtɛ:tyóˑh.

[Drum beat] (349) ta: neˀ ti shɔ: ne waˀakwatóisyók, neˀ nɛ:kɛ: ne
kato:kéˑh, he nɔ:yoˀtéˑɔk, ne ska:t hɛská:hóˀ, he nɛyónishéˀt,
[sung] kwá: híh.

[Song: *yowihiyah* etc., as on p. 90]

9. The Trees

(350) ta: tɛ:nɔténɔ:ɔnyóh, ti n e:kétyohkwakwe:kóh. (351) wai
nɛ: he niyáwɛˀóh, ne saˀníkóɛˀ. (352) neˀ wai ne seˀóh, neˀ ti n
ɛyotehatɔní:ak, héˑowe ˀoˀkóɛja:táˑt. (353) neˀ n ɛyothɔtóni:ak,
nɛtyóhsawáˀk. (354) neˀ ti ˀáeˀ, ˀeyakoyaˀtakehashǽˀkɛ:ɔk ne
ˀɔ:kwéh, ne yóɛjaˀkéh, ˀoˀtyɔtawɛ:nyéˑ. (355) nɛ: he tekhni:
naˀtesaye:ɛ he teyoœwe:nyéˑh, héˑowe yɔɛjatéˀ. (356) neˀ wai ne seˀɔ
kato:kɛ: shɔ: he nɛyɔnishéˀséˑk, nɛyoˀtáiɛhséˑk. (357) ta:kato:kɛ:
háeˀkwa nɛyónishéˀt, ˀo:n ɛkánɔˀnós, ne tekœ:wɛ:nyéˑ. (358) ta:
neˀ wai ne seˀóh, neˀ ti nɛ:kéˑh, ˀeyakoyaˀtataiaˀtahkóˑɔk n o:nɛ
ˀɛkánɔˀnós, teyoœwɛ:nyéˑh, héˑowe yɔɛjatéˀ, neˀho wai nisaˀni-
kɔɛwéˀóh. (359) ta: neˀ wai ne seˀóh, neˀ ne tkaye:íˀ. (360) neˀ
ti ne tkaye:íˀ, háeˀkw ɛyótihsɛnɔyɛ:tɔ:k nɛ: ˀɛwɔtí:otɔnyóˑk. (361)
ˀɛyotehatɔní:ak hɛyóɛja:téˑkˀ (362) ta: neˀho háeˀkwa nisaye:ɛ neˀ
ne sæ:kwéh. (363) nɛ: ne seˀóh, neˀ ti n ɛkakwe:níˀ, ˀonóhkwaˀshǽˀ,
ˀeyakotɔˀseˀóˑɔk ne ˀɔ:kwéh, ne yóɛjaˀkéh, ˀoˀtyɔtawɛ:nyéˑ. (364)
nɛ: ˀothɔtɔ:ni: héˑowe yɔɛjata:tyéˀ. (365) ta: neˀ wai ne tkaye:iˀ
kakwe:kɔ ˀotíhsɛnɔyɛ:tóˀ. (366) neˀ ne yeyɛtéihko:wáˑh, tɛˀétiˀkwa
nɔˀootóˀtéˀ, neˀ waˀéihsa:kháˀ, kahatakɔ: hɛyótkɔ:ták. (367) neˀ
sɛˀɛ ne tkaye:íˀ, sheya:wi: ˀoyaˀtowéhtashǽˀ, ˀeyeyɛtéiá:k, ti

believe that the whole thing still continues to function unchanged. And indeed we give thanks again that it all is continuing. (349) And now we ask only that it will continue in the same manner for the period of another year.

9. The Trees

(350) And the entire group is thankful. (351) This is what you intended. (352) You decided, "There will be forests growing on the earth. (353) It will begin with the brush. (354) It too will be of assistance to the people moving about on the earth." (355) You made two winds on the earth. (356) You decided, "It will always be just at a certain time that it will become warm. (357) And at a certain time, too, the wind will become cold." (358) And this is what you decided: "They will use it for heat when the wind becomes cold on the earth." That is what you intended. (359) And indeed this is what you decided. (360) "They will indeed also have names, the trees that will be standing about, (361) the forests growing on the earth." (362) And this also you did: you chose one. (363) You decided, "It can be a medicine to assist the people moving about on the earth, (364) the brush growing about on the earth. (365) And indeed they all have names. (366) People know well what kind of tree it is, when they go to look for it in the woods. (367) For indeed you gave them the power of thought, so that they will know which

ni:ká:ʔ, n ɛyakoyáʔtake:háʔ, ʔɛtkáiwatiyɔ:téʔ, kiʔshéh.   (368) ta:
  4   2   4   2   3   2 31

neʔ wai ne tkaye:íʔ, toʔoiwánɔʔko:wás, honɔtyǽ:ʔtahkɔ́h, he niyóto-
  4   2   3   2   3   2

ʔkta:tyéʔ.   (369) ta:neʔ kho he nisaye:éh.   (370) neʔ wai ne seʔɔ́h,
 3   31   2   3 31   2   4

tkaye:iʔ aeʔ ɛkæ:kóʔ, neʔho ʔɛtkháwihtak ʔɛyɔkashǽ:ʔseʔne ʔɔ:kwéh,
 2   4   2

ne teyakotawɛnyé:h.   (371) wai nɛ: he nisaye:éh, neʔ ne kɛɔtato:-
 2 3   31   2   2   2

ké:h, neʔ sæ:kwéh.   (372) neʔ aeʔ nɛ :yɔtɔʔéshɔnyɔ́:ʔ, n o:n ɛyɔ́t-
 4   2   3   31   2   4   2

kathóʔ, ʔɛtka:nekáiʔt, kato:kɛ: he niyó:waʔkéh.   (373) ta:neʔ wai
 4   2   2   3   31   2

nɛ: ne wahtáʔ, ʔakwa:tɔ́h.   (374) toʔoiwánɔʔko:wás, watí:otɔnyɔ́ʔ,
 4 2 3 31   2   4   2   4

neʔho nɛ: kahatakɔ:shɔ́ʔ.   (375) ta:neʔ háeʔkwa ne toʔoiwánɔʔko:-
 2   3   31   2

wás, tohka:ʔa niyókweʔta:ké:h, yeiwastéistháʔ (376) neʔ ne ʔoʔkak-
 4   4   2 3 31   2

we:níʔ, kɛs waʔɔ́hkeotɔ́:ʔ, n o:nɛ wa:sé:ʔ, sayoʔtáie tɔsakæ:wɛnyé:ʔ,
 4   2

he yɔejatéʔ.   (377) ta:neʔ wai he nisaye:éh.   (378) neʔ wai ne ʔi:sé:h,
 2 3   31   2   3 31   2   4

neʔ ti kɛs n ɛyéhsɛnɔ:níʔ, n ɛtwatyéehták, ʔɛyɔ:stéʔt.   (379) neʔ wai
 2   4   2   4   2 3 31   2

ne ʔi:sé:h, neʔ ne ʔowæ:nɔ́ʔ, ʔakwas hɛwɔ:tɔ́ʔ.   (380) neʔ nɛ: n
 4   2   4   2   3 31   2

ɛyɔ́te:wa:téʔ, n ɛtwɔtyéehták, n ɛyéhsɛnɔ:níʔ.   (381) neʔ ti næ:
 4   2   4   2 3   31   2

nɛ:ké:h, ʔɛyéke:ya:téʔ, n o:n ɛwɔ:yawéthæ: shésʔa: jistɔtáʔshǽʔ,
 4   2   4   2   4

neʔho wai nisaye:éh.   (382) ta:neʔ wai nɛ:ké:h, ʔɛka:nekakaʔɔs-
 2   3   31   2   4   2

tahkɔ́:ɔk, n o:nɛ ʔɛɔtí:ek, nɛ: shesʔá:h, ʔeotiyaʔtayéisták, tɛ:nɔté-
 2   2   2   4   2   4   2 3

nɔ:ɔnyɔ́:ʔ.   (383) ta:neʔho wai nɛ: niyáwɛʔɔ́h, ne saʔníkɔ́eʔ.   (384)
 31   2   4   2   3 31

ta:neʔ wai ne seʔɔ́h, n ɛtwɔtyéehták, hɛyé:nekɔ:nét, nɛ: wahtáʔ.
 2   4   2   4   2   21

(385) neʔ wai ne seʔɔ́h, neʔ hekáyaʔtí:h, n ɛyɔtɔʔéshɔnyɔ́:ʔ.   (386) nɛ:
 2   4   2   4   2   3 31

he koyaʔtakɔ́hsothaʔ tkaye:íʔ, ʔo:nɛ ʔaeʔ sayótkathóʔ, he niyó:waʔke
                                  2

nisáiwa:ɔ́ʔ.   (387) neʔ ti ne tkaye:íʔ, ʔonɔ́hkwaʔshǽʔ, ti yako:tɔ́:ʔs,
 3   31   2   4   2   4   2   4

ne teyakotawɛnyé:h, neʔho wai niyáwɛʔɔ ne saʔníkɔ́eʔ.   (388) ta:neʔ
 2   3   2   3 31   2

wai ne tkaye:íʔ, he niyótoʔkta:tyéʔ, toʔoiwánɔʔko:was hɛnɔtyǽ:-
 4   2   4   2   4   2

ʔtahkwaʔ ne ʔɔ:kwe teyakotawɛnyé:h.   (389) ta:neʔ kwa:ne ʔakwé:h,
                    3   31   2   4

one will be helpful when they may be badly off. (368) And indeed it continues unchanged; they are using it up to the present time. (369) And this also is what you did. (370) You decided, "I will indeed again choose one that will cause the people moving about to remember me." (371) This is what you did: you chose a certain tree. (372) "Again they will be grateful, when they see the sap dripping at a certain time." (373) And this we call the maple. (374) It continues unchanged: the trees are standing there in the forests. (375) And it continues also that a few persons pay attention to them. (376) It is always possible to tap them, when the wind becomes warm on the earth each new time. (377) And this is what you did. (378) You said, "They will store it away, first boiling it down." (379) You said, "It will become sugar. (380) They will put away the first of it; they will store it away. (381) They will get it out when the strawberries begin to appear." [53] That is what you did. (382) "And it will be a flavoring for them when they gather the strawberries. They will use it for their gatherings of thanksgiving." (383) And this is what you intended. (384) You decided, "It will begin when they drink the maple." (385) You decided, "They will simply be grateful, (386) those who remain, when they see it again," at the time which you set for the ceremonies. (387) "It will indeed be available as a medicine to those who are moving about." That is what you intended. (388) And it is true: it continues unchanged up to the present time. The people moving about are using it. (389)

---

[53] Lit. '(when) the berries will be between (the leaves)'.

ʔóiwakwe:kóh, ʔahsɔ toʔoiwánɔʔko:was ʔotí:wahtɛ:tyó:h. (390) ta:
$_2$ $_4$ $_2$ $_3$ $_{31}$ $_2$

nya:wɛ ti ʔahsɔ tkaye:í?, ʔahsɔ ʔóiwakwe:kɔ ʔohtɛ:tyó:h, he nisaʔ-
$_4$ $_2$ $_4$ $_2$

nikɔɛwɛ́ʔóh. (391) ta: neʔ ti hekáyaʔtí:h, ne tɔtayakwáɛ?. (392) neʔ
$_3$ $_{31}$ $_2$ $_4$ $_2$ $_3$ $_{31}$ $_2$

ti ne waʔakwatóisyók, nɛ: ne kato:kɛ́:h, he nɔ:yoʔtɛ́:ɔk, nɛ: ne ska:t
$_4$ $_2$ $_4$ $_2$ $_4$ $_2$

hɛská:hóʔ, he neyónishéʔt, [sung] kwá: híh.
$_4$ $_2$ $_3$ $_2$ $_2$ $_{31}$

[Song: to:kɛs neʔho watókothaʔ koneho:ɔʔ etc., as on p. 100]

10. The Animals

(393) ta onɛ wai ʔɔkwáhsawa:tyéʔ, teyɔkwaténɔ:nyɔtyéʔ, he
$_2$ $_4$ $_2$ $_4$ $_2$

nyo:ʔnikɔɛwɛ́ʔɔh, n o:tyɛ:nóʔktaʔóh. (394) neʔ ti ne tɛ:nɔténɔ:ɔn-
$_4$ $_2$ $_{31}$ $_2$

yóh, hekɛ́tyohkwakwe:kóh. (395) wai nɛ: he nisaye:éh, hɛ́:ɔwe
$_4$ $_2$ $_3$ $_{31}$ $_2$ $_4$ $_2$ $_3$

yɔɛjatéʔ. (396) neʔ wai ne seʔóh, neʔ ti ne ʔɛkyáʔtata:thó:ʔ, nɛ:
$_{31}$ $_2$ $_4$ $_2$ $_4$ $_2$

kanyó:ʔ, ʔɛkatakhenɔtyéʔsɛ́:k. (397) neʔho nɛ: kahatakɔ:shóʔ,
$_4$ $_2$ $_3$ $_{31}$ $_2$ $_4$

ʔɛkatakhenɔtyéʔsɛ́:k. (398) neʔ ti ne ʔaténɔʔshæ̂ʔ, ti yakotɔʔseʔó:ɔk
$_2$ $_3$ $_{31}$ $_2$ $_4$

ne ʔɔ:kwéh, teyakotawɛnyé:h. (399) neʔ ti ne nikanyoʔtáʔsʔá:h,
$_4$ $_2$ $_3$ $_{31}$ $_2$ $_4$

nɛtyóhsawáʔk. (400) neʔho nɛ: ʔotehatóʔktatyéʔ, ʔɛwɔtitakhenɔ́t-
$_2$ $_3$ $_{31}$ $_2$ $_4$ $_2$ $_3$

yeʔsɛ́:k. (401) ʔo:nɛ nɛ: he niyótoʔkta:tyéʔ, ʔo:nɛ tejakwaká:néː?,
$_{31}$ $_2$ $_4$ $_2$ $_4$

kanyóʔtowa:nɛ́s. (402) nɛ: he nisaye:ɛ seʔóh, neʔ ti n ɛska:tkáʔ,
$_2$ $_3$ $_{31}$ $_2$ $_4$ $_2$ $_4$

ʔɛkanyoʔtowanéʔsɛ́:k. (403) neʔ ɛkakwe:níʔ, ʔaténɔʔshæʔ o:nɔtɔʔ-
$_2$ $_3$ $_{41}$ $_2$ $_4$ $_2$ $_3$

seʔó:ɔk. (404) ta: tkaye:íʔ, he niyótoʔkta:tyéʔs, teyakwaká:néː?,
$_3$ $_1$ $_2$ $_4$ $_2$ $_3$

katákhenɔ:tyéʔs, ʔo:nɛ kanyóʔtowa:nɛ́s. (405) ta: neʔ wai ne
$_2$ $_4$ $_2$ $_3$ $_{31}$ $_2$

seʔóh, neʔ ti næ: ne kakwe:kóh, háeʔkwa ʔɛyótihsɛnɔyɛ:tó:k. (406)
$_4$ $_2$ $_4$ $_2$ $_3$ $_{31}$

neʔho wai niyóʔtɛ́:h, ne ʔɔ:kwe teyakotawɛnyé:h. (407) neʔ wai
$_2$ $_4$ $_2$ $_3$ $_{31}$ $_2$

ne hɛʔɛ taʔa:yokwe:níʔ, na:yakéʔ, nɛ:ta neʔ nɛ: shaʔka:t hó:ɔwe
$_4$ $_2$ $_4$ $_2$

twakékɛ:nóʔ, shaʔtewatiyaʔtóʔtɛ́:h, nɛ: kanyo:ʔ katákhenɔ:tyéʔs.
$_4$ $_2$ $_4$ $_2$ $_3$ $_{31}$

(408) ta: neʔ wai shɔ: hekáyaʔti: n ɛyéyashó:ʔ, he nɔʔkayaʔtóʔtéʔ,
$_2$ $_4$ $_2$ $_4$

ʔo:nɛ ko:kɛ́:h. (409) ta: nɛ: he niyótoʔkta:tyéʔ, toʔoiwánɔʔko:wás,
$_2$ $_3$ $_{31}$ $_2$ $_4$ $_2$ $_3$

And we believe that it all still continues to function unchanged. (390) And now indeed again there is thanks that it all still continues as you intended. (391) And we simply say it here again. (392) We ask that it will continue in the same manner for the period of another year.

10. The Animals

(393) And now we are going along giving thanks for what the Creator intended. (394) The entire group is thankful. (395) This is what you did on the earth. (396) You decided, "I shall establish various animals to run about. (397) There in the forests they will be running about. (398) They will be available as food to the people moving about. (399) It will begin with the small animals. (400) There at the edges of the forests they will be running about." (401) Now at the present time we see again the large animals. (402) For what you did was to decide, "I shall again provide the large animals, (403) which can be available to them as food." (404) And indeed up to the present time we see the large animals running about. (405) And you decided, "They too will all have names." (406) For this is how it is, where the people are moving about. (407) It would be impossible for people to say, "This is the same one I saw there before." For they look alike, the animals running about. (408) But people will simply give the names of the type of animals that they see. (409) And up to the present time it continues unchanged; they

ʔaténɔʔshǽʔ, ʔɔkwátɔʔse:ʔɔ́h. (410) ka:ɛkwa nikɛɔtyéʔ, neʔ ne
tkaye:íʔ, neʔ nɛ:kɛ ʔɛka:nekakaʔɔ́stak n o:nɛ ʔis ʔoʔsyaʔtakwe-
niyóʔhéʔt. (411) ta: he niyótoʔkta:tyéʔ, ʔakwe: ʔóiwakwe:kɔ́h,
ʔahsɔ ʔohtɛ:tyɔ́:h. (412) nɛ: seʔɔ neʔ ti tɛ:neʔnikɔɛwɛnyáʔtha:k
nɛ: wa:tɔ hotiskɛʔɛ́kehtɔ hotiyaʔtá:ni:yɔ́h. (413) nɛ: he nisaye:ɛ
seʔɔ́h, neʔ ti næ: to:neʔnikɔɛwɛnyáʔtɔ:ɔk nɛ:kɛ: he nɛ:we:ʔ ɛkanɔʔ-
nóstha:k heyɔ́eja:té:k. (414) neʔho nɛ: kaetiʔkwá:ɔwe kahatakɔ:
neʔho hɛ:nɔtsistakéːɔʔ. (415) ta: neʔ kwa: nɛ: he niyótoʔkta:tyéʔ,
toʔoiwánɔʔko:wás. (416) hoti:wayéistɔ wa:t otiskɛʔɛ́kehtɔ hoti-
yaʔtá:ni:yɔ́h. (417) neʔ tɛ:neʔnikɔɛwɛnyáʔtháʔ, nɛ: kanyɔ́:ʔ, katák-
henɔ:tyéʔs, hɛ́:ɔwe yɔɛjatéʔ. (418) ta: ʔakwe: ti ʔóiwakwe:kɔ
ʔahsɔ ʔohtɛ:tyɔ: he ni:yɔ: saiwihsáʔɔ́h. (419) ta: nya:wɛ ti ʔahsɔ
tkaye:íʔ, ʔóiwakwe:k ohtɛ:tyɔ: he nisaʔnikɔɛwéʔɔ́h. [Drum beat]
(420) ta: waʔakwatɔ́isyɔk ti hekáyaʔtí:h, neʔ ne kato:kéːh, he nɔ:yoʔ-
tɛ́:ɔk, nɛ: ne ska:t hɛská:hóʔ, he nɛyɔ́nishéʔt, [sung] kwá: híh.

[Song: *nya:wɛh* etc., as on p. 87]

11. The Birds

(421) ta: tɛ:nɔténɔ:ɔnyɔ́h, neʔ n e:kétyohkwakwe:kɔ́h. (422) wai
nɛ: he nisaye:éh, seʔɔ neʔ ti néh, tɛyonɔteʔsætɛsyɔtyéʔse:k jiʔtɛʔɔshɔ́ʔɔ
niyɔɛjákɛ:yá:t. (423) neʔho ti næ: hetkɛ heyawenɔ́:ɔk, he nitká-
shatɔ:tyéʔs, nɛyótoʔktáʔk. (424) neʔ háeʔkwa ne seʔɔ́h, kato:kɛ:
he niyó:waʔkéh, ʔo:nɛ neʔho to:nɔtawenyé:ák. (425) neʔ n o:n
ɛyoʔtáiéɔk, ne tɛyoæwɛ:nyéːh, ta: neʔho wai to:nɔtawenyé:ak, neʔho
wai nisaʔnikɔɛwéʔɔ́h. (426) ta: neʔ ne tkaye:íʔ, he niyótoʔkta:tyéʔ,
hoti:wayéistɔ háeʔkwáh. (427) neʔ háeʔkwa ne nikajiʔtáʔsʔá:h, si
nikájiʔtáʔs, niyo:tɔ́ʔk, sasyɔ:ní:h. (428) neʔ háeʔkwa ne seʔɔ́h,

are available to us as food. (410) And indeed from time to time they will serve as a flavoring for the soup, when something is done for your benefit.[54] (411) And up to the present time we believe that it all still continues. (412) You decided, "They will always be a source of amusement for those who are called warriors, whose bodies are strong." (413) What you did was to decide, "It will be a source of amusement for them whenever it becomes cold on the earth, (414) wherever in the forest they put down their fires." (415) And up to the present time it continues unchanged. (416) They are doing as they should, those who are called warriors, whose bodies are strong. (417) They are using the animals running about on the earth as a source of amusement. (418) And we believe that it all still continues, all that you planned. (419) And now again there is thanks that it all continues as you intended. (420) And we ask simply that it may continue in the same manner for the period of another year.

11. The Birds

(421) And the entire group is thankful. (422) This is what you did: you decided, "Birds will spread their wings from just above the earth, (423) extending upward as high as the clouds." (424) You decided also, "At a certain time they will move about there. (425) When the wind is warm, then it is that they will move about." That is what you intended. (426) And it is true: up to the present time they too are performing their obligation. (427) And you made the birds, from the small ones to the larger ones. (428) You decided

---

[54] I.e. when a ceremony is performed.

tkaye:i? aténɔ?shæ? ɛyɔkwatɔ?se?ɔ́:ɔ́k. (429) ta: ne? wai ne se?ɔh,
ne? ti ne tkaye:í?. (430) nɛ: he niyó?tɛ́:h, teyoæwɛ:nyɛ́:h, hɛ́:ɔwe
yɔɛjatɛ́?. (431) ne? n o:nɛ ?ɛskanɔ?nós, he teyoæwɛ:nyɛ́:h, ta: ne?
wai hɛ́:ɔwe tyo?táie: ?ɛshɛ́nɔtkɔ:ták. (432) ta onɛ ne ?ɔ:kwéh,
tsiyakokwɛ́:ɔ́?, næ: tkaye:í?. (433) ne? n o:nɛ tɔtayo?táiéh, he
teyoæwɛ:nyɛ́:h, ta onɛ wai sa:tiyá?ta?ti:hɛ́?t, ha?tá:tiwɛnɔ:kɛ́:h,
saɛnɔtí?stáɛ?, hatiwɛni:yó:h. (434) ta onɛ wai he ni:yɔ: koya?ta-
kɔ́hsothá?, ne ?ɔ:kwéh. (435) ?o:nɛ sayewɛnɔ́:ɔk, ?o:nɛ sawati:yɔ́?,
ji?tɛ?ɔshɔ́?ɔ watiwɛni:yó:h. (436) ta: ne?ho wai ne tkaye:í?, ?is
wáɔsashá:a?t, koya?takɔ́hsothá?, tkaye:i? o:nɛ sayɔ́tkathó?. (437)
ne? wai n o?tyɔtɛnɔ́:nyɔ́:?, hekáya?ti: skɛ:nɔ? yɛnɔ́htɔnyɔ́h. (438)
ta: ne? wai háe?kwa ne se?ɔ́h, ne? ne kakwe:kɔ ti n ɛyótihsɛnɔyɛ:-
tɔ́:k. (439) ne? ti ne tkaye:í?, yeyɛtéihko:wá:h, he nɔ?kaya?tó?tɛ́?,
n o:nɛ wa?e:kɛ́?. (440) ta: tkaye:í?, nɛ: he?ɛ te?sáiwakɔ:tɔ́h, he?ɛ
tɔ?ɔ́sa:tikwe:ní?, hotiya?takɔhsóthá?, ne kakwe:k ɔ́:sa:tiya:shɔ́:?,
he niyotihsɛ́nɔ?tɛ́:h, ?ɔkwɛ́?ɔwe:khá:?. (441) ta: ne? kwa: ne ?ak-
wɛ́:h tkaye:i? ahsɔ ?óiwakwe:kɔ ?otí:wahtɛ:tyɔ́:h, he nisa?ni-
kɔɛwɛ́?ɔ́h. [Drum beat.] (442) ta: nya:wɛ ti ?ahsɔ tkaye:i? óiwak-
we:k ohtɛ:tyɔ: he nisa?nikɔɛwɛ́?ɔh, ne?ho wai nɛyó?tɛ:ɔ́k, n ɔkwa?-
nikɔ́ɛ?, [sung] kwá: híh.

[Song: *yowihiyah* etc., as on p. 90]

12. The "Sisters"

(443) ta: tɛ:nɔtɛ́nɔ:ɔnyɔ́h, ti n e:kétyohkwakwe:kɔ́h. (444) wai
nɛ:kɛ́:h, he nisaye:ɛ se?ɔ́h, hɛ́:ɔw ɛyɔ́ɛja:tɛ́:k, ne?ho ti ?ɛka:tká?,
ne skɛ:nɔ́?, ?ɛ:nɛnɔhtɔnyɔ́:ɔk. (445) ne?ho ti ?óiwakwe:kɔ́h, to:-

moreover, that they would indeed be available to us as food. (429) And this you decided. (430) The way the wind is on the earth, (431) when the wind becomes cold again, then it is that they will head back to where it is warm. (432) But the people remain where they are. (433) When the wind becomes warm again, then they return. With all their voices they sing once more their beautiful songs. (434) And then all those people who remain (435) hear their voices again, when the birds with their beautiful voices return. (436) And then indeed they remember you, those who are left, when indeed they see them again. (437) They simply are thankful that they are happy. (438) And you decided also, "They all will have names." (439) People do indeed know well what kind they are when they see them. (440) And indeed it does not escape you that those who remain are no longer able to name them all, to give their Indian names. (441) And indeed we believe that it all still functions as you intended. (442) And again there is thanks that it all continues as you intended. And our minds will continue to be so.

12. The "Sisters"

(443) And the entire group is thankful. (444) This is what you did: you decided, "I shall leave on the earth for their happiness (445) all the things that they will be harvesting." That is what you in-

tihkwéɔtyé?₄, ne?ho₂ wai nisa?nikɔɛwé?ɔ́h₃ ₃₁. (446) ta: ne?₂ wai ne tka-

ye:í?₄, n o:nɛ₂ tsa?ka:yɔ́?₄, ka?níkɔ:iyó:h₂ ₃ ₃₁. (447) ?o:nɛ wai nɛ:kɛ́:h₂ ₄,

?ɔkwatokɛ́hsɛ:?₂, ?ɔkhí:owi: satɛ́hɔ?shɛ́?₄ ₂, he nɛyó?tɛ:ɔ́k₂, n o:nɛ: nɛ́?₃ ₂ ₄,

?ɛyákwathyo:wí?₂ ₃. (448) ne?₃₁ wai n ɛyakwatɔ́:ɔk₂, ne?₄ ne tewɛnɔté:-₂

nɔ:té:?₄ ₂, ?akyɔ́hehkɔ n o:nɛ ne?h₃ ₃₁ ɛyákwathyo:wí?₂. (449) ta: tkaye:i?

wai nɛ:kɛ́:h₄ ₂, satká?wɛ́h₄ ₂, hɛ́:owe yɔɛjaté?₃ ₂₁. (450) ne?₂ ne se?ɔ́h, ?o:nɛ₂

honɔ:hɔ́?₄ ₂, to:nɔtáte?nya:ɛ?₄ ne ?ɔ:kwéh, ne teyakotawɛnyé:h₂ ₃ ₃₁. (451)

ne?₂ ne yɔɛjakɔ: ?ɛɔtiyé:ɔk₄, ?a:hɔ?₂ ti wɔtotyáhse:k ne?ho wai nisa?ni-

kɔɛwé?ɔ́h₃ ₃₁. (452) ta: nɛ: he niyóto?kta:tyé?₂, teyakwaká:nɛ́:?₄ ₂, ?otɔ:-₄ ₂ ₃

ní:h₃₁. (453) nɛ: ?ɔkyɔishæ:niyéhkɔ́h₂, ha?tewɛ:níshæké:h₄ ₂ ₃₁. (454)

ha?téwahsɔtaké:h₂, ne?₂ ɔkwatyǽ:?tahkɔ́h₃ ₃₁. (455) ta onɛ tkaye:í?₂,

?ahs ɔkwaya?tá:ni:yɔ́h₂, ne yɔ́ɛja?kɛ́h₄ ₂, teyɔkwatawɛnyé:h₂ ₃ ₃₁. (456) ta:₂

ne?ho wai ni:ká:?₄, ?áɔ?e:sát₂ ₃ ₃₁. (457) nɛ: kato:kɛ: ne ti nisaye:ɛ́h₂ ₄,

tesa?sɛhtɔ:tyé?₂ ₄ ₂, ne skɛ:nɔ? i:kɛ: ?a:yakwɛnɔhtónyɔ́:ɔk₄, nɛ: nɛ:kɛ́:h₂ ₄,

?ɔkwæ:hkɔ́:tyé?₂ ₃ ₃₁. (458) ta: ne?₄ ti hekáya?tí:h₂, n atɔ́?eshɔ:nyɔ́k₄,

satká?wɛ́h₂ ₄, hɛ́:owe yɔɛjaté?₂ ₃ ₃₁. (459) ta: nya:wɛ ti ?ahsɔ tkaye:í?₄,

?ɔ́iwakwe:k ohtɛ:tyɔ́:h₂ ₄, he ni:yɔ: saiwihsá?ɔ́h₃ ₃₁. [Drum beat] (460)

ta: ne?₂ ti shɔ: ne wa?akwatɔ́isyɔ́k₃₁. (461) ne?₂ ti nɛ:kɛ: ne kato:kɛ:

he nɔ:yo?té:ɔk₄ ₂, nɛ: ne ska:t hɛská:hɔ́?₄ ₂ ₃ ₂, he nɛyónishɛ́?t₂, [sung] kwá:₂

híh₃₁.

[Song: *wihiyah yowihiyah* etc., as on p. 94]

13. The Four Rituals

(462) ta onɛ wai ?ɔkwáhsawá:tyé?₄ ₄₁ ₂ ₃, ne?₂ hekáya?tí:h₅, n ɔkwátɔ?ɛ́:-₅ ₄₂

sɛ́h₃ ₂, he nioyɛno?tɛ?hɛ́?ɔh₄ ₃ ₂ ₃ ₂, n o:tyɛ:nɔ́?ktaʔɔ hɛ́ tyɔhe?₄ ₂ ₁ ₃. (463) ta:

hawe:?ɔ́ wáih₅ ₂₃, ke:i niyɔ́iwá:kɛ́:h₃ ₃ ₄ ₄₂, ?ɛkayɛ́:tá?k₂ ₄ ₄₁ ₂, hɛ́:ow ɛyɔ́ɛja:té:k₃ ₂ ₃ ₄ ₄₁.

(464) ne?₅ ti nɛ́:kɛ́:h₅₂ ₃, teyɔkhnɔ:nyɔ?táhkwá:k₂ ₃ ₄ ₂₃, ne ?ɔ́:kwéh₄ ₄₂, ne₃ ₂

tended. (446) And indeed when the Good Message came, (447) then it was explained to us. Your helpers told us the way it would be when we refer to them. (448) We shall say "the Sisters, our sustenance" when we talk about them. (449) And indeed you left them on the earth. (450) You decided, "The people moving about will take care of themselves. (451) They will put them in the earth and they will mature of their own accord." That is what you intended. (452) And up to the present time we see them growing. (453) They strengthen our breath every day. (454) Every night we are using them. (455) And now indeed we are still strong, we who move about on the earth. (456) And therefore let there be gratitude (457) that you are doing it in the same way, providing [55] them for our happiness, for us who are passing through. (458) And there is simply gratitude that you left them on the earth. (459) And again there is thanks that it all continues, all that you planned. (460) And we ask only (461) that it will continue in the same manner for the period of another year.

13. The Four Rituals

(462) And now we are going along giving thanks; we are simply grateful for the works of Our Creator. (463) And he decided, "The Four Rituals will be there on the earth. (464) The people moving

---

[55] Lit. 'dropping, letting fall'.

yóɛjáʔkɛ́h, ʔoʔtyɔtawe:nyɛ́:ʔ. (465) ta: neʔ wai ne tkaye:íʔ, neʔ
_{3 4 2   4   41   4   5 4}

n ostówæʔkó:wá:h, konéoɔ́ʔ, kanɛ:hwɛ́ʔkó:wá:h, ʔatɔ́:wɛ́ʔ, neʔ
_{52 3   3 412   3   4 42 3   4 41 2 3}

ke:i niyóiwá:kéʔh, hotkáʔwɛ́h. (466) neʔ tɛyɔkhnɔ:nyɔʔtáhkwá:k,
_{4 42 3   3 4   41   5   25 3}

hawé:ʔɔ́h, n o:tyɛ:nóʔktaʔɔ́h. (467) ta: nɛ́ʔ wáih, ʔotí:wahtɛ́:tyɔ́:h,
_{3 41 2   4 3 4   31   4   5 23   3 4   4 2}

wɛ:níshæté?. (468) n e:káyáʔtí:h, n ɔkwátɔʔé:sɛ́h, he nioyɛnoʔ-
_{2 3   31   5   23   3   41 2   3   2 3}

tɛʔhéʔɔ́h. (469) hawe:ʔɔ́ tih, neʔ ne konéoɔʔ, tekaɛnókɛhkéh. (470)
_{2 4 41   3   5 3   3   53   3   5 2 41}

ʔɛwó:tɔ́ʔ, neʔho ʔɛtyewɛní:tkéʔt, niyókweʔtá:ké:h, koyaʔtakɔ́h-
_{3 31 2   3   4   41 2   2 3 4   41 2   2   3}

sothá?. (471) ta: nɛ́ʔ wáih, ʔɔkwatyæ:ʔtahkɔ́:tyéʔ, ʔɔkwathyo-
_{31   3 5   23   3   4   41 2   3}

wíatyeʔ. (472) ta: neʔ wai he nioʔnikɔɛwéʔɔh, n o:tyɛ:nóʔktaʔɔ hé
_{42 1   4   5   4 31 3   2 4}

tyɔheʔ. (473) ta: nya:wɛ ti ʔahsɔ tkáye:íʔ, ʔóiwakwe:k ohtɛ́:tyɔ́:h,
_{2 1   4   5   2 3   3   4   41 2}

he nioiwíhsaʔɔ́h. (474) ta: waʔakwatóisyók, ti hekáyaʔtí:h, nɛ: ne
_{2 3   31   4   52 3   3   4 41 2   4}

kato:kɛ́:h, he nɔ:yoʔtɛ́:ɔ́k, ne ska:t hɛská:hóʔ, he nɛyónisheʔt.
_{52 3   3   4   412   2 3   31 2   2   4 1}

[sung] kwá: híh.
_{31 31}

[Song: *yowihiyah* etc., as on p. 90]

14. The Wind

(475) ta: tɛ:notɛ́nɔ:ɔnyɔ́h, neʔ n e:kétyohkwakwé:kɔh. (476)
_{4   5   5 2 3   3   4 2 1}

ʔo:nɛ wai wa:éʔ, ʔoʔkyɛné:táʔt, ʔoʔkóeja:tá:tʔ (477) ta: neʔ ti
_{4   5   5   5 2 3   3 4   41   4}

ne tkaye:íʔ, hawé:ʔɔ́h, ʔɛwɔkatɛhɔʔshe:táʔk tíh. (478) neʔ ne
_{5   4 5 2 3   2 3   41 4   41   4}

hekæ:hkwéʔskwá: nɔʔwó:tíh, neʔho hosyɔ:ní:h. (479) neʔ ti næ:
_{5   5 2 3   3 4   41   4}

ʔɛyotaʔéoɔ́:k, skɛnɔ́ʔɔ: nɛtyoyé:ɔ́k, ʔɛyotkahatɔ́:ɔ́k. (480) neʔho
_{5 2 3   3 4 3   412   2 3   2   4 41   4}

ti næ: ʔɛtyawehtɔ́:tyéʔ, ne tɛkæ:wɛ́:nyéʔ, skɛ:noʔ ɛyɛnɔhtɔ́:nyɔ́:ʔ,
_{52 3   3   4 41 2   2 3 2 4   41 2}

ʔɔ:kwéh, ʔoʔtyɔtawe:nyéʔ. (481) ta: tkaye:íʔ, wai he niyóto?ktá:-
_{42 4   4   41   3   5   4 5 52}

tyéʔ, neʔ n ɔkwaʔnikɔiyóstáhkɔ́h, he niyóʔhastéʔ, teyoæwe:nyé:h.
_{3 3   4   41 2   2   4 2 3   3   31}

(482) hɛʔɛ neʔho teʔóʔtɛ́:h, ná:yoʔhá:stɛ́:k, ta:kæ:wényéʔ, héʔɔwe
_{5   2 3   41 2   41 2   4   41 2   4}

ni:wáʔ, twanɔkenyɔ́ʔ, wa:t ɔkwéʔɔ:wɛ́h. (483) ta: neʔho nɛ:
_{41 2   3 1 2   2   3   31   4}

niyóʔtɛ́:h, ʔɔkhí:owí:h, hatiɔyáʔké:onɔʔ. (484) neʔ wai ne hó:nɛ́:h,
_{5 23   3 4   23   3 2 4 1   5   52 3}

about on the earth will use them for thanking me." (465) And indeed they are the Feather Dance, the Thanksgiving Dance, the Bowl Game, and the Personal Chant, the Four Rituals which he provided. (466) "They will use them for thanking me," the Creator decided. (467) And the rituals are in progress today. (468) We are simply grateful for his creations. (469) He decided on the konéoɔ̓ between the songs. (470) "They will come to recite it, the people who remain." (471) And we are using it; we are reciting it. (472) And that is what Our Creator intended. (473) And again there is thanks indeed that it all continues as he planned. (474) And we ask simply that it will continue in the same manner for the period of another year.

14. The Wind

(475) And the entire group is thankful. (476) Now he thought, "I have finished the creation of the earth." (477) And indeed he decided, "I shall have helpers." (478) In the west he made it. (479) It would be covered by a veil; slowly it would move and revolve. (480) From there the wind would be coming, and the people moving about would be happy. (481) And indeed up to the present time we are content with the strength of the wind. (482) It is not such that the wind would be strong, where those of us who are called Indians dwell. (483) And it is so: the Sky Dwellers told us. (484)

ne? ti ne ?ákwé:h, ?ɛyɔ́tkathɔ́?, ne shenɔ́:kshɔ?. (485) n o:nɛ
4   23   3 4   23   3   41   4

tsiɔwó:wi:atyé? shetwakowá:néh, kanyotáiyo?. (486) ne? wai ne
5   2 3   4   41 2   3   41   5   4

hɔwéɔhsé:h, ne? ne ?akwé:h, ?ɛyɔ́tkatho? shenɔ́:kshɔ́?, n o:ɛtɔ́:k-
52 3   4   12   2 3   2   4 41 2   3 2 4

wá:h. (487) né? nɛ:kɛ:h, ne?ho nɛya:wéh. (488) ne? n ɛkakwé:ní?
41   5   23   4   41   5   51 4

tɛkæ:wé:nyé:?, ?ɛyɔ́?hastéh. (489) ne? ti kho ne ?ákwé:h, ne? ne
41 2   2   3   41   5   23   3

ká:ɛkwáh, n a:?tɛkaké:sé:?, hé:ɔwéh, yɔɛjaté?. (490) ta: né:h, he
4 1   2   4   41 2   4 1 2   3   41   4   5   5

niyóto?ktá:tyé?, ?ɔkwaya?takɔhsóthá?. (491) ?o:né wáih, twatká:-
4 5   52 3   3   4 41   3 5   23   3   41

thwás, ne?ho niyá:wés, ne? shɔ́: n í?, n ɔkwátæ?swí:yó:h, hɛ?ɛ ne?ho
2   3   41 2   5   52 3   3   41 2   3

te?á:wés, hé:ɔw ɔkwákwé:ɔ́?. (492) ne? kwa: ne tkáye:í?, ?ɛhni:-
41 2   3   2   3   31   5   2 3   2 4

wakwáihsí?, ne?ho niyá:wɛs. (493) ta: káiwakwení:yó? waih, he
41 2   2 3   2 41   5   52 3   2   3

nyo:tiyé:éh, hatiɔyá?ké:ónɔ?. (494) ne? wai ne hó:né:h, ne? ne
412   3 2 4   41   5   52 3   3

heyó:éh, ne? ɔkwatkáɛɔ?. (495) ne? hɛ?ɛ sí:kwá:h, thá:yo?há:stéh,
412   3 2 4   41   3   41 2   3   41 2

?a:watkáhatɔ́h. (496) ta: ne?ho tí shɔ́:h, nitká:té?, n ɔkwa?nikɔi-
3   4 41   3   5   23   3   41 2   2

yóstahkɔ́h. (497) ta: ?áɔ?e:sát, hekáya?tí:h. (498) ta: nya:wɛ ti
4   41   3 5   2 3   2 3   41   4

?ahsɔ tkayé:í?, ?ohté:tyɔ́:h, he nioiwíhsa?ɔ́h, n o:tyɛ:nɔ́?kta?ɔ́h.
  5 2 3   3   41 2   3   4 1 2   3   2 3   31

[Drum beat] (499) ta:ne? ti ne wa?akwatɔ́isyɔ́k, ne? nɛ: ne katɔ́:ké:h,
             4   52 3   4   41 2

he nɔ:yo?té:ɔ́k, nɛ: né ska:t hɛská:hó?, nɛyónishé?t, [sung] kwá: híh.
2 3   412   3   4   2   3   41 2   2 4 1 2   31 31

[Song: *to:kɛs ne?ho watɔ́kotha? koneho:ɔ?* etc., as on p. 100]

15. The Thunderers

(500) ta: tɛ:nɔténɔ:ɔnyɔ́h, ne? n e:kétyohkwakwe:kɔ́h. (501)
      2   4   2   3   31

wai nɛ: he nisaye:éh, se? ɛwɔkatéhɔ?she:tá?k, hekæ:hkwé?skwa:
2   4   2   4   2   2

nɔ?wɔ:tíh, ?é:ni?tyɔ:tá?k. (502) ne? ti næ: ne?ho tɛ:nɔtawenyé:?,
4 2   3 2   3   31   2   4

hé:ɔwe nikáshatɔ:tyé?s. (503) ne? ti næ: ne ?o:nekasé:?, ?ɛɔtía-
2   3   31   2   2   4 2

wi?sé:k, ne?ho wai né:h, nisa?nikɔewé?ɔ́h. (504) ta: ne? wai ?ae?
4   2   2 3   2 3   31   2

ne tkaye:í?, ?ɔkwatokéhsé:?. (505) ne? wai ne se?ɔ́h, ne? ne kanɔ:-
   4   2   3 31   2   4 2

kshǽ?, n o:nɛ ne ?ɛyakwathyónya:né?, ?ɛɔtiyá?taté:k. (506) ta:
4   2   4   2 3   31   2

They said, "We believe that your kinsmen will see it." (485) It was when they were telling our great one, Handsome Lake. (486) They told him, "We believe that your kinsmen will see it in the future. (487) This will happen. (488) The wind can become strong. (489) And we believe that it will scrape off everything on the earth." (490) And up to the present time we who remain (491) see the way it happens. We are the ones who have good luck; it does not happen in the spots where we are located. (492) We can indeed attest to what happens. (493) For it is true what the Sky Dwellers said. (494) They said, "It is the most important thing for us to watch, (495) that it does not become too strong in its revolving." (496) And it is just the right strength, that we are content. (497) And let there simply be gratitude. (498) And indeed again there is thanks that it continues as the Creator planned. (499) And we ask that it will continue in the same manner for the period of another year.

15. The Thunderers

(500) And the entire group is thankful. (501) This is what you did: you decided, "I shall have helpers who live in the west. (502) They will move about among the clouds, (503) carrying fresh water." That is what you intended. (504) And this too was indeed explained to us. (505) You decided that there will be a relationship when we want to refer to them. (506) And we say "our grandparents, *hiˀnɔˀ*,

neʔ nɛː n akwaːtóh, neʔne ʔakhíhsoːt hiʔnɔ́ʔ, hatiwɛnotatyéʔs. (507)

neʔ wai nɛː seʔɔ́h, neʔ n oːnekaséːʔ, ʔɛɔtíawiʔseːk ʔéɔtiɛtosæːhseːk he niːyɔː satkáʔwɛ ʔaːhɔʔ watɔːníh. (508) neʔ kho ne seʔɔ́h, neʔ ti n oːnekaséːʔ, ʔoːnɔnyaːnɔtyéʔséːk. (509) nɛː ʔotíhahtɛtyɔkwéh, nɛː kho kaːnekɛɔnyɔ́ʔ, kaːnekowaːnés. (510) nɛː kho ʔoːnékitkɛː- shɔ́ʔ, seʔɔ ʔoːnekaseːʔ ti yonɔtɔ́ʔseʔɔ́ːɔk. (511) taː neʔ kh aeʔkwa sheiwakéistaníːh, nɛː ʔakhíhsoːt hiʔnɔ́ʔ, hatiwɛnotatyéʔs. (512) nɛː he nisayeːéh, neʔ wai ne yɔɛjakɔː hesáːa nɛː ne kanyɔ́ʔtowaːnés. (513) neʔ shɔː ʔaːkakwɛːníʔ, ʔɔːsayákohtɛːtyeːt ne ʔɔːkwe teyako- tawɛnyéːh. (514) nɛː ne ʔáːyɔtkaːthɔ́ʔ, he niyoyaʔtánæːækwát. (515) taː neʔ wai sheiwakéistaːniː hotítoːækɔneʔho yɔɛjakɔ́ːh. (516) taː ʔakweː háeʔkwa hotiːwayéistɔ he niyóiwaʔ hatiːwayɛtáhkɔ́h. (517) taː nyaːwɛ ti ʔahsɔ tkayeːíʔ, ʔohtɛːtyɔ́ːh, he nisaʔnikɔɛwéʔɔ́h. [Drum beat] (518) taː neʔ ti ne waʔakwatɔisyɔ́k, katoːkéːh, he nɔːyoʔtéːɔk, nɛː ne skaːt hɛskáːhɔ́ʔ, nɛyónishéʔt, [sung] kwáː híh.

[Song: *wihiyah yowihiyah* etc., as on p. 94]

16. The Sun

(519) taː tɛːnɔténɔːɔnyɔ́h, neʔ n eːkétyohkwakweːkɔ́h. (520) wai nɛː he nisayeːéh, seʔɔ ti neʔ ti n ɛkéɔyaːtéːk, hetkɛ noːtinɔ́ʔɛːɛtíh, ne ʔɔːkwéh, teyakotawɛnyéːh. (521) neʔ wai ne seʔɔ́h, neʔ ti n ɛwɔkatɛhɔʔshɛːtáʔk, héːɔw ɛkéɔyaːtéːk. (522) neʔ ti næː neʔho toːtawényeːák, héːɔw ɛkéɔyaːtéːk. (523) neʔ ti næː ʔɛkaiwayɛtáh- kɔ́ːɔk, toːhathéʔtɔ́ːɔk, he nɔʔkeyɛnóʔtɛʔhéʔt, héːɔwe yɔɛjatéʔ. (524) neʔ ne katoːkɛː heːkwaː ʔɛthéhtahkwáːk, katoːkɛː kho heːkwáːh, hɛː- etháːk. (525) taː neʔ wai ne seʔɔ́h, neʔ ti ne ʔɛwéːnishætenyɔ́ːk, ti ʔɛkayasɔ́ːɔk. (526) taː tkayeːíʔ, wai nɛː ʔɔkwéːnishæːtéʔ, wáiwaye:-

the Thunderers." (507) You decided that they will always carry fresh water and sprinkle the gardens, all the things that you provided that grow of their own accord. (508) And you decided also that they will always furnish fresh water (509) for the flowing rivers and the ponds and lakes, (510) and the springs as well. You decided that fresh water will always be available to them.[56] (511) And you also gave our grandparents, *hiʔnoʔ*, the Thunderers, an added responsibility. (512) This is what you did: under the earth you put the large animals. (513) For it might be that the people moving about could die (514) of fright if they saw them. (515) And you gave them [57] the added responsibility of holding them down under the earth.[58] (516) And we believe that they too are carrying out the responsibility that was assigned them. (517) And again there is thanks indeed that it continues as you intended. (518) And we ask that it will continue in the same manner for the period of another year.

16. The Sun

(519) And the entire group is thankful. (520) This is what you did: you decided, "There will be a sky above the heads of the people moving about." (521) You decided, "I shall have a helper in the sky. (522) There in the sky he will move about. (523) It will be his responsibility to make it light for my creations on the earth. (524) He will always come from a certain direction, and he will always go in a certain direction." (525) And you decided, "They will be called 'days'." (526) And it is true: he is doing what he is

---

[56] I.e. to the plants.
[57] I.e. the Thunderers.
[58] There is a tradition that large animals, too frightening for people to look upon, were put underground by the Creator, who assigned the Thunderers to see that they stayed there.

ís, ne?ho hotǽ?neta:ktɔ hέ:ɔwe kéɔyaté?. (527) ta: ne? kwa: ne se?ɔ
4   2   3   21   2

kanɔ:kshǽ?, n o:nɛ ne? ɛyɔthyonyá:nέ?, ne ?ɔ:kwéh, teyakotawɛn-
4   2   4   2   4   2 3

yé:h. (528) ta: ne? wai nɛ: ?ɛte:kha:? shakwáhji? kǽ:hkwá:?.
31   2   3   31

(529) ta: ne? wai ne ?óiwake: nɔ: næ: hehsi:wakéistani: ?óiwakwe:kɔ
           2

tha?akwáiwayɛte:íh. (530) ta: næ: shɔ: niyoiwa? ɔkwénɔhtɔ́?, ta:
3   31   2   4   2

?akwe: ?óiwakwe:kɔ hoiwayéistóh. (531) ne? ne tkaye:i? teyohat-
              3   31   2

hétsi:yo: ?o:nɛ ne?ho ?o?tyakwatawɛnye:? hέ:ɔwe yɔejaté?. (532)
                                        3   31

ne? kho ne tkaye:i? o?táiɛ: teyoæwɛ:nyé:h, ne? haiwayétahkóh.
2   4   2   3   31

(533) ne? ne tkaye:í?, ?o?wenɔtóhɔhtɛ:tí?, he ni:yɔ: ?is satká?wɛ
     2   4   2   4   2

?a:hɔ? watɔ:ni hέ:ɔwe yɔejaté?. (534) ta: ne? ti næ: ?akwe: ?óiwak-
              3   31   2

wɛ:kɔ hoiwayéistóh. (535) ta: nya:wɛ ti ?ahsɔ tkaye:í?, ?óiwakwe:kɔ
3   31   2   4   2

hoiwayeistó:tyé?s, he niyóiwa? hehsíɔta:s?óh. [Drum beat] (536) ta:
4   2   3   31   2

ne? ti hekáya?ti: ne wa?akwatóisyók. (537) ne? ti nɛ:kɛ: ne kato:kɛ:
                  3   31   2

he nɔ:yo?té:ɔk, nɛ: ne ska:t hɛská:hó?, he neyónishé?t, [sung] kwá:
4   2   4   2   4   2   3

híh.
31

[Song: *nya:wɛh* etc., as on p. 87]

17. The Moon

(538) ta: tɛ:nɔténɔ:ɔnyóh, ne? n e:kétyohkwakwe:kóh. (539)
     2   4   2   3   31

wai nɛ: he nisaye:éh, hέ:ɔwe kéɔyaté?. (540) ne? wai ne ?o?kí?,
2   4   2   3   31   2   4

ne? ne kato:kɛ: he nisaye:éh. (541) ne? ne kato:kɛ: he neyónishé?t,
2   3 31   2   4

teyohathéhsé:k, hέ:ɔw ɛyóɛja:té:k, ta on ɛswóte:ɔnós. (542) ne?
2   4   2   4   2   3   31   2

wai ne se?óh, ne? ti neh, ?eyakoya?táɛ?he?sé:k, ne ?ɔ:kwéh, ne
4   2   2   4   2   4   2

teyakotawɛnyé:h, n o:n ɛwóte:ɔnós. (543) ne? ti ne ha?tɛskayé-
              2   3   31   2

ta?sé?, he yeyá?tayɛtatyé?, ne?ho wai nisa?nikɔɛwé?óh. (544) ta:
4   2   4   2   3   31   2

ne? kwa: ne se?óh, ne?ho ki?shɛ neya:wéh. (545) ne? ne kǽɛti?kwa
         4   2   3   31   2

niyo:wé?, tayakohsóta?ís. (546) ta: ne? wai ne se?óh, ne? ne thika:-
4   2   3   31   2   4   2

supposed to do today, attached there to the sky. (527) And you decided, "There will be a relationship when they want to refer to it, the people moving about." (528) It is "our elder brother, the sun". (529) And you gave him the responsibility for various things, if we were only aware of everything. (530) For we know but a small amount, but we believe that he has done all that he was obligated to do. (531) There is indeed beautiful daylight now for us who move about on the earth. (532) And indeed the warm wind is also his responsibility. (533) Indeed all the things are flourishing that you left on the earth to grow of their own accord. (534) And we believe that he has done all that he was obligated to do. (535) And again there is thanks indeed that he is carrying out the entire assignment that you gave him. (536) And we ask only (537) that it will continue in the same manner for the period of another year.

17. *The Moon*

(538) And the entire group is thankful. (539) This is what you did in the sky. (540) As I said, you did it in a certain way. (541) "For a certain period it will be light on the earth, and then it will become dark again." (542) You decided, "The people moving about will rest when it becomes dark. (543) Their bodies will then return to normal." That is what you intended. (544) And you decided, "It will perhaps happen (545) that they will run into darkness somewhere at a distance." (546) And you decided, "There will be another

té?, ti ?eskǽ:hkwá:a?k, hɛ́:ow ɛkéɔya:té:k.   (547) ne? ti háe?kwa
 4   2   4   2   3   31   2

næ: ne ha?tɛyakoshɛtá?ɔ:ɔk?a teyakohathe?tɔ́:ɔk.   (548) ?ɛkakwe:-
                                                              2

ní?, ?eyakoya?tatókɛsták, ne ?ɔ:kwe teyakotawɛnyé:h, hɛ́:ow ɛjótkɔ:-
 4   2   2   2

ták, hɛ́:owe tyakoyaké?ɔ́h.   (549) ta: ne?ho wai ne tkaye:í?, ?oiwa-
    2   3   31   2   4   2

yeistɔ́:tyé?s, he niyóto?kta:tyé?.   (550) ta: ne? wai ne kanɔ:kshæ?
 4   2   3   31   2

háe?kwa sɔ:ni: hɛ́:owe yeyá?taté?.   (551) ne? wai nɛ: ne se?ɔ́h, ne?
                        3   31   2   4   2

n akhíhso:t sɔ́ɛkha:? kǽ:hkwá:?, ne?ho neyakwaye:há:k, n o:nɛ
                          4   2   3

ne?h ɛyákwathyo:wí?.   (552) ta: ne? wai ne tkaye:í?, koiwayeistɔ́:-
 3   21   2   4   2

tyé?s, he niyóto?kta:tyé?.   (553) nɛ: he nisaye:éh, ne? næ: ne tɛka-
 4   2   3   31   2   4   2

tenyóhsé:k, he niyó?té:h, ?otæhkwahtɛ:tyɔ́:h.   (554) ne? ti næ: n
 4   2   4   2   3   31   2

ɛwɔtɛ:ní?to?kthá:k, ne?ho wai nisaye:éh.   (555) ne? ti næ: ?eyakote-
 4   2   3 31   2

nɔ?kæ:htashɛtáhkɔ:ɔk ne ?ɔ:kwe he neyakotkɛistɔ́:tyé?, ne?ho wai
                                                  4   2

nisa?nikɔɛwé?ɔ́h.   (556) ta: nɛ: ne? kho háe?kwa yeiwayétahkɔ́h.
 3   31   2   3   31

(557) nɛ: he nisaye:ɛ yeya?taté?, ne wɛnɔ́thɔwi:sas ne?ho ?etya-
      2   4   2

wehtɔ́:tyé? wa:se:? teotitá?ɔ:ɔtye? n a:tiksa?shɔ́?ɔ́h.   (558) ta:
                                   3   31   2

tkaye:i? hae?kwa koiwayéistɔ koti:wahtétya?tɔ he niyóto?kta:tye?

he niyóiwa? shéiɔta:s?ɔ́h.   (559) ta: ne? wai ne hekáya?tí:h, ?akwe:
            3   31   2   4   2

?ɔ́iwakwe:kɔ koiwayéistɔ he niyóiwá?, shéiɔta:s?ɔ́h.   (560) ta: nya:-
                                4   3   31

wɛ ti ?ahsɔ tkaye:i? oiwakwe:k ohtɛ:tyɔ: he nisa?nikɔɛwé?ɔ́h.   (561)
                                                  3   31

ta: wa?akwatɔ́isyok ti hekáya?ti: nɛ: ne kato:kɛ: he nɔ:yo?té:ɔk,
 2   4

ne ska:t hɛská:hɔ́, he nɛyónishe?t, [sung] kwá: híh.
 2   4 2 3 2   2 31

[Song: *wihiyah yowihiyah* etc., as on p. 94]

18. The Stars

(562) ta: teyɔkwaténɔ:nyɔtyé?, ne? ɔkwathyowíatyé?, nioyɛno?tɛ?-
      3   4 41   2   3   31   2   2   2

hé?ɔ́h, hotyɛ:nó?kta?ɔ hé tyɔhe?.   (563) ta: hawe:?ɔ́ waih, hɛ́:ow
 3 12 3 2 3   2   4   1   3   4 3

ɛkéɔyá:té:k, n o:tyɛ:nó?kta?ɔ́h.   (564) ne? wai ne tkáye:í?, ?ɛka-
 1 4 41 12 3 1 3   31   4   2   3

jistánohkwa:ɔ́?, n o:n ɛwɔ́té:ɔnos.   (565) ne? ti n ɛkajihsɔ?tahsí:-
 4   4 1 2 3   2 3 4 1   4   41

orb in the sky. (547) It will be a sort of guide for their steps, providing them with light. (548) It will be able to direct the people moving about back to their homes, to where they came from. (549) And it is true: it is carrying out its responsibility up to the present time. (550) And you also made a relationship with respect to her. (551) You decided, " 'Our grandmother, the moon', that is what they will say when they refer to her." (552) And it is true: she is carrying our her responsibility up to the present time. (553) This is what you said: "The moon will change its form as it goes along. (554) It will always come to the end of a phase." That is what you said. (555) "People will use her to measure by as they are moving along." That is what you intended. (556) And this too is her added responsibility. (557) You made it so that new infants, the children, will come from the women. (558) And indeed she is continuing to perform her obligation too, up to the present time, the responsibility you assigned her. (559) And we believe simply that she is carrying out the entire assignment that you gave her. (560) And again there is thanks indeed that it all continues as you intended. (561) And we ask simply that it will continue in the same manner for the period of another year.

18. *The Stars*

(562) And we are being thankful, speaking of the works of Our Creator. (563) And the Creator decided, "In the sky (564) there will be stars when it becomes dark. (565) Stars will indeed be ar-

æ?k, hé:ɔw ɛkéɔya:té:k. (566) ne? ti yakotya?tasyɔnya?táhkɔ́:ɔ́k,
2 3 1 3 31 2 1 3 312

n o:n ɛyɔtotáhsí?, nɛ: ?ethíhsó:t, sɔ́ekhá:?, kǽ:hkwá:?. (567) ta
3 2 4 12 3 12 31 12 2 31 3

?oiwakéistɔ háe?kwáh, hati:wayɛtáhkóh. (568) tkaye:i?, hoiwayɛɔn-
4 41 12 2 3 2 1 3 41 3 4 4

yá:nɔ́?, ?ɛyakotɛnɔ?kæ:htashɛtáhkɔ:ɔ́k, né ?ɔ:kwéh, teyakotawɛn-
41 12 3 2 3 412 4 1 2 3

yé:h. (569) nɛ: he nyo:yé:ɛ́h, hawé:?ɔ́h, ne? ne kakwé:kóh, ?ɛyóhse-
41 4 412 3 41 2 4 41 3 3

nɔyé:tɔ́:k, he ní:yɔ́:h, ?ɛyojihsɔ́?tǽ:?k. (570) ne? ti ne ?ɛyeye-
31 23 3 12 3 2 31 4 4

téiá:k, ne ?ɔ́:kwéh, teyakotawɛnyé:h. (571) ?ɛkakwé:ní?, háe?k-
412 4 41 23 3 31 4 41 3 31

wáh, né?, ?ɛyakoya?tatókɛsták, ?ɛyakohsɔ́ta?ís, ne?hó waíh, nio?ni-
12 3 3 1 3 4 1 12 3 2 3 1 12 3 12 2

kɔɛwé?ɔh. (572) ta: ne? kwa: ne tkaye:í?, hoti:wayéistóh, he
4 1 4 5 4 5 51 2 4

niyóiwá? nǽ:h, hakɔiɔtas?ɔ́h. (573) ne? wai nǽ: ne?hóh, tayawehtɔ́:-
41 3 2 2 4 41 5 3 3 4

tyé?. (574) nɛ: he hawé:?ɔ́h, ?ɛyoti:nekahsɔ́nye?sé:k, he ni:yɔ:
41 5 52 3 3 4 3 4 3 12 3 2

hotká?wɛ ?a:hɔ́? watɔ́:nih. (575) ne? nɛ: ne hawé:?ɔ́h, ne? nɛ:
4 1 4 41 3 4 3 4 41 23 3

tkáye:í?, ?ɛwɔti:nékehá:k, he niwáhsɔ:tí:s. (576) ta: ne? ne tka-
2 3 2 4 23 2 3 31 4 5

ye:i? setéhjiáh, ?etwatya?tákeskó?, ne? wai ne tkáye:í?, teyáɔkó:h,
4 5 4 5 12 2 3 4 1 2 3 4 1 2 3 31 2

ne ?asté:kwá:h. (577) ne? ne tkaye:i? o?á:yé?, ne ?asté:kwá:h.
3 2 4 41 5 52 3 3 2 4 41

(578) ne? ne?ho tayawehtɔ́:tyé?, watí:neké:ha? tkáye:í?, nɛ:né?hóh,
5 4 5 52 3 2 3 41 3 4 1 2 4 2

hati:wayɛtáhkóh, kajihsɔ?táhsí:a?. (579) ta: ?itwe: wai háe?kwáh,
1 2 8 2 3 4 4 1 4 5 4 52 3

hoti:wayéistóh, he niyóiwá?, hati:wayɛtáhkóh. (580) tkaye:í?,
1 3 31 2 2 31 2 2 3 2 3 31 2 4

háe?kwa kéɔnyɔ́?, ?ahsóh, ne koya?takóhsothá?, kotɛnɔ?kæ:htashe-
4 41 3 2 3 2 3 4

táhkóh, ne teyakotáwɛnyé:h, ne ?ɔ:kwéh. (581) ta: ne? wai ne
2 3 4 1 2 3 31 4 5

tkaye:i? áɔ?e:sát, nɛ: he niyóiwá?, hawé:?ɔ́h, ne? ɛyakotɛnɔ?kæ:-
52 3 3 41 2 3 41 2 3

htashɛtáhkɔ́:ɔk. (582) ta:nya:wɛ ti ?ahsɔ́ tkáye:í?, hoti:wayéistóh,
4 1 4 5 2 3 2 3 41 2

nɛ: he niyóto?ktá:tyé?, he niyóiwá?, hati:wayɛtáhkóh. [Drum beat]
3 2 3 31 2 2 31 2 2 3 2 3 31

(583) ta:ne? ti hekáya?tí:h, ne wa?akwatɔisyók. (584) ne? nɛ:ké:h,
4 5 23 3 2 4 41 5 5 23

ne katɔ́:ké:h, he nɔ:yo?té:ɔ́k, ne ska:t hɛská:hó?, he nɛyónishé?t,
3 4 23 3 4 412 3 2 41 2 3 4 1 2

[sung] kwá: híh.
41 41

[Song: *nya:wɛh* etc., as on p. 87]

rayed in the sky." (566) Our grandmother, the moon, will be clothed in stars when she appears. (567) And they too have a responsibility that is theirs. (568) Indeed he indicated some of them to be used for measuring by the people moving about. (569) This is what he did: he decided, "They will all have names, all the stars that are there. (570) And the people moving about will know them. (571) They too can be used for guidance when people run into darkness." That is what he intended. (572) And it is true: they are carrying out their responsibility, the assignment he gave them. (573) And this is due to them. (574) He decided that all the things he left to grow of their own accord would enjoy water. (575) He decided "Indeed they will drink throughout the night." (576) And it is true: in the morning when we arise it is indeed wet outside. (577) There is indeed dew outside. (578) It is indeed because of them that they drink; it is the responsibility of the stars. (579) And we believe that they too have performed their obligation, the responsibility that is theirs. (580) There are indeed still a few people left moving about who measure by them. (581) And let there indeed be gratitude that he decided that people would use them for measuring. (582) And again there is thanks indeed that they have performed their obligation up to the present time, the responsibility that is theirs. (583) And we ask simply (584) that it will continue in the same manner for the period of another year.

19. Handsome Lake

(585) ta onε wai né:h, nityókwe'tá:ké:h, 'ɔkwaya'tayéi'óh. (586)
　　3　　　　5　　5　　　　　52　3　　3　　　　4 41

ne' wai né'hóh, tayɔkwawεnitké'ó:ɔtyé', 'ɔkwatɔ'eshɔnyó:tyé', nio-
5　　　52 3　　3　　　4　　5 5 2 3　2　3　　4　　42 3　2

yεno'tε'hé'ɔh, n o:tyε:nó'kta'óh.　(587) ta: ne' wai ne tkáye:í',
3　　4 2　　3　　2 3　　31　　　　4　　　　　5　　　5 2 3

ne' næ: ne sha'ka:t 'ó:kwéh, teyɔkwatawεnyé:nó'.　(588) ne' wai
4　3　　3 4　　42 3　　3　　　　4 41　　　　5

ne waoyé:nó:', 'onóhsotaiyó:'.　(589) ne' wái neh, wáonɔktané:tá:k,
2 5 3　　2 3　　4 41　　　5　　52 3　　42 3

'o'yóshæké:', ta:ε'tákwεhtá:'.　(590) ta: ne'ho wai niyó'té:h, ne'
2 3　　12　　3 2 3　　41　　　4　　　　5 23　　4

ne 'í:éh, só:ká:', ha'tekakó:t, hayá'taté'.　(591) ne' nε:kε: hosyó:-
4 23　42　34　　4　23　2 3　　31　　5　　　　　52

ní:h, he niyó'té:h, to:tawε:nyé:h.　(592) kho nε: he niyó'té:h,
3　　3　4 23　　3　　　41　　　　4　5　　　23

hotóhɔhté:tyó:h.　(593) kho nε: he niyó'té:h, hotkáthwé:ɔtyé',
3　　4　41　　　4　5　　　　3　3　4 2　3

hé:ɔwe yɔejaté'.　(594) ta: ne' wai ne tkáye:í', hatɔisyóhkwá'.
4 3 4　　41　　　4　　　　5　　2 3　　3 2　4　　41

(595) ne' kho ne shatathewáthá'.　(596) ta onε wai nε:ké:h, ne'ho
4　1　2　　1　2　3　31　　　4　　　　5　4

niyó'té:h, ho'níkɔé', hotyε:nó'kta'óh.　(597) tkaye:i' ta:ka:næh-
5 23　　3　4 23　1　3　　31　　　4　　5

jí:wéh, niyakotyé:éh, ne 'ó:kwéh, shakótká'wéh, teyakotawεnyé:h.
52 3　　4　　4 23　4　42　3　　3 4　41 3　4　　　41

(598) ne' ne 'a:yé:', he'ε te'kátká'hóh, te'skayεtáhkóh, ne hoti'-
4　　5　　5　52 3　4　3 2 3　12　3　2 3

nikóé'.　(599) kwá shó:h, thiyotye:éh.　(600) ta onε ti nε:ké: wá:é',
4 1　　　4　12　3　4 41　　　4　　　　5　52 3

to'óiwató:ké:h, ne' ne'ho 'ɔ:takyó'ták, 'ɔ:sakhé:owí', ne 'ó:kwéh,
3 4　42 3　　4　1　2　3　4 2 3　4 42　3

kheyátka'wéh.　(601) nε: hɔkwéh, thakí:wayé:ní:h, ha'tewε:níshæ-
3 4　　41　　5　　　3　3 4　42 3　3　4 2

ké:h, ha'téwahsɔtaké:h.　(602) ta onε wai né: né'hóh, thakɔyatén-
3　3 4　41　　　4　　　5　23　3　4

yehtóh, hotéhɔ'shé', ke:i nye:nɔtí:h.　(603) né' waíh, hɔwɔowíatyé:',
1 2　2 3　2　2 3　41　　5　23　3　41 23

shetwakowá:néh, kanyotáiyó', twató:k.　(604) ne' wai né:ké:h, he
3　4 41 3　4 3　41 3　3　　5　4　41 23　3

tyonóhsaté:kéh, tá:hsawé', ne' hothyówi:átyé', na'o't hɔwɔowíatye'.
4 41 2 3　12　4　4 51 3　3　　　41

(605) he nεjakwayé:ók, ne 'o:εtó:kwá:h.　(606) ta: ne' wai ne
4　　5 2 3　3　4 1 4　41　　4

tkaye:í', taohtεtyó:tyé', ka:o' nithawe:nó:h.　(607) tkaye:í' wai
5　54　　51 23　2 3　31　　　4 5

næ: twayεté:íh, ne'ho nókhóh, héohtεtyó:h.　(608) ta: né' kwá: ne
4　5 13　3　4 3　23　31　　4　5　51 3

tkaye:í' itwé:h, hoiwayéistóh.　(609) ne'ho wai ne ye:í' ska:é',
1　3 3　12　2 3　31　　5　　2 3　4　2 3

19. Handsome Lake

(585) And now those of us who have gathered (586) are expressing our gratitude for the works of the Creator. (587) And indeed he was among us people who moved about. (588) Illness took hold of him. (589) For a number of years he was confined to bed, lying helpless. (590) And the way things were, he thought that there must be someone there (591) who made it the way it was when he was moving about, (592) and the way his health was then. (593) And the way things were he was looking about on the earth. (594) And then indeed he prayed, (595) and repented. (596) And then, the way things were in the mind of the Creator, (597) he saw well indeed how the people he had left to move about were acting. (598) It seemed that nowhere was there any longer any guidance for their minds. (599) It was simply not as it should be. (600) And then he thought, "It might be better for me to tell them through him, the people whom I left, (601) through this man who is concentrating on me every day and every night." (602) And then he sent his helpers, the Four Beings. (603) They spoke to him, our great one, whom we used to call Handsome Lake. (604) And he began at Cornplanter. He told about the things that they had told him. (605) We shall continue to do it that way in the future. (606) And indeed he traveled on, coming this way. (607) Indeed we know that he was from here.[59] (608) And indeed we believe that he performed

---

[59] Handsome Lake's mother is said to have been a Tonawanda woman, and to have been buried near the present longhouse.

nɔʔyóshæké:ʔ. (610) neʔ né:ké:h, waɛɔyákɛʔták, neʔ shako:wíatyéʔs,
2 3   31   4 41 23   3 1 3 1   12   3   41   12

ne shakónɔkshɔ́ʔ, he nioʔnikóʔté:h, n o:tyɛ:nóʔktaʔóh. (611) ta: neʔ
2   3   12 1 2   3 12   n o 2 3   31   4

wai ne kanɔktiyóʔkéh, neʔho heoyaʔtyénɛʔóh. (612) ta: ʔitwé: waíh,
5 4 51 23   2 3 23 2 4 3 31   4   5   23

ʔóiwakwé:kɔ́h, hoiwayéistóh. (613) neʔ wai jɔkwatyǽ:ʔtahkɔ́h, tet-
3 31 12   2   3 31   5   1 23   2

hotwenéhtóh, n o:tyɛ:nóʔktaʔóh. (614) ta: ʔɛswe:hɛ́:k tíh, waʔak-
3 12   3 1 3   31   4   5   3   4

watyɛ:nɔ́:níʔ, ʔo:né:néʔ, ʔoʔtsakwanɔ́:nyó:ʔ, nɛ: kanyotaiyoʔ akwå-
4 1 3   2 3 12 3   41   2   4   3 4

tɔ́:k, ta: neʔho wai neyóʔtɛ:ɔ́k, n ɔkwaʔnikɔ́eʔ. [Drum beat]
2   3   4 2   3 1 2   2 3 2 31

[Song: *yowihiyah* etc., as on p. 90]

20. The Four Beings

(615) ta: hawe:ʔɔ́ wáih, hotyɛ:nóʔktaʔɔ hé tyɔheʔ. (616) neʔ ti
3   4 3   2 3 2   4 2 1   4

n ɛwɔkatého ʔshe:táʔk tíh, ke:i niyóʔkweʔtá:ké:h. (617) neʔ wai nɛ:
5 3   3 4   41   5   45

tɛshakonéʔnyátɔ́:ʔ, né ʔɔ:kwéh, ne yóɛjaʔkéh. (618) ʔoʔtyɔtawé:-
4   5   23   4 2   3   2 3 4 41   4   41

nyé:ʔ, ʔoʔtyɔ́tɔɛjine:hsɔ́:ʔ. (619) neʔ wai ne haʔté:yɔ: niyotyé:éh,
3 3   31   5   52 4   413

hɛ́:owe yɔɛjatá:tyeʔ. (620) neʔ wai ne hɛʔɛ taʔa:kakwé:níʔ, ne
4 1 3   41   5   52 3   2

koyaʔtoská ʔah, ta:yakotawenyé:ák. (621) neʔ ne næ: shɔ: ká:téʔ,
4   42   3   2 4 41   5   52 3

n ɛyakotí:watyé:ɔ́ʔ, ne ʔɔ́:kwéh, teyakotawenyé:h. (622) ta: neʔ
2 3 2 4   413   4 41 2   3   41   5

wai ne hawé:ʔóh, ke:i niyɔ́kweʔtá:ké:h, ʔɛkatɛhɔ́ʔshé:ʔ, neʔ tɛsha-
52 3 4   41 2   3 4   2   3 2

konéʔnyatɔ́:ʔ. (623) ta: neʔ háeʔkwáh, hakɔiwakéistaní:h, hɔwe-
3   31   4   5   3   3 2 4   41 3

nɔtkáeɔ́ʔ, nɛ: he ní:yó:h, hotého ʔshéʔ, tɛyókhisnyé:k, ne yóɛjaʔkéh.
412   2   31 2   2 4 1 2   2 3   2   1 3   31

(624) ta: neʔ háeʔkwa nɛ́: he niyótoʔktá:tyeʔ itwé:h, hoti:wayéistóh,
4   5   52 4   23 2 3   31 2

he niyóiwáʔ, hati:wayɛtáhkɔ́h. (625) neʔ ne tkaye:íʔ ɛtwákaʔé:-
2 3 2 2 3 2 4 41   4   5   52

yó:ʔ, n ɛthenɛʔnéoʔktéʔ, ʔɛkayé:táʔk, n atyéɔshǽʔ. (626) ta: neʔ
3 3   41 2 3   3 1 2   2 3 31   4

n a:ʔtewɛ:níshæké:h, haʔtéwahsɔtaké: teyókɛshɔ́ʔ, hwaʔɔkhí:atyéʔ
5 2 3   4   34 3 4 1 2   2 3 4 1 2

ne skɛ:nóʔ i:ké:h, ʔaetwenóhtɔnyɔ́:ʔ. (627) ta: neʔho wai ni:ká:ʔ,
2 31 3 3 12 3   41   4   5

ʔáɔʔe:sát, hoti:wayéistóh, he niyóiwáʔ, hakɔiɔtasʔóh. (628) ta:
52   3 4 41 2   2 4 2 3 31   4

nya:wɛ ti ʔahsɔ́ tkáye:íʔ, ʔóiwakwe:k ohtɛ:tyɔ́:h, nioʔnikɔewéʔɔh.
5   523   2 3 31 2 2   4

his obligation. (609) For 16 years (610) he labored, telling his kins-men the intentions of the Creator. (611) And at Onondaga he collapsed. (612) And we believe that he did all that he was obligated to do. (613) We are still following the message sent down by the Creator. (614) And give it your thought, that we may do it properly: we now give thanks for him whom we called Handsome Lake. And our minds will continue to be so.

20. The Four Beings

(615) And this is what Our Creator decided. (616) "I shall have as helpers the Four Beings. (617) They will protect the people on the earth, (618) who are moving about across the earth. (619) Everything is going on on the earth. (620) It is impossible for people to move about alone. (621) It is inevitable that they will have accidents, the people moving about." (622) And he decided, "The Four Beings, my helpers, will protect them." (623) And he also gave them the responsibility of watching over all his appointed helpers that look after us on the earth. (624) And we believe also that up to the present time they are carrying out their responsibility. (625) Indeed we notice that accidents occur which are beyond our reach. (626) And every day and every night they are showing us the way to happiness. (627) And therefore let there be gratitude that they are carrying out the responsibility he assigned them. (628) And again there is thanks indeed that it still continues as he intended. (629)

[Drum beat]   (629) ta: ne? ti shɔ: ne wa?akwatɔ́isyók, ne? ne: ne
        4   52   3   5   4

kató:ké:h, he nɔ:yo?té:ók, nɛ: ne ska:t hɛská:hó?, he nɛyónishe?t.
52   3   3   4   4 1 2   2   3   31 2   2   4 1

[Song: *nya:wɛh* etc., as on p. 87]

21. The Creator

(630) ta: niyóto?ktá:tyé?, ne? ɔkwathyowíatyé?, teyɔkwaténɔ:n-
        3   4   41   2   3   41   2   2   3   31

yɔtyé?, hawe:?ɔ tɛyɔtɛnɔ:nyó:ók, hekáyá?tí:h, ne ?ó:kwéh, ?o?tyɔ-
    2   3   4   4 1 2   2   3   12   3   31   2   3

tawé:nye:?.   (631) nɛ: ti?kwa na?áhtɛ?éh, ?eyakotkáthwé:ɔtyé?,
    41   4   5   5   5 1   2

nɔ?keyɛnó?té?he?t.   (632) ta: ne?ho wai ?ó:néh, niká:wí?s, ?o:nɛ:
2   4 41   4   4   51 2   2 41 2   2   3

ne? ne?ho hetwá:yɔ? he nyo:?nikɔɛwé?ɔh.   (633) hawe:?ó waih,
4   4 3   41 2   2   3   2   4 1   4   5   3

ne?ho ti hejáko?kthá:k, n ɛyɔtɔ?eshɔnyó:ók, ne ?ó:kwéh, ne yóɛja?kéh.
3   4 1   12 3   412   4 41   2   2   3   31

(634) nɛ: hetkɛ n í? nɔ?kéɔyá:tíh, ne?ho né:h, hɛskí?tyó:ta?k. (635)
    4   5   51 2   2   2   3   2   3   31

ne?ho ti hejáko?kthá:k, n ɛyóto?é:shó:?, yóɛja?ke ?ɛyóhsahá:k.
4   5 2   2 3   41 2   2   3   31

(636) né? shó:h, n ɛyɔtɔ?eshɔnyó:ók, ne? ɛyakothyówi:ák, he nɔ?-
    4   23   3   412   3   4 1 2   3

keyɛnó?tɛ?hé?t.   (637) ta: ?etwáiwaye:ís waíh, nɛ: swé?óh, ?i? ɛka-
2 3   31   4   5   12   3   3 12 3   3   2

yakéhták, n e:twawɛnɔkwe:kóh.   (638) né? shó:h, ?etwáthyó:wí?,
1 3   12   3   31   4   23   2   3   31   2

nyo:yeno?tɛ?hé?ɔh, ?atɔ?eshó:nyók, ?atwɛnɔtá:kshǽ?, totétwáɛ?.
2   3   2   2   3   31 2   2   3   31   2   2 3   31

(639) ta: nɛ:ta nityókwe?tá:ké:h, káiwaya:só shó:h.   (640) ne? ne
    4   5 52   3   4   41 4   41   4

ské:nɔ? twɛnóhtɔnyóh, nɛ: né:wá?, ?otí:wahté:tyó:h.   (641) ta: ne?
41 3   2 3   1   2   3   41 2   2 3   31

ti ne ?eswé:hé:k, ne? kɛ ne wa?akwatyé:nó:ní?, ?o:nɛ: né?, ?o?tsak-
5   52 3   4   41 2   4   12   3   2

wanó:nyó:?, n o:tye:nó?kta?ɔ h akyɔ:hé?, ta: ne?ho wai nɛyó?tɛ:ók,
41 2   4   3   4   1   2   3   4 1 2

n ɔkwa?nikóɛ?.   [Drum beat]
3   41

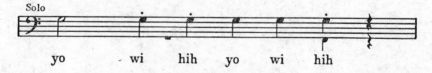

Solo

yo   wi   hih   yo   wi   hih

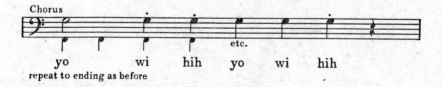

Chorus

etc.

yo   wi   hih   yo   wi   hih
repeat to ending as before

And we ask only that it will continue in the same manner for the period of another year.

21. *The Creator*

(630) And we have been speaking along up till now, giving thanks; for he decided, "The people moving about will simply be thankful (631) for whatever things they see that I created." (632) And now that brings it up to where we are, according to the way he intended it. (633) He decided, "The people on the earth will end their gratitude (634) with me, above the sky where I shall dwell. (635) There they will always end their gratitude, having begun on the earth. (636) They will simply express their gratitude, telling about what I created." (637) And we have done what we were supposed to do. You [60] decided that all our words would issue from me. (638) We simply told about his creations, and repeated our gratitude and our hope.[61] (639) And we here can at least claim (640) that we are happy at this ceremony today. (641) And give it now your thought, that we may do it properly: we now give thanks to him, Our Creator. And our minds will continue to be so.

---

[60] Plural; addressed to those present, and specifically the Faith Keepers.
[61] That each item would continue to function.

22. The Singers

(642) ta onε ti né:h, nikεtyohkóʔté:h, ʔó:néh, ʔetwáiwaye:ís.
4   5   5   4   5   23   4   3   3   4   41

(643) né: sweʔóh, ʔiʔ εkayakéhták, n e:twawenɔkwe:kóh. (644) ta:
5   2 3   3   4   12   3   31   4

neʔ n akwás haʔtékyáʔtí:h, neʔ ne katóʔeshó:nyóh, he skε:nɔʔ né:
5   4   5   23   3   4 3 41   23   3   2   3

ʔíʔ, kenóhtɔnyóh. (645) nε: he ʔeswé:ʔ, ʔiʔ εkaiwayεtáhkó:ók, neʔhó
12   2 3   31   4   1   23   3   4   4 23   2   3

tεktáʔt. (646) hé:ɔwe n o:néh, tεkaεnókεhkéh. (647) neʔh εkayakéhták,
31   4   4 2 3   3   4   41   4   3   4 23

hetwawenɔkwé:kóh, ʔatóʔeshó:nyɔk. (648) ta: tekwánɔ:ɔnyɔ ti ne
4   42 3   2 3   41   4   5   2   3

swǽ:ʔseshε? swatí:ót, nε: hé ʔeswé:ʔ, neʔh εkayakéhták, n e:yak-
4   2   3   423   4   5   2   23   3   2   4 23   4

wawenɔkwé:kóh, hé kyaʔtá:teʔ. (649) ta onε ti nε: jǽ:ʔseshéʔ,
42 3   4   41   4   5   2   23

káεnóʔ, kaiwayétahkóh. (650) neʔho wai nyo:ye:éh, hotyε:nóʔkta-
31 3   2   3   3 1   3   4   4   3   4   2

ʔóh, neʔ ne há:hóʔ, neʔhó nyo:ye:éh. (651) ʔíʔ nε:kε: shɔkwa-
3   4   42 3   2 3   31   5   4

yaʔtæ:kwáɔʔ, tiʔkwa naʔáhtεʔéh, ʔeyɔkwayeʔheʔó:ók, ne yóεjaʔkéh.
5   23   3   4   2 3   3   4   3 4 23   2   3   31

(652) ta: ʔis ne: jǽʔseshéʔ, jienɔkwé:nyó:h, nε: nikaεnóʔté:h, wá:tóh,
4   5   2   3   3   41   23   3   2 3   4   23   32 3

konéɔɔʔ. (653) ta: neʔ n esní:wayé:ís, heʔε teʔkanó:óʔ, n o:nε
2 4 1   4   5   523   3   4   4 23   2   3

waʔetsiyéʔnyatá:t. (654) ta:neʔ ti hekáyáʔtí:h, ne tɔta:tíeʔ. (655)
2 3 2 4   41   4   5   23   3   2   41

neʔ hekáyaʔtí:h, ne waʔétsiejéɔnyó:ʔ, n o:εtó:kwá:h, ʔoʔwé:nishæ-
5   2   3   3   4   42   23   3   4   23   2   3

tenyó:tyéʔ, nε: neʔho nɔ:yoʔtéɔtyeʔ ná:kε:ók, teʔkanó:óʔ, jiʔníkɔéʔ,
31 23   4   54   5   2 3   3   4 423   2   4 23

nesháti ʔnyátatyéʔ ki ʔshéh, he jiyáʔtatéʔ. (656) neʔ wai ne toʔoi-
2   3   1   3   1   12   3   1   3   31   4

wánɔʔkó:wás, teyɔkwaténɔ:nyɔtyéʔ, he ni:y oiwihsáʔhóʔ, n o:tyε:-
5   52 3   2 3   4 1   23   2   3   31   23   3   2

nóʔktaʔóh, ta: ʔis ti ʔo:nε sakáiwayεtá:théʔt, tó:tiʔkwa neskaεnó-
3   2 3   4   5   52 3   3   4   3 4

keʔhéʔt, neʔho ti netwátkwe:níʔ, tetwawεní:tkéʔt, ta: neʔho wai
1   23   3   4   2   23   3   31 2   3

neyóʔtε:ók, n ɔkwaʔnikóεʔ, tá: neʔhoh.
4   2 3   2   3   23   4   3 1

THANKSGIVING DANCE

PART THREE: FINAL SONG GROUP

Repetition of Songs V, VI, VII, VIII, IX, X, XI, XII, XIII, XIV, XV, XXII, XXIII, XXV, and XXVI from Part One.

22. The Singers

(642) And now we in this group have fulfilled our obligation. (643) You decided that all our words would issue from me. (644) And certainly I myself, expressing the gratitude, am happy. (645) You decided that it would be my responsibility to stand up (646) here in the middle of the song, (647) that all our words of gratitude would issue from me. (648) And I thank you, the moiety partners, the Faith Keepers, that you decided that all the words would issue from me. (649) And now for you two moiety partners whose responsibility is the song. (650) This is what the Creator did; this is what he himself did. (651) He chose certain of us to learn certain things on the earth. (652) And you two moiety partners are able to do the songs, these songs called *konéoɔ?*. (653) And you fulfilled your obligation, did not hold back when they extended their hands to you.[62] (654) And they simply repeat it here. (655) They simply give you encouragement, that in future days your minds may not hold back when perhaps they extend their hands to you again. (656) It continues unchanged. We are giving thanks for the works of the Creator. And it is now up to you again: how many more songs there will be. That is all the speaking we can do. And our minds will continue to be so. That is it.

---

[62] When the Faith Keepers asked you to be the singers.

EXCERPTS FROM OTHER PERFORMANCES

EXCERPTS FROM THE TOBACCO INVOCATION

Final Sentences from Sections Dealing with the Wind

. . . (657) ta: neʔ ti ʔáeʔ, n oyéʔkwaʔɔ:wéh, waʔakwatyǽ:ʔták.

(658) neʔ ne ʔoʔtyakwanó:nyɔ́:ʔ, nɛ: héːɔwe ʔotáʔeoɔ́h, tyotatɔ:-ní:h, teyoæwe:nyé:h, ta: neʔho wai neyóʔtɛ:ɔ́k, nɛ: ne saʔníkɔ́ɛʔ.

. . . (659) ta: neʔ ti ʔáeʔ, ne ʔoyéʔkwaʔɔ:wéh, ʔoʔkáyeʔkweotéʔ.

(660) neʔ nɛ: ne waʔakwatɔ́isyɔ́k, nɛ: ne kato:kéːh, shɔ́: nɔ:yoʔtéːɔk.

(661) neʔho shɔ: nɛ:kéːh, nɔ:taka:té:k, ne teyoæwe:nyéːh, nɔ:-yɔkwaʔnikɔiyostahkɔ́:ɔk. (662) nɛ: he skɛ:nɔ́ʔ, ʔakwénɔhtɔ:nyɔ́h, neʔho shɔ: he niyóʔhastéʔ, teyoæwe:nye: ne skɛ:nɔ́ʔ, ʔi:kéːh, ʔakwénɔhtɔ:nyɔ́h. (663) ta: waʔakwatɔ́isyɔk ti nǽːh, kato:kéː shɔːh, nɔ:yoʔtéːɔk, n o:ɛtɔ́:kwaːh, ʔoʔwéːnishætenyɔ:tyéʔ, ta: neʔho wai neyóʔtɛ:ɔ́k, ne saʔníkɔ́ɛʔ.

EXCERPT FROM A SECOND RECORDING OF THE THANKSGIVING SPEECH BY CORBETT SUNDOWN

Section Dealing with the Wind

(664) ta onɛ wai nyo:ye:éh, hotyɛ:nóʔktaʔɔ he tyɔhéʔ, tkaye:iʔ hawe:ʔɔ́h, neʔ o:néh, ʔoʔkyɛnɛ:táʔt, ʔɛyɔ́eja:té:k. (665) ta onɛ ti neʔ ne haʔtekakɔ́:t, wai hɛʔɛ taʔáyoska:sthéʔt, neʔho shɔ:h, nɔ:yoʔtéːɔk. (666) ta: neʔ wai ne haʔtekakɔ́:t, ʔɛkésyɔ:níʔ, neʔ ne tɛkæ:-we:nyéːʔ, héːɔw ɛyɔ́eja:té:k. (667) ta: neʔ wai ne hekæ:hkwéʔskwáːh, nɔʔwɔ:tíh, neʔho hosyɔ:níːh, ʔotáʔeoɔ́h, skenɔ́ʔɔ́:h, nityoye:éh, ʔotkahatɔ́:h. (668) neʔho ʔotatɔ:níːh, ta onɛ teyoæwe:nyéːh, ta onɛ

. . . (657) And again we use the tobacco. (658) We give thanks for the thing that is covered by a veil, where the wind is formed. And your mind will continue to be so.

. . . (659) And again the tobacco smoke rises. (660) We ask that it will continue in the same manner. (661) That the wind will be just so strong that we are content. (662) We are happy; the wind is just so strong that we are happy. (663) And we ask that it will continue in the same manner in future days. And your mind will continue to be so.

(664) And now this is what Our Creator did: indeed he decided, "Now I have finished the creation of the earth. (665) And now it must not be by itself in just this way. (666) And I must make the wind on the earth." (667) And in the west he made the thing that is covered by a veil. Slowly it moves and revolves. (668) And now the wind is formed there, and now we who move about on the earth

skɛ:nɔʔ twɛnóhtɔnyóh, ne yóɛjaʔkéh, teyɔkwatawɛnyé:h. (669) neʔho
_{4 2 4 2 3 31 2}

shɔ: kho nitka:téʔ, ne teyoæwɛ:nyé:h, n ɔkwaʔnikɔiyóstahkóh, ʔɔk-
_{4 2 4 2 4 2}

yɔishǽ:ni:yóh, hawe:ʔóh, neʔho neyóʔtɛ:ók, ne yóɛjaʔkéh, shɔkwát-
_{4 2 4 2 4 2 2 3}

kaʔwéh. (670) ta onɛ ʔáeʔ, ʔɔkwatokéhsé:ʔ, ʔɔkhí:owí:h, hatiɔyáʔ-
_{31 2 4 2 4 2 2 3}

ke:onóʔ. (671) neʔ wai ne ho:néːh, ʔakwe: neʔ wai nɛ:kéːh, neʔ
_{31 2 4 2 4 2}

ɛyótkathóʔ, ne shenɔ:kshóʔ, n o:ɛtó:kwá:h. (672) neʔ kiʔshɛ neʔho
_{4 2 4 2 31 2}

neya:wéh, neyóʔhastéh, tɛkæ:we:nyé:ʔ, hé:ɔwe yɔejata:tyéʔ. (673)
_{4 2 4 2 3 31}

ta: neʔ wai ne ʔakwé:h, neʔ ne ka:ɛkwáh, n a:ʔtɛkakɛ:séːʔ, hé:ɔwe
_{2 4 2 2 4 2}

yɔejatéʔ, neʔ kho ne ʔɛkaiwáhtóʔt, hé:ɔwe nɛ:kéːh, koʔníkɔ:iyó:h,
_{4 2 4 2 4 2 4}

kokwé:ɔnyóʔ, neʔho wai nɛ:kéːh, ʔakwé:h, niyɔkwaʔníkoʔté:h.
_{2 4 2 4 2 4 2 4 31}

(674) ta: neʔho wai nyo:tiye:éh, hatiɔyáʔke:onóʔ, ʔɔkhí:owí:h, ta:
_{2 4 2 4 2 4 2}

tkaye:íʔ, twaiwakwáihsós, we:níshæte:nyóʔ, neʔ ne tkaye:íʔ, ʔetwát-
_{4 2 4 2 4 2 4 2}

kathóʔ, ʔo:né neʔho niya:wés, ne ka:ɛkwá nɔʔtkakɛ:séːʔ, kokwé:ɔn-
_{4 2 4 2 4 2 4 2 3}

yóʔ. (675) ta: ʔɔkwatæʔswi:yó:h, wai n íʔ, heʔɛ taʔaetwakwe:níʔ,
_{31 2 4 2 4 2 4}

ʔáetwatka:thóʔ, ʔahsóh, nɛ:kɛ: niyótoʔkta:tyéʔ, he nó:yoʔha:stéh,
_{2 4 2 4 2 4 2 4}

takæ:we:nyé:ʔ, na:yɔkwatowe:hták. (676) ta:neʔho wai ni:ká:ʔ, ne
_{2 4 2 3 21 2 4 2}

ʔáɔʔe:sát, nɛ:kɛ: n ɛtwatɔʔéshɔnyó:k, skɛ:nóʔ, n iʔ shɔ: twɛnóhtɔnyóh.
_{4 2 4 2 4 2 3 31}

(677) ta: ʔɛswe:héːk, ti waʔakwatyɛ:nɔ:níʔ, nɛ: ne ʔoʔtyakwanó:n-
_{2 4 2 4 2}

yó:ʔ, nɛ: tyotáʔeoóh, teyoæwɛ:nyé:h, ta: neʔho wai neyóʔtɛ:ók, n
_{4 2 4 2 4 2}

ɔkwaʔnikóɛʔ.
_{2 41}

EXCERPTS FROM THE THANKSGIVING SPEECH BY SOLON JONES

Section Dealing with the Wind

(678) ta onɛ wáih, hawe:ʔóh. (679) neʔ néh, teyoæwɛnyé:ak nɛ:
_{3 4 3 1 2 4 2 3}

hé yɔejatéʔ. (680) neʔho shɔ: khó nɛtka:té:k. (681) nɛ:kɛ: ʔi:-
_{4 3 31 2 4 3 21 2}

ké:h, sɔ:ka:ʔ tha:yakótowe:hták. (682) ta: neʔho næ: niyóʔté:h.
_{4 2 31 2 4 31}

(683) nɛ: tewaktatyéʔ. (684) ta: neʔho næ: sí:kwá:h, nitwáteʔ-
_{2 31 2 4 2}

are happy. (669) And the wind is just the strength for us to be content with it; it strengthens our breath. He decided it would be so, with us whom he left on the earth. (670) And again it was explained to us; the Sky Dwellers told us. (671) They said, "We believe that your kinsmen will see that in the future (672) it may happen that the wind will become strong over the earth. (673) And we believe that it will scrape off everything on the earth and will destroy people's homes and property. That is what we believe, what is on our minds." (674) And that is what the Sky Dwellers said, what they told us. And indeed we can attest to it; in these days it is true: we see it happen, that it scrapes off all their homes. (675) But we ourselves are fortunate. We are not able to see it yet, up to the present time: that the wind would become so strong as to harm us. (676) And therefore let there be gratitude. We shall be grateful that we ourselves, at least, are happy. (677) And give it your thought, that we may do it properly: we now give thanks for the thing that is covered by a veil, for the wind. And our minds will continue to be so.

(678) And now he decided, (679) "There will be wind on the earth. (680) And it will be just so strong, (681) so that no one will be harmed." (682) And the way things are, (683) surrounding us

hastɔ́?. (685) ne?ho nɛ:kɛ́:h, ?ɛyakotówehták, né ?ɔ:kwéh. (686)
4 31   2   4   2   4   4 3   21

yeksá?shɔ?ɔ yekɛhjishɔ́?ɔh. (687) ne?ho kwa: hɛ́:ɔwéh, ?ɔkwákwɛ:ɛ́?
2   4 1   2   3 2   3

nɛ: tyɔkwé?ɔ:wéh. (688) ta: ne?ho thikɛɔ ?aikɛ́:h, nɛ:kɛ: he ni-
2   4 3   21   2   4   2

káyɛthá?, ne sí:kwa: niyó?hasté?, héh, teyoæwɛ:nyé:h. (689) ta:
3 2 4   2   4 3 4   4   2   31   2

ne? ti ?ae? óiwá?. (690) ne? kho ne tkaye:i? wai ?ɔkhí:owí:h. (691)
3   43   21   2   4 3   21

hɛ́:ɔwe nɛ:kɛ́:h, twatatɔ:níh, nɛ: héh, teyoæwɛ:nyé:h. (692) ne?
2   4   2   4   2 4   2 3   31   2

ne wa:tɔ wáih, né?, néh, ?otá?eoóh. (693) ta: ne?ho nɛ:kɛ́:h, tyo-
4   4   3   2 3 2   41   2   3   2

tatɔ:ní:h, teyoæwɛ:nyé:h, he yɔɛjata:tyé?. (694) ta: ne? n ɛtwa-
4   2   3   3   31   2

tyɛ:nɔ:ni? n ɔkwa?nikɔɛ?. (695) ?o:nɛ ?o?titwanɔ́:nyɔ́:?, hɛ́:ɔwéh,
41   2   4   2   4

twatatɔ:níh, teyoæwɛ:nyé:h, nɛ: he yɔɛjata:tyé?, ta: ne? he nɛyó?-
2   4   2   4   2   4   2

tɛ:ɔk nɛ: ?ɔkwa?nikɔɛ?.
41

(684) it is stronger (685) and brings harm to people, (686) to children and old people. (687) But where we Indians are living (688) the wind strikes with less force. (689) And another thing. (690) They told us this, also. (691) Where the wind is formed, (692) it is called the thing that is covered by a veil. (693) And there it is formed, the wind over the earth. (694) And we shall do what we should with our minds. (695) We now give thanks for the place where it is formed, the wind over the earth. And our minds will continue to be so.

GRAMMATICAL COMMENTARY

This commentary is based on the analysis published in Chafe (1960–61). References to paragraphs in that work are made in square brackets.

Seneca has seven vowels: *i*, *e*, *æ*, *a*, *o*, *ε*, and *ɔ*. The last two are nasalized. There are nine consonants: *n*, *w*, *y*, *t*, *k*, *s*, *j*, *h*, and *ʔ* (glottal stop). The stops *t* and *k* are voiced before a vowel and before *n*, *w*, and *y*. The affricate *j* is phonetically [*dz*]. Vowel length is written with a colon, stress with an acute accent mark. There are at most five distinctive pitches (see below), which are written, from low to high, with the numbers 1 to 5 under the letters. The pitch remains level until a new pitch is indicated. Juncture between phrases is written with a comma, between sentences with a period. The two are distinguished by relative length of pause. Word space has no phonological significance but is simply a guide to word boundaries, except that after *t*, *k*, and *s* it indicates interword juncture, phonetically similar to plus juncture in English.

Seneca words are classified as verbs, nouns, and particles. Except for some elliptical forms, verbs (*kihsa:s* 'I'm looking for it') and nouns (*kahsíʔtaʔ* 'my foot') contain a stem (-*ihsa:s*, -*ahsíʔtaʔ*) preceded by a pronominal prefix (*k-* 'first person'). The latter may be subjective (as above), objective (*ʔakihsa:s* 'it sees me'), or transitive (*hakihsa:s* 'he sees me'). The stem consists of at least a root (-*ihsa[:k]*- 'look for', -*ahsíʔta-* 'foot') followed by an aspect suffix (-*s* 'iterative') or noun suffix (-*ʔ* 'simple noun suffix'). The root may be modified by a root suffix (*kihsa:khɔh* 'I'm looking for things'), an incorporated noun root (*kyaʔtihsa:s* 'I'm looking for the body'), a reflexive or reciprocal morpheme, or any combination of these. A modified root is called a base. The aspect suffix may also be modified in several ways (*kihsa:skwaʔ* 'I used to look for it'). Finally, this entire structure may be modified by a modal prefix (*ʔεkihsa:k* 'I will look for it'), a primary prefix (*skihsa:s* 'I'm looking for it again'), a secondary prefix (*nikihsa:s* 'how I look for it'), or several prefixes of unique distribution (*teʔkihsa:s* 'I don't look for it'). There are a few attributive suffixes which modify the entire structure that precedes them: *kihsásko:wa:h* 'I'm a great one at looking for things'.

While no thorough syntactic analysis of Seneca has been made, several factors relating to syntax can be discussed. These include the morphophonemic variation found at the borders of juxtaposed words, or external sandhi, and the two syntactic styles which are represented in these texts.

146

The class of sandhi alternates which can be designated 'formal' and associated with the formal morphological style [27.1] is easily described. A word that ends in *h* before juncture occurs without this *h* before a following word: see the first three words of sentence 2, *ta: neⁿho wai* (*niotiye:ɛh*), which are in isolation *ta:h*, *neⁿhoh*, and *waih*. Interword juncture occurs after *t*, *k*, and *s* when another word directly follows. Since its presence can be inferred from the word boundaries, which are marked by word space, there is no need for a special notation. It is found, for example, between *ⁿethíhso:t* and *sɔekha:ⁿ* in sentence 138. Finally, when a word that ends with *ⁿ* precedes a word beginning *ⁿ*, only one *ⁿ* is actually present. The convention is followed of writing it at the end of the first word and omitting it at the beginning of the second: see *neⁿ ɛyakaɔⁿesháhseⁿ* in sentence 6, where the second word is in isolation *ⁿɛyakaɔⁿesháhseⁿ*. Compare in the same sentence *ne ⁿɔ:kweh*, where the first word is *neh* in isolation.

There is a second class of sandhi alternates which can be termed 'colloquial' and associated with the colloquial style of [27]. This style is distinguished by the absence of word-initial *ⁿ* or *h* after a word that would end in *h* in isolation. In the following list of alternations included in this style, *a* stands for any vowel and *o* for any second vowel:

In Isolation:	In Sequence:
(a) - - - ah ⁿo- - -	- - - o- - -
(b) - - - ah ⁿo:- - -	- - - o:- - -
(c) - - - ah ho(:)- - -	- - - o:- - -
(d) - - - a:h ⁿo(:)- - -	- - - a o- - -

An example of (a) is *n ɔkhí:owi:h* (*neh*, *ⁿɔkhí:owi:h*) in sentence 2; of (b), *neⁿh o:nɛh* (*neⁿhoh*, *ⁿo:nɛh*) in sentence 33; of (c), *n o:tyɛ:nóⁿk-taⁿɔh* (*neh*, *hotyɛ:nóⁿktaⁿɔh*) in sentence 9; of (d), *ta onɛh* (*ta:h*, *ⁿo:nɛh*) in sentence 1. In (a), however, if the first vowel is *i*, it, rather than the second vowel, remains: *ti yakotɔⁿseⁿɔ́:ɔk* (*tih*, *ⁿɛyakotɔⁿseⁿɔ́:ɔk*) in sentence 65.

There are in Seneca at least three speaking styles that are distinguished solely by their patterns of pitch and stress. Two of them, which will be referred to as 'chanting' and 'preaching', are exemplified in these texts. The third is the style of normal conversation, and it is represented here only in the Epilogue to the Thanksgiving Speech.

Chanting is the characteristic style for rituals of this sort. It is followed throughout the Thanksgiving Speech and in sections 2 to 12 and 15 to 17 of the Thanksgiving Dance. It utilizes only pitches 1 to 4. In it, nearly all of the phrases which are not sentence-final begin on pitch 2 and remain there until the end of the phrase, where there is a rise to pitch 4. This rise is accompanied by stress, which is in addition to the morphological stress on the word, if there is one. The position of the phrase-final stress and rise to pitch 4 is as follows: it occurs on the next to last vowel of the phrase if that vowel (a) is directly followed (without intervening length) by the phrase-final vowel, or (b) is separated from the latter only by length and is at the same time either identical with it or morphologically stressed. An example of (a) is *wáih* in sentence 5. Examples of (b) are *to:nɛ²ni-kɔɛwɛnyá²tɔ́:ɔk* in sentence 63, and *²ɛyot²eohtɔní:ak* in sentence 20. Otherwise the stress and rise is on the last vowel of the phrase (see examples passim).

In the sentence-final phrase there is most commonly a rise to pitch 3 at some (apparently nondistinctive) point during the phrase and a fall to pitch 1 on the last vowel (or vowel sequence), which is again stressed.

Other patterns occur in chanting, but those described above are overwhelmingly the most frequent and characteristic.

Preaching is conspicuous as the style in which the Good Message of Handsome Lake is recited. It occurs in other rituals too, and is found in sections 1, 13, 14, and 18 to 22 of the Thanksgiving Dance recorded here. Its alternation with chanting seems to have some semantic function, indicating, although not consistently, the beginning of a major subdivision of the text. Here, at least, it signals the first section of the entire text, and the shift from terrestrial to celestial items at section 13 (cf. p. 7).

Preaching utilizes five pitches. Its patterns are more intricate and varied than those of the chanting style, but several characteristic features can be easily described.

Probably its most characteristic feature is an added stress that immediately precedes the usual phrase-final stress. In phrases that are not sentence-final this stress is accompanied by a falling pitch, with a partial rise on the phrase-final stress. Typical pitch patterns are 523, 423, and 412, the last two usually preceded by a phrase containing the first. In the sentence-final phrase there is very often a rise to pitch 4 before the end of the phrase, with a fall from 4 to 1 on the final vowel. Many sentences contain an initial phrase which begins on pitch 4 and ends with a rise to pitch 5. All of these above-mentioned patterns are exemplified in sentence 465. Variations of them, and some entirely different patterns, can be found throughout the sections of the Thanksgiving Dance containing this style.

The structure of each word in the texts will now be described. A boldface number is given to each word for purposes of cross reference. The following abbreviations are used:

asp., aspect
attr., attributive
augment., augmentative [20.2] [63]
caus., causative [13.3, 5, 7]
charact., characterizer [20.4]
cisloc., cislocative [21]
coin., coincident [25.3]
coll., colloquial
cont., continuative [18]
contr., contrastive [25.4]
dat., dative [13.12]
desc., descriptive [5.6–7]
dimin., diminutive [20.3]
direct., directive [13.2]
dist., distributive [13.10]
du., dual
dupl., duplicative [22.1]
ell., elliptical
even., eventuative [16]
excl., exclusive
ext., external [7.5]
fem., feminine [6.1, 7]
fut., future [8.5]
iden., identical
impv., imperative [5.10–11]
inch., inchoative [13.5, 8–9]
incl., inclusive
incorp., incorporated
indef., indefinite [7.3]
indic., indicative [8.6]
inst., instrumental [13.11]
int., internal [7.5]
intens., intensifier [13.16]

iter., iterative [5.8–9]
lit., literally
loc., locative
masc., masculine [6.1, 6]
mod., modal
neg., negative [23]
neut., neuter [6.1, 8]
nn., noun
nom., nominalizer [12]
nonmasc., nonmasculine
obj., objective
oppos., oppositive [13.4, 6]
opt., optative [8.4]
part., partitive [25.2]
pers., person
pl., plural
plur., pluralizer [20.7]
popul., populative, [20.5]
pref., prefix
prim., primary
prog., progressive [17]
punc., punctual [8.2]
purp., purposive [13.15]
recip., reciprocal [15]
refl., reflexive [15]
repet., repetitive [21]
rt., root
sec., secondary
spl., simple [7.5]
subj., subjective
suff., suffix
trans., transient [13.14]
transloc., translocative [24]
vb., verb

---

[63] Only the most important morpheme references are cited in this list. A complete general index to Chafe (1960–61) can be found in [30.1].

Thanksgiving Speech

(1)

1. **ta:h** 'and' (sentence connective)
2. **ʔo:nɛh** 'now, then, at a specific time'
3. **tih** 'now, at this moment'
4. **nikɛtyohkóʔtɛ:h** 'the way the group is'

> Vb. base: vb. rt. *-óʔtɛ-* 'be of a certain kind, in a certain condition'; incorp.
> nn. rt. *-ityóhkw-* [3.12, 6.8] 'group, crowd'
> Asp. suff.: *-h* 'desc.'
> Subj. pref.: *-kɛ-* 'neut.'
> Sec. pref.: *ni-* 'part.' (usual with this vb. rt.)

5. **waʔɔkwayáʔtaye:ih** 'we (pl.) gather'

> Vb. base: vb. rt. *-yei-* 'be right'; rt. suff. *-ʹh-* 'inch. II'; incorp. nn. rt.
> *-yáʔta-* 'body' (together meaning 'gather', usually with reference to a
> religious gathering)
> Asp. suff.: *-∅* 'punc.'
> Obj. pref.: *-ɔkwa-* 'we (pl.)'
> Mod. pref.: *wa-* 'indic.'

(2)

6. **neʔhoh** 'that, there'
7. **waih** 'just, precisely'
8. **niotiye:ɛh** 'what they (masc.) did'

> Vb. rt.: *-ye-* 'do'
> Asp. suff.: *-ɛ́h* 'desc.'
> Obj. pref.: *-ʹoti-* 'they (masc.)'
> Sec. pref.: *ni-* 'part.'

9. **hatiɔyáʔke:onɔʔ** 'the Sky Dwellers (masc. pl.)'

> Nn. rt.: *-(y)ɔ́:ya-* [3.21, 6.3] 'sky'
> Nn. suff.: *-ʹʔkɛ́-* 'ext. loc.'
> Subj. pref.: *hati-* 'they (masc. pl.)'
> Attr. suff.: *-ʹonɔ́ʔ* 'popul.'

10. **neʔ** 'it is that . . .' (followed by a predication; usually untranslated, as here)
11. **neh** 'the' (often untranslatable, as here)
12. **ʔɔkhí:owi:h** 'they told us'

> Vb. rt.: *-ʹ(hy)owi-* [6.3] 'tell'
> Asp. suff.: *-h* 'desc.'
> Trans. pref.: *ʔɔkhi-* 'they . . . us'

13. **ʔɛyɔkwayɛ:taʔk** 'we (pl.) shall continue to have it'

> Vb. rt.: *-yɛta-* 'have'
> Asp. suff.: *-ʹʔ-* 'desc.'; *-k* 'cont.'
> Obj. pref.: *-yɔkwa-* 'we (pl.)'
> Mod. pref.: *ʔɛ-* 'fut.'

14. kanɔɔhkwá'shæ' 'love'

Nn. base: vb. rt. -noɔ́hkwa- 'love'; -'ɂshæ- 'nom.'
Nn. suff.: -'ɂ 'spl. nn. suff.'
Subj. pref.: ka- 'neut.'

15. yɔ́ɛja'keh 'on the earth'

Nn. rt.: -ɔ́ɛja- 'earth'
Nn. suff.: -'ɂkɛ́h 'ext. loc.'
Subj. pref.: y- 'neut.'

16. teyɔkwatawɛnye:h 'we (pl.) are moving about'

Vb. base: vb. rt. -awɛnye- 'stir, move about'; -at- 'refl.' (yields intransitive meaning)
Asp. suff.: -h 'desc.'
Obj. pref.: -yɔkw- 'we (pl.)'
Other pref.: te- 'dupl.' (usual with this rt.)

See also **1.**

(3)

17. 'ɛtyotyéɛhtɔ:ɔk 'it will continue to be first'

Vb. base: vb. rt. -yeɛ́ht- 'instigate; (with refl. and cisloc.) be first'; -at- [10.8] 'refl.'
Asp. suff.: -ɔ́- 'desc.'; -ak [3.14] 'cont.'
Obj. pref.: -yo- 'neut.'
Mod. pref.: 'ɛ- 'fut.'
Prim. pref.: -t- 'cisloc.'

18. 'ɛyakoya'tayéihse' 'people will come and gather'

Vb. base: -yáɂta-yei- 'gather' **(5)**; -'hs- 'trans.'
Asp. suff.: -ɛ́' 'purp.'
Obj. pref.: -yako- 'fem.' (here 'people, they' [6.1])
Mod. pref.: 'ɛ- 'fut.'

19. 'ɛtyɔtawɛ:nye:' 'people will move about there'

Vb. base: -at-awɛnye- 'move about' **(16).**
Asp. suff.: -' 'punc.'
Subj. pref.: -y[ɔ]- 'fem.'
Mod. pref.: 'ɛ- 'fut.'
Prim. pref.: -t- 'cisloc.'

20. 'ɔ:kweh 'person', here 'people'

Nn. rt.: -ɔkwe- 'person'
Nn. suff.: -'h- 'spl. nn. suff.'
Subj. pref.: '- 'indef.'

See also **1, 7, 10, 11, 15.**

(4)

21. nityóhsa:ʔ 'how it begins'

Vb. rt.: -ahsaw- [3.10] 'begin'
Asp. suff.: -ʔ 'desc.'
Obj. pref.: -yo- 'neut.'
Prim. pref.: -t- 'cisloc.' (very often with this rt.)
Sec. pref.: ni- 'part.'

22. teyʃkweʔta:ke:h 'two people'

Vb. base: vb. rt. -ake- 'be separate entities' (used in enumeration); incorp.
    nn. rt. -ɔkweʔta- 'person' (incorp. allomorph of -ɔkwe-; cf. 20)
Asp. suff.: -h 'desc.'
Subj. pref.: -y- 'indef.'
Other pref.: te- 'dupl.' (here meaning 'two')

23. tɛ:yatate:kɛʔ 'they (masc. du.) will see each other'

Vb. base: vb. rt. -kɛ- 'see'; -atate- 'recip.'
Asp. suff.: -ʹʔ 'punc.'
Subj. pref.: -ʹ:y- 'they (masc. du.)'
Mod. pref.: -ɛ- 'fut.'
Other pref.: t- 'dupl.'

24. tyotyéɛhtɔh 'it is first'

Iden. with 17 except that cont. and fut. are lacking.

25. hotí:wa:yɛʔ 'they (masc.) have the obligation'

Vb. base: vb. rt. -yɛ- 'have'; incorp. nn. rt. -(C)i:wa- 'matter, affair', here
    'obligation'
Asp. suff.: -ʹʔ 'desc.'
Obj. pref.: hoti- 'they (masc.)'

26. wáonɔʔe:sha 'it pleases them (masc.), they are grateful'

Vb. rt.: -ɔʔesha- 'please, gratify'
Asp. suff.: -ʹʔ 'punc.'
Obj. pref.: -ʹon- 'them (masc.)'
Mod. pref.: wa- 'indic.'

27. skɛ:nɔʔ 'it is well, healthy (mentally and physically)'
28. yɛnʃhtɔnyɔh 'people think', with skɛ:nɔʔ 'people are happy'

Vb. base: vb. rt. -(ɛ)nʃhtɔ- 'know'; rt. suff. -nyɔ- 'dist.' (together meaning
    'think')
Asp. suff.: -ʹh 'iter.'
Subj. pref.: y- 'fem.'

See also **1, 6, 7, 10**

(5)

29. tɛ:yatahnʃ:nyɔ:ʔ 'they (masc. du.) will greet each other'

Vb. base: -nʃɔnyɔ- 'rejoice in, greet, thank'; -atah- 'recip.'
Asp. suff.: -ʔ 'punc.'
Subj. pref.: -ʹ:y- 'they (masc. du.)'
Mod. pref.: -ɛ- 'fut.'
Other pref.: t- 'dupl.' (usual with this rt.)

30. nɛ:h 'this'

31. hɛ:ni:wá²hotɛ² 'they (masc. du.) will take up the matter there'

> Vb. base: vb. rt. *-a²hot-* 'attach, add on'; incorp. nn. rt. *-(C)i:w-* 'matter'
> Asp. suff.: *-é²* 'punc.'
> Subj. pref.: *-':ni-* 'they (masc. du.)'
> Mod. pref.: *-ɛ-* 'fut.'
> Other pref.: *h-* 'transloc.'

32. hiyá²ti:h 'they (masc. du.) alone'

> Vb. base: vb. rt. *-i-* 'make up the total'; incorp. nn. rt. *-yá²t-* 'body' (often, as here, simply indicating that living beings are involved)
> Asp. suff.: *-h* 'desc.'
> Subj. pref.: *hi-* 'they (masc. du.)'

33. honóti:wa:te² 'their (masc.) subject matter'

> Vb. base: vb. rt. *-te-* 'be present'; incorp. nn. rt. *-(C)i:wa-* 'matter'; *-at-* [3.14] 'refl.'
> Asp. suff.: *-'²* 'desc.'
> Obj. pref.: *hon-* 'their (masc.)'

See also **1, 7, 10, 11.**

(6)

34. nioye:ɛh 'what he did'

> Iden. with 8 except for obj. pref. *-'o-* 'masc.'

35. hotyɛ:nó²kta²ɔh 'the Creator', lit. 'he has fashioned it'

> Vb. base: vb. rt. *-ó²kta-* 'come to the end'; rt. suff. *-'²-* 'inch. I'; incorp. nn. rt. *-yɛɛn-* (with this vb. rt. yields meaning 'fashion'); *-at-* 'refl.'
> Asp. suff.: *-óh* 'desc.'
> Obj. pref.: *ho-* 'masc.'

36. heh 'there, where'

37. tyɔhe² 'we (incl. pl.) are alive' (**35–37** together are translated 'Our Creator')

> Vb. rt.: *-ɔhe-* 'be alive'
> Asp. suff.: *-'²-* 'desc.'
> Subj. pref.: *ty-* 'we (incl. p.)'

38. hawe:²ɔh 'he decided'

> Vb. rt.: *-e²ɔ-* 'decide, ordain'
> Asp. suff.: *-'h-* 'desc.'
> Obj. pref.: *haw-* 'masc.'

39. ²ɛyakaɔ²esháhse² 'people will come to express their gratitude'

> Vb. base: vb. rt. *-ɔ²esha-* 'gratify'; rt. suff. *-'hs-* 'trans.'
> Asp. suff.: *-é²* 'purp.'
> Obj. pref.: *-yaka-* 'fem.'
> Mod. pref.: *²ɛ-* 'fut.'

40. hekáya⁷ti:h 'it is all that there is, simply'

Vb. stem iden. with **32.**
Subj. pref.: *-ka-* 'neut.'
Other pref.: *he-* 'transloc.' (here indicating completeness)

41. teyakotawɛnye:h 'people are moving about'

Iden. with **16** except for obj. pref. *-yako-* 'fem.'

See also **1, 6, 7, 10, 11, 15.**

(7)

42. nɛ:kɛ:h 'this, that'

43. nityókwe⁷ta:ke:h 'how many of us people there are'

Vb. stem iden with **22.**
Subj. pref.: *-ty-* 'we (incl. pl.)'
Sec. pref.: *ni-* 'part.'

44. ⁷ɔkwaiwáyɛstɔh 'we (pl.) have the obligation'

Vb. base: vb. rt. *-yɛ-* 'have'; rt. suff. *-ˈst-* 'caus.-inst.'; incorp. nn. rt.
-(C)ɨ:wa- 'matter, obligation'
Asp. suff.: *-óh* 'desc.'
Obj. pref.: *⁷ɔkwa-* 'we (pl.)'

45. ⁷ɛyɔkwatɔ⁷esɛ́:ɔk 'we (pl.) shall continue to be grateful'

Vb. base: vb. rt. *-ɔ⁷es-* 'please, gratify' (formally distinct from the vb.
rt. in **26, 39**); *-at-* 'refl.'
Asp. suff.: *-ɛ́-* 'desc.'; *-ak* 'cont.'
Obj. pref.: *-yɔkw-* 'we (pl.)'
Mod. pref.: *⁷ɛ-* 'fut.'

See also **1, 5, 7.**

(8)

46. khoh 'and, also'

47. niyó⁷tɛ:h 'the way it is'

Vb. rt.: *-ó⁷tɛ-* 'be in a certain condition' (cf. **4**)
Asp. suff.: *-h* 'desc.'
Subj. pref.: *-y-* 'neut.'
Sec. pref.: *ni-* 'part.'

48. kanɔtakwɛ́hta:⁷ 'community', lit. 'town laid out flat'

Vb. base: vb. rt. *-kwɛ́hta-* 'lay out flat'; incorp. nn. rt. *-nɔta-* 'town'
Asp. suff.: *-⁷* 'desc.'
Subj. pref.: *ka-* 'neut.'

49. hɛ⁷ɛh 'no, not'

50. tɔ⁷ókwa:ɔkɛh 'we (pl.) have not heard'

Vb. rt.: *-áɔ(:)k-* 'hear'
Asp. suff.: *-ɛ́h* 'desc.'
Obj. pref.: *-⁷ɔkw-* 'we (pl.)'
Other pref.: *tɔ⁷-* [27.5] 'negative'

51. kano:ɔ^ʔ 'it is difficult'

Vb. rt.: -noɔ- 'be difficult'
Asp. suff.: -'ʔ 'desc.'
Subj. pref.: ka- 'neut.'

52. kiʔshɛh 'perhaps, maybe'
53. nɔ:yotyé:ɔk 'how it might continue to happen accidentally'

Vb. rt.: -atyeɔ- 'happen accidentally or unexpectedly'
Asp. suff.: -'Ø- 'desc.'; -ak [3.14,19,20] 'cont.'
Obj. pref.: -yo- 'neut.'
Mod. pref.: -aa- [3.14] 'opt.'
Sec. pref.: n- 'part.'

See also **6, 11, 30.**

(9)

54. kakéɔta:tye^ʔ 'it is laid down all along'

Vb. rt.: -kéɔt- 'lay down'
Asp. suff.: -Ø 'desc.'; -atye- 'prog.'; -'ʔ 'desc.'
Subj. pref.: ka- 'neut.'

55. koyá^ʔto:ækhɔ^ʔ 'it is holding people down here and there'

Vb. base: vb. rt. -ɔæk- 'hold down'; rt. suff. -hɔ- 'dist.' ('here and there');
incorp. nn. rt. -yá²t-'body' (cf. **32**)
Asp. suff.: -'ʔ 'desc.'
Obj. pref.: ko- 'fem.'

56. ʔonɔ́hsotaiyɔ:^ʔ 'disease'

Vb. rt.: -nɔhsotaiyɔ- 'make sick'
Asp. suff.: -ʔ 'desc.'
Obj. pref.: ²o- 'neut.'

57. kwa:h 'even, especially'
58. ha:hɔ^ʔ 'he himself'

Nn. rt.: -hɔ- 'emphatic third person'
Nn. suff.: -'ʔ 'spl. nn. suff.'
Obj. pref.: ha- 'masc.' [28.4]

59. næ:h 'emphatically, certainly'
60. kaiwayétahkɔh 'it is a responsibility, obligation'

Vb. base: vb. rt. -yɛta- 'have'; rt. suff. -'hkw- [3.12] 'inst.'; incorp. nn. rt.
-(C)í:wa- 'matter, responsibility'
Asp. suff.: -ɔ́h 'desc.'
Subj. pref.: ka- 'neut.'

See also **1, 6, 7, 10, 11, 30, 35, 47.**

(10)

61. ni:ka:? 'what is in it', here 'therefore'

> Vb. rt.: -(C)- 'put in, incorporate in'
> Asp. suff.: -ʔ 'desc.'
> Subj. pref.: -ka- 'neut.'
> Sec. pref.: ni- 'part.'

62. ʔáɔʔe:sat 'let it cause gratification, let there be gratitude'

> Vb. base: vb. rt. -ɔʔesa- 'gratify'; rt. suff. -'ht- [3.6] 'caus. I'
> Asp. suff.: -Ø 'impv.'
> Obj. pref.: ʔa- 'neut.'

63. ʔɛyɔkyɔʔéshahse:k 'we (pl.) shall continue to be grateful'

> Vb. rt.: -ɔʔesha- 'gratify'
> Asp. suff.: -'hs- 'iter.'; -ek 'cont.'
> Obj. pref.: -yɔky- 'we (pl.)'
> Mod. pref.: ʔɛ- 'fut.'

64. nɔ́ʔkɛ:? 'behind, afterward'

65. ʔɔkwayaʔtakɔhsóhtɔ:ɔtyeʔ 'we (pl.) are remaining'

> Vb. base: vb. rt. -kɔhsóht- 'remain'; incorp. nn. rt. -yáʔta- 'body'
> Asp. suff.: -ɔ́- 'desc.'; -atye- 'prog.'; -'ʔ 'desc.'
> Obj. pref.: ʔɔkwa- 'we (pl.)'

66. káiwaya:sɔh 'it is claimed', lit. 'the matter is called'

> Vb. base: vb. rt. -yas- 'call, name'; nn. rt. -(C)i:wa- 'matter'
> Asp. suff.: -ɔ́h 'desc.'
> Subj. pref. ka- 'neut.'

67. ʔiʔ 'I, me, we, us'

68. ʔɛtwiʔ 'we (incl. pl.) shall say'

> Vb. rt.: -i- 'say'
> Asp. suff.: -'ʔ 'punc.'
> Subj. pref.: -tw- 'we (incl. pl.)'
> Mod. pref.: ʔɛ- 'fut.'

69. twɛnɔ́htɔnyɔh 'we (incl. pl.) think'

> Iden. with 28 except for subj. pref. tw- 'we (incl. pl.)'

See also **1, 6, 7, 10, 11, 27, 30, 36.**

(11)

70. ʔɛswe:he:k 'you (pl.) will continue to think'

> Vb. rt.: -ehe- 'think, give thought'
> Asp. suff.: -Ø- 'desc.'; -k 'cont.'
> Subj. pref.: -sw- 'you (pl.)'
> Mod. pref.: ʔɛ- 'fut.'

71. kɛh emphasizes meaning of preceding word (sometimes of following word)

72. tayakwatye:ɛt 'it's first for us (excl. pl.)'

>Vb. base iden. with **17.**
>Asp. suff.: -∅ 'punc.'
>Subj. pref.: -yakwa- 'we (excl. pl.)'
>Mod. pref.: -a- 'indic.'
>Prim. pref.: t- 'cisloc.'

73. ʔoʔtyakwatáhnɔ:ɔnyɔ:ʔ 'we (excl. pl.) greet each other'

>Vb. stem iden with **29.**
>Subj. pref.: -yakw- 'we (excl. pl.)'
>Mod. pref.: ʔoʔ- 'indic.'
>Other pref.: -t- 'dupl.'

74. nɛyóʔtɛ:ɔk 'it will continue to be so'

>Vb. rt.: -óʔtɛ- 'be in a certain condition'
>Asp. suff.: -∅- 'desc.'; -ak 'cont.'
>Subj. pref.: -y- 'neut.'
>Mod. pref.: -ɛ- 'fut.'
>Sec. pref.: n- 'part.'

75. ʔɔkwaʔnikʒɛʔ 'our (pl.) minds'

>Nn. rt.: -ʔnikʒɛ- 'mind'
>Nn. suff.: -'ʔ 'spl. nn. suff.'
>Obj. pref.: ʔɔkwa- 'our (pl.)'

See also **1, 3, 6, 7, 10, 11, 30, 67.**

(12)

76. nyo:ye:ɛh coll. for **34.**

77. ʔɛkʒeja:ta:t 'I shall establish the earth'

>Vb. base: vb. rt. -te- [13.5] 'be present, in place'; rt. suff. -at- 'caus. II'
>(together meaning 'establish'); incorp. nn. rt. -ʒeja- 'earth'
>Asp. suff.: -∅ 'punc.'
>Subj. pref.: -k- '1st pers.'
>Mod. pref.: ʔɛ- 'fut.'

78. tɛyɔtawɛ:nye:ʔ 'people will move about'

>Iden. with **19** except for t- 'dupl.' and lack of -t- 'cisloc.'

See also **1, 6, 7, 11, 20, 30, 35–8.**

(13)

79. wa:se:ʔ 'it is new'

>Vb. rt.: -ase- 'be new'
>Asp. suff.: -ʔ 'desc.'
>Subj. pref.: w- 'neut.'

80. **teyakotáɔ:ɔtyeˀ** 'people are coming to be standing'

> Vb. base: vb. rt. *-ta-* 'stand'; rt. suff. *-ˀʔ-* 'inch. I'
> Asp. suff.: *-ɔ́-* 'desc.'; *-atye-* 'prog.'; *-ˀʔ* 'desc.'
> Obj. pref.: *-yako-* 'fem.'
> Other pref.: *te-* 'dupl.'

81. **hɛ́:ɔweh** 'where'

82. **ˀɛyɔ́ɛja:te:k** 'the earth will continue to be there'

> Vb. base: vb. rt. *-te-* 'be present'; incorp. nn. rt. *-ɔ́ɛja-* 'earth'
> Asp. suff.: *-Ø-* 'desc.'; *-k* 'cont.'
> Subj. pref.: *-y-* 'neut.'
> Mod. pref.: *ˀɛ-* 'fut.'

See also **3, 6, 11, 20, 30, 46.**

(14)

83. **kanɔ:kshæˀ** 'relationship'

> Nn. base: vb. rt. *-nɔk-* 'be related'; *-shæ-* 'nom.'
> Nn. suff.: *-ˀʔ* 'spl. nn. suff.'
> Subj. pref.: *ka-* 'neut.'

84. **n o:nɛh** 'when'

> *neh* (11) *ˀo:nɛh* (2)

85. **ˀɛyɔthyonyá:neˀ** 'people are going to tell about it'

> Vb. base: vb. rt. *-hyonya-* 'tell'; rt. suff. *-ˀ:n-* 'trans.'; *-at-* 'refl.' (yields meaning 'tell about')
> Asp. suff.: *-éʔ* 'purp.'
> Subj. pref.: *-y[ɔ]-* 'fem.'
> Mod. pref.: *ˀɛ-* 'fut.'

86. **ˀɛ:nɔtɔ́:ɔk** 'they (masc. pl.) will continue to say'

> Vb. rt. *-atɔ-* 'say'
> Asp. suff.: *-ˀØ-* 'iter.'; *-ak* 'cont.'
> Subj. pref.: *-ˀɛn-* 'they (masc. pl.)'
> Mod. pref.: *ˀɛ-* 'fut.'

87. **ˀakhínoˀɛh** 'we (excl.) have her as mother, our mother'

> Vb. rt.: *-nóʔɛ-* 'have as mother'
> Asp. suff.: *-ˀh* 'desc.'
> Trans. pref.: *ˀakhi-* 'we (excl.) . . . her'

88. **teyɔkwɛ:hsiˀtakɛˀsǽhkɔh** 'we (pl.) have it as a support for our feet'

> Vb. base: vb. rt. *-kɛˀsǽhkw-* 'put a support under'; incorp. nn. rt. *-ahsiˀta-* [15.4]; *-(ɛ)ɛ-* 'refl.'
> Asp. suff.: *-ɔ́h* 'desc.'
> Obj. pref.: *-yɔkw-* 'we (pl.)'
> Other pref.: *te-* 'dupl.'

See also **1–3, 10, 11, 82.**

(15)

89. tkaye:i? 'indeed, in fact, actually'

Vb. rt.: -yei- 'be right'
Asp. suff.: -'? 'desc.'
Subj. pref.: -ka- 'neut.'
Prim. pref.: t- 'cisloc.'

90. ?ɔkwatyǽ:?tahkɔh 'we (pl.) use it'

Coll. for ?ɔkwatyɛ̀ǽ?tahkɔh [27.2]
Vb. base: vb. rt. -yeæ- 'do'; rt. suff. -'?ta- 'caus. I' (yields meaning 'use'),
   -'hkw- 'inst.'; -at- 'refl.'
Asp. suff.: -ɔ̀h 'desc.'
Obj. pref.: ?ɔkw- 'we (pl.)'

91. ha?tewɛ:níshæke:h 'every day'

Vb. base: vb. rt. -ake- [14.4] 'be separate entities'; incorp. nn. rt. -ɛ́:nishæ-
   'day'
Asp. suff.: -h 'desc.'
Subj. pref.: -w- 'neut.'
Other pref.: -te- 'dupl.', ha?- 'transloc.' (indicating completeness, 'every')

92. ha?téwahsɔtake:h 'every night'

Iden. with **91** except for incorp. nn. rt. -ahsɔt- 'night'

93. yɔɛjate? 'the earth'

Vb. base: vb. rt. -te- 'be present'; incorp. nn. rt. -ɔ́ɛja- 'earth'
Asp. suff.: -'? 'desc.'
Subj. pref.: y- 'neut.'

See also **1, 6, 7, 10, 11, 16, 81.**

(16)

94. teyɔkwahkwɛ́ɔtye? 'we are lifting'

Vb. rt.: -'hkw- 'lift'
Asp. suff.: -ɛ́- 'desc.'; -atye- 'prog.'; -'? 'desc.'
Obj. pref.: -yɔkwa- 'we (pl.)'
Other pref.: te- 'dupl.' (usual with this rt.)

95. ?i:kɛ:h 'this, here'

See also **6, 11, 27, 30, 46, 69, 81, 93.**

(17)

96. ?itwe:h 'we (incl. pl.) think, believe'

Vb. rt.: -e- 'think, believe'
Asp. suff.: -h 'desc.'
Subj. pref.: ?itw- [6.11] 'we (incl. pl.)'

97. ʔóiwakwe:kɔh 'the whole matter, everything'

Vb. base: vb. rt. -*kwek*- 'be the whole of'; incorp. nn. rt. -(C)*i:wa*- 'matter'
Asp suff.: -*ɔh* 'desc.'
Obj. pref.: *ʔo*- 'neut.'

98. koiwayéistɔh 'she has done what she was obligated to do'

Vb. base: vb. rt. -*yei*- 'be right'; rt. suff. -'*st*- 'caus.-inst.'; incorp. nn. rt.
-(C)*i:wa*- 'matter, obligation'
Asp. suff.: -*ɔh* 'desc.'
Obj. pref.: *ko*- 'fem.'

99. ʔethíno?ɛh 'we (incl.) have her as mother, our mother'

Iden. with 87 except for trans. pref. *ʔethi*- 'we (incl.) . . . her'

100. niyóiwaʔ 'what responsibility'

Nn. rt.: -(C)*i:wa*- 'matter, responsibility'
Nn. suff.: -'*ʔ* 'spl. nn. suff.'
Obj. pref.: -*yo*- 'neut.'
Prim. pref.: *ni*- 'part.'

101. shakoiɔ́tas?ɔh 'he has given her an assignment'

Vb. base: vb. rt. -*ɔ(:)ta*- 'attach'; incorp. nn. rt. -(C)*i*- 'matter, assign-ment'
Asp. suff.: -'*s?*- 'even.'; -*ɔh* 'desc.'
Trans. pref.: *shako*- 'he . . . her'

102. waʔakwatyɛ:nɔ:niʔ 'we (excl. pl.) do it properly'

Vb. base: vb. rt. -*ɔ(:)ni*- 'make'; incorp. nn. rt. -*yɛɛn*- (together meaning 'do properly'; cf. 35); -*at*- 'refl.'
Asp. suff.: -'*ʔ* 'punc.'
Subj. pref.: -*ʔakw*- 'we (excl. pl.)'
Mod. pref.: *wa*- 'indic.'

103. ʔo:nɛ: 'now'

ʔo:nɛh (2); the final vowel length is anomalous, but occurs consistently in this one context.

104. ʔoʔtyakwanɔ́:nyɔ:ʔ 'we (excl. pl.) thank'

Vb. rt.: -*nɔɔnyɔ*- 'thank'
Asp. suff.: -*ʔ* 'punc.'
Subj. pref.: -*yakwa*- 'we (excl. pl.)'
Mod. pref.: *ʔoʔ*- 'indic.'
Other pref.: -*t*- 'dupl.'

See also **1, 3, 6, 7, 10, 11, 30, 36, 61, 62, 70, 74, 75, 88.**

(18)

See **1, 2, 7, 30, 35, 76.**

(19)

105. ʔɛyotʔeohtɔní:ak 'plants will continue to grow'

> Vb. base: vb. rt. -ɔ(:)ni- 'make'; incorp. nn. rt. -ʔeóht- 'plant'; -at-
> 'refl.' (with this vb. rt. yields meaning 'grow')
> Asp. suff.: -ʹØ- 'desc.'; -ak 'cont.'
> Obj. pref.: -yo- 'neut.'
> Mod. pref.: ʔɛ- 'fut.'

See also **3, 7, 10, 11, 38, 81, 82, 89.**

(20)

106. kakwe:kɔh 'the whole, all'

> Vb. rt.: -kwek- 'be the whole of'
> Asp. suff.: -ɔ́h 'desc.'
> Subj. pref.: ka- 'neut.'

107. ʔɛyótihsɛnɔyɛ:tɔ:k 'they (nonmasc.) will continue to have names'

> Vb. base: vb. rt. -yɛt- 'have'; rt. suff. -ɔ- 'dist.' incorp. nn. rt. -hsɛnɔ-
> 'name'
> Asp. suff.: -Ø- 'desc.'; -k 'cont.'
> Obj. pref.: -yoti- 'they (nonmasc.)'
> Mod. pref.: ʔɛ- 'fut.'

108. ni:yɔ:h 'how many'

> Vb. rt.: -ɔ- 'be a certain amount'
> Asp. suff.: -h 'desc.'
> Subj. pref.: -y- 'neut.'
> Sec. pref.: ni- 'part.'

See also **10, 11, 36, 82, 89, 105.**

(21)

109. kato:kɛ:h 'it is certain, specific, the same'

> Vb. rt.: -tokɛ- 'be certain, etc.'
> Asp. suff.: -h 'desc.'
> Subj. pref.: ka- 'neut.'

110. niyó:waʔkeh 'at a specific time'

> Nn. rt.: -ʹ:wa- 'specific time'
> Nn. suff.: -ʹʔkɛ́h 'ext. loc.'
> Obj. pref.: -yo- 'neut.'
> Sec. pref.: ni- 'part.'

111. tɛwɛnɔɛjotkáʔwahse:k 'they (nonmasc. pl.) will always emerge
from the earth'

> Vb. base: vb. rt. -otkáʔw- 'emerge from'; incorp. nn. rt. -ɔ́ɛj- 'earth'
> Asp. suff.: -áhs- 'iter.'; -ek 'cont.'
> Subj. pref.: -wɛn- 'they (nonmasc. pl.)'
> Mod. pref.: -ɛ- 'fut.'
> Other pref.: t- 'dupl.'

112. ʔaːhɔʔ 'itself, themselves', here 'of their own accord'

   Nn. stem iden. with **58.**
   Obj. pref.: *ʔa-* 'neut.'

113. ʔɛwɔtotyáhseːk 'it will always grow to maturity'

   Vb. rt.: *-atoty-* [3.14] 'grow to maturity'
   Asp. suff.: *-ɑ́hs-* 'iter.'; *-ek* 'cont.'
   Subj. pref.: *-w-* 'neut.'
   Mod. pref.: *ʔɛ-* 'fut.'

See also **2, 3, 10, 11, 36.**

(22)

114. ʔonɔhkwaʔshǽʔshɔʔɔh 'medicines'

   Nn. rt.: *-nɔhkwaʔshæ-* 'medicine'
   Nn. suff.: *-´ʔ-* 'spl. nn. suff.'
   Obj. pref.: *ʔo-* 'neut.'
   Attr. suff.: *-shɔ́ʔɔ́h* 'plur.'

115. ʔoːnɔtɔʔseʔɔ́ːɔk 'it will continue to be available to them (masc.) in abundance'

   Coll. for *ʔeonɔtɔʔseʔɔ́ːɔk* [26.2]
   Vb. rt.: *-atɔʔseʔ-* 'be available in abundance'
   Asp. suff.: *-ɔ́-* 'desc.'; *-ak* 'cont.'
   Obj. pref.: *-´on-* 'they (masc.)'
   Mod. pref.: *ʔɛ-* [3.16] 'fut.'

116. ʔoʔtyɔtawɛːnyeːʔ 'people move about'

   Iden. with **78** except for mod. pref. *ʔoʔ-* 'indic.'

117. nioʔnikɔɛwɛ́ʔɔh 'what he intended', lit. 'how his mind fell'

   Vb. base: vb. rt. *-ɛ-* 'fall'; rt. suff. *-´ʔ-* 'inch. I'; incorp. nn. rt. *-ʔnikɔɛ-* 'mind'
   Asp. suff.: *-ɔ́h* 'desc.'
   Obj. pref.: *-´o-* 'masc.'
   Sec. pref.: *ni-* 'part.'

See also **3, 6, 7, 10, 11, 15, 20, 42.**

(23)

118. niyótoʔktaːtyeʔ 'up to the present time'

   Vb. base: vb. rt. *-óʔkt-* 'come to the end, extend to a certain point'; *-at-* 'refl.'
   Asp. suff.: *-Ø-* 'desc.'; *-atye-* 'prog.'; *-´ʔ* 'desc.'
   Obj. pref.: *-yo-* 'neut.'
   Sec. pref.: *ni-* 'part.'

See also **1, 7, 10, 11, 30, 36, 89, 90.**

(24)

119. háɔnya:nɔ² 'he made them'

> Vb. base: vb. rt. -ɔnya- 'make'; rt. suff. -':nɔ- 'dist.'
> Asp. suff.: -'² 'desc.'
> Obj. pref.: ha- 'masc.'

See also **11, 30, 35, 114.**

(25)

120. tɛyakohkwéɔtye² 'people will be lifting'

> Vb. stem iden. with **94** except for final asp. suff. -'² 'punc.'
> Obj. pref.: -yako- 'fem.'
> Mod. pref.: -ɛ- 'fut.'
> Other pref.: t- 'dupl.'

121. ²ɛwɔtihsí:æ²k 'they (nonmasc. pl.) will continue to be distributed'

> Vb. rt.: -hsiaæ- [5.4] 'stand in array, be distributed'
> Asp. suff.: -'²- 'desc.'; -k 'cont.'
> Subj. pref.: -wati- 'they (nonmasc. pl.)'
> Mod pref.: ²ɛ- 'fut.'

See also **6, 38, 74, 82, 114.**

(26)

122. ²ɛyakóæ²se² 'it will catch up with people'

> Vb. base: vb. rt. -(C)æ²- 'catch up with'; rt. suff. -se- 'dat.'
> Asp. suff.: -'² 'punc.'
> Obj. pref.: -yako- 'fem.'
> Mod. pref.: ²ɛ- 'fut.'

123. kanɔ́:kte:shæ² 'illness'

> Nn. base: vb. rt. -nɔ́ɔkte- 'feel sickly'; -shæ- 'nom.'
> Nn. suff.: -'² 'spl. nn. suff.'
> Subj. pref.: ka- 'neut.'

124. ²ɛkayɛ:ta²k 'it will continue to be there'

> Iden. with **13** except for subj. pref. -ka- 'neut.' (with subj. pref. this rt. means 'be put down, be there')

125. ²ɛyakoyá²take:ha² 'it will assist people'

> Vb. rt.: -ya²takeh- 'assist'
> Asp. suff. -á² 'punc.'
> Obj. pref.: -yako- 'fem.'
> Mod. pref.: ²ɛ- 'fut.'

See also **1, 3, 6, 7, 10, 11, 15, 34, 35, 38, 41.**

(27)

126. haʔteyonóhkwaʔshæ:kɛ:h 'all the medicines'

> Vb. base: vb. rt. -ake- [14.4] 'be separate entities'; incorp. nn. rt.
> -nɔhkwaʔshæ- 'medicine'
> Asp. suff.: -h 'desc.'
> Obj. pref.: -yo- 'neut.'
> Other pref.: -te- 'dupl.', haʔ- 'transloc.' (cf. **91, 92**)

127. hotkáʔwɛh 'he left, provided'

> Vb. rt.: -atkáʔw- 'leave, provide'
> Asp. suff.: -éh 'desc.'
> Obj. pref.: ho- 'masc.'

128. ʔɛyɔkwayaʔtakehashǽʔkɛ:ɔk 'it will be our assistance in the future'

> Vb. base: vb. rt. -ʔkéɔk- 'be there in the future' (?); incorp. nn. base:
> vb. rt. -yaʔtakeha- 'assist'; -shæ- 'nom.'
> Asp. suff.: -Ø 'punc.'
> Obj. pref.: -yɔkwa- 'our (pl.)'
> Mod. pref.: ʔɛ- 'fut.'

See also **1, 7, 10, 11, 81, 93.**

(28)

See **1, 6, 35, 46, 76.**

(29)

129. ʔotʔéohtɔ:ni:h 'plants are growing'

> Vb. base iden. with **105.**
> Asp. suff.: -h 'desc.'
> Obj. pref.: ʔo- 'neut.'

130. ʔɛkaʔeohtatókɛ:ɔk 'there will continue to be a certain plant'

> Vb. base: vb. rt. -tokɛ- 'be certain, specific'; incorp. nn. rt. -ʔeóhta-
> 'plant'
> Asp. suff.: -'Ø- 'desc.'; -ak 'cont.'
> Subj. pref.: -ka- 'neut.'
> Mod. pref.: ʔɛ- 'fut.'

131. ʔɛwɔ:yaníyɔtha:k 'berries will always hang'

> Vb. base: vb. rt. -niyɔt- 'hang'; incorp. nn. rt. -á:ya- [3.14] 'berries, fruit'
> Asp. suff.: -h- 'iter.'; -ak 'cont.'
> Subj. pref.: -w- 'neut.'
> Mod. pref.: ʔɛ- 'fut.'

See also **7, 10, 11, 30, 36, 38, 47, 81, 93, 109, 110.**

(30)

132. ʔɛtkháwihtak 'I shall then bring it about, cause it'

Vb. base: vb. rt. -*hawi*- 'carry', with cisloc. 'bring'; rt. suff. -*'ht*- 'caus.
I'; -*'hkw*- 'inst.' (the entire base meaning 'bring about')
Asp. suff.: -*∅* 'punc.'
Subj. pref.: -*k*- '1st pers.'
Mod. pref.: *ʔɛ*- 'fut.'
Prim. pref.: -*t*- 'cisloc.'

133. ʔɛyɔkasháe:ʔse:k 'people will always remember me'

Vb. base: vb. rt. -*ashaæ*- [5.4] 'take cognizance of'; rt. suff. -*'ʔ*- 'inch. I'
(together meaning 'remember')
Asp. suff. -*s*-'iter.'; -*ek* 'cont.'
Trans. pref.: -*yɔk*- 'people . . . me'
Mod. pref.: *ʔɛ*- 'fut.'

See also **3, 6, 10, 11, 15, 20, 116.**

(31)

134. kɛs 'repeatedly, each time'

135. ʔɛyɔtɔʔéshɔnyɔ:ʔ 'people will repeatedly be grateful'

Vb. base: vb. rt. -*ɔʔes*- 'gratify'; rt. suff. -*hɔ*- 'dist.', -*nyɔ*- 'double dist.'
[13.10]; -*at*- 'refl.'
Asp. suff.: -*ʔ* 'punc.'
Subj. pref.: -*y[ɔ]*- 'fem.'
Mod. pref.: *ʔɛ*- 'fut.'

136. ʔɛyɔ́tkathoʔ 'people will see'

Vb. rt. -*atkathw*- 'see'
Asp. suff.: -*óʔ* 'punc.'
Subj. pref.: -*y[ɔ]*- 'fem.'
Mod. pref.: *ʔɛ*- 'fut.'

137. ʔɛwɔ́:yaniyɔ:tɛʔ 'berries will hang'

Iden. with **131** except for asp. suff. -*éʔ* 'punc.'

138. niyɔɛjákɛ:ya:t 'above the earth'

Vb. base: vb. rt. -*kɛ́:yat*- 'put on top of, above'; incorp. nn. rt. -*ɔeja*-
'earth'
Asp. suff.: -*∅* 'punc.'
Subj. pref.: -*y*- 'neut.'
Sec. pref.: *ni*- 'part.'

See also **3, 10, 11, 84.**

(32)

139. hotíyastɔh 'they (masc.) call it'

> Vb. base: vb. rt. -*yas*- 'call'; rt. suff. -*t*- 'caus. I'
> Asp. suff.: -*ɔh* 'desc.'
> Obj. pref.: *hoti*- 'they (masc.)'

140. shésʔa:h 'wild strawberry'

> Vb. base (?): vb. rt. -*sʔáa*- 'be small'; incorp. nn. rt. -*she*- (not found elsewhere)
> Asp. suff.: -ʹ*h* 'desc.'

See also **1, 7, 9–11, 30.**

(33)

141. jistɔtáʔshæʔ 'strawberry'

> Ell. for *ʔojistɔtáʔshæʔ* [26.6]
> Nn. base: vb. rt. -*ɔta*- 'attach'; incorp. nn. rt. -*jist*- 'ember'; -ʹ*ʔshæ*- 'nom.'
> Nn. suff.: -ʹ*ʔ* 'spl. nn. suff.'
> (Obj. pref.: *ʔo*- 'neut.')

142. ʔɛtwáyastha:k 'we (incl. pl.) shall always call it'

> Vb. base iden. with **139.**
> Asp. suff.: -*h* 'iter.'; -*ak* 'cont.'
> Subj. pref.: -*twa*- 'we (incl. pl.)'
> Mod. pref.: *ʔɛ*- 'fut.'

See also **1, 2, 6, 7, 10, 11, 15, 16, 67.**

(34)

143. ʔɛtwátkathoʔ 'we (incl. pl.) see'

> Vb. stem iden. with **136.**
> Subj. pref.: -*tw*- 'we (incl. pl.)'
> Mod. pref.: *ʔe*- 'indic.'

144. naʔtetyoʔtáiɛ:h 'when it is warm again there'

> Vb. rt.: -*aʔtaiɛ*- 'be warm, hot'
> Asp. suff.: -*h* 'desc.'
> Obj. pref.: -*yo*- 'neut.'
> Prim. pref.: -*t*- 'cisloc.'
> Other pref.: -*te*- 'dupl.'
> Sec. pref.: *naʔ*- 'part.' (a variant of *nɔʔ*- in this speaker's idiolect)

145. teyoæwɛ:nye:h 'the wind', lit. 'the wind is stirring'

> Vb. base: vb. rt. -*awɛnye*- 'stir'; incorp. nn. rt. -(*C*)*æ*- 'wind' [14.4]
> Asp. suff.: -*h* 'desc.'
> Obj. pref.: -*yo*- 'neut.'
> Other pref.: *te*- 'dupl.'

146. ʔoʔwá:yaniyɔ:tɛʔ 'berries hang'

Iden. with **137** except for mod. pref. *ʔoʔ-* 'indic.'

See also **1, 7, 30, 36, 89, 93, 141.**

(35)

147. ʔetwatyǽ:ʔtak 'we (incl. pl.) use it'

Vb. base iden. with **90.**
Asp. suff.: *-Ø* 'punc.'
Subj. pref.: *-tw-* 'we (incl. pl.)'
Mod. pref.: *ʔe-* 'indic.'

148. hetwá:nekɔ:nɛt 'we (incl. pl.) swallow the drink'

Vb. base: vb. rt. *-ɔnɛht-* 'swallow'; incorp. nn. rt. *-ʼ:nek-* 'drink'
Asp. suff.: *-Ø* 'punc.'
Subj. pref.: *-twa-* 'we (incl. pl.)'
Mod. pref.: *-e-* 'indic.'
Other pref.: *h-* 'transloc.' (usual with this rt.)

149. ʔɛyekɔ:tak 'people will direct it toward, take it to'

Vb. base: vb. rt. *-kɔta-* 'perform an irrevocable act'; rt. suff. *-ʼhkw-* 'inst.'
 (together meaning 'direct toward')
Asp. suff.: *-Ø* 'punc.'
Subj. pref.: *-ye-* 'fem.'
Mod. pref.: *ʔɛ-* 'fut.'

150. koyaʔtayéistha? 'where people gather, meeting place'

Vb. base: *-yáʔta-yei-* 'gather' **(5)**; rt. suff. *-ʼst-* 'caus.-inst.'
Asp. suff.: *-háʔ* 'iter.'
Obj. pref.: *ko-* 'fem.'

151. tɛyénɔ:ɔnyɔ:ʔ 'people will give thanks'

Vb. stem iden. with **104.**
Subj. pref.: *-ye-* 'fem.'
Mod. pref.: *-ɛ-* 'fut.'
Other pref.: *t-* 'dupl.'

152. haʔteyɔkwéʔtake:h 'all the people'

Iden. with **91** except for incorp. nn. rt. *-ɔkweʔta-* 'person'

153. koyaʔtakɔ́hsotha? 'people remain'

Vb. base iden. with **65.**
Asp. suff.: *-háʔ* 'iter.'
Obj. pref.: *ko-* 'fem.'

154. tɛyɔtɛnɔ́:nyɔ:ˀ 'people will be thankful'

> Vb. base: vb. rt. -nɔ́ɔnyɔ- 'thank'; -atɛ- 'refl.' (together meaning 'be thankful')
> Asp. suff.: -ˀ 'punc.'
> Subj. pref.: -y[ɔ]- 'fem.'
> Mod. pref.: -ɛ- 'fut.'
> Other pref.: t- 'dupl.'

See also **1, 6, 7, 10, 11, 36, 38, 46, 76, 84, 89, 108, 134, 136, 146.**

(36)

155. ˀoˀkáiwaye:ih 'it comes to pass'

> Vb. base: vb. rt. -yei- 'be right'; rt. suff. -´h- 'inch. II'; nn. rt. -(C)i:wa- 'matter' (the entire base meaning 'come to pass')
> Asp. suff.: -∅ 'punc.'
> Subj. pref.: -ka- 'neut.'
> Mod. pref.: ˀoˀ- 'indic.'

156. nɔˀwe:ˀ 'while, during, since'

157. tetyoˀtáiɛsˀɔh 'it eventually becomes warm again there'

> Vb. rt.: -aˀtaiɛ- 'be warm'
> Asp. suff.: -´sˀ- 'even.'; -ɔ́h 'desc.'
> Obj. pref.: -yo- 'neut.'
> Prim. pref.: -t- 'cisloc.'
> Other pref.: te- 'dupl.'

158. ˀoˀtitwaténɔ:ɔnyɔ:ˀ 'we (incl. pl.) are thankful'

> Vb. stem iden. with **154.**
> Subj. pref. -tw- 'we (incl. pl.)'
> Mod. pref.: ˀoˀ- 'indic.'
> Other pref.: -ti- 'dupl.'

See also **1, 7, 10, 11, 36, 89, 93, 97.**

(37)

159. ska:t 'one'

160. waˀakwayɛ:ˀ 'we (excl. pl.) put down, establish'

> Vb. rt.: -yɛ- 'put down, establish'
> Asp. suff.: -ˀ 'punc.'
> Subj. pref.: -ˀakwa- 'we (excl. pl.)'
> Mod. pref.: wa- 'indic.'

161. ˀɔkwánɔhkwa:ˀshæ̀ˀ 'our medicines'

> Nn. rt.: -nɔhkwaˀshæ- 'medicine'
> Nn. suff.: -´ˀ 'spl. nn. suff.'
> Obj. pref.: ˀɔkwa- 'our (pl.)'

See also **1, 3, 6, 7, 10, 11, 30, 36, 42, 70, 71, 74, 75, 104, 108, 129.**

(38)

162. ꞓyo:nekítkꜱshɔ:k 'there will continue to be water emerging here
     and there, to be springs'

> Vb. base: vb. rt. -itkꜱ- 'emerge'; rt. suff. -shɔ- 'dist.'; incorp. nn. rt.
> -ʹ:nek- 'water'
> Asp. suff.: -∅- 'desc.'; -k 'cont.'
> Obj. pref.: -yo- 'neut.'
> Mod. pref.: ꞓꜱ- 'fut.'

See also **1, 3, 6, 7, 10, 11, 34–38, 81, 82.**

(39)

163. ꞓyojinɔ́:yaꞁtꜱɔnyɔ:k 'there will continue to be arteries on it'

> Vb. base: vb. rt. -(Cæ)- 'be on'; rt. suff. -ɔ- 'dist.', -nyɔ- 'double dist.';
> incorp. nn. rt. -jinɔ́:yaꞁta- [14.4] 'artery, vein'
> Asp. suff.: -∅- 'desc.'; -k 'cont.'
> Obj. pref.: -yo- 'neut.'
> Mod. pref.: ꞓꜱ- 'fut.'

164. ꞓyotihahtꜱtyɔ́kwa:ɔk 'rivers will continue to flow'

> Vb. base: vb. rt. -ahtꜱty- 'move, flow'; rt. suff. -ɔkwa- 'oppos.', -ʹɔ-
> 'dist.'; incorp. nn. rt. -ih- 'river'; -at- 'refl.'
> Asp. suff.: -∅- 'desc.'; -k 'cont.'
> Obj. pref.: -yo- 'neut.'
> Mod. pref.: ꞓꜱ- 'fut.'

165. yɔꜱjakɔ:shɔꞁ 'under the earth plurally'

> Nn. rt.: -ɔ́ꜱja- 'earth'
> Nn. suff.: -kɔ- 'int. loc.'
> Subj. pref.: y- 'neut.'
> Attr. suff.: -shɔ́ꞁ 'plur.'

166. nꜱyoæhtɔ́:ɔk 'how it will continue to pass by'

> Vb. rt.: -ʹ(h)æht- 'pass by'
> Asp. suff.: -ɔ́- 'desc.'; -ak 'cont.'
> Obj. pref.: -yo- 'neut.'
> Mod. pref.: -ꜱ- 'fut.'
> Sec. pref.: n- 'part.'

See also **3, 10, 11, 30, 46, 81, 93.**

(40)

167. ꞓká:nekꜱɔnyɔ:k 'there will continue to be waters on it'

> Vb. base: vb. rt. -(Cæ)- 'be on'; rt. suff. -ɔ- 'dist.', -nyɔ- 'double dist.';
> incorp. nn. rt. -ʹ:neka- [14.4] 'water'
> Asp. suff.: -∅- 'desc.'; -k- 'cont.'
> Subj. pref.: -ka- 'neut.'
> Mod. pref.: ꞓꜱ- 'fut.'

168. ʔɛka:nekowanɛ́ʔseːk 'there will always be large waters'

> Vb. base: vb. rt. -owanɛ- 'be large'; incorp. nn. rt. -ʼ:nek- 'water'
> Asp. suff.: -ʼʔs- 'iter.'; -ek 'cont.'
> Subj. pref.: -ka- 'neut.'
> Mod. pref.: ʔɛ- 'fut.'

169. tɛwɔtiyenɔwɔ́ʔkhɔːk 'they (nonmasc. pl.) will continue to work hand in hand'

> Vb. rt.; -yenɔwɔ́ʔkhɔ- 'hold on to', with dupl. 'work hand in hand'
> Asp. suff.: -∅- 'desc.'; -k 'cont.'
> Subj. pref.: -wati- 'they (nonmasc. pl.)'
> Mod. pref.: -ɛ- 'fut.'
> Other pref.: t- 'dupl.'

170. nɔʔkeyenóʔtɛʔheʔt 'how I fashion it'

> Vb. base: vb. rt. -óʔtɛ- 'be of a certain kind'; rt. suff. -ʼʔhɛ́ʔ- 'inch· I'; incorp. nn. rt. -y(C)ɛn- 'cause, custom' (the entire base meaning 'fashion, create')
> Asp. suff.: -t 'punc.'
> Subj. pref.: -ke- '1st pers.'
> Mod. pref.: -aʔ- [3.14] 'indic.'
> Sec. pref.:   n- 'part.'

171. ʔoʔkɔ́ɛjaːtaːt 'I establish the earth'

> Iden. with 77 except for mod. pref. ʔoʔ- 'indic.'

172. ʔɛyotishátɛʔseːk 'there will always be moisture falling'

> Vb. base: vb. rt. -ɛ- 'fall'; rt. suff. -ʼʔ- 'inch. I'; incorp. nn. rt. -shat- 'fog, mist, moisture'
> Asp. suff.: -s- 'iter.'; -ek 'cont.'
> Obj. pref.: -yoti- 'they (nonmasc.)'
> Mod. pref.: ʔɛ- 'fut.'

See also **1, 3, 10, 11, 36, 46, 89.**

(41)

173. ʔoːnekaseːʔ 'fresh water'

> Vb. base: vb. rt. -ase- 'be new, fresh'; incorp. nn. rt. -ʼ:nek- 'water'
> Asp. suff.: -ʔ 'desc.'
> Obj. pref.: ʔo- 'neut.'

174. ʔɔkwátɔʔseːʔɔh 'it is available in abundance to us (pl.)'

> Vb. rt.: -atɔʔseʔ- 'be available in abundance'
> Asp. suff.: -ɔ́h 'desc.'
> Obj. pref.: ʔɔkw- 'us (pl.)'

175. ʔɔkwaʔnikɔiyóstahkɔh 'it contents us (pl.)'

> Vb. base: vb. rt. -iyo- 'be good'; rt. suff. -ʼsta- 'caus.-inst.', -ʼhkw- 'inst.'; incorp. nn. rt. -ʔnikɔ́- 'mind' (the entire base meaning 'content, satisfy')
> Asp. suff.: -ɔ́h 'desc.'
> Obj. pref.: ʔɔkwa- 'us (pl.)'

176. háe?kwah 'also, too, in addition, moreover'
177. honɔ́tɔ?se:?ɔh 'it is available in abundance to them (masc.)'

Iden. with 174 except for obj. pref. *hon-* 'them (masc.)'

See also **1, 10, 11, 15, 16, 30, 36, 46, 67, 89, 108, 127.**

(42)

See **1, 7, 10, 11, 36, 89, 90, 118.**

(43)

178. ?ɛtwatyǽ:?tak 'we (incl. pl.) shall use it'

Iden. with 147 except for mod. pref. *?ɛ-* 'fut.'

179. ?ɛtwatya?tákesko? 'we (incl. pl.) shall arise'

Vb. base: vb. rt. *-keskw-* 'raise'; incorp. nn. rt. *-yá?ta-* 'body'; *-at-* 'refl.'
Asp. suff.: *-ó?* 'punc.'
Subj. pref.: *-tw-* 'we (incl. pl.)'
Mod. pref.: *?ɛ-* 'fut.'

180. tɛjawɛtɔ:ti? 'day will open, dawn again'

Vb. base: vb. rt. *-ɔ(:)ty-* 'open'; incorp. nn. rt. *-ɛt-* 'day'
Asp. suff.: *-i?* 'punc.'
Obj. pref.: *-yaw-* 'neut.'
Mod. pref.: *-ɛ-* 'fut.'
Prim. pref.: *-[j]-* 'repet.'
Other pref.: *t-* 'dupl.'

181. ?o:nekanos 'water'

Vb. base: vb. rt. *-no-* 'be cold'; nn. rt. *-´:neka-* 'water'
Asp. suff.: *-´s* 'iter.'
Obj. pref.: *?o-* 'neut.'

See also **7, 10, 11, 24, 79, 84, 147.**

(44)

See **1, 7, 62, 89.**

(45)

182. ?oiwayei?ɔ́:tye?s 'it is coming to pass'

Vb. base iden. with 155.
Asp. suff.: *-ɔ́-* 'desc.'; *-atye-* 'prog.'; *-´?s* 'iter.'
Obj. pref.: *?o-* 'neut.'

183. nyo:?nikɔɛwɛ́?ɔh 'what he intended'

Coll. for 117.

See also **35–37.**

(46)

184. ʔoːnékitkɛːshɔʔ 'the springs'

> Vb. base iden. with **162**.
> Asp. suff.: -ʹʔ 'desc.'
> Obj. pref.: ʔo- 'neut.'

185. ʔojinɔːyáʔtɛɔnyɔʔ 'the arteries on it'

> Vb. base iden. with **163**.
> Asp. suff.: -ʹʔ 'desc.'
> Obj. pref.: ʔo- 'neut.'

186. ʔotíhahtɛtyɔkwɛh 'the rivers'

> Vb. base iden. with **164** except for lack of dist.
> Asp. suff.: -ɛ́h 'desc.'
> Obj. pref.: ʔo- 'neut.'

187. kaːnekɛɔnyɔʔ 'waters on it'

> Vb. base iden. with **167**.
> Asp. suff. -ʹʔ 'desc.'
> Subj. pref.: ka- 'neut.'

188. kaːnekowaːnɛs 'large waters'

> Vb. base iden. with **168**.
> Asp. suff.: -ʹs 'iter.'
> Subj. pref.: ka- 'neut.'

See also **1, 3, 6, 7, 10, 11, 30, 46, 70, 74, 75, 102–4.**

(47)

See **1, 2, 7, 30, 34, 35.**

(48)

189. ʔɛyotehatɔníːak 'forests will continue to grow'

> Iden. with **105** except for incorp. nn. rt. -hat- 'forest'

See also **3, 7, 10, 11, 38, 81, 82, 89.**

(49)

190. ʔɛyakoyaʔtakehashǽʔkɛːɔk 'it will be people's assistance'

> Iden. with **128** except for obj. pref. -yako- 'fem.'

See also **7, 10, 11, 15, 20, 89, 116, 189.**

(50)

191. shɔ:h 'just, only'
192. nɛyɔnishéʔse:k 'the length of time it will always become'

    Vb. base: vb. rt. -*is*- 'be long'; rt. suff. -*héʔ*- 'inch. I'; incorp. nn. rt.
       -*ɔn*- 'period of time'
    Asp. suff.: -*s*- 'iter.'; -*ek* 'cont.'
    Subj. pref.: -*y*- 'neut.'
    Mod. pref.: -*ɛ*- 'fut.'
    Sec. pref.: *n*- 'part.'

193. tɛkæ:wɛ:nye:ʔ 'the wind will stir'

    Vb. base iden. with **145.**
    Asp. suff.: -*ʔ* 'punc.'
    Subj. pref.: -*kæ*- 'neut.'
    Mod. pref.: -*ɛ*- 'fut.'
    Other pref.: *t*- 'dupl.'

194. nɛyoʔtáiɛhse:k 'when it always will be warm'

    Vb. rt.: -*aʔtaiɛ*- 'be warm'
    Asp. suff.: -*ʹhs*- 'iter.'; -*ek* 'cont.'
    Obj. pref.: -*yo*- 'neut.'
    Mod. pref.: -*ɛ*- 'fut.'
    Sec. pref.: *n*- 'part.'

195. nikáiwi:s 'how long a matter'

    Vb. base: vb. rt. -*is*- 'be long'; nn. rt. -(*C*)*i:w*- 'matter'
    Asp. suff.: -∅ 'desc.'
    Subj. pref.: -*ka*- 'neut.'
    Sec. pref.: *ni*- 'part.'

196. ʔɛkánɔʔnos 'when it will become cold'

    Vb. base: vb. rt. -*nɔ́ʔno*- 'be cold'; rt. suff. -*ʹst*- [3.4] 'caus.-inst.' (here
      with inch. meaning)
    Asp. suff.: -∅ 'punc.'
    Subj. pref.: -*ka*- 'neut.'
    Mod. pref.: -*ɛ*- 'fut.'
    Sec. pref.: *n*- 'part.'

See also **1, 7, 10, 11, 30, 38, 89, 109, 176.**

(51)

197. ʔo:tiyaʔtataiaʔtahkɔ́:ɔk 'it will continue to provide heat for them'

    Coll. for *ʔeotiyaʔtataiaʔtahkɔ́:ɔk*
    Vb. base: vb. rt. -*taia*- 'be warm'; rt. suff. -*ʹʔta*- 'caus. I', -*ʹhkw*- 'inst.';
      incorp. nn. rt. -*yáʔta*- 'body'
    Asp. suff.: -*ɔ́*- 'desc.'; -*ak* 'cont.'
    Obj. pref.: -*ʹoti*- 'them (masc.)'
    Mod. pref.: *ʔɛ*- [3.16] 'fut.'

See also **1, 6, 7, 10, 11, 30, 35, 81, 82, 89, 117, 189.**

(52)

198. to?oiwánɔ?ko:was 'it continues unchanged'

> Coll. for *te?oiwánɔ?ko:was* [27.5]
> Vb. base: vb. rt. *-nɔ̆?kow-* (with neg.) 'be capable of anything'; incorp.
>   nn. rt. *-(C)í:wa-* 'matter' (together meaning 'continue unchanged')
> Asp. suff.: *-ás* 'iter.'
> Obj. pref.: *-?o-* 'neut.'
> Other pref.: *te-* 'neg.'

199. tohka:?ah 'a few'

200. ?ɔkwaya?tataia?táhkɔh 'we (pl.) are using it for heat'

> Vb. base iden. with **197.**
> Asp. suff.: *-ɔ́h* 'desc.'
> Obj. pref.: *?ɔkwa-* 'we (pl.)'

201. ?otéhatɔ:ni:h 'forests are growing'

> Vb. base iden. with **189.**
> Asp. suff.: *-h* 'desc.'
> Obj. pref.: *?o-* 'neut.'

See also **1, 7, 10, 30, 36, 42, 81, 89, 93, 118.**

(53)

202. ?othɔtɔ:ni:h 'trees are growing'

> Iden. with **201** except for incorp. nn. rt. *-hɔt-* 'tree, brush'

See also **1, 6, 10, 46, 76, 81, 93, 114, 119, 176.**

(54)

203. ?ɛkakwe:ni? 'it will be possible'

> Vb. rt.: *-kweny-* 'be possible'
> Asp. suff.: *-í?* 'punc.'
> Subj. pref.: *-ka-* 'neut.'
> Mod. pref.: *?ɛ-* 'fut.'

204. ?ɛyakotɔ?se?ɔ́:ɔk 'it will continue to be available to people in abundance'

> Vb. rt.: *-atɔ?se?-* 'be available in abundance'
> Asp. suff.: *-ɔ́-* 'desc.'; *-ak* 'cont.'
> Obj. pref.: *-yako-* 'fem.'
> Mod. pref.: *?ɛ-* 'fut.'

See also **11, 15, 20, 38, 114, 116, 176.**

(55)

205. ʔaeʔ 'again'

206. ʔɛkɛɔtatokɛ́:ɔk 'there will continue to be a certain tree'

     Vb. base: vb. rt. *-tokɛ-* 'be certain, specific'; incorp. nn. rt. *-(y)ɔta-* 'tree'
     Asp. suff.: *-'Ø-* 'desc.'; *-ak* 'cont.'
     Subj. pref.: *-kɛ-* 'neut.'
     Mod. pref.: *ʔɛ-* 'fut.'

207. ʔɛyakoshǽ:ʔseʔ 'it will remind people'

     Vb. base: vb. rt. *-ashæ-* 'take cognizance of'; rt. suff. *-'ʔ-* 'inch. I' (cf. **133**), *-se-* 'dat.'
     Asp. suff.: *-'ʔ* 'punc.'
     Obj. pref.: *-yako-* 'fem.'
     Mod. pref.: *ʔɛ-* 'fut.'

208. ʔɛyɔkashǽ:ʔseʔ 'people will remember me'

     Iden. with **207** except for trans. pref. *-yɔk-* 'people . . . me'

See also **1, 6, 10, 11, 30, 38, 41, 42, 46, 57, 67, 76, 132.**

(56)

209. ʔɛwɔtí:otɔnyɔ:k 'trees will always be standing here and there'

     The length in *i:o* is inconsistent with [3.21]. Apparently this word is a recent change < * *ʔɛwɔtiɛɔtɔnyɔ:k*, analyzable as follows:
     Vb. base: vb. rt. *-ot-* 'stand upright'; rt. suff. *-ɔ-* 'dist.', *-nyɔ-* 'double dist.'; incorp. nn. rt. *-'(h)ɛ-* 'tree'
     Asp. suff.: *-Ø-* 'desc.'; *-k* 'cont.'
     Subj. pref.: *-wati-* 'they (nonmasc. pl.)'
     Mod. pref.: *ʔɛ-* 'fut.'

210. wahtaʔ '(hard) maple'

     Nn. rt.: *-áhta-* 'maple'
     Nn. suff.: *-'ʔ* 'spl. nn. suff.'
     Subj. pref.: *w-* 'neut.'

211. ʔɛtka:nekái ʔse:k 'sap will always flow there'

     Vb. base: vb. rt. *-'(h)i-* 'spill'; rt. suff. *-'ʔ-* 'inch. I'; incorp. nn. rt. *-':neka-* 'water, sap'
     Asp. suff.: *-s-* 'iter.'; *-ek* 'cont.'
     Subj. pref.: *-ka-* 'neut.'
     Mod. pref.: *ʔɛ-* 'fut.'
     Prim. pref.: *-t-* 'cisloc.'

212. ʔɛyowǽnɔ:ek 'it will continue to be sweet'

     Vb. base: vb. rt. *-(C)e-* 'put in'; incorp. nn. rt. *-wænɔ-* 'sugar' (together meaning 'be sweet')
     Asp. suff.: *-Ø-* 'desc.'; *-k* 'cont.'
     Obj. pref.: *-yo-* 'neut.'
     Mod. pref.: *ʔɛ-* 'fut.'

See also **10, 11, 30, 42, 81, 82.**

(57)

213. **tɛtyoˀtáiɛh** 'it will become warm again there'

> Vb. base: vb. rt. -aˀtaiɛ- 'be warm'; rt. suff. -ˀh- 'inch II'
> Asp. suff.: -Ø 'punc.'
> Obj. pref.: -yo- 'neut.'
> Mod. perf.: -ɛ- 'fut.'
> Prim. pref.: -t- 'cisloc.'
> Other pref.: t- 'dupl.' (here 'again')

214. **ˀɛtka:nekáiˀt** 'sap will flow there'

> Iden. with **211** except for asp. suff. -t 'punc.'

215. **ˀó:nɔˀe:shaˀ** 'they (masc.) will be grateful'

> Coll. for ˀéonɔˀe:shaˀ
> Vb. rt.: -ɔˀesha- 'gratify'
> Asp. suff.: -ˀ 'punc.'
> Obj. pref.: -ˀon- 'they (masc.)'
> Mod. pref.: ˀɛ- 'fut.'

216. **hɛnɛ́nɔhtɔ:nyɔh** 'they (masc. pl.) think'

> Iden. with **28** except for subj. pref. hɛn- 'they (masc. pl.)'

217. **nɛ:tah** 'this, that'

218. **hɔsáka:eˀ** 'the time arrives again'

> Vb. rt.: -(h)e- 'arrive (of time)'
> Asp. suff.: -ˀ 'punc.'
> Subj. pref.: -ka- 'neut.'
> Mod. pref.: -ɔ-a- 'indic.'
> Prim. pref.: -s- 'repet.'
> Other pref.: h- 'transloc.' (usual with this rt.)

219. **tɛshátisnye:ˀ** 'they (masc. pl.) will attend to it again'

> Vb. rt.: -snye- 'attend to'
> Asp suff.: -ˀ 'punc.'
> Subj. pref.: -hati- 'they (masc. pl.)'
> Mod. pref.: -ɛ- 'fut.'
> Prim. pref.: -s- 'repet.'
> Other pref.: t- 'dupl.' (usual with this rt.)

220. **watí:otɔnyɔˀ** 'trees are standing here and there'

> Iden. with **209** except for lack of -k 'cont.' and of ˀɛ- 'fut.'

See also **1–3, 10, 11, 27, 36, 42, 84, 89, 93, 134, 205, 210.**

(58)

221. **niyɔ́kweˀta:ke:h** 'how many people there are'

> Iden. with **43** except for subj. pref. -y- 'indef.'

222. hoti:wastéistɔh 'they (masc.) have noticed it'

> Vb. base: vb. rt. -asteist- 'manage, arrange'; incorp. nn. rt. -(C)i:w- 'matter' (together meaning 'notice, pay attention to')
> Asp. suff.: -ɔ́h 'desc.'
> Obj. pref.: hoti- 'they (masc.)'

223. hɛnɔ́hke:othaʔ 'they (masc. pl.) tap the tree'

> Vb. base: vb. rt. -ot- 'stand upright'; incorp. nn. rt. -ahke- 'chip' (together meaning 'tap a tree')
> Asp. suff.: -háʔ 'iter.'
> Subj. pref.: hɛn- 'they (masc. pl.)'

224. wá:tihsɛnɔ:niʔ 'they (masc. pl.) store it'

> Vb. base: vb. rt. -ɔ(:)ni- 'make'; incorp. nn. rt. -hsɛn- 'name' (together meaning 'store, put away')
> Asp. suff.: -ʔ 'punc.'
> Subj. pref.: -ʹati- 'they (masc. pl.)'
> Mod. pref.: wa- 'indic.'

225. ʔowæ:nɔʔ 'sugar'

> Nn. rt.: -wænɔ- 'sugar'
> Nn. suff.: -ʹʔ 'spl. nn. suff.'
> Obj. pref.: ʔo- 'neut.'

See also **1, 10, 11, 15, 20, 30, 38, 41, 89, 198, 204.**

(59)

226. ʔahsɔh 'still, yet'

See also **1, 89, 90, 118, 198.**

(60)

227. ʔohtɛ:tyɔ:h 'it is continuing'

> Vb. rt. -ahtɛty- 'travel, continue on'
> Asp. suff.: -ɔh 'desc.'
> Obj. pref.: ʔo- 'neut.'

228. nioiwíhsaʔɔh 'the way he planned it'

> Vb. base: vb. rt. -ihsáʔ- 'create'; incorp. nn. rt. -(C)i:w- 'matter' (together meaning 'plan, promise to do')
> Asp. suff.: -ɔ́h 'desc.'
> Obj. pref.: -ʹo- 'masc.'
> Sec. pref.: ni- 'part.'

See also **1, 6, 35, 36, 61, 62, 97, 205, 226.**

(61)

See **1, 3, 6, 7, 10, 11, 70, 74, 75, 81, 93, 102–4, 201.**

(62)

229. ʔɛkyáʔtata:thɔ:ʔ 'I shall establish various types'

Vb. base: vb. rt. -te- 'be present'; rt. suff. -at- 'caus. II' (cf. 77), -hɔ- 'dist.'; incorp. nn. rt. -yáʔta- 'body, form'
Asp. suff.: -ʔ 'punc.'
Subj. pref.: -k- '1st pers.'
Mod. pref.: ʔɛ- 'fut.'

230. kanyo:ʔ 'wild animal'

Vb. rt.: -nyo- 'be wild (of animals or plants)'
Asp. suff.: -ʔ 'desc.'
Subj. pref.: ka- 'neut.'

231. ʔɛkatakhenɔtyéʔse:k 'they will always be running about'

Vb. base: vb. rt. -takhe- 'run'; rt. suff. -nɔ- 'dist.'
Asp. suff.: -Ø- 'desc.'; -tye- 'prog.'; -ʔs 'iter.'; -ek 'cont.'
Subj. pref.: -ka- 'neut.'
Mod. pref.: ʔɛ- 'fut.'

See also 1–3, 7, 10, 11, 35–38, 76, 82, 89.

(63)

232. to:nɛʔnikɔɛwɛnyáʔtɔ:ɔk 'they (masc.) will continue to use it as a source of amusement'

Coll. for teonɛʔnikɔɛwenyáʔtɔ:ɔk
Vb. base: vb. rt. -awenya- [24.4] 'stir'; rt. suff. -ʔʔt- 'caus. I'; incorp. nn. rt. -ʔnikɔɛ- 'mind'; -ɛ- 'refl.'
Asp. suff.: -ɔ́- 'desc.'; -ak 'cont.'
Obj. pref.: -ʹon- 'they (masc.)'
Mod. pref.: -ɛ- 'fut.'
Other pref.: te- 'dupl.'

233. wa:tɔh 'it says, it is called'

Vb. rt.: -atɔ- 'say'
Asp. suff.: -ʹh 'iter.'
Subj. pref.: w- 'neut.'

234. hotiskɛʔɛ́kehtɔh 'they (masc.) are warriors'

Vb. rt.: -skɛʔɛkéht- 'be a warrior'
Asp. suff.: -ɔ́h 'desc.'
Obj. pref.: hoti- 'they (masc.)'

235. hotiyaʔtá:ni:yɔh 'their (masc.) bodies are solid, tough'

Vb. base: vb. rt. -ʹ:niy- 'be solid, tough'; incorp. nn. rt. -yáʔta- 'body'
Asp. suff.: -ɔ́h 'desc.'
Obj. pref.: hoti- 'their (masc.)'

See also 7, 10, 11, 30, 42, 89.

(64)

236. hakɔ́kɛ:yatani:h 'he provided it for them'

Vb. base: vb. rt. -kɛ́:yata- 'put up, provide'; rt. suff. -ni- 'dat.'
Asp. suff.: -h 'desc.'
Trans. pref.: hakɔ- 'he . . . them'

237. katákhenɔ:tye²s 'they are running about'

Iden. with **231** except for lack of -ek 'cont.' and ²ɛ- 'fut.'

238. tɛ:nɛ²nikɔɛwɛnyá²tha:k 'they (masc. pl.) will always use it as a source of amusement'

Iden. with **232** except for asp. suff. -h- 'iter.' and subj. pref. -'ɛn- 'they (masc. pl.)'

See also **10, 11, 30, 38, 59, 230, 234, 235.**

(65)

239. ²atɛ́nɔ²shæ² 'food'

Nn. base: nn. rt. -nɔ²shæ- (?); ²atɛ- 'refl.' [15.6]
Nn. suff.: -'² 'spl. nn. suff.'

See also **1, 3, 10, 11, 15, 20, 41, 204.**

(66)

240. tetwáka:ne:² 'we (incl. pl.) have seen'

Vb. rt.: -ká:ne- 'see, look at'
Asp. suff.: -² 'desc.'
Subj. pref.: -twa- 'we (incl. pl.)'
Other pref.: te- 'dupl.' (usual with this rt.)

241. nikanyo²tá²s²a:h 'small animals'

Vb. base: vb. rt. -²s²áa- 'be small'; incorp. nn. rt. -nyó²ta- 'animal'
Asp. suff.: -'h 'desc.'
Subj. pref.: -ka- 'neut.'
Sec. pref.: ni- 'part.'

242. hatítakhenɔtye²s 'they (masc. pl.) are running about'

Iden. with **237** except for subj. pref. hati- 'they (masc. pl.)'

243. niyoteháto²kta:tye²s 'along the edges of the forests'

Vb. base: vb. rt. -ó²kt- 'come to the end, extend to the edge'; incorp. nn. rt. -hat- 'forest'; -ate- 'refl.'
Asp. suff.: -∅- 'desc.'; -atye- 'prog.'; -'²s 'iter.'
Obj. pref.: -yo- 'neut.'
Sec. pref.: ni- 'part.'

244. kahatakɔ:shɔˀ 'within the forests'

    Nn. rt.: -*hata*- 'forest'
    Nn. suff.: -*kɔ*- 'int. loc.'
    Subj. pref.: *ka*- 'neut.'
    Attr. suff.: -*sh3ˀ* 'plur.'

See also **1, 2, 6, 30, 36, 46, 89, 118.**

(67)

245. tejitwaká:ne:ˀ 'we (incl. pl.) see again'

    Iden. with **240** except for addition of prim. pref. -*ji*- 'repet.'

246. kanyóˀtowa:nɛs 'large animals'

    Vb. base: vb. rt. -*owanɛ*- 'be large'; incorp. nn. rt. -*nyoˀt*- 'animal'
    Asp. suff.: -ˊ*s* 'iter.'
    Subj. pref.: *ka*- 'neut.'

247. hɛnɔtkɛˀɔ́:neˀs 'they (masc. pl.) appear momentarily'

    Vb. base: vb. rt. -*atkɛˀɔ*- 'appear momentarily'; rt. suff. -ˊ:*n*- 'trans.'
    Asp. suff.: -*ɛ̂ˀs* 'iter.'
    Subj. pref.: *hɛn*- 'they (masc. pl.)'

See also **1, 2, 36, 42, 57, 118.**

(68)

248. to:kwah 'so many'

249. nɔˀyóshæke:ˀ 'how many years'

    Vb. base: vb. rt. -*ake*- 'be separate entities'; incorp. nn. rt. -*oshæ*- 'winter, year'
    Asp. suff.: -*ˀ* 'punc.'
    Subj. pref.: -*y*- 'neut.'
    Mod. pref.: -*aˀ*- [3.14] 'indic.'
    Sec. pref.: *n*- 'part.'

250. teˀjitwakɛh 'we (incl. pl.) don't see it any longer'

    Vb. rt.: -*kɛ*- 'see'
    Asp. suff.: -ˊ*h* 'iter.'
    Subj. pref.: -*twa*- 'we (incl. pl.)'
    Prim. pref.: -*ji*- 'repet.'
    Other pref.: *teˀ*- 'neg.'

See also **7, 11, 49, 84, 89, 246.**

(69)

251. niyótoˀkta:tyeˀs 'up to the present time'

    Iden. with **118** except for asp. suff. -ˊ*ˀs* 'iter.'

252. jɔkwátɔˀse:h 'it is available to us (pl.) again in abundance'

> Vb. rt.: *-atɔˀse-* 'be available in abundance' (formally distinct from *-atɔˀseˀ-*; cf. 174)
> Asp. suff.: *-h* 'desc.'
> Obj. pref.: *-yɔkw-* 'us (pl.)'
> Prim. pref.: [ʝ]- 'repet.'

See also **1, 2, 30, 57, 89, 118, 237, 239, 245, 246.**

(70)

See **1, 7, 35–37, 90, 117.**

(71)

See **1, 3, 6, 7, 10, 11, 36, 42, 61, 62, 70, 74, 75, 89, 97, 102–104, 117, 226, 227, 230, 237.**

(72)

See **1, 6, 34–37.**

(73)

253. tɛyonɔteˀsætɛsyɔtyéˀse:k 'they (nonmasc.) will always be spreading their wings'

> Vb. base: vb. rt. *-ɔ(:)ty-* 'throw open'; incorp. nn. base: vb. rt. *-ˀsætɛ-* 'stretch (as on a frame)'; *-sy-* [14.2] 'nom.'; *-ate-* 'refl.'
> Asp. suff.: *-éˀs-* 'iter.'; *-ek* 'cont.'
> Obj. pref.: *-yon-* 'they (nonmasc.)'
> Mod. pref.: *-ɛ-* 'fut.'
> Other pref.: *t-* 'dupl.'

254. nɛyóto ˀktaˀk 'it will continue to extend to the limit'

> Vb. base: *-óˀkta-* [18.3 end] 'come to the end, extend to the limit'; *-at-* 'refl.'
> Asp. suff.: *-'ˀ-* 'desc.'; *-k* 'cont.'
> Obj. pref.: *-yo-* 'neut.'
> Mod. pref.: *-ɛ-* 'fut.'
> Sec. pref.: *n-* 'part.'

See also **7, 10, 11, 38, 89, 138, 229.**

(74)

255. hæ:ˀkwah 'also, in addition'

> Variant of **176.**

256. ˀɛɔtiyásɔ:ɔk 'they (masc. pl.) will continue to be called'

> Vb. rt. *-yas-* 'call'
> Asp. suff.: *-ó-* 'desc.'; *-ak* 'cont.'
> Subj. pref.: *-'ati-* 'they (masc. pl.)'
> Mod. pref.: *ˀɛ-* 'fut.'

See also **1, 10, 11, 230.**

(75)

257. nɛyóhsawaˀk 'how it will continue to begin'

> Vb. rt.: -ahsawa- 'begin'
> Asp. suff.: -ˊˀ- 'desc.'; -k 'cont.'
> Obj. pref.: -yo- 'neut.'
> Mod. pref.: -ɛ- 'fut.'
> Sec. pref.: n- 'part.'

258. nitkáshatɔ:tyeˀs 'where the mist falls, in the clouds'

> Vb. base: vb. rt. -ɔ(:)ty- 'throw open, fall (of rain, snow, mist, etc.)';
> incorp. nn. rt. -shat- 'moisture, mist'
> Asp. suff.: -ɛˀs 'iter.'
> Subj. pref.: -ka- 'neut.'
> Prim. pref.: -t- 'cisloc.'
> Sec. pref.: ni- 'part.'

See also **10, 11, 138, 254.**

(76)

259. hotíhsɛnɔye:tɔˀ 'they (masc.) have names'

> Vb. base: vb. rt. -yɛt- 'have'; rt. suff. -ɔ- 'dist.'; incorp. nn. rt. -hsɛnɔ-
> 'name'
> Asp. suff.: -ˊˀ 'desc.'
> Obj. pref.: hoti- 'they (masc.)'

260. jiˀtɛˀɔshɔ́ˀɔh 'birds'

> Vb. base: vb. rt. -ɛˀɔ- (?); incorp. nn. rt. -jiˀt- 'bird' (cf. jiˀtɛ́ˀɔ:h 'bird')
> Attr. suff.: -shɔ́ˀɔh 'plur.'

261. teyonɔteˀsætɛ́syɔtyeˀs 'they (nonmasc.) are spreading their
wings'

> Iden. with **253** except for lack of -ek 'cont.' and of -ɛ- 'fut.'

See also **1, 10, 11, 30, 88, 106, 176.**

(77)

262. nya:tijiˀtaˀsˀá:h 'small birds'

> Coll. for niatijiˀtaˀsˀá:h [27.3]
> Iden. with **241** except for incorp. nn. rt. -jiˀta- 'bird' and subj. pref.
> -ˊati- 'they (masc. pl.)'

263. nɛyɔ́nisheˀt 'the length of time it will become'

> Iden. with **192** except for asp. suff. -t- 'punc.'

264. to:nɔtawɛnyé:ak 'they (masc.) will continue to move about'

> Coll. for teonɔtawɛnyé:ak
> Vb. base: vb. rt. -awɛnye- 'stir'; -at- 'refl.'
> Asp. suff.: -ˊØ- 'desc.'; -ak 'cont.'
> Obj. pref.: -ˊon- 'they (masc.)
> Mod. pref.: -ɛ- 'fut.'
> Other pref.: t- 'dupl.'

265. ʔɛshɛnɔtká:ɛkoʔ 'they (masc. pl.) will turn back'

> Vb. base: vb. rt. *-kaáɛkw-* 'turn back'; *-at-* 'refl.'
> Asp. suff.: *-óʔ* 'punc.'
> Subj. pref.: *-hɛn-* 'they (masc. pl.)'
> Prim. pref.: *-s-* 'repet.' (here 'back')
> Mod. pref.: *ʔɛ-* 'fut.'

266. hé:kwa:h 'toward there, in that direction'

> *heh* 'there' (36), *-kwah* 'toward' [26.8]

267. tyone:nɔʔ 'where it is warm'

> Vb. rt.: *-nenɔ-* 'be warm (of weather)'
> Asp. suff.: *-ʔ* 'desc.'
> Obj. pref.: *-yo-* 'neut.'
> Prim. pref.: *t-* 'cisloc.'

268. hɛshɛ:ne:ʔ 'they (masc. pl.) will go back there'

> Vb. base: vb. rt. *-e-* 'go'; rt. suff. *-n-* [3.10] 'direct.'
> Asp. suff.: *-ʔ* 'punc.'
> Subj. pref.: *-hɛn-* 'they (masc. pl.)'
> Mod. pref.: *-ɛ-* 'fut.'
> Prim. pref.: *-s-* 'repet.'
> Other pref.: *h-* 'transloc.'

See also **1, 2, 6, 7, 10, 11, 30, 36, 38, 57, 89, 109.**

(78)

269. ʔɛshatiyáʔtaʔti:heʔt 'they (masc. pl.) will come around again'

> Vb. base: vb. rt. *-aʔti-* 'lean'; rt. suff. *-héʔ-* 'inch. I'; incorp. nn. rt.
>   *-yáʔt-* 'body' (the entire base meaning 'arrive, come around')
> Asp. suff.: *-t* 'punc.'
> Subj. pref.: *-hati-* 'they (masc. pl.)'
> Mod. pref.: *ʔɛ-* 'fut.'
> Prim. pref.: *-s-* 'repet.'

270. haʔtewatiwɛnɔ:ke:h 'all their (nonmasc. pl.) voices'

> Vb. base: vb. rt. *-ake-* 'be separate entities'; incorp. nn. rt. *-wɛn-* 'voice'
> Asp. suff.: *-h* 'desc.'
> Subj. pref.: *-wati-* 'their (nonmasc. pl.)'
> Other pref.: *-te-* 'dupl.'; *haʔ* 'transloc.'

271. ʔɛswɛnɔtíʔstaɛʔ 'they (nonmasc. pl.) will sing, chatter again'

> Vb. base: vb. rt. *-(C)-* 'put in'; incorp. nn. rt. *-iʔsta-* 'noise'; *-at-* 'refl.'
>   (the entire base meaning 'chatter')
> Asp. suff.: *-éʔ* 'punc.'
> Subj. pref.: *-wɛn-* 'they (nonmasc. pl.)'
> Mod. pref.: *ʔɛ-* 'fut.'
> Prim. pref.: *-s-* 'repet.'

272. watiwɛni:yoʔs 'their (nonmasc. pl.) beautiful voices'

> Vb. base: *-iyo-* 'be beautiful'; incorp. nn. rt. *-wɛn-* 'voice, word'
> Asp. suff.: *-ʔs* 'iter.'

Subj. pref.: *wati*- 'their (nonmasc. pl.)'

See also **1, 10, 11, 36, 93, 213.**

(79)

273. tɛkáhkwaˀt 'it will lift'

Vb. base: vb. rt. -ˀ*hkwa*- 'lift'; rt. suff. -ˀ*ˀt*- 'caus. I'
Asp. suff.: -*Ø* 'punc.'
Subj. pref.: -*ka*- 'neut.'
Mod. pref.: -*ɛ*- 'fut.'
Other pref.: *t*- 'dupl.'

274. hotiˀnikɔ́ɛˀ 'their (masc.) minds'

Iden. with **75** except for obj. pref. *hoti*- 'their (masc.)'

275. hotiyaˀtakɔhsótha? 'they (masc.) remain'

Vb. base: vb. rt. -*kɔhsóht*- [3.6] 'remain'; incorp. nn. rt. -*yáˀta*- 'body'
(cf. **65**)
Asp. suff.: -*háˀ* 'iter.'
Obj. pref.: *hoti*- 'they (masc.)'

276. nikajiˀtáˀsˀa:h 'small birds'

Iden. with **262** except for subj. pref. -*ka*- 'neut.'

See also **1, 2, 7, 10, 30, 36, 108, 269.**

(80)

See **1, 6, 11, 30, 57, 76, 174, 176, 239, 260, 261.**

(81)

See **30, 89, 90, 174, 176, 239, 260, 261.**

(82)

277. hoti:wayéistɔh 'they (masc.) are performing their obligation'

Iden. with **98** except for obj. pref. *hoti*- 'they (masc.)'

278. hoti:wayɛtáhkɔh 'their (masc.) responsibility'

Iden. with **60** except for obj. pref. *hoti*- 'their (masc.)'

See also **1, 36, 57, 96, 100, 106, 176.**

(83)

279. ˀoˀkiˀ 'I said'

Vb. rt.: -*i*- 'say'
Asp. suff.: -ˀ*ˀ* 'punc.'
Subj. pref.: -*k*- '1st pers.'
Mod. pref.: ˀ*oˀ*- 'indic.'

280. nɔ:tiyá?to?tɛ? 'what their (masc. pl.) type is'

> Vb. base: vb. rt. *-ó?tɛ-* 'be of a certain kind'; incorp. nn. rt. *-yá?t-* 'body'
> Asp. suff.: *-'?* 'punc.'
> Subj. pref.: *-'ati-* 'their (masc. pl.)'
> Mod. pref.: *-a-* [3.14] 'indic.'
> Sec. pref.: *n-* 'part.'

See also 7, 36, 106, 259.

(84)

See 1, 3, 6, 7, 10, 11, 30, 70, 74, 75, 102–104, 260, 261.

(85)

See 1, 2, 7, 35–37, 76.

(86)

281. ?i:eh 'he thought'

> Vb. rt.: *-e-* 'think, decide'
> Asp. suff.: *-h* 'desc.'
> Subj. pref.: *?i-* 'masc.' [6.11]

282. ?ɛka:tka? 'I shall leave it'

> Vb. rt.: *-atka-* 'leave, provide'
> Asp. suff.: *-'?* 'punc.'
> Subj. pref.: *-k-* '1st pers.'
> Mod. pref.: *?ɛ-* 'fut.'

283. honɔ:hɔ? 'they (masc.) themselves'

> Iden. with 58 except for obj. pref. *hon-* 'they (masc.)'

284. to:nɔtátɛ?nya:ɛ? 'they (masc.) will take care of themselves'

> Coll. for *teonɔtátɛ?nya:ɛ?*
> Vb. base: vb. rt. *-(C)-* 'put in'; incorp. nn. rt. *-?nya-* 'hand' (together meaning 'take care of'); *-atatɛ-* 'recip.'
> Asp. suff.: *-ɛ?* 'punc.'
> Obj. pref.: *-'on-* 'they (masc.)'
> Mod. pref.: *-ɛ-* 'fut.'
> Other pref.: *t-* 'dupl.'

See also 1, 2, 7, 10, 11, 20, 41, 81, 89, 93.

(87)

285. yɔɛjakɔ:h 'in the earth'

> Iden. with 165 except for lack of *-sh5?* 'plur.'

286. ?ɛɔtiyɛ́:ɔk 'they (masc. pl.) will always put it down'

> Vb. rt.: *-ye-* 'put down'
> Asp. suff.: *-'∅-* 'iter.'; *-ak* 'cont.'
> Subj. pref.: *-'ati-* 'they (masc. pl.)'
> Mod. pref.: *?ɛ-* 'fut.'

287. to:tihkwéɔtyeʔ 'they (masc.) will be harvesting it', lit. 'lifting it'

> Coll. for *teotihkwéɔtyeʔ*
> Vb. rt.: -ʹhkw- 'lift'
> Asp. suff.: -ɛ́- 'desc.'; -atye 'prog.'; -ʹʔ 'punc.'
> Obj. pref.: -ʹoti- 'they (masc.)'
> Mod. pref.: -ɛ- 'fut.'
> Other pref.: t- 'dupl.'

288. ʔɛ:nɛnɔhtɔnyɔ́:ɔk 'they (masc. pl.) will always think'

> Iden. with **216** except for addition of -*ak* 'cont.' and of mod. pref. *ʔɛ*- 'fut.'

See also **3, 6, 10, 11, 27, 112, 113.**

(88)

See **1, 7, 36, 59, 89, 118, 240.**

(89)

289. teyonɔɛjotká̱ʔwɛh 'they (nonmasc.) emerge from the earth'

> Vb. base iden. with **111.**
> Asp. suff.: -ɛ́h 'desc.'
> Obj. pref.: -*yon*- 'they (nonmasc.)'
> Other pref.: *te*- 'dupl.'

290. ʔɛyɔkwaʔnikɔ́iyostak 'it will bring us (pl.) contentment'

> Iden. with **175** except for asp. suff. -∅ 'punc.' and addition of mod. pref. *ʔɛ*- 'fut.'

291. tɔta:weʔ 'it comes again'

> Vb. rt.: -*e*- 'come'
> Asp. suff.: -ʹʔ 'punc.'
> Subj. pref.: -*w*- 'neut.'
> Mod. pref.: -ɔ-a- 'indic.'
> Prim. pref.: -*t*- 'cisloc.'
> Other pref.: *t*- 'dupl.' (here 'again')

292. tɛskate:niʔ 'it will change again'

> Vb. rt.; -*teny*- 'change'
> Asp. suff.: -*iʔ* 'punc.'
> Subj. pref.: -*ka*- 'neut.'
> Mod. pref.: -ɛ- 'fut.'
> Prim. pref.: -*s*- 'repet.'
> Other pref.: *t*- 'dupl.' (usual with this rt.)

See also **2, 10, 103, 145, 240.**

(90)

293. ʔɔkyɔishæ:niyéhkɔh 'it strengthens our breath'

> Vb. base: vb. rt. -ʔ:niye- 'be solid, strong'; rt. suff. -ʼhkw- 'inst.'; incorp.
> nn. rt. -ɔishæ- 'breath'
> Asp. suff.: -ɔ́h 'desc.'
> Obj. pref.: ʔɔky- 'our (pl.)'

See also **1, 7, 10.**

(91)

294. tsaʔka:nɔʔ 'when it came, arrived'

> Vb. rt.: -yɔ- 'arrive'
> Asp. suff.: -ʼʔ 'punc.'
> Subj. pref.: -ka- 'neut.'
> Mod. pref.: -aʔ- 'indic.'
> Sec. pref.: ts- 'coin.'

295. kaʔníkɔ:lyo:h 'good-mindedness', here referring to the Good
Message of Handsome Lake

> Vb. base: vb. rt. -iyo- 'be good'; incorp. nn. rt. -ʔnikɔ́- 'mind'
> Asp. suff.: -h 'desc.'
> Subj. pref.: ka- 'neut.'

296. ʔɔkwatokéhse:ʔ 'it was explained to us (pl.)'

> Vb. base: vb. rt. -tokɛ- 'be straight'; rt. suff. -ʼhse- 'dat.' (together
> meaning 'set straight, explain to')
> Asp. suff.: -∅ 'desc.'; -ʔ 'past' (?)
> Obj. pref.: ʔɔkwa- 'us (pl.)'

297. ʔɛkæ:tyéʔse:k 'it will always be included'

> Vb. rt.: -(C)æ- 'put in'
> Asp. suff.: -∅- 'desc.'; -atye- 'prog.'; -ʼʔs- 'iter.'; -ek 'cont.'
> Subj. pref.: -kæ- 'neut.'
> Mod. pref.: ʔɛ- 'fut.'

298. ʔotí:wahtɛ:tyɔ:h 'the ceremony is performed'

> Vb. base: vb. rt. -ahtɛty- 'travel, operate'; incorp. nn. rt. -(C)i:w- 'matter,
> ceremony'; -at- 'refl.'
> Asp. suff.: -ɔh 'desc.'
> Obj. pref.: ʔo- 'neut.'

299. ke:ih 'four'

300. niyóiwa:ke:h 'how many ceremonies'

> Vb. base: vb. rt. -ake- 'be separate entities'; incorp. nn. rt. -(C)i:w-
> 'ceremony'
> Asp. suff.: -h 'desc.'
> Obj. pref.: -yo- 'neut.'
> Sec. pref.: ni- 'part.'

See also **1, 2, 7, 10, 11, 84, 176.**

(92)

301. ʔonɔtɔ́isyɔhkɔh 'they asked'

> Vb. base: vb. rt. -ɔisyɔ́hkw- 'persist'; -at- 'refl.' (together meaning 'ask, request, pray, hope')
> Asp. suff.: -ɔ́h 'desc.'
> Obj. pref.: ʔon- 'they (nonmasc.)'

302. tɛwɛnɔtɛ́:nɔtæʔk 'they (nonmasc. pl.) will continue to be sisters (to each other)'

> Vb. rt.: -atɛ́:nɔtæ- 'be siblings'
> Asp. suff.: -ʼʔ- 'desc.'; -k 'cont.'
> Subj. pref.: -wɛn- 'they (nonmasc. pl.)'
> Mod. pref.: -ɛ- 'fut.'
> Other pref.: t- 'dupl.' (usual with this rt.)

303. tewáti'nya:ʔ 'they (nonmasc. pl.) are taking care of it'

> Vb. base: vb. rt. -(C)- 'put in'; incorp. nn. rt. -ʔnya- 'hand' (cf. 284)
> Asp. suff.: -ʔ 'desc.'
> Subj. pref.: -wati- 'they (nonmasc. pl.)'
> Other pref.: te- 'dupl.'

See also **7, 10, 11, 30, 46, 59, 81, 91.**

(93)

304. niyo:weʔ 'how far it is (in distance or, as here, time)'

> Vb. rt.: -we- 'be a certain distance'
> Asp. suff.: -ʼʔ 'desc.'
> Obj. pref.: -yo- 'neut.'
> Sec. pref.: ni- 'part.'

305. ʔotɔ́ʔɔh 'it became, there arose'

> Vb. rt.: -atɔ́ʔ- 'become'
> Asp. suff.: -ɔ́h 'desc.'
> Obj. pref.: ʔo- 'neut.'

306. watiyaʔta:teʔ 'their (nonmasc. pl.) bodies are present', here, 'between them'

> Vb. base: vb. rt. -te- 'be present', incorp. nn. rt. -yáʔta- 'body'
> Asp. suff.: -ʼʔ 'desc.'
> Subj. pref.: wati- 'their (nonmasc. pl.)'

307. nɛtwátɔ:ɔk 'how we (incl. pl.) shall always say it'

> Vb. rt.: -atɔ- 'say'
> Asp. suff.: -ʼØ- 'iter.'; -ak 'cont.'
> Subj. pref.: -tw- 'we (incl. pl.)'
> Mod. pref.: -ɛ- 'fut.'
> Sec. pref.: n- 'part.'

308. tewɛnɔtɛ́:nɔ:teʔ 'they (nonmasc. pl.) are sisters'

> Iden. with **302** except for lack of -k 'cont.' and of mod. pref. -ɛ- 'fut.'

309. tyɔhéhkɔh 'we (incl. pl.) use it for living, our sustenance'

Vb. base: vb. rt. -ɔhe- 'be alive'; rt. suff. -'hkw- 'inst.'
Asp. suff.: -ɔ́h 'desc.'
Subj. pref.: ty- 'we (incl. pl.)'

310. ʔɛtwathyonyá:neʔ 'we (incl. pl.) are going to tell about it'

Iden. with 85 except for subj. pref. -tw- 'we (incl. pl.)'

See also **1, 2, 6, 7, 10, 30, 36, 83.**

(94)

311. ʔɔkwaʔnikɔ́:iyo:h 'we (pl.) are satisfied'

Iden. with **175** (cf. also **290**) except for lack of -'sta- 'caus.-inst.' and of -'hkw- 'inst.'

312. ʔotɔ:ni:h 'it is growing'

Vb. base: vb. rt. -ɔ(:)ni- 'make'; -at- 'refl.' (cf. **105**)
Asp. suff.: -h 'desc.'
Obj. pref.: ʔo- 'neut.'

See also **1, 7, 10, 11, 42, 89, 118, 240.**

(95)

313. nɔʔtewɛnɔ́tɛ:nɔ:te:ʔ 'how they (nonmasc. pl.) are sisters'

Iden. with **308** except for addition of sec. pref. nɔʔ- 'part.'

314. ʔakyɔ́hehkɔh 'we (excl. pl.) use it for living'

Iden. with **309** except for subj. pref. ʔaky- 'we (excl. pl.)'

See also **1, 3, 6, 7, 10, 11, 70, 74, 75, 102–4.**

(96)

315. taʔakakwe:niʔ 'it can't be'

Coll. for teʔakakwe:niʔ [27.5]
Vb. rt.: -kweny- 'be able'
Asp. suff.: -iʔ 'punc.'
Subj. pref.: -ka- 'neut.'
Mod. pref.: -ʔa- 'indic.'
Other pref.: te- 'neg.'

316. nɔ:yoʔtɛ́:ɔk 'it might continue to be so'

Iden. with **74** except for mod. pref. -aa- [3.14] 'opt.'

See also **1–3, 6, 7, 10, 11, 35–38, 49, 76, 191.**

(97)

See **1, 3, 7, 10, 11, 38, 39.**

(98)

317. haʔtekakɔːt 'it must be'

    Vb. rt. *-kɔ(ː)t-* 'perform an irrevocable act'
    Asp. suff.: *-Ø* 'desc.'
    Subj. pref.: *-ka-* 'neut.'
    Other pref.: *-te-* 'dupl.'; *haʔ-* 'transloc.' (together indicating complete-
    ness or inevitability)

318. tɛyoæwɛnyéːak 'the wind will continue to stir'

    Iden. with **145** except for addition of *-ak* 'cont.' and of mod. pref. *-ɛ-*
    'fut.'

319. ʔeotiyaʔtaːníyɔːɔk 'their (masc.) bodies will continue to be
    strong'

    Iden. with **235** except for addition of *-ak* 'cont.' and of mod. pref. *ʔɛ-*
    'fut.'

320. ʔoʔthɛnɔtawɛnyeːʔ 'they (masc. pl.) move about'

    Iden. with **116** except for subj. pref. *-hɛn-* 'they (masc. pl.)'

321. ʔoʔkhéyatkaʔ 'I left them'

    Vb. rt.: *-atka-* 'leave, provide'
    Asp. suff.: *-ʼʔ* 'punc.'
    Trans. pref.: *-khey-* 'I . . . them'
    Mod. pref.: *ʔoʔ-* 'indic.'

See also **1, 3, 10, 11, 20, 81, 171.**

(99)

322. hosyɔːniːh 'he made it'

    Vb. rt.: *-ʼsyɔ(ː)ni-* 'make, fix, prepare'
    Asp. suff.: *-h* 'desc.'
    Obj. pref.: *ho-* 'masc.'

323. ʔotáʔeoɔh 'it's covered with a veil'

    Vb. base: vb. rt. *-o-* 'cover'; incorp. nn. rt. *-aʔa(æ)-* [14.4] 'veil'; *-at-*
    'refl.'
    Asp. suff.: *-ɔh* 'desc.'
    Obj. pref.: *ʔo-* 'neut.'

324. hekæːhkwɛ́ʔskwaːh 'toward where the sun sets, the west'

    Vb. base: vb. rt. *-ɛ-* 'fall'; rt. suff. *-ʼʔ-* 'inch.'; incorp. nn. rt. *-(C)æhkw-*
    'sun'
    Asp suff.: *-s-* 'iter.'
    Subj. pref.: *-kæ-* 'neut.'
    Other pref.: *he-* 'transloc.'
    Enclitic: *-kwah* 'toward'

325. nɔʔwɔ:tih 'on which side'

> Vb. base: vb. rt. -ati- 'be on a certain side'; rt. suff.: -'h 'inch. II'
> Asp. suff.: -∅ 'punc.'
> Subj. pref.: -w- 'neut.'
> Mod. pref.: -aʔ- 'indic.'
> Sec. pref.: n- 'part.'

326. skɛnɔ́ʔɔ:h 'slowly'

327. nityoye:ɛh 'how it goes, moves'

> Vb. rt.: -ye- 'do', with cisloc. 'go, move'
> Asp. suff.: -ɛh 'desc.'
> Obj. pref.: -yo- 'neut.'
> Prim. pref.: -t- 'cisloc.'
> Sec. pref.: ni- 'part.'

328. ʔotkahatɔ́:h 'it revolves'

> Vb. base: vb. rt. -kahatɔ́- 'revolve'; -at- 'refl.'
> Asp. suff.: -ɔ́h 'desc.'
> Obj. pref.: ʔo- 'neut.'

See also **1, 7, 10, 11.**

(100)

329. tyotatɔ:ni:h 'it forms there'

> Vb. base: vb. rt. -ɔ(:)ni- 'make'; -atat- 'recip.' (together meaning 'form')
> Asp. suff.: -h 'desc.'
> Obj. pref.: -yo- 'neut.'
> Prim. pref.: t- 'cisloc.'

330. ʔɔkyɔishǽ:ni:yɔh 'it strengthens our breath'

> Iden. with **293** except for lack of -'hkw- 'inst.'

See also **1, 2, 6, 7, 10, 15, 16, 27, 36, 42, 69, 89, 145.**

(101)

331. nitka:teʔ 'how much it is present there, how strong it is'

> Vb. rt.: -te- 'be present'
> Asp. suff.: -'ʔ 'desc.'
> Subj. pref.: -ka- 'neut.'
> Prim. pref.: -t- 'cisloc.'
> Sec. pref.: ni- 'part.'

See also **6, 11, 27, 46, 69, 95, 145, 175, 191.**

(102)

332. ho:nɛ:h 'they (masc.) said'

> Vb. rt.: -ɛ- 'say'
> Asp. suff.: -h 'desc.'
> Obj. pref.: hon- 'they (masc.)'

333. ʔakwe:h 'we (excl. pl.) think'

> Iden. with 96 except for subj. pref. *ʔakw-* 'we (excl. pl.)'

334. shenɔ:kshɔʔ 'you have them as kinsmen'

> Vb. rt.: *-nɔk-* 'have as kinsman'
> Asp. suff.: *-Ø-* 'desc.'
> Trans. pref.: *she-* 'you . . . them'
> Attr. suff.: *-shɔ́ʔ* 'plur.'

See also **1, 7, 9–12, 57, 136.**

(103)

335. ʔo:ɛtɔ:h 'it is ahead, in the future'

> Vb. rt.: *-ʹɛt-* 'be ahead'
> Asp. suff.: *-ɔh* 'desc.'
> Obj. pref.: *ʔo-* 'neut.'

336. ʔoʔwɛ́:nishætenyɔ:tyeʔ 'days are present all along'

> Vb. base: vb. rt. *-te-* 'be present'; rt. suff. *-nyɔ-* 'dist.'; incorp. nn. rt.
> *-ɛ́:nishæ-* 'day'
> Asp. suff.: *-Ø-* 'desc.'; *-tye-* 'prog.'; *-ʹʔ* 'punc.'
> Subj. pref.: *-w-* 'neut.'
> Mod. pref.: *ʔoʔ-* 'indic.'

337. nɛya:wɛh 'how it will happen'

> Vb. rt.: *-ɛ́h-* 'happen'
> Asp. suff.: *-Ø* 'punc.'
> Obj. pref.: *-yaw-* 'neut.'
> Mod. pref.: *-ɛ-* 'fut.'
> Sec. pref.: *n-* 'part.'

338. ʔɛtyakwɛʔnéoʔktɛʔ 'it will then be beyond our (excl. pl.) reach, control'

> Vb. rt.: *-ɛʔneóʔkt-* 'be unable to reach'
> Asp. suff.: *-ɛ́ʔ* 'punc.'
> Subj. pref.: *-yakw-* 'we (excl. pl.)'
> Mod. pref.: *ʔɛ-* 'fut.'
> Prim. pref.: *-t-* 'cisloc.'

339. heyó:eh 'it is time'

> Vb. rt.: *-ʹe-* 'arrive (of time)'
> Asp. suff.: *-h* 'desc.'
> Obj. pref.: *-yo-* 'neut.'
> Other pref.: *he-* 'transloc.' (usual with this rt.)

340. ʔɔkwatkáɛɔʔ 'we (pl.) are watching it'

> Vb. rt. *-atkáɛɔ-* 'watch, observe'
> Asp. suff.: *-ʹʔ* 'desc.'
> Obj. pref.: *ʔɔkw-* 'we (pl.)'

See also **6, 10, 11, 30, 52.**

(104)

341. nεyóʔhastεh 'how strong it will become'

> Vb. base: vb. rt. -ʔhast- 'be strong, powerful'; rt. suff.: -éh- 'inch. II'
> Asp. suff.: -∅ 'punc.'
> Obj. pref.: -yo- 'neut.'
> Mod. pref.: -ε- 'fut.'
> Sec. pref.: n- 'part.'

342. ʔewótkaha:tɔh 'it will revolve'

> Vb. base: vb. rt. -kahatóh- 'revolve'; -at- 'refl.'
> Asp. suff.: -∅ 'punc.'
> Subj. pref.: -w- 'neut.'
> Mod. pref.: ʔε- 'fut.'

343. ka:εkwah 'very, extremely, excessively'

344. haʔtεkakε:seʔ 'it will scrape everything'

> Vb. rt.: -kεse- 'scrape'
> Asp. suff.: -ʔ 'punc.'
> Subj. pref.: -ka- 'neut.'
> Mod. pref.: -ε- 'fut.'
> Other pref.: -t- 'dupl.'; haʔ- 'transloc.' (together meaning everything')

See also **7, 10, 11, 52, 81, 93, 332.**

(105)

345. ʔεyakotówehtak 'it will cause harm to people'

> Vb. base: vb. rt. -oweht- 'disturb'; rt. suff. -ʔhkw- 'inst.'; -at- 'refl.' (the
> entire base meaning 'cause harm to')
> Asp. suff.: -∅ 'punc.'
> Obj. pref.: -yako- 'fem.'
> Mod. pref.: ʔε- 'fut.'

346. nyo:tiye:εh 'what they (masc.) did'

> Coll. for 8.

See also **6, 7, 10, 11, 20, 41, 52, 193, 332, 340.**

(106)

347. ʔεtwaiwakwáihsiʔ 'we (incl. pl.) shall attest to it'

> Vb. base: vb. rt. -kwáihs- 'straighten out'; incorp. nn. rt. -(C)í:wa-
> 'matter' (together meaning 'attest to')
> Asp. suff.: -íʔ 'punc.'
> Subj. pref.: -twa- 'we (incl. pl.)'
> Mod. pref.: ʔε- 'fut.'

348. niya:wεs 'how it happens'

> Vb. rt.: -éh- 'happen'
> Asp. suff.: -s 'iter.'
> Obj. pref.: -yaw- 'neut.'
> Sec. pref.: ni- 'part.'

349. ʔoʔkaiwâhtɔʔt 'it destroys'

> Vb. base: vb. rt. -ahtɔ- 'lose'; rt. suff. -ʔt- 'caus. I' (together meaning 'make disappear, destroy'); incorp. nn. rt. -(C)ᵢ:w- 'matter'
> Asp. suff.: -Ø 'punc.'
> Subj. pref.: -ka- 'neut.'
> Mod. pref.: ʔoʔ- 'indic.'

350. hotiʔnikɔ́:iyo:h 'they (masc.) are content'

> Iden. with **311** except for obj. pref. hoti- 'they (masc.)'

351. ʔoʔkakwe:niʔ 'it is possible, it can'

> Iden. with **315** except for lack of ta- 'neg.'

352. waʔóʔhastɛh 'it becomes strong'

> Iden. with **341** except for mod. pref. wa- 'indic.' and lack of n- 'part.'

353. ʔoʔtkæ:wɛ:nye:ʔ 'the wind stirs'

> Iden. with **193** except for mod. pref. ʔoʔ- 'indic.'

See also **1, 6, 10, 11, 30, 42, 81, 89, 118, 134.**

(107)

354. niyóʔhasteʔ 'how strong it is'

> Vb. rt.: -ʔhaste- 'be strong'
> Asp. suff.: -ʔ 'desc.'
> Obj. pref.: -yo- 'neut.'
> Sec. pref.: ni- 'part.'

See also **1, 10, 11, 27, 36, 57, 67, 69, 145, 175, 191.**

(108)

See **1, 3, 6, 7, 11, 70, 74, 75, 102, 104, 145, 323, 328.**

(109)

355. ʔɛwɔkatɛ́hɔʔshɛ:taʔk 'I shall continue to have helpers'

> Vb. base: vb. rt. -ɛta- 'have'; incorp. nn. base: vb. rt. -háʔ- [3.14] 'hire, assign'; -sh- 'nom.'; -atɛ- 'refl.'
> Asp. suff.: -ʔ- 'desc.'; -k 'cont.'
> Obj. pref.: -wak- '1st pers.'
> Mod. pref.: ʔɛ- 'fut.'

356. ʔɛthɛ́niʔtyɔ:taʔk 'they (masc. pl.) will continue to dwell there'

> Vb. rt.: -iʔtyɔ(:)ta- 'dwell'
> Asp. suff.: -ʔ- 'desc.'; -k 'cont.'
> Subj. pref.: -hɛn- 'they (masc. pl.)'
> Mod. pref.: ʔɛ- 'fut.'
> Prim. pref.: -t- 'cisloc.'

See also **1, 2, 6, 35–38, 59, 76, 324, 325.**

(110)

357. ʔɛthɛnehtáhkwa:k 'they (masc. pl.) will always come from there'

> Vb. base: vb. rt. *-ehta-* 'come from'; rt. suff. *-ʼhkw-* 'inst.'
> Asp. suff.: *-Ø-* 'iter.'; *-ak* 'cont.'
> Subj. pref.: *hen-* 'they (masc. pl.)'
> Mod. pref.: *ʔɛ-* 'fut.'
> Prim. pref.: *-t-* 'cisloc.'

358. tɛ:nɔtawɛnye:ʔ 'they (masc. pl.) will move about'

> Iden. with **78** except for subj. pref. *-ʼɛn-* 'they (masc. pl.)'

359. nikáshatɔ:tyeʔs 'as the moisture falls'

> Iden. with **258** except for lack of prim. pref. *-t-* 'cisloc.'

360. ʔɛɔtíawiʔse:k 'they (masc. pl.) will always carry it'

> Vb. rt.: *-ʼ(h)awi-* 'carry'
> Asp. suff.: *-ʼʔs-* 'iter.'; *-ek* 'cont.'
> Subj. pref.: *-ʼati-* 'they (masc. pl.)'
> Mod. pref.: *ʔɛ-* 'fut.'

See also **3, 6, 10, 36, 59, 173.**

(111)

361. ʔɛ́ɔtiɛtosæ:hse:k 'they (masc. pl.) will always sprinkle the gardens'

> Vb. base: vb. rt. *-osæ-* 'sprinkle'; incorp. nn. rt. *-ʼ(h)ɛt-* 'garden'
> Asp. suff.: *-hs-* 'iter.'; *-ek* 'cont.'
> Subj. pref.: *-ʼati-* 'they (masc. pl.)'
> Mod. pref.: *ʔɛ-* 'fut.'

362. watɔ:nih 'it grows'

> Iden. with **312** except for asp. suff. *-ʼh* 'iter.' and subj. pref. *w-* 'neut.'

See also **10, 11, 30, 36, 81, 93, 108, 112, 127.**

(112)

363. nɛ:nɔtɔ́:ɔk 'how they (masc. pl.) will always say it'

> Iden. with **307** except for subj. pref. *-ʼɛn-* 'they (masc. pl.)'

364. ʔethíhso:t 'we (incl.) have them as grandparents, our grandparents'

> Vb. rt.: *-ʼhsot-* 'have as grandparent'
> Asp. suff.: *-Ø* 'desc.'
> Trans. pref.: *ʔethi-* 'we (incl.) . . . them'

365. hiʔnɔʔ (a name; see p. 9)

366. hatiwɛnotatyeʔs 'they (masc. pl.) are speaking out, spreading the word'

>   Vb. base: vb. rt. -*ot*- 'stand upright'; incorp. nn. rt. -*wɛn*- 'voice' (together
>   meaning 'speak out')
>   Asp. suff.: -Ø-'desc.'; -*atye*- 'prog.'; -ʔs 'iter.'
>   Subj. pref.: *hati*- 'they (masc. pl.)'

367. nɛɔtiye:ha:k 'how they (masc. pl.) will always do it'

>   Vb. rt.: -*ye*- 'do'
>   Asp. suff.: -*h*- 'iter.'; -*ak* 'cont.'
>   Subj. pref.: -'*ati*- 'they (masc. pl.)'
>   Mod. pref.: -*ɛ*- 'fut.'
>   Sec. pref.: *n*- 'part.'

See also 1, 3, 6, 7, 10, 11, 30, 38, 57, 83–85.

(113)

368. heakɔyátkaʔwɛh 'he left them there'

>   Vb. rt.: -*atkáʔw*- 'leave, provide'
>   Asp. suff.: -*ɛ́h* 'desc.'
>   Trans. pref.: -*akɔy*-'he . . . them'
>   Other pref.: *he*- 'transloc.'

See also 1, 6, 7, 10, 11, 324, 357.

(114)

369. nɛyóʔhaste:k 'how strong it will continue to be'

>   Vb. rt.: -ʔ*haste*- 'be strong'
>   Asp. suff.: -Ø- 'desc.'; -*k* 'cont.'
>   Obj. pref.: -*yo*- 'neut.'
>   Mod. pref.: -*ɛ*- 'fut.'
>   Sec. pref.: *n*- 'part.'

370. ʔɛyakoʔnikɔiyostáhkɔ:ɔk 'it will continue to satisfy people'

>   Vb. base iden. with 175.
>   Asp. suff.: -ɔ́- 'desc.'; -*ak* 'cont.'
>   Obj. pref.: -*yako*- 'fem.'
>   Mod. pref.: ʔ*ɛ*- 'fut.'

371. honɔ́teʔshæʔ 'their (masc.) grandchildren'

>   Nn. base: vb. rt. -*ate*- 'be grandparent to'; -ʔ*shæ*- 'nom.'
>   Nn. suff.: -ʔ 'spl. nn. suff.'
>   Obj. pref.: *hon*- 'their (masc.)'

See also 1, 6, 10, 11, 20, 41, 89.

(115)

372. niyokɛhíso:ɔtye⁷ 'all through the summer'

> Vb. base: vb. rt. *-is-* 'be long'; incorp. nn. rt. *-kɛh-* 'summer'
> Asp. suff.: *-ó-* 'desc.'; *-atye-* 'prog.'; *-'⁷* 'desc.'
> Obj. pref.: *-yo-* 'neut.'
> Sec. pref.: *ni-* 'part.'

373. to:nɔtawɛnye:h 'they (masc.) are moving about'

> Coll. for *teonɔtawɛnye:h*
> Iden. with **16** except for obj. pref. *-'on* 'they (masc.)'

374. honónya:nɔ:tye⁷s 'they (masc.) are making things'

> Vb. base: vb. rt. *-ɔnya-* 'make'; rt. suff. *-':nɔ-* 'dist.'
> Asp. suff.: *-Ø-* 'desc.'; *-tye-* 'prog.'; *-'⁷s* 'iter.'
> Obj. pref.: *hon-* 'they (masc.)'

See also **1, 6, 30, 36, 46, 173, 186–188, 277, 359.**

(116)

375. ⁷o⁷tyethinó:nyɔ:⁷ 'we (incl.) thank them'

> Iden. with **104** except for trans. pref. *-yethi-* 'we (incl.) . . . them'

See also **1, 3, 6, 7, 10, 11, 30, 70, 74, 75, 102, 103, 364–366.**

(117)

376. ⁷ɛkéɔya:te:k 'sky will continue to be there'

> Vb. base: vb. rt. *-te-* 'be present, in place'; incorp. nn. rt. *-(y)ó:ya-* 'sky'
> Asp. suff.: *-Ø-* 'desc.'; *-k* 'cont.'
> Subj. pref.: *-kɛ-* 'neut.'
> Mod. pref.: *⁷ɛ-* 'fut.'

377. hetkɛh 'above, overhead'

378. na⁷akonó⁷ɛ:tih 'on which side of people's heads'

> Vb. base: vb. rt. *-ati-* 'be on a certain side'; rt. suff. *-'h-* 'inch. II'; incorp.
> nn. rt. *-nɔ⁷ɛɛ-* 'head'
> Asp. suff.: *-Ø* 'punc.'
> Obj. pref.: *-⁷ako-* 'fem.'
> Mod. pref.: *-a-* 'indic.'
> Sec. pref.: *n-* 'part.'
> Cf. **144, 325.**

See also **1, 2, 7, 10, 11, 20, 35–38, 76, 116.**

(118)

See **7, 10, 11, 36, 176, 317, 355, 376.**

(119)

379. hɔwɔiɔ́tasˀɔh 'he gave him an assignment'

    Iden. with 101 except for trans. pref. *hɔwɔ-* 'he . . . him'

380. hotǽˀnɛta:ktɔh 'he is attached, stuck on'

    Vb. base: vb. rt. *-(C)æ̂netak-* 'stick on'; rt. suff. *-t-* 'caus. I'; *-at-* 'refl.'
    Asp. suff.: *-ɔ́h* 'desc.'
    Obj. pref.: *ho-* 'masc.'

381. kέɔyateˀ 'the sky'

    Iden. with 376 except for lack of *-k* 'cont.' and of mod. pref. *ˀɛ-* 'fut.'
    Cf. 93.

See also 1, 7, 10, 11, 81, 89.

(120)

382. to:tawɛ́nye:ak 'he will continue to move about'

    Iden. with 264 except for obj. pref. *-ˊo-* 'masc.'

383. tɔɛjíyaˀktha:k 'he will always cross the earth'

    Vb. base: vb. rt. *-iyáˀk-* 'cross'; rt. suff. *-t-* 'caus. I'; incorp. nn. rt. *-ɔ́ɛj-* 'earth'
    Asp. suff.: *-h-* 'iter.'; *-ak* 'cont.'
    Subj. pref.: *-ˊa-* 'masc.'
    Mod. pref.: *-ɛ-* 'fut.'
    Other pref.: *t-* 'dupl.' (usual with this vb. rt.)
    The initial morph sequence *t-ɛ-a-ɔɛj-* occurs as *tɔɛj-*.

384. nɛthe:tha:k 'how he will always come'

    Vb. rt.: *-eht-* 'come from'
    Asp. suff.: *-h-* 'iter.'; *-ak* 'cont.'
    Subj. pref.: *-h-* 'masc.'
    Mod. pref.: *-ɛ-* 'fut.'
    Prim. pref.: *-t-* 'cisloc.'
    Sec. pref.: *n-* 'part.'

385. hɛ:etha:k 'he will always go there'

    Vb. stem iden. with 384 (with transloc. means 'go')
    Subj. pref.: *-ˊØ-* 'masc.'
    Mod. pref.: *-ɛ-* 'fut.'
    Other pref.: *h-* 'transloc.'

See also 6, 10, 30, 46, 109, 267.

(121)

386. ˀɛte:kha:ˀ 'diurnal'

    ˀɛ:teh 'day'
    Attr. suff.: *-khaˀ* 'charact.'

387. shetwáhji? 'we (incl. pl.) have him as older brother, our older brother'

> Vb. rt.: -'hji- 'have as older sibling'
> Asp. suff.: -'? 'desc.'
> Trans. pref.: shetwa- 'we (incl. pl.) . . . him'

388. kǽ:hkwa:? 'sun, moon is in it' (in the sky)

> Vb. base: vb. rt. -(C)- 'put in'; incorp. nn. rt. -(C)ǽhkwa- 'sun, moon'
> Asp. suff.: -? 'desc.'
> Subj. pref.: kæ- 'neut.'

See also 1, 10, 11, 30, 57, 76, 83, 84, 176, 307, 310.

(122)

389. hoiwayéistɔh 'he has done what he was obligated to do'

> Iden. with **98** except for obj. pref. ho- 'masc.'

390. teyohathétsi:yo:h 'the beautiful daylight'

> Vb. base: vb. rt. -iyo- 'be beautiful'; incorp. nn. base: vb. rt. -hathe- 'be light'; -ts- 'nom.'
> Asp. suff.: -h 'desc.'
> Obj. pref.: -yo- 'neut.'
> Other pref.: te- 'dupl.' (usual with -hathe-)

See also 1, 2, 6, 27, 69, 81, 89, 380, 381.

(123)

391. ?onɔtɔhɔ́htɛtyɔ:h 'they (nonmasc.) are flourishing'

> Vb. base: vb. rt. -ahtɛty- 'travel, operate'; incorp. nn. rt. -ɔh- 'life'; -at 'refl.'
> Asp. suff.: -ɔh 'desc.'
> Obj. pref.: ?on- 'they (nonmasc.)'

392. hɔwɔiwakɛ́istani:h 'he gave him the assignment, responsibility'

> Vb. base: vb. rt. -kɛista- 'move'; rt. suff. -ni- 'dat.'; incorp. nn. rt. -(C)í:wa- 'matter, responsibility' (the entire base meaning 'give responsibility, authority')
> Asp. suff.: -h 'desc.'
> Trans. pref.: hɔwɔ- 'he . . . him'

393. ?ɛɔ?táia?tha:k 'he will always make it warm'

> Vb. base: vb. rt. -a?tata- 'be warm'; rt. suff. -'?t- 'caus. I'
> Asp. suff.: -h- 'iter.'; -ak 'cont.'
> Subj. pref.: -'∅- 'masc.'
> Mod. pref.: ?ɛ- 'fut.'

394. ʔɛwɛnɔtɔ́hɔhtɛ:tiʔ 'they (nonmasc. pl.) will flourish'

    Vb. base iden. with **391**.
    Asp. suff.: -tʔ 'punc.'
    Subj. pref.: -wɛn- 'they (nonmasc. pl.)'
    Mod. pref.: ʔɛ- 'fut.'

See also 1, 2, 7, 10, 11, 27, 30, 36, 81, 82, 89, 96, 97, 108, 112, 127, 176, 362, 389.

(124)

See 1, 7, 36, 96, 100, 118, 379, 389.

(125)

395. ʔɛtsakwanɔ́:nyɔ:ʔ 'we (excl. pl.) shall thank him there'

    Vb. rt.: -nɔ́ɔnyɔ- 'thank'
    Asp. suff.: -ʔ 'punc.'
    Trans. pref.: -sakwa- 'we (excl. pl.) . . . him'
    Mod. pref.: ʔɛ- 'fut.'
    Prim. pref.: -t- 'cisloc.'

396. shakwáhjiʔ 'our (excl. pl.) elder brother'

    Iden. with **387** except for trans. pref. *shakwa-* 'we (excl. pl.) . . . him'

See also 1, 3, 6, 7, 10, 11, 30, 70, 74, 75, 102, 386, 388.

(126)

397. ʔɛwɔtɛ́ɔnostha:k 'it will always make shade'

    Vb. base: vb. rt. -atɛ́ɔno- 'be shady'; rt. suff. -ʹst- 'caus.-inst.'
    Asp. suff.: -h- 'iter.'; -ak 'cont.'
    Subj. pref.: -w- 'neut.'
    Mod. pref.: ʔɛ- 'fut.'

See also 1–3, 7, 35–38, 42, 76, 82, 109, 191, 263.

(127)

398. ʔɛwɛ́:nishætenyɔ:k 'days will continue to be there'

    Vb. base: vb. rt. -te- 'be present'; rt. suff. -nyɔ- 'dist.'; incorp. nn. rt. -ɛ́:nishæ- 'day'
    Asp. suff.: -Ø- 'desc.'; -k 'cont.'
    Subj. pref.: -w- 'neut.'
    Mod. pref.: -ʔɛ- 'fut.'

See also 46, 109, 263.

(128)

399. ta:ka:nǽhji:wɛh 'he saw well'

    Coll. for *teaka:nǽhji:wɛh*
    Vb. base: vb. rt. -ká:næ- 'see, look at'; rt. suff. -hjï:w- 'intens.'
    Asp. suff.: -ɛ́h 'desc.'
    Subj. pref.: -ʹa- 'masc.'
    Other pref.: te- 'dupl.' (usual with this rt.)

400. kotatya'takehá:nɔ' 'people helped, took care of themselves'

Vb. base: vb. rt. *-ya'takeha-* 'help'; rt. suff. *-':nɔ-* 'dist.'; *-atat-* 'recip.'
Asp. suff.: *-'?* 'desc.'
Obj. pref.: *ko-* 'fem.'

See also **1, 7, 10, 11, 20, 41, 89.**

(129)

401. 'ɛyɔtɔ́ishɛ:ɔk 'people will always rest'

Vb. rt.: *-atɔishɛ-* 'rest'
Asp. suff.: *-'Ø-* 'iter.'; *-ak* 'cont.'
Subj. pref.: *-y[ɔ]-* 'fem.'
Mod. pref.: *'ɛ-* 'fut.'

402. nɛ:we:' 'while, during'

See also **1, 3, 6, 7, 10, 11, 36, 38, 183, 397.**

(130)

403. káɛti'kwah 'wherever'

404. 'ɛtyakohsɔ́ta'is 'people will run into darkness there'

Vb. base: vb. rt. *-a'ist-* 'run into, puncture'; incorp. nn. rt. *-ahsɔt-* 'darkness, night'
Asp. suff.: *-Ø* 'punc.'
Obj. pref.: *-yako-* 'fem.'
Mod. pref.: *'ɛ-* 'fut.'
Prim. pref.: *-t-* 'cisloc.'

See also **1, 6, 10, 11, 52, 57, 304, 337.**

(131)

405. thika:te' 'another one'

Vb. rt.; *-te-* 'be present'
Asp. suff.: *-'?* 'desc.'
Subj. pref.: *-ka-* 'neut.'
Sec. pref.: *thi-* 'contr.'

406. 'ɛkǽ:hkwa:a'k 'a moon will continue to be in it'

Vb. base: vb. rt. *-(C)æ-* [5.4] 'put in'; incorp. nn. rt. *-(C)æhkwa-* 'moon, sun'
Asp. suff.: *-'?-* 'desc.'; *-k* 'cont.'
Subj. pref.: *-kæ-* 'neut.'
Mod. pref.: *'ɛ-* 'fut.'

See also **1, 10, 11, 57, 81, 355, 376.**

(132)

407. sɔekha:' 'nocturnal'

sɔeh 'night'
Attr. suff.: *-kha'* 'charact.'
Cf. **386.**

408. ha⁷tɛyakoshɛtá⁷ɔ:ɔk⁷ah 'it will continue to be a sort of guide for people's steps'

> Vb. rt.: -ashɛtá²- 'tread, step'
> Asp. suff.: -ɔ́- 'desc.'; -ak 'cont.'
> Obj. pref.: -yako- 'fem.'
> Mod. pref.: -ɛ- 'fut.'
> Other pref.: -t- 'dupl.'; ha²- 'transloc.'
> Attr. suff.: -²áh 'dimin.'

409. tɛyakohathe⁷tɔ́:ɔk 'it will continue to bring people light'

> Vb. base: vb. rt. -hathe- 'be light'; rt. suff. -'²t- 'caus. I'
> Asp. suff.: -ɔ́- 'desc.'; -ak 'cont.'
> Obj. pref.: -yako- 'fem.'
> Mod. pref.: -ɛ- 'fut.'
> Other pref.: t- 'dupl.'

See also **6, 10, 30, 203, 363, 364, 367, 388.**

(133)

410. ⁷ɔkwatɛnɔ⁷kæ:htashɛ́tahkɔh 'we (pl.) are using it for measuring'

> Coll. for ²ɔkwatɛnɔ²keæhtashɛ́tahkɔh
> Vb. base: vb. rt. -ɛta- 'put down'; rt. suff. -'hkw- 'inst.'; incorp. nn. base:
>   vb. rt. -atɛnɔ²keæhta- 'try'; -'sh- 'nom.' (together meaning 'measure-
>   ment'; with -ɛta-, 'measure')
> Asp. suff.: -ɔ́h 'desc.'
> Obj. pref.: ²ɔkw- 'we (pl.)'

411. nɛyɔkwatkɛistɔ́:tye⁷ 'as we (pl.) shall be moving along'

> Vb. base: vb. rt. -kɛist- 'move'; -at- 'refl.'
> Asp. suff.: -ɔ́- 'desc.'; -atye- 'prog.'; -'² 'punc.'
> Obj. pref.: -yɔkw- 'we (pl.)'
> Mod. pref.: -ɛ- 'fut.'
> Sec. pref.: n- 'part.'

See also **1, 7, 10, 11, 15, 16, 36, 89.**

(134)

412. tɛkatenyɔ́hse:k 'it will always change'

> Vb. rt.: -teny- 'change'
> Asp. suff.: -ɔ́hs- 'iter.'; -ek 'cont.'
> Subj. pref.: -ka- 'neut.'
> Mod. pref.: -ɛ- 'fut.'
> Other pref.: t- 'dupl.'

413. ⁷otæhkwahtɛ:tyɔ:h 'the moon is traveling'

> Vb. base: vb. rt. -ahtɛty- 'travel'; incorp. nn. rt. -(C)æhkw- 'sun, moon';
>   -at- 'refl.'
> Asp. suff.: -ɔh 'desc.'
> Obj. pref.: ²o- 'neut.'

414. ʔɛwɔtɛ:níʔtoʔktha:k 'the moons always come to an end'

> Vb. base: vb. rt. -*óʔkt*- 'come to the end'; incorp. nn. rt. -*ɛ̀:níʔt*- 'month,
> moon (as a period of time)'; -*at*- 'refl.'
> Asp. suff.: -*h*- 'iter.'; -*ak* 'cont.'
> Subj. pref.: -*w*- 'neut.'
> Mod. pref.: *ʔɛ*- 'fut.'

See also **3, 7, 10, 11, 30, 36, 38, 47, 139.**

(135)

415. ʔɔkwatkɛ́istɔ:ɔtyeʔ 'we (pl.) are moving along'

> Iden. with **411** except for final -*ʔ* 'desc.' in asp. suff. and lack of mod.
> and sec. prefs.

See also **1, 7, 10, 11, 15, 16, 36, 42, 47, 89, 118, 226, 410.**

(136)

416. tayawehtɔ́:tyeʔ 'it is coming from there'

> Vb. rt.: -*eht*- 'come from'
> Asp. suff.: -*ɔ́*- 'desc.'; -*atye*- 'prog.'; -*ʔ* 'punc.'
> Obj. pref.: -*yaw*- 'neut.'
> Mod. pref.: -*a*- 'indic.'
> Prim. pref.: *t*- 'cisloc.'

417. to:titáʔɔ:ɔtyeʔ 'they (masc.) are coming to stand, taking their
places'

> Coll. for *teotitáʔɔ:ɔtyeʔ*
> Vb. base: vb. rt. -*ta*- 'stand'; rt. suff. -*ʔ*- 'inch. I'
> Asp. suff.: -*ɔ́*- 'desc.'; -*atye*- 'prog.'; -*ʔ* 'desc.'
> Obj. pref.: -*oti*- 'they (masc.)'
> Other pref.: *te*- 'dupl.'

418. saʔ diminutive particle
419. niɛnɔhɔ́ʔsʔah 'little children'

> Vb. rt.: -*ɔh*- 'be alive'
> Asp. suff.: -*ɔ́ʔs*- 'iter.'
> Subj. pref.: -*ɛn*- 'they (masc. pl.)'
> Attr. suff.: -*ʔáh* 'dimin.'

See also **1, 6, 57, 81, 93, 96, 99, 176, 198, 306.**

(137)

420. shakoiwakɛ́istani:h 'he gave her the assignment, responsibility'

> Iden. with **392** except for trans. pref. *shako*- 'he . . . her'

See also **1, 6, 7, 36, 61, 96–98, 100.**

(138)

See **1–3, 6, 7, 10, 11, 30, 70, 74, 75, 102, 103, 364, 375, 388, 407.**

(139)

See 1, 2, 7, 35–37, 76.

(140)

421. ˀɛkajihsɔˀtahsí:æˀk 'the stars will continue to stand in array'

> Vb. base: vb. rt. -hstaæ- (cf. 121) 'stand in array'; incorp. nn. rt. -jihsɔ́ˀta-
> 'star'
> Asp. suff.: -ˀˀ- 'desc.'; -k 'cont.'
> Subj. pref.: -ka- 'neut.'
> Mod. pref.: ˀɛ- 'fut.'

See also 7, 10, 11, 36, 38, 81, 89, 176, 376, 397, 402.

(141)

422. naˀáhtɛˀɛh 'things'
423. hakɔiɔ́tasˀɔh 'he gave them an assignment'

> Iden. with 101 except for trans. pref. hakɔ- 'he . . . them'

See also 1, 6, 10, 11, 36, 74, 109, 176.

(142)

424. ˀɛyótihsɛnɔyɛ:taˀk 'they (nonmasc.) will continue to have names'

> Iden. with 107 except for lack of -ɔ- 'dist.'

425. ˀojistanóhkweɔˀ 'speckles, stars in it'

> Vb. base: vb. rt. -(Cæ)- 'put in'; rt. suff. -ɔ- 'dist.'; incorp. nn. rt. -jista-
> nóhkwa- [14.4] 'speckle'
> Asp. suff.: -ˀˀ 'desc.'
> Obj. pref.: ˀo- 'neut.'

See also 7, 36, 38, 81, 106, 108, 176, 381.

(143)

426. ˀɛkaiwayɛ́ɔnya:nɔ:k 'it will indicate things'

> Vb. base: vb. rt. -yɛɔnya- 'indicate'; rt. suff. -ˀ:nɔ- 'dist.'; incorp. nn.
> rt. -(C)ɪ̃:wa- 'matter, thing'
> Asp. suff.: -∅- 'desc.'; -k 'cont.'
> Subj. pref.: -ka- 'neut.'
> Mod. pref.: ˀɛ- 'fut.'

427. ˀɛyakotɛnɔˀkæ:htashɛtáhkɔ:ɔk 'people will continue to use it for measuring'

> Iden. with 410 except for addition of -ak 'cont.' to asp. suff. and of mod.
> pref. ˀɛ- 'fut.' and obj. pref. -yako- 'fem.'

428. ˀɛyakohsɔ́taˀis 'people will run into darkness'

> Iden. with 404 except for lack of -t- 'cisloc.'

429. ʔatháinɔʔkeh 'on the journey'

> Vb. base: vb. rt. *-inɔ-* 'go'; incorp. nn. rt. *-há-* 'road'; *ʔat-* 'refl.' [15.6]
> Nn. suff.; *-ʔkéh* 'ext. loc.' [26.4]

430. koyǽ:ʔtɔh 'people use it'

> Coll. for *koyǽʔtɔh*
> Vt. base: vb. rt. *-yeǽ-* 'do'; rt. suff. *-ʔt-* 'caus. I' (together meaning 'use')
> Asp. suff.: *-ɔ́h* 'desc.'
> Obj. pref.: *ko-* 'fem.'

See also 1, 6, 10, 11, 20, 30, 41, 46, 52, 89, 176, 337.

(144)

431. ʔɛyɔtkɔskáhatɛʔ 'people will turn up their faces'

> Vb. base: vb. rt. *-kahat-* 'turn (up)'; incorp. nn. rt. *-kɔ́hs-* [3.6] 'face';
> *-at-* 'refl.'
> Asp. suff.: *-ɛ́ʔ* 'punc.'
> Subj. pref.: *-y[ɔ]-* 'fem.'
> Mod. pref.: *ʔɛ-* 'fut.'

432. ʔɛyakoyaʔtatókɛstak 'it will set people straight'

> Vb. base: vb. rt. *-tokɛ-* 'be straight'; rt. suff. *-ʔst-* 'caus.-inst.', *-ʔhkw-*
> 'inst.'; incorp. nn. rt. *-yáʔta-* 'body'
> Asp. suff.: *-Ø* 'punc.'
> Obj. pref.: *-yako-* 'fem.'
> Mod. pref.: *ʔɛ-* 'fut.'

433. ʔɛjɔ́tkɔ:tak 'people will go directly back'

> Vb. base: vb. rt. *-kɔta-* 'perform an irrevocable act'; rt. suff. *-ʔhkw-* 'inst.'
> (together meaning 'direct toward'); *-at-* 'refl.'
> Asp. suff.: *-Ø* 'punc.'
> Subj. pref.: *-y[ɔ]-* 'fem.'
> Mod. pref.: *ʔɛ-* 'fut.'
> Prim. pref.: *-[j]-* 'repet.'

434. hɛ:ɔwé:kwa:h 'toward where'

> *hɛ́:ɔweh* 'where' (81)
> Enclitic: *-kwah* 'toward' [26.8]

435. tetyakoʔníkɔhka:nyɛh 'it bites people's minds back there, their
home'

> Vb. base: vb. rt. *-kany-* 'bite'; incorp. nn. rt. *-ʔnikɔ́h-* 'mind'
> Asp. suff.: *-ɛ́h* 'desc.'
> Obj. pref.: *-yako-* 'fem.'
> Prim. pref.: *-t-* 'cisloc.'
> Other pref.: *te-* 'dupl.'

See also 1, 6, 7, 10, 59, 89, 425.

(145)

436. hati:wayɛtáhkɔh 'their (masc. pl.) responsibility'

Iden. with **60** except for subj. pref. *hati-* 'their (masc. pl.)'

See also **1, 10, 30, 118, 176.**

(146)

437. ʔotɛɔnóstɔh 'it is in shadow'

Vb. base: vb. rt. *-atɛɔno-* 'be shady'; rt. suff. *-ʹst-* 'caus.-inst.'
Asp. suff.: *-ɔ́h* 'desc.' (cf. **397**)
Obj. pref.: *ʔo-* 'neut.'

438. ʔɛ́ɔtisha:tɛt 'they (masc. pl.) will cause moisture to fall'

Vb. base: vb. rt. *-ɛ-* 'fall'; rt. suff. *-ʹht-* 'caus. I'; incorp. nn. rt. *-shat-* 'moisture'
Asp. suff.: *-∅* 'punc.'
Subj. pref.: *-ʹati-* 'they (masc. pl.)'
Mod. pref.: *ʔɛ-* 'fut.'

See also **10, 30, 36, 81, 93, 108, 112, 127, 362, 402.**

(147)

439. ʔoti:nekáhsɔnyeʔs 'they (nonmasc.) savor the water'

Vb. base: vb. rt. *-hsɔny-* 'savor'; incorp. nn. rt. *-ʹ:neka-* 'water'
Asp. suff.: *-éʔs* 'iter.'
Obj. pref.: *ʔoti-* 'they (nonmasc.)'

440. niwáhsɔ:ti:s 'how long the night is'

Vb. base: vb. rt. *-is-* 'be long'; incorp. nn. rt. *-ahsɔ(:)t-* 'night'
Asp. suff.: *-∅* 'desc.'
Subj. pref.: *-w-* 'neut.'
Sec. pref.: *ni-* 'part.'

441. ʔojihsɔʔtáhsi:aʔ 'the stars standing in array'

Vb. stem iden. with **421** except for lack of *-k* 'cont.'
Obj. pref.: *ʔo-* 'neut.'

See also **1, 6, 10, 30, 36, 81, 89, 108, 112, 127, 362, 381, 416.**

(148)

See **1, 6, 7, 10, 11, 70, 74, 75, 81, 96, 100, 102, 103, 176, 277, 375, 381, 436, 441.**

(149)

442. tɛshakonɛˀnyatɔ:ˀ 'they (masc.) will protect people'

> Vb. base: vb. rt. -t- 'stand'; rt. suff. -ɔ- 'dist.'; incorp. nn. rt. -ˀnya-
> 'hand'; -ɛ- 'refl.' (the entire base meaning 'protect')
> Asp. suff.: -ˀ 'punc.'
> Trans. pref.: -shakon- 'they (masc.) . . . people'
> Mod. pref.: -ɛ- 'fut.'
> Other pref.: t- 'dupl.'

See also 1–3, 7, 10, 11, 15, 20, 35–38, 116, 221, 299, 355.

(150)

443. taˀáyoska:stheˀt 'it can't be alone, doesn't work by itself'

> Coll. for teˀáyoska:stheˀt
> Vb. base: vb. rt. -oska- 'be only'; rt. suff. -st- 'caus.-inst.'; -héˀ- 'inch. I'
> Asp. suff.: -t 'punc.'
> Subj. pref.: -y- 'neut.'
> Mod. pref.: -ˀa- 'indic.'
> Other pref.: te- 'neg.'

444. hotiyaˀtóskaˀah 'only them (masc.), nothing but them'

> Vb. base: vb. rt. -oskáˀa- (variant of -oska-) 'be only'; incorp. nn. rt.
> -yáˀt- 'body'
> Asp. suff.: -ˀh 'desc.'
> Obj. pref.: hoti- 'them (masc.)'

445. taonɔtawénye:ak 'they (masc.) might continue to move about'

> Iden. with 264 except for mod. pref. -aa- [3.21] 'opt.'

See also 7, 49, 89, 399.

(151)

446. haˀte:yɔ:h 'everything'

> Vb. rt.: -ɔ- 'be a certain amount'
> Asp. suff.: -h 'desc.'
> Subj. pref.: -y- 'neut.'
> Other pref.: -te- 'dupl.; haˀ- 'transloc.'

447. niyotye:ɛh 'what's being done, is going on'

> Vb. base: vb. rt. -ye- 'do'; -at- 'refl.'
> Asp. suff.: -ɛh 'desc.'
> Obj. pref.: -yo- 'neut.'
> Sec. pref.: ni- 'part.'

448. yɔɛjata:tyeˀ 'along the earth'

> Vb. base: vb. rt. -t- 'be present'; incorp. nn. rt. -ɔeja- 'earth'
> Asp. suff.: -Ø- 'desc.'; -atye- 'prog.'; -ˀ 'desc.'
> Subj. pref.: y- 'neut.'

449. ʔɛthɛnɔtawɛnye:ʔ 'they (masc. pl.) will move about there'

>   Iden. with **19** except for subj. pref. -hɛn- 'they (masc. pl.)'

See also **6, 7, 10, 11, 36, 89.**

(152)

450. ka:teʔ 'it's there', with preceding particles 'it's right there, imminent'

>   Vb. rt.: -te- 'be present'
>   Asp. suff.: -ʔ 'desc.'
>   Subj. pref.: ka- 'neut.'

451. ʔɛyakotye:ɔʔ 'it will happen to people accidentally'

>   Vb. rt.: -atyeɔ- 'happen accidentally to'
>   Asp. suff.: -ʔ 'punc.'
>   Obj. pref.: -yako- 'fem.'
>   Mod. pref.: ʔɛ- 'fut.'

See also **10, 11, 15, 20, 41, 59, 191.**

(153)

452. ʔɛyakotí:watye:ɔʔ 'people will have accidents'

>   Vb. base: vb. rt. -atyeɔ- 'happen accidentally to'; incorp. nn. rt. -(C)í:w- 'matter'; -at- 'refl.'
>   Asp. suff.: -ʔ 'punc.'
>   Obj. pref.: -yako- 'fem.'
>   Mod. pref.: ʔɛ- 'fut.'

453. ʔɛthɛnɛʔnéoʔktɛʔ 'it will then be beyond their (masc. pl.) control'

>   Iden. with **338** except for subj. pref. -hɛn- 'their (masc. pl.)'

See also **10, 11, 15, 20, 41.**

(154)

454. twaiwakwáihsɔs 'we (incl. pl.) attest to it'

>   Iden. with **347** except for asp. suff. -ɔ́s 'iter.' and lack of mod. pref. ʔɛ- 'fut.'

See also **1, 6, 11, 15, 16, 30, 36, 46, 47, 89, 93, 337, 452, 453.**

(155)

455. ʔɔwɛnɔ́tkaɛɔʔ 'they will watch them (masc.)'

>   Vb. rt.: -atkáɛɔ- 'watch'
>   Asp. suff.: -ʔ 'punc.'
>   Trans. pref.: -ʔɔwɛn- 'they . . . them (masc.)'
>   Mod. pref.: ʔɛ- 'fut.'

456. hotɛ́hɔʔshɛʔ 'his helpers'

> Vb. base iden. with **355**.
> Asp. suff.: -ʼʔ 'desc.'
> Obj. pref.: *ho-* 'masc.'

457. nikɛ́tyohkwa:ke:h 'how many groups'

> Vb. base: vb. rt. *-ake-* 'be separate entities'; incorp. nn. rt. *-ityóhkw-* 'group'
> Asp. suff.: *-h* 'desc.'
> Subj. pref.: *-kɛ-* 'neut.'
> Sec. pref.: *ni-* 'part.'

See also **1, 10, 11, 46, 89, 95, 176, 233, 299, 436.**

(156)

458. tɛ́ɔtisnye:k 'they (masc. pl.) will continue to look after it'

> Vb. rt.: *-snye-* 'look after, attend to'
> Asp. suff.: *-Ø-* 'desc.'; *-k* 'cont.'
> Subj. pref.: -ʼ*ati-* 'they (masc. pl.)'
> Mod. pref.: *-ɛ-* 'fut.'
> Other pref.: *t-* 'dupl.'
> Cf. **219.**

459. shɔkwátkaʔwɛh 'he has left us (pl.)'

> Iden. with **127** except for trans. pref. *shɔkw-* 'he . . . us (pl.)'

460. ʔɛyɔkwaʔnikɔiyostáhkɔ:ɔk 'it will continue to content us (pl.)'

> Iden. with **290** except for asp. suff. *-ɔ́-* 'desc.'; *-ak* 'cont.'

See also **30, 81, 93.**

(157)

461. nyɛ:nɔti:h '(four) of them (masc. pl.) in all'

> Coll. for *nienɔti:h*
> Vb. base: vb. rt. *-i-* 'make up the total'; *-at-* 'refl.'
> Asp. suff.: *-h* 'desc.'
> Subj. pref.: -ʼ*ɛn-* 'they (masc. pl.)'
> Sec. pref.: *ni-* 'part.'

462. teyɔkhiyɛ́ʔnyatɔʔ 'they protect us'

> Vb. base iden. with **442**.
> Asp. suff.: -ʼʔ 'desc.'
> Trans. pref.: *-yɔkhiy-* 'they . . . us'
> Other pref.: *te-* 'dupl.'

See also **1, 30, 36, 96, 100, 176, 233, 277, 278, 299.**

(158)

See **1, 6, 7, 10, 11, 27, 30, 61, 62, 69, 70, 74, 75, 96, 103, 159, 160, 299, 375, 456, 461, 462.**

(159)

See **1, 2, 7, 30, 35–37, 76.**

(160)

463. nio⁷nikó⁷tɛ:h 'what the state of his mind was'

    Vb. base: vb. rt. *-ó⁷tɛ-* 'be in a certain state'; incorp. nn. rt. *-⁷nik-* 'mind'
    Asp. suff.: *-h* 'desc.'
    Obj. pref.: *-'o-* 'masc.'
    Sec. pref.: *ni-* 'part.'

See also **3, 6, 7, 10, 11, 36, 38, 89, 317, 337.**

(161)

464. sha⁷ka:t 'it's the same thing', here 'among'

    Coll. for *tsa⁷ka:t* [27.9]
    Vb. rt.: *-t-* 'stand'
    Asp. suff.: *-Ø* 'punc.'
    Subj. pref.: *-ka-* 'neut.'
    Mod. pref.: *-a⁷-* 'indic.'
    Sec. pref.: *ts-* 'coin.'

465. teyɔkwatawɛnyé:nɔ⁷ 'we (pl.) were moving about'

    Iden. with **16** except for addition of *-':n⁵⁷* 'past'

See also **7, 10, 11, 30, 81, 89, 93.**

(162)

466. waoye:nɔ:⁷ 'it took hold of him'

    Vb. rt.: *-yenɔ-* 'take hold of'
    Asp. suff.: *-⁷* 'punc.'
    Obj. pref.: *-'o-* 'masc.'
    Mod. pref.: *wa-* 'indic.'

467. wáonɔktanɛ:ta:k 'it confined him to bed'

    Vb. base: vb. rt. *-nɛtak-* 'attach'; incorp. nn. rt. *-nɔkta-* 'bed'
    Asp. suff.: *-Ø* 'punc.'
    Obj. pref.: *-'o-* 'masc.'
    Mod. pref.: *wa-* 'indic.'

See also **7, 10, 11, 56, 89.**

(163)

468. ⁷o⁷yóshæke:⁷ 'it was years'

    Vb. base: vb. rt. *-ake-* 'be separate entities'; incorp. nn. rt. *-oshæ-* 'winter, year'
    Asp. suff.: *-⁷* 'punc.'
    Subj. pref.: *-y-* 'neut.'
    Mod. pref.: *⁷o⁷-* 'indic.'

469. ta:ɛʔtákwɛhta:ʔ 'he lay helpless'

> Vb. base: vb. rt. -kwɛ́hta- 'lay flat'; incorp. nn. rt. -iʔta- 'feces' (as incorp.
> nn. rt. serves simply to intensify meaning)
> Asp. suff.: -ʔ 'desc.'
> Subj. pref.: -'ɛ- 'masc.'
> Mod. pref.: -aa- [3.21] 'opt.' [8.1, fn. 15]
> Other pref.: t- 'dupl.'

See also **7, 10, 11.**

(164)

470. ta:tɛnɔ́:nyɔ:ʔ 'he was thankful then'

> Vb. base: vb. rt. -nɔ́ɔnyɔ- 'thank'; -atɛ- 'refl.'
> Asp. suff.: -ʔ 'punc.'
> Subj. pref.: -'Ø- 'masc.'
> Mod. pref.: -a- 'indic.'
> Prim. pref.: t- 'cisloc.'

471. wahsɔtate:nyɔʔ 'nights'

> Vb. base: vb. rt. -te- 'be present'; rt. suff. -nyɔ- 'dist.'; incorp. nn. rt.
> -ahsɔta- 'night'
> Asp. suff.: -'ʔ 'desc.'
> Subj. pref.: w- 'neut.'

472. wɛ:níshæte:nyɔʔ 'days'

> Iden. with **471** except for nn. rt. -ɛ́:nishæ 'day'

473. sɔ:ka:ʔ 'someone'
474. hayáʔtateʔ 'he is there'

> Iden. with **306** except for subj. pref. ha- 'masc.'

475. hotkáthwɛ:ɔtyeʔ 'he was seeing it'

> Vb. rt.: -atkathw- 'see'
> Asp. suff.: -ɛ́- 'desc.'; -atye- 'prog.'; -'ʔ 'desc.'
> Obj. pref.: ho- 'masc.'

See also **1, 6, 7, 11, 36, 46, 47, 108, 281, 317, 322.**

(165)

476. tethácehaʔ 'he puts it on it there again, thereupon'

> Vb. rt.: -'(h)e- 'put on'
> Asp. suff.: -háʔ 'iter.'
> Subj. pref.: -ha- 'masc.'
> Prim. pref.: -t- 'cisloc.'
> Other pref.: te- 'dupl.'

477. shatathewáthaʔ 'he repents', lit. 'punishes himself again'

> Vb. base: vb. rt. -hewáht- 'punish'; -atat- 'recip.'
> Asp. suff.: -háʔ 'iter.'
> Subj. pref.: -h- 'masc.'
> Prim. pref.: s- 'repet.'

478. hoyέʔhihseʔs 'he comes to do wrong'

Vb. base: vb. rt.-yέʔhi- 'err'; rt. suff. -ʹhs- 'trans.'
Asp. suff.: -έʔs 'iter.'
Obj. pref.: ho- 'masc.'

479. to:tawε:nye:h 'he moved about'

Coll. for teotawε:nye:h
Iden. with 16 except for obj. pref. -ʹo- 'masc.'

See also 1, 6, 10, 11, 15, 36, 42, 46, 106, 108, 281.

(166)

480. to:tεnɔ́:nyɔʔ 'he was thankful'

Coll. for teotεnɔ́:nyɔʔ
Vb. base iden. with 470.
Asp. suff.: -ʹʔ 'desc.'
Obj. pref.: -ʹo- 'masc.'
Other pref.: te- 'dupl.'

481. tiʔkwah 'whatever'
482. wá:tkathoʔ 'he saw'

Vb. rt.: -atkathw- 'see'
Asp. suff.: -óʔ 'punc.'
Subj. pref.: -ʹØ- 'masc.'
Mod. pref.: wa- 'indic.'

See also 1, 10, 11, 57, 79, 89, 91, 422.

(167)

483. nɔʔɔ:wεh 'what happened'

Iden. with 337 except for mod. pref. -a- [3.14] 'indic.'

484. sεʔʒεh 'because, for what reason', here 'how'
485. niyakotye:εh 'how people acted'

Iden. with 447 except for obj. pref. -yako- 'fem.'

See also 1, 2, 6, 7, 10, 11, 15, 20, 35, 36, 42, 89, 399.

(168)

486. ʔa:yε:ʔ 'it seems, apparently'
487. teʔkátkaʔhoh 'nowhere'
488. teʔskayεtáhkɔh 'there is no longer any guidance'

Vb. base: vb. rt. -yεta- 'set down'; rt. suff. -ʹhkw- 'inst.'
Asp. suff.: -ɔ́h 'desc.'
Subj. pref.: -ka- 'neut.'
Prim. pref.: -s- 'repet.'
Other pref.: teʔ- 'neg.'

489. koˀníkɔɛˀ ‘people’s minds’

Iden. with **75** except for obj. pref. *ko-* ‘fem.’

See also **10, 11, 41, 49.**

(169)

490. thakɔyatɛ́nyehtɔh ‘he sent them here’

Vb. rt.: *-atɛnyeht-* ‘send’
Asp. suff.: *-ɔ́h* ‘desc.’
Trans. pref.: *-hakɔy-* ‘he . . . them’
Prim. pref.: *t-* ‘cisloc.’

491. hɔwɔwɛnɛ:ˀɔh ‘they told him’

Vb. rt.: *-wɛnɛɛˀ-* ‘tell’
Asp. suff.: *-ɔ́h* ‘desc.’
Trans. pref.: *hɔwɔ-* ‘they . . . him’

492. shetwakowa:nɛh ‘our (incl. pl.) great one’

Vb. rt.: *-kowanɛ-* ‘be great’
Asp. suff.: *-ˊh* ‘desc.’
Trans. pref.: *shetwa-* ‘we (incl. pl.) . . . him’

493. twatɔ́:k ‘we (incl. pl.) used to say’

Vb. rt.: *-atɔ-* ‘say’
Asp. suff.: *-ˊ∅-* ‘iter.’; *-ák* ‘past’
Subj. pref.: *twa-* ‘we (incl. pl.)’

494. kanyotaiyoˀ ‘Handsome Lake’

Vb. base: vb. rt. *-iyo-* ‘be beautiful’; incorp. nn. rt. *-nyota-* ‘lake’
Nn. suff.: *-ˊˀ* ‘spl. nn. suff.’ [26.4]
Subj. pref.: *ka-* ‘neut.’

495. tsaˀto:tawɛnye:h ‘when he moved about’

Coll. for *tsaˀteotawɛnye:h*
Iden. with **479** except for addition of sec. pref. *tsaˀ-* ‘coin.’

See also **1–3, 6, 10, 30, 456, 483.**

(170)

496. ˀɛtsɔ́kwa:owiˀ ‘he will tell us (pl.) again’

Vb. rt.: *-ˊ(hy)owi-* ‘tell’
Asp. suff.: *-ˊˀ* ‘punc.’
Trans. pref.: *-sɔkwa-* ‘he . . . us (pl.)’
Mod. pref.: *ˀɛ-* ‘fut.’
Prim. pref.: *-t-* ‘repet.’

497. nɛjakwayé:ɔk ‘how we (excl. pl.) shall continue to do it again’

Vb. rt.: *-ye-* ‘do’
Asp. suff.: *-ɛ́-* ‘desc.’; *-ak* ‘cont.’ (*-yé-ɛ-ak* occurring as *-yé:ɔk*)
Subj. pref.: *-yakwa-* ‘we (excl. pl.)’
Mod. pref.: *-ɛ-* ‘fut.’
Prim. pref.: *-[j]-* ‘repet.’
Sec. pref.: *n-* ‘part.’

498. ʔo:ɛtɔ́:kwa:h 'in the future'

> *ʔo:ɛtɔ:h* 'it is ahead' (335)
> Enclitic: *-kwah* 'toward'

See also **7, 10, 11, 42, 392.**

(171)

499. hothyówi:atyeʔ 'he was telling about it'

> Vb. base: vb. rt. *-ʼ(hy)owi-* 'tell'; *-at-* 'refl.' (cf. 85)
> Asp. suff.: *-ʼØ-* 'desc.'; *-atye-* 'prog.'; *-ʼʔ* 'desc.'
> Obj. pref.; *ho-* 'masc.'

500. nya:wɛnóʔtɛ:h 'the manner of his words'

> Coll. for *niawɛnóʔtɛ:h*
> Vb. base: vb. rt. *-óʔtɛ-* 'be of a certain kind'; incorp. nn. rt. *-wɛn-* 'word'
> Asp. suff.: *-h* 'desc.'
> Subj. pref.: *-ʼa-* 'masc.'
> Sec. pref.: *ni-* 'part.'

See also **1, 7, 10, 11, 35, 36, 468.**

(172)

501. niyóʔtɛ:ɔtyeʔ 'the way it was, went along'

> Vb. rt.: *-óʔtɛ-* 'be in a certain state'
> Asp. suff.: *-ʼØ-* 'desc.'; *-atye-* 'prog.'; *-ʼʔ* 'desc.'
> Subj. pref.: *-y-* 'neut.'
> Sec. pref.: *ni-* 'part.'

502. haʔtɔsa:yoskwɛ́hta:at 'he fell back to a prone position, collapsed'

> Vb. base: vb. rt. *-ɛ́htaæ-* [5.4] 'lay flat'; rt. suff. *-ʼht-* 'caus. I'; incorp.
> nn. rt. *-(h/:)yoskw-* 'belly'
> Asp. suff.: *-Ø* 'punc.'
> Subj. pref.: *-ʼa-* 'masc.'
> Mod. pref.: *-ɔ-a-* 'indic.'
> Prim. pref.: *-s-* 'repet.'
> Other pref.: *-t-* 'dupl.'; *haʔ-* 'transloc.'

503. hoɔyakɛ́ʔtɔ:ɔtyeʔs 'he was laboring'

> Vb. rt.: *-(y)ɔ́:yakɛ́ʔt-* 'force to labor'
> Asp. suff.: *-ɔ́-* 'desc.'; *-atye-* 'prog.'; *-ʼʔs* 'iter.'
> Obj. pref.: *ho-* 'masc.'

See also **1, 6, 7, 10, 36, 42, 304.**

(173)

504. nikɛɔtyeʔ 'how things go along in it, occasionally'

> Vb. base: vb. rt. *-(Cæ)-* 'put in'; rt. suff. *-ɔ-* 'dist.'
> Asp. suff.: *-Ø-* 'desc.'; *-tye-* 'prog'; *-ʼʔ* 'desc.'
> Subj. pref.: *-kɛ-* 'neut.'
> Sec. pref.: *ni-* 'part.'

505. sayókwathɔ:tɛh 'we (pl.) come to hear it again'

> Vb. base: vb. rt.-*athɔ(:)t-* 'hear'; rt. suff. *-ɛ́h-* 'inch II'
> Asp. suff.: *-Ø* 'punc.'
> Obj. pref.: *-yɔkw-* 'we (pl.)'
> Mod. pref.: *-a-* 'indic.'
> Prim. pref.: *s-* 'repet.'

See also 1, 2, 7, 10, 11, 35, 36, 42, 62, 89, 343, 500.

(174)

See 1, 6, 7, 10, 61, 62, 226–228.

(175)

506. ʔoʔtsakwanɔ́:nyɔ:ʔ 'we (excl. pl.) thank him'

> Vb. rt.: *-nɔ́ɔnyɔ-* 'thank'
> Asp. suff.: *-ʔ* 'punc.'
> Trans. pref.: *-sakwa-* 'we (excl. pl.) . . . him'
> Mod. pref.: *ʔoʔ-* 'indic.'
> Other pref.: *-t-* 'dupl.'
> Cf. 395.

507. ʔakwátɔ:k 'we (excl. pl.) used to say'

> Iden. with **493** except for subj. pref. *ʔakw-* 'we (excl. pl.)'

See also 1, 3, 6, 7, 11, 30, 70, 74, 75, 102, 494.

(176)

See 1, 2, 7, 35–37, 76.

(177)

508. nɔʔkɛ́ɔya:tih 'on which side of the sky'

> Vb. base: vb. rt. *-ati-* 'be on a certain side'; rt. suff. *-ʔh-* 'inch. II'; incorp.
> nn. rt. *-(y)ɔ́:y-* 'sky'
> Asp. suff.: *-Ø* 'punc.'
> Subj. pref.: *-kɛ-* 'neut.'
> Mod. pref.: *-aʔ-* 'indic.'
> Sec. pref.: *n-* 'part.'

509. hɛskíʔtyɔ:taʔk 'I shall continue to dwell there again'

> Vb. rt.: *-iʔtyɔ(:)ta-* 'dwell'
> Asp. suff.: *-ʔ* 'desc.'; *-k* 'cont.'
> Subj. pref.: *-k-* '1st pers.'
> Mod. pref.: *-ɛ-* 'fut.'
> Prim. pref.: *-s-* 'repet.'
> Other pref.: *h-* 'transloc.'

510. hɛjáko?ktha:k 'people will always come back to the end there'

> Vb. rt.: *-6?kt-* 'come to the end'
> Asp. suff.: *-h-* 'iter.'; *-ak* 'cont.'
> Subj. pref.: *-yak-* 'fem.'
> Mod. pref.: *-ɛ-* 'fut.'
> Prim. pref.: *-[j]* 'repet.'
> Other pref.: *h-* 'transloc.'

See also 3, 6, 7, 11, 15, 38, 67, 89, 154, 377.

(178)

511. ?ɛyakoyɛ:ta?k 'people will continue to have it'

> Vb. rt.: *-yɛta-* 'have'
> Asp. suff.: *-'?-* 'desc.'; *-k* 'cont.'
> Obj. pref.: *-yako-* 'fem.'
> Mod. pref.: *?ɛ-* 'fut.'

512. ?atɔ́?eshɔ:nyɔk 'gratitude'

> Vb. base: vb. rt. *-ɔ?es-* 'gratify'; rt. suff. *-ɔh-* 'dist.', *-nyɔ-* 'double dist.',
> *-'hkw-* 'inst.' *?at-* 'refl.' [15.6]
> Asp. suff.: *-∅-* 'impv.'

513. ?ɛyakotkáthwɛ:ɔtye? 'people will be seeing it'

> Vb. rt.: *-atkathw-* 'see'
> Asp. suff.: *-ɛ́-* 'desc.'; *-atye-* 'prog.'; *-'?* 'punc.'
> Obj. pref.: *-yako-* 'fem.'
> Mod. pref.: *?ɛ-* 'fut.'

514. ?ɛyotɔníatye? 'it will be growing'

> Vb. base iden. with **312.**
> Asp. suff.: *-'∅-* 'desc.'; *-atye-* 'prog.'; *-'?* 'punc.'
> Obj. pref.: *-yo-* 'neut.'
> Mod. pref.: *?ɛ-* 'fut.'

See also 6, 7, 10, 11, 36, 40, 46, 108, 117, 170, 171, 191.

(179)

515. tɛyɔtɛnɔ:nyɔ́:ɔk 'people will always be thankful'

> Iden. with **154** except for asp. suff. *-'∅-* 'iter.'; *-ak* 'cont.'

See also 3, 11, 14, 15, 20, 40, 116, 511.

(180)

516. ?ɛyɔ́hsaha:k 'people will always begin'

> Vb. rt.: *-ahsaw-* 'begin'
> Asp. suff.: *-h-* 'iter.'; *-ak* 'cont.'
> Subj. pref.: *-y[ɔ]-* 'fem.'
> Mod. pref.: *?ɛ-* 'fut.'

517. tayenɔ́:nyɔ:ɔk 'people always thank then'

> Vb. stem iden. with 515 except for lack of -atɛ- 'refl.'
> Subj. pref.: -ye- 'fem.'
> Mod. pref.: -a- 'indic.'
> Prim. pref.: t- 'cisloc.'

518. kotkáthwaʔɔh 'people have come to see it'

> Vb. base: vb. rt. -atkathwa- 'see'; rt. suff. -ʾʔ- 'inch. I'
> Asp. suff.: -ɔ́h 'desc.'
> Obj. pref.: ko- 'fem.'

See also **6, 36, 81, 82, 108.**

(181)

519. hɛyéahse:k 'people will always take it there'

> Vb. rt.: -ʾ(h)a- 'take'
> Asp. suff.: -hs- 'iter.'; -ek 'cont.'
> Subj. pref.: -ye- 'fem.'
> Mod. pref.: -ɛ- 'fut.'
> Other pref.: h- 'transloc.'

See also **6, 377, 509, 510.**

(182)

520. ʔɛwɔkathɔtehjí:wɛ:ɔk 'I shall continue to listen carefully'

> Vb. base: vb. rt. -athɔte- 'listen'; rt. suff. -hjɪ:w- 'intens.'
> Asp. suff.: -ɛ́- 'desc.'; -ak 'cont.'
> Obj. pref.: -wak- '1st pers.'
> Mod. pref.: ʔɛ- 'fut.'

521. ʔɛyeiwa:notátyeʔse:k 'people will always be saying, preaching',
lit. 'piling up words'

> Vb. base: vb. rt. -ʾ:nota- 'pile up'; incorp. nn. rt. -(C)i:wa-'matter, word'
> Asp. suff.: -∅- 'desc.'; -tye- 'prog.'; -ʾʔs- 'iter.'; -ek 'cont.'
> Subj. pref.: -ye- 'fem.'
> Mod. pref.: ʔɛ- 'fut.'

See also **3, 11, 20, 41.**

(183)

522. tɛkheka:næhji:wɛ́:ɔk 'I shall continue to watch them carefully'

> Vb. base: vb. rt. -ká:næ- 'see, watch'; rt. suff. -hjɪ:w- 'intens.'
> Asp. suff.: -ɛ́- 'desc.'; -ak 'cont.'
> Trans. pref.: -khe- 'I . . . them'
> Mod. pref.: -ɛ- 'fut.'
> Other pref.: t- 'dupl.'

523. nɛyakotyéːɔk 'how people will continue to act'

> Iden. with **485** except for addition of *-ak* 'cont.' and of mod. pref. *-ɛ-* 'fut.'

See also **10, 11, 15, 20, 36, 46, 89.**

(184)

See **1, 6, 7, 10, 11, 27, 30, 43, 69, 89, 96, 118.**

(185)

See **1, 6, 11, 27, 36, 46, 61, 62, 66, 68, 69.**

(186)

524. ʔakyɔːheʔ 'we (excl. pl.) are alive'

> Iden. with **37** except for subj. pref. *ʔaky-* 'we (excl. pl.)'

See also **1–3, 6, 7, 10, 11, 35, 36, 70, 71, 74, 75, 103, 159, 160, 506.**

(187)

525. niwátkwenyɔs 'what is possible'

> Vb. base: vb. rt. *-kweny-* 'be possible'; *-at-* 'refl.'
> Asp. suff.: *-ɔ́s* 'iter.'
> Subj. pref.: *-w-* 'neut.'
> Sec. pref.: *ni-* 'part.'

526. honeːʔɔh 'they (masc.) decided'

> Iden. with **38** except for obj. pref. *hon-* 'they (masc.)'

527. kaiwatéhkɔh 'usage, custom, ritual'

> Vb. base: vb. rt. *-te-* 'be present'; rt. suff. *-ʼhkw-* 'inst.'; incorp. nn. rt. *-(C)íːwa-* 'matter, ritual'
> Asp. suff.: *-ɔ́h* 'desc.'
> Subj. pref.: *ka-* 'neut.'

528. niwakeyɛ́ʔheʔɔh 'what I learned'

> Vb. base: vb. rt. *-y(C)ɛ-* 'know'; rt. suff. *-ʼʔhɛ́ʔ-* 'inch. I'
> Asp. suff.: *-ɔ́h* 'desc.'
> Obj. pref.: *-wake-* '1st pers.'
> Sec. pref.: *ni-* 'part.'

See also **1, 3, 6, 11, 18, 30, 36, 39, 42, 67, 124, 139, 191, 335, 346, 498.**

(188)

See **1, 6.**

Thanksgiving Dance

(189)

529. ʔoʔwa:tɔʔ 'it became'

> Vb. rt.: -atɔ́ʔ- 'become'
> Asp. suff.: -∅ 'punc.'
> Subj. pref.: -w- 'neut.'
> Mod. pref.: ʔoʔ- 'indic.'

530. hɔkatɔ́isyɔhkwa:ni:h 'they have requested me'

> Vb. base: vb. rt. -ɔisyɔ́hkwa- 'persist'; -at- 'refl.' (together meaning 'ask, request'); rt. suff. -ni- 'dat.'
> Asp. suff.: -h 'desc.'
> Trans. pref.: hɔk- 'they . . . me'

531. honɛ:ʔséshɛʔ 'they (masc.) are in opposite moieties'

> Vb. base: vb. rt. -ɛ- 'establish'; incorp. nn. base: -ɛɛʔse- 'be cousins'; -ʹsh- 'nom.'
> Asp. suff.: -ʹʔ 'desc.'
> Obj. pref.: hon- 'they (masc.)'

532. honɔ́ti:ɔt 'the Faith Keepers', lit. 'they (masc.) have the ceremonies on them, attached to them'

> Vb. base: vb. rt. -ɔ(:)t- 'attach'; incorp. nn. rt. -i- 'matter, ceremony'; -at- 'refl.'
> Asp. suff.: -∅ 'desc.'
> Obj. pref.: hon- 'they (masc.)'

See also **1–3, 11, 30, 60, 67, 233.**

(190)

533. hɛkayakéhtak 'it will go straight out'

> Vb. base: vb. rt. -yakɛ- 'take out'; rt. suff. -ʹhta- 'caus. I', -ʹhkw- 'inst.'
> Asp. suff. -∅ 'punc.'
> Subj. pref.: -ka- 'neut.'
> Mod. pref.: -ɛ- 'fut.'
> Other pref.: h- 'transloc.'

534. heyakwawɛnɔkwe:kɔh 'all our (excl. pl.) words'

> Vb. base: vb. rt. -kwek- 'be all of'; incorp. nn. rt. -wɛnɔ- 'word'
> Asp. suff.: -ɔ́h 'desc.'
> Subj. pref.: -yakwa- 'our (excl. pl.)'
> Other pref.: he- 'transloc.'

535. kyaʔta:teʔ 'my body is present'

> Vb. base: vb. rt. -te- 'be present'; incorp. nn. rt. -yáʔta- 'body'
> Asp. suff.: -ʹʔ 'desc.'
> Subj. pref.: k- '1st pers.'

536. niyáwɛʔɔh 'what happened'

> Vb. rt.: -ɛ́ʔ- 'happen'
> Asp. suff.: -ɔ́h 'desc.'
> Obj. pref.: -yaw- 'neut.'
> Sec. pref.: ni- 'part.'

See also 3, 6, 7, 42, 81, 274, 526.

(191)

537. katanitɛ:sthaʔ 'I plead forgiveness'

> Vb. base: vb. rt. -itɛ- 'show pity'; rt. suff. -st- 'caus.-inst.'; -atan- 'recip.' (the entire base meaning 'plead forgiveness')
> Asp. suff.: -hấʔ 'iter.'
> Subj. pref.: k- '1st pers.'

538. ʔɛyɔkwáiwɛʔs 'we (pl.) will inadvertently drop (part of) the ritual'

> Vb. base: vb. rt. -ɛ- 'fall'; rt. suff. -ʔs- 'dat.' (together, with obj. pref., meaning 'drop inadvertently'); incorp. nn. rt. -(C)i:w- 'matter, ritual'
> Asp. suff.: -∅ 'punc.'
> Obj. pref.: -yɔkwa- 'we (pl.)'
> Mod. pref.: ʔɛ- 'fut.'

539. heyawe:nɔ:h 'it goes there', here 'the way it goes'

> Vb. base: vb. rt. -e- 'go'; rt. suff. -n- 'direct.'
> Asp. suff.: -ɔh 'desc.'
> Obj. pref.: -yaw- 'neut.'
> Other pref.: he- 'transloc.'

540. sɛ:nɔh 'don't''

541. ʔáeswe:h 'you (pl.) might think'

> Vb. rt.: -e- 'think, believe'
> Asp. suff.: -h 'impv.'
> Subj. pref.: -sw- 'you (pl.)'
> Mod. pref.: ʔae- 'opt.' (rather than the usual fut. [8.5])

542. kwaʔ see 543.

543. tha:aye:ʔ with **kwaʔ** 'he did it intentionally'

> Vb. rt.: -ye- 'do'
> Asp. suff.: -ʔ 'punc.'
> Subj. pref.: -ʔa- 'masc.'
> Mod. pref.: -a- 'indic.'
> Sec. pref.: th- 'contr.'

544. swayɛte:ih 'you (pl.) know'

> Vb. rt.: -yetei- 'know'
> Asp. suff.: -h 'desc.'
> Subj. pref.: swa- 'you (pl.)'

545. sɛhkɛh see 546

546. thiyótɔʔɔh with **sɛhkeh** 'it isn't normal, isn't the way it should be'

> Vb. rt.: *-atɔ́ʔ-* 'become'
> Asp. suff.: *-ɔ́h* 'desc.'
> Obj. pref.: *-yo-* 'neut.'
> Sec. pref.: *thi-* 'contr.'

547. tewakyaʔtowehtɔ́:tyeʔs 'I am pondering along, my thoughts'

> Vb. base: vb. rt. *-oweht-* 'disturb'; incorp. nn. rt. *-yáʔt-* 'body' (together, with dupl., meaning 'ponder')
> Asp. suff.: *-ɔ́-* 'desc.'; *-atye-* 'prog.'; *-ʔʔs* 'iter.'
> Obj. pref.: *-wak-* '1st pers.'
> Other pref.: *te-* 'dupl.'

See also **1, 3, 6, 10, 11, 36, 52, 89, 191, 337, 472.**

(192)

548. ʔɛswáʔhɔtɛʔ 'you (pl.) will put it together', here 'fill it in'

> Vb. rt.: *-aʔhɔt-* 'put together'
> Asp. suff.: *-ɛ́ʔ* 'punc.'
> Subj. pref.: *-sw-* 'you (pl.)'
> Mod. pref.: *ʔɛ-* 'fut.'

549. tyɔ:kwah 'if'

550. nɛyɔkwayáʔtawɛh 'how it will happen to us (pl.)'

> Vb. base: vb. rt. *-wɛ́h-* 'happen'; incorp. nn. rt. *-yáʔta-* 'body'
> Asp. suff.; *-Ø* 'punc.'
> Obj. pref.: *-yɔkwa-* 'us (pl.)'
> Mod. pref.: *-ɛ-* 'fut.'
> Sec. pref.: *n-* 'part.'

551. ʔɛtyono:ɔʔ 'it will be deficient, have something lacking'

> Vb. rt.: *-noɔ-* 'be difficult', with obj. and cisloc. 'be deficient'
> Asp. suff.: *-ʔ* 'punc.'
> Obj. pref.: *-yo-* 'neut.'
> Mod. pref.: *ʔɛ-* 'fut.'
> Prim. pref.: *-t-* 'cisloc.'

552. heyóti:wi:nɔ:h 'the ritual goes there', here 'the way the ritual goes, progresses'

> Vb. base: vb. rt. *-in-* 'go somewhere'; incorp. nn. rt. *-(C)i:w-* 'matter' ritual'; *-at-* 'refl.'
> Asp. suff.: *-ɔh* 'desc.'
> Obj. pref.: *-yo-* 'neut.'
> Other pref.: *he-* 'transloc.'

553. swáiwayɛte:ih 'you (pl.) know the ritual'

> Iden. with **544** except for addition of incorp. nn. rt. *-(C)i:wa-* 'matter' ritual'

See also **1, 6, 10, 11, 52, 89, 191.**

(193)

554. takatyéɛhtak 'what I begin with'

> Vb. base: vb. rt. *-yeɛhta-* 'instigate'; rt. suff. *-'hkw-* 'inst.'; *-at-* 'refl.'
> Asp. suff.; *-Ø* 'punc.'
> Subj. pref.: *-k-* '1st pers.'
> Mod. pref.: *-a-* 'indic.'
> Prim. pref.: *t-* 'cisloc.'

555. wa:iˀ 'I thought, so far as I am concerned'

556. ˀɛkátɔ:isyɔk 'I will request'

> Vb. base: vb. rt. *-ɔisyɔhkw-* 'persist'; *-at-* 'refl.' (cf. **350**)
> Asp. suff.: *-Ø* 'punc.'
> Subj. pref.: *-k-* '1st pers.'
> Mod. pref.: *ˀɛ-* 'fut.'

557. ná:kɛ:ɔk 'it wouldn't be'

558. kwistɛˀ 'anything'

559. toˀóˀtɛ:h 'it isn't in that state'

> Coll. for *teˀóˀtɛ:h*
> Vb. rt.: *-óˀtɛ-* 'be in a certain state'
> Asp. suff.: *-h* 'desc.'
> Obj. pref.: *-ˀ-* 'neut.'
> Other pref.: *te-* 'neg.'

560. swaˀníkɔɛˀ 'your (pl.) minds'

> Iden. with **75** except for obj. pref. *swa-* 'your (pl.)'

See also **1, 3, 10, 42, 49.**

(194)

See **1, 7, 10, 30, 35–38, 78, 81, 82.**

(195)

561. shɔkyɔ:ni:h 'he made us (pl.)'

> Vb. rt.: *-ɔ(:)ni-* 'make'
> Asp. suff.: *-h* 'desc.'
> Trans. pref.: *shɔky-* 'he . . . us (pl.)'

See also **1, 6, 7, 10, 11, 16, 20, 89, 93, 459.**

(196)

562. nɔ:h 'perhaps, at least'

563. wɛ:níshæteˀ 'today'

> Iden. with **472** except for lack of *-nyɔ-* 'dist.'

564. né:waˀ 'the present time'

See also **1, 6, 7, 16, 27, 42, 66, 390.**

(197)

See **1, 6, 11, 30, 36, 46–53, 89.**

(198)

See **1, 5, 27, 36, 43, 69, 106, 317.**

(199)

565. twayɛte:ih 'we (incl. pl.) know'

> Iden. with **544** except for subj. pref. *twa-* 'we (incl. pl.)'

See also **7, 10, 11, 89, 106.**

(200)

566. teyɔkwatɛ́:nishæyɛtɔ⁷ 'all the days we (pl.) have'

> Vb. base: vb. rt. *-yɛt-* 'have'; rt. suff. *-ɔ-* 'dist.'; incorp. nn. rt. *-ɛ́:nishæ-*
> 'day'; *-at-* 'refl.'
> Asp. suff.: *-⁷* 'desc.'
> Obj. pref.: *-yɔkw-* 'we (pl.)'
> Other pref.: *te-* 'dupl.'

See also **7, 10, 11, 15, 16, 191.**

(201)

567. ⁷ɔkwaya⁷takɔhsótha⁷ 'we (pl.) remain'

> Iden. with **153** except for obj. pref. *⁷ɔkwa-* 'we (pl.)'

568. hɔsétwa:aho⁷ 'through another of our (incl. pl.) cycles, another
year'

> Vb. rt.: *-'(h)ahw-* 'go through a cycle'
> Asp. suff.: *-ó⁷* 'punc.'
> Subj. pref.: *-twa-* 'we (incl. pl.)'
> Mod. pref.: *-ɔ-e-* 'indic.'
> Prim. pref.: *-s-* 'repet.'
> Other pref.: *h-* 'transloc.' (usual with this rt.)

569. nyóiwa:ɔ⁷ 'how he has spaced the ceremonies'

> Coll. for *nióiwa:ɔ⁷*
> Vb. base: vb. rt. *-(C)-* 'put in'; rt. suff. *-ɔ-* 'dist.'; incorp. nn. rt. *-(C)i:wa-*
> 'matter, ceremony'
> Asp. suff.: *-⁷* 'desc.'
> Obj. pref.: *-'o-* 'masc.'
> Sec. pref.: *ni-* 'part.'

See also **1, 2, 7, 10, 11, 35–37, 62, 89, 203, 216, 220, 225.**

(202)

570. ʔɛyakoti:wahtɛtyaʔtɔ́:ɔk 'people will continue their ceremonies'

> Vb. base: vb. rt. -*ahtɛtya*- 'travel, continue'; rt. suff. -'*ʔt*- 'caus. I'; incorp.
> nn. rt. -(C)*i:w*- 'matter, ceremony'; -*at*- 'refl.'
> Asp. suff.: -*ɔ́*- 'desc.'; -*ak* 'cont.'
> Obj. pref.: -*yako*- 'fem.'
> Mod. pref.: *ʔɛ*- 'fut.'

See also 7, 10, 11, 15, 20, 127, 299, 300.

(203)

See 3, 6, 7, 10, 11, 36, 38, 40, 117, 170, 171, 191, 513, 515.

(204)

571. ʔatɔisyɔ́hkwaʔshæʔ 'request, hope'

> Nn. base: vb. rt. -*ɔistɔ́hkwa*- 'persist'; *ʔat*- 'refl.' (cf. 530); -*ʔshæ*- 'nom.'
> Nn. suff.: -'*ʔ* 'spl. nn. suff.'

See also 1, 3, 6, 11, 30, 36, 46, 109, 316, 512, 526, 533, 535.

(205)

572. tyɔkwa:yɔ:h 'we (pl.) entered here'

> Vb. rt.: -*yɔ*- 'arrive, enter'
> Asp. suff.: -*h* 'desc.'
> Obj. pref.: -*yɔkwa*- 'we (pl.)'
> Prim. pref.: *t*- 'cisloc.'

See also 1, 3, 46, 67, 70, 71, 221.

(206)

See 7, 27, 66, 69, 279.

(207)

See 1, 3, 6, 7, 11, 67, 70, 72–75, 102.

(208)

See 1, 2, 5, 42, 43.

(209)

See 6, 7, 10, 11, 20, 35–38, 78, 82.

(210)

See 3, 6, 42, 46, 79, 80, 82.

(211)

See 1, 3, 6, 7, 10, 11, 36, 38, 74, 83–85.

(212)

573. ˀɛyɔ́tɔːɔk 'people will continue to say'

Iden. with **86** except for subj. pref. -y[ɔ]- 'fem.'

See also **3, 6, 7, 10, 11, 30, 38, 84, 85, 87, 88, 117.**

(213)

574. ˀɔkwɛ́ːnishæːteˀ '(in) our (pl.) day'

Iden. with **563** except for obj. pref. *ˀɔkw-* 'our (pl.)'

575. hoˀtitwatawɛnyeːˀ 'we (incl. pl.) move about there'

Vb. stem iden. with **19.**
Subj. pref.: *-tw-* 'we (incl. pl.)'
Mod. pref.: *-oˀ-* 'indic.'
Other pref.: *-ti-* 'dupl.'; *h-* 'transloc.'

576. háɔɛjatatɔh 'he established the earth'

Vb. base iden. with **77.**
Asp. suff.: *-ɔ́h* 'desc.'
Obj. pref.: *ha-* 'masc.'

See also **1, 7, 10, 81, 89, 147.**

(214)

577. tɛyakotawɛnyéːak 'people will continue to move about'

Iden. with **41** except for addition of *-ak* 'cont.' to asp. suff. and of mod.
pref. *-ɛ-* 'fut.'

See also **10, 11, 36, 38, 82, 89, 147, 228.**

(215)

See **1, 7, 10, 11, 36, 89, 96, 98, 100, 101.**

(216)

578. ˀóiwakeːh 'separate responsibilities'

Iden. with **300** except for lack of sec. pref. *ni-* 'part.'

579. hoiwakháhsɔkwɛh 'he divided the responsibilities'

Vb. base: vb. rt. *-kháhs-* 'divide'; rt. suff. *-ɔkw-* 'oppos.I'; incorp. nn. rt
-(C)iːwa- 'matter, responsibility'
Asp. suff.: *-ɛ́h* 'desc.'
Obj. pref.: *ho-* 'masc.'

580. yeiwayɛ́tahkɔh 'her responsibility'

Iden. with **60** except for subj. pref. *ye-* 'fem.'

581. teyɔ́khisnye⁷ 'she is looking after us'

> Vb. rt.: -snye- 'look after'
> Asp. suff.: -'⁷ 'desc.'
> Trans. pref.: -yɔkhi- 'she . . . us'
> Other pref.: te- 'dupl.' (usual with this rt.)

See also **7, 10, 11, 15, 16, 42, 59.**

(217)

582. kaya:sɔh 'it is called', here 'it can be said, claimed' (cf. **66**)

> Vb. rt.: -yas- 'call'
> Asp. suff.: -ɔ́h 'desc.'
> Subj. pref.: ka- 'neut.'

See also **1, 6, 11, 42, 57, 118, 198, 311, 564.**

(218)

See **1, 3, 10, 11, 70, 71, 87, 88, 102, 103, 375.**

(219)

583. tɔtétwaɛ⁷ 'we (incl. pl.) say it here again'

> Vb. rt.: -'(h)ɛ- 'say'
> Asp. suff.: -'⁷ 'punc.'
> Subj. pref.: -twa- 'we (incl. pl.)'
> Mod. pref.: -ɔ-e- 'indic.'
> Prim. pref.: -t- 'cisloc.'
> Other pref.: t- 'dupl.'

584. wa⁷akwatɔ́isyɔk 'we (excl. pl.) ask'

> Vb. stem iden. with **556.**
> Subj. pref.: -⁷akw- 'we (excl. pl.)'
> Mod. pref.: wa- 'indic.'

585. hɛská:ho⁷ 'it will be another cycle, year'

> Vb. rt.: -'(h)ahw- 'go through a cycle' (cf. **568**)
> Asp. suff.: -ó⁷ 'punc.'
> Subj. pref.: -ka- 'neut.'
> Mod. pref.: -ɛ- 'fut.'
> Prim. pref.: -s- 'repet.'
> Other pref.: h- 'transloc.'

See also **1, 6, 10, 11, 30, 36, 46, 70, 71, 102, 109, 159, 316.**

(220)

586. ⁷ɔkwaya⁷tayéi⁷ɔh 'we (pl.) have gathered'

> Iden. with **5** except for asp. suff. -ɔ́h 'desc.' and lack of mod. pref. wa-
> 'indic.'

See also **1, 2, 42, 43.**

(221)

See **7, 10, 11, 35–38.**

(222)

587. ʔɛyɔtɔʔeshɔnyɔ́:ɔk 'people will always be grateful'

Iden. with **135** except for asp. suff. -'Ø- 'iter.'; -ak 'cont.'

See also **7, 10, 11, 15, 40, 41.**

(223)

588. ʔɛɔtiyáʔtate:k 'they (masc. pl.) will continue to be present'

Vb. base: vb. rt. -te- 'be present'; incorp. nn. rt. -yáʔta- 'body'
Asp. suff.: -Ø- 'desc.'; -k 'cont.'
Subj. pref.: -'ati- 'they (masc. pl.)'
Mod. pref.: ʔɛ- 'fut.'

589. hatikowa:nɛs 'the chiefs', lit. 'they (masc. pl.) are great'

Vb. rt.: -kowanɛ- 'be great'
Asp. suff.: -'s 'iter.'
Subj. pref.: hati- 'they (masc. pl.)'

See also **1, 3, 7, 10, 11, 30, 38, 233, 531.**

(224)

590. ʔɛkaiwayɛtáhkɔ:ɔk 'it will continue to be a responsibility'

Iden. with **60** except for addition of -ak 'cont.' and of mod. pref. ʔɛ- 'fut.'

591. koshɛnɔnyáshæʔ 'people's security'

Nn. rt.: -ashɛnɔnyáshæ- 'security'
Nn. suff.: -'ʔ 'spl. nn. suff.'
Obj. pref.: ko- 'fem.'

See also **3, 10, 11, 15, 30, 41, 59, 458.**

(225)

592. ʔo:ti:weʔnɔní:ak 'they (masc.) will continue to make it round, roll it up'

Coll. for ʔeoti:weʔnɔní:ak
Vb. rt.: -:weʔnɔ(:)ni- 'make round'
Asp. suff.: -'Ø- 'desc.'; -ak 'cont.'
Obj. pref.: -'oti- 'they (masc.)'
Mod. pref.: ʔɛ- 'fut.'

593. honítyohkwaʔ 'their (masc.) group, the people'

Nn. rt.: -ityóhkwa- 'group'
Nn. suff.: -'ʔ 'spl. nn. suff.'
Obj. pref.: hon- 'their (masc.)'

See also **10, 11, 60, 176, 274.**

(226)

594. heyáoska:ˀah 'all it is'

> Vb. rt.: -oskaˀa- 'be only'
> Asp. suff.: -ʼh 'desc.'
> Obj. pref.: -ya- 'neut.'
> Other pref.: he- 'transloc.'

595. thakɔyawi:h 'he gave it to them'

> Vb. rt.: -awi- 'give'
> Asp. suff.: -h 'desc.'
> Trans. pref.: -hakɔy- 'he . . . them'
> Prim. pref.: t- 'cisloc.' (here indicates 'give temporarily, hand to')

See also **3, 10, 11, 59, 295.**

(227)

596. tɛɔtiˀnyæ:hkɔ́:ɔk 'they (masc. pl.) will continue to look after it'

> Vb. base: vb. rt. -(C)æ- 'put in'; rt. suff. -ʼhkw- 'inst.'; incorp. nn. rt.
> -ˀnya- [5.4] 'hand' (the entire base meaning 'look after')
> Asp. suff.: -ɔ́- 'desc.'; -ak 'cont.'
> Subj. pref.: -ʼati- 'they (masc. pl.)'
> Mod. pref.: -ɛ- 'fut.'
> Other pref.: t- 'dupl.'

597. ˀa:yɛnɔhtɔnyɔ́:ɔk 'people might always think'

> Iden. with **28** except for addition of -ak 'cont.' and of mod. pref. ˀaa-
> 'opt.'

See also **6, 7, 10, 11, 27, 42, 59, 76, 95, 593.**

(228)

598. hatíhsi:aˀ 'they (masc. pl.) are standing in array, in an organized group'

> Vb. rt.: -hsia- 'stand in array'
> Asp. suff.: -ˀ 'desc.'
> Subj. pref.: hati- 'they (masc. pl.)'

See also **1, 7, 11, 30, 118, 198, 233, 531, 589.**

(229)

See **6, 11, 36, 89, 100, 346, 436.**

(230)

599. tyáwɛˀɔh 'at all times'

600. tá:ti'nya:? 'they (masc. pl.) are looking after it'

    Coll. for *téati?nya:?*
    Vb. base: vb. rt. -(*C*)- 'put in'; incorp. nn. rt. -*?nya*- 'hand' (cf. **596**)
    Asp. suff.: -*?* 'desc.'
    Subj. pref.: -*'ati*- 'they (masc. pl.)'
    Other pref.: *te*- 'dupl.'

601. yekɛhjishɔ́'ɔh 'the old people'

    Vb. rt.: -*kɛ́hji*- 'be old'
    Asp. suff.: -*∅*- 'desc.'
    Subj. pref.: *ye*- 'fem.'
    Attr. suff.: -*shɔ́?ɔh* 'plur.'

602. yeksá'shɔ'ɔh 'the children'

    Nn. rt.: -*ksa*- 'child'
    Nn. suff.: -*'?*- 'spl. nn. suff.'
    Subj. pref.: *ye*- 'fem.'
    Attr. suff.: -*shɔ́?ɔh* 'plur.'

603. tayékɔhsɔtatye? 'those yet unborn', lit. 'people's faces attached all along'

    Vb. base: vb. rt. -*ɔt*- 'attach'; incorp. nn. rt. -*kɔ́hs*- 'face'
    Asp. suff.: -*∅*- 'desc.'; -*atye*- 'prog.'; -*'?* 'punc.'
    Subj. pref.: -*ye*- 'fem.'
    Mod. pref.: -*a*- 'indic.'
    Prim. pref.: *t*- 'cisloc.'

See also **7, 10, 11, 27, 30, 46, 95, 226, 597.**

(231)

604. to:nɔtí'stya'kɔh 'they (masc.) do the talking'

    Coll. for *teonɔtí?stya?kɔh*
    Vb. base: vb. rt. -*yá?k*- 'break'; incorp. nn. rt. -*i?st*- 'noise'; -*at*- 'refl.'
    (the entire base meaning 'do the talking')
    Asp. suff.: -*ɔh* 'desc.'
    Obj. pref.: -*'on* 'they (masc.)'.
    Other pref.: *te*- 'dupl.'

605. 'ɛyakoyá'taye:ih 'people will gather'

    Vb. stem iden. with **5.**
    Obj. pref.: -*yako*- 'fem.'
    Mod. pref.: *?ɛ*- 'fut.'

606. kaeti'kwá:ɔweh 'wherever, anywhere'
See also **1, 10, 11, 30, 46, 89.**

(232)

607. hotí:we'nɔ:ni:h 'they (masc.) have rolled it up'

    Iden. with **592** except for lack of -*ak* 'cont.' and of mod. pref. *?ɛ*- 'fut.'

608. nyo:tikwe:nyɔ:h 'what is possible for them (masc.)'

 Coll. for *niotikwe:nyɔ:h*
 Vb. rt.: *-kweny-* 'be possible'
 Asp. suff.: *-ɔh* 'desc.'
 Obj. pref.: *-'oti-* 'them (masc.)'
 Sec. pref.: *ni-* 'part.'

See also **10, 11, 36, 489, 593.**

(233)

609. hotíkeɔtatyeʔs 'they (masc.) keep laying it down'

 Vb. rt.: *-kéɔt-* 'lay down'
 Asp. suff.: *-Ø-* 'desc.'; *-atye-* 'prog.'; *-'ʔs* 'iter.'
 Obj. pref.: *hoti-* 'they (masc.)'

See also **10, 11, 27, 42, 95, 597.**

(234)

See **1, 7, 10, 11, 35, 38.**

(235)

610. teɔtiyenɔwɔ́ʔkhɔ:k 'they (masc. pl.) will continue to help each other'

 Vb. rt.: *-yenɔwɔ́ʔkhɔ-* 'hold onto', with dupl. 'work together'
 Asp. suff.: *-Ø-* 'desc.'; *-k* 'cont.'
 Subj. pref.: *-'ati-* 'they (masc. pl.)'
 Mod. pref.: *-ɛ-* 'fut.'
 Other pref.: *t-* 'dupl.'

See also **3, 10, 11, 42, 59, 233, 531, 532, 590.**

(236)

611. ʔɛ́ɔta:ayɛ:ʔ 'he will whisper'

 Vb. rt.: *-atáayɛ-* 'whisper'
 Asp. suff.: *-ʔ* 'punc.'
 Subj. pref.: *-'Ø-* 'masc.'
 Mod. pref.: *ʔɛ-* 'fut.'

612. hotí:ɔt 'the Faith Keeper'

 Iden. with **532** except for obj. pref. *ho-* 'masc.'

613. tɛʔɛ́tiʔkwah 'whatever'

614. hɛníʔtyɔʔ 'they (masc. pl.) stay, are there'

 Vb. rt.: *-iʔtyɔ-* 'stay'
 Asp. suff.: *-'ʔ* 'desc.'
 Subj. pref.: *hɛn-* 'they (masc. pl.)'

See also **3, 6, 10, 11, 36, 42, 422, 463, 589.**

(237)

615. kɛtyóhkwaɛh 'in the middle of the group, in public'

> Vb. base: vb. rt. -ʻ(h)ɛ- 'be in the middle of'; incorp. nn. rt. -ityóhkwa- 'group'
> Asp. suff.: -ʻh 'desc.'
> Subj. pref.: kɛ- 'neut.'

616. ʔó:thæ:k 'he will be the speaker'

> Coll. for ʔéothæ:k
> Vb. rt.: -thaæ- 'speak'; rt. suff. -ʻhkw- 'inst.'
> Asp. suff.: -∅ 'punc.'
> Obj. pref.: -ʻo- 'masc.'
> Mod. pref.: ʔɛ- 'fut.'

617. hakowanɛh 'the chief'

> Iden. with **589** except for asp. suff. -ʻh 'desc.' and subj. pref. ha- 'masc.'

See also **3, 10, 11, 30, 60.**

(238)

See **1, 6, 7, 47, 89, 198, 298, 565.**

(239)

618. hotitakwâihsɔ:h 'they (masc.) have set it straight'

> Vb. rt.: -takwaths- 'set straight'
> Asp. suff.: -ɔh 'desc.'
> Obj. pref.: hoti- 'they (masc.)'

See also **10, 11, 36, 47, 97, 227, 299, 300, 589.**

(240)

See **1, 7, 10, 11, 89, 97, 117, 197, 227.**

(241)

619. nya:wɛh 'thanks, thank you'
See also **1, 3, 11, 30, 89, 226, 233, 276, 589.**

(242)

See **1, 3, 10, 11, 584.**

(243)

620. ʔaotiyaʔtakɔhsótha:k 'they (masc.) might continue to remain'

> Vb. base iden. with **65.**
> Asp. suff.: -h- 'iter.'; -ak 'cont.'
> Obj. pref.: -ʻoti- 'they (masc.)'
> Mod. pref.: ʔaa- 'opt.'

See also **11, 30, 36, 109, 159, 316, 585.**

(244)

621. tayɔkwawɛnitkɛ́ʔɔːɔtyeʔ 'we (pl.) are speaking along'

> Vb. base: vb. rt. *-itkɛ-* 'emerge'; rt. suff. *-'ʔ-* 'inch. I'; incorp. nn. rt. *-wɛn-* 'word'
> Asp. suff.; *-ɔ́-* 'desc.'; *-atye-* 'prog.'; *-'ʔ* 'punc.'
> Obj. pref.: *-yɔkwa-* 'we (pl.)'
> Mod. pref.: *-a-* 'indic.'
> Prim. pref.: *t-* 'cisloc.'

See also **1, 2, 7, 30, 40, 90, 512.**

(245)

622. tsaːyɛnɛːtaʔt 'when he finished the creation'

> Vb. base: vb. rt. *-ɛtáʔ-* 'finish'; incorp. nn. rt. *-yɛn-* 'creation'
> Asp. suff.: *-t* 'punc.'
> Subj. pref.: *-'a-* 'masc.'
> Mod. pref.: *-a-* 'indic.'
> Sec. pref.: *ts-* 'coin.'

See also **1, 2, 7, 11, 30, 35, 81, 84, 93, 117.**

(246)

See **1, 3, 7, 10, 11, 38, 355.**

(247)

See **11, 20, 30, 41, 81, 93, 464.**

(248)

623. ʔɛɔtiːwakéskwahseːk 'they (masc. pl.) will always get up the ceremonies'

> Vb. base: vb. rt. *-keskw-* 'raise'; incorp. nn. rt. *-(C)iːwa-* 'matter, ceremony, etc.'
> Asp. suff.: *-áhs-* 'iter.'; *-ek* 'cont.'
> Subj. pref.: *-'ati-* 'they (masc. pl.)'
> Mod. pref.: *ʔɛ-* 'fut.'

624. ʔoʔkatatiːwakéːɔs 'I laid down the ceremonies for myself'

> Vb. base: vb. rt. *-kéɔ-* 'lay down'; incorp. nn. rt. *-(C)iːwa-* 'matter, ceremony'; *-atat-* 'recip.'
> Asp. suff.: *-s* 'iter.'
> Subj. pref.: *-k-* '1st pers.'
> Mod. pref.: *ʔoʔ-* 'indic.'

See also **3, 6, 7, 10, 11, 59, 117, 299, 300, 590.**

(249)

625. twaːtɔh 'we (incl. pl.) say'

> Iden. with **233** except for subj. pref. *tw-* 'we (incl. pl.)'

See also **1, 7, 10, 11, 30, 531, 532.**

(250)

626. hotá'ɛnɔ:te' 'his pole is there'

> Vb. base: vb. rt. *-te-* 'be present'; incorp. nn. rt. *-a'ɛnɔ-* 'pole'; *-at-* 'refl.'
> Asp. suff.: *-'ʔ* 'desc.'
> Obj. pref.: *ho-* 'masc.'

See also **6, 7, 10, 11, 35, 42, 198, 598.**

(251)

627. taoti:wayeistɔ́:tye' 'they (masc.) are accomplishing their task'

> Vb. base iden. with **98.**
> Asp. suff.: *-ɔ́-* 'desc.'; *-atye-* 'prog'; *-'ʔ* 'punc.'
> Obj. pref.: *-'oti-* 'they (masc.)'
> Mod. pref.: *-a-* 'indic.'
> Prim. pref.: *t-* 'cisloc.'

628. hɔsakaiwaihsɔ́:ne' 'the ceremonies come to spill out again, are due'

> Vb. base: vb. rt. *-'(h)i-* 'spill'; rt. suff. *-'hsɔ-* 'dist.', *-':n-* 'trans.'; incorp. nn. rt. *-(C)i:wa-* 'matter, ceremony'
> Asp. suff.: *-ɛ́ʔ* 'purp.'
> Subj. pref.: *-ka-* 'neut.'
> Mod. pref.: *-ɔ-a-* 'indic.'
> Prim. pref.: *-s-* 'repet.'
> Other pref.: *h-* 'transloc.'

629. wa:ɛne:' 'they (masc. pl.) decide'

> Vb. rt.: *-e-* 'think, decide'
> Asp. suff.: *-ʔ* 'punc.'
> Subj. pref.: *-'ɛn-* 'they (masc. pl.)'
> Mod. pref.: *wa-* 'indic.'

630. ho'tkaye:ih 'it is the proper thing', here 'proper time'

> Vb. base: vb. rt. *-yei-* 'be proper'; rt. suff. *-'h-* 'inch. II'
> Asp. suff.: *-Ø* 'punc.'
> Subj. pref.: *-ka-* 'neut.'
> Mod. pref.: *-oʔ-* 'indic.'
> Other pref.: *-t-* 'dupl.'; *h-* 'transloc.'

See also **2, 10, 11, 89.**

(252)

631. wa:ti:wakésko' 'they (masc. pl.) get up the ceremony'

> Vb. base iden. with **623.**
> Asp. suff.: *-ɔ́ʔ* 'punc.'
> Subj. pref.: *-'ati-* 'they (masc. pl.)'
> Mod. pref.: *wa-* 'indic.'

632. honɔtwɛníhsaʔɔh 'they (masc.) announce it', lit. 'complete their word'

> Vb. base: vb. rt. *-ihsáʔ-* 'complete'; incorp. nn. rt. *-wɛn-* 'word'; *-at-* 'refl.'
> Asp. suff.: *-ɔ́h* 'desc.'
> Obj. pref.: *hon-* 'they (masc.)'

633. tetkáiwayɛɔni:h 'a ceremony is then indicated'

> Vb. base: vb. rt. *-yɛɔni-* 'indicate'; nn. rt. *-(C)í:wa-* 'matter, ceremony'
> Asp. suff.: *-h* 'desc.'
> Subj. pref.: *-ka-* 'neut.'
> Prim. pref.: *-t-* 'cisloc.'
> Other pref.: *te-* 'dupl.'

See also **1, 2, 7, 10, 30, 103, 422, 613.**

(253)

634. taoti:wakéskwɛ:ɔtyeʔ 'they (masc.) are getting up the ceremonies'

> Vb. base iden. with **623.**
> Asp. suff.: *-ɛ́-* 'desc.'; *-atye-* 'prog.'; *-ʼʔ* 'punc.'
> Obj. pref.: *-ʼoti-* 'they (masc.)'
> Mod. pref.: *-a-* 'indic.'
> Prim. pref.: *t-* 'cisloc.'

See also **1, 7, 11, 30, 89, 233, 532.**

(254)

635. nikaye:ɛh 'how it is done'

> Vb. rt.: *-ye-* 'do'
> Asp. suff.: *-ɛ́h* 'desc.'
> Subj. pref.: *-ka-* 'neut.'
> Sec. pref.: *ni-* 'part.'

636. tsaʔtetkáɛɔ:teʔ 'the trees are of equal height'

> Vb. base: vb. rt. *-te-* 'be present'; incorp. nn. rt. *-ʼ(h)ɛɔ-* 'tree'
> Asp. suff.: *-ʼʔ* 'desc.'
> Subj. pref.: *-ka-* 'neut.'
> Prim. pref.: *-t-* 'cisloc.'
> Sec. pref.: *tsaʔ-* 'coin.'
> Other pref.: *-te-* 'dupl.'

See also **6, 7, 10, 11, 30, 176, 233, 531, 532.**

(255)

637. tɛkawɛnɔʔtihéʔseʔ 'there will be consent'

> Vb. base: vb. rt. *-aʔtí-* 'lean'; rt. suff. *-héʔ-* 'inch. I', *-se-* 'dat.'; incorp. nn. rt. *-wɛn-* 'word' (the entire base meaning 'be in agreement')
> Asp. suff.: *-ʼʔ* 'punc.'
> Subj. pref.: *-ka-* 'neut.'
> Mod. pref.: *-ɛ-* 'fut.'
> Other pref.: *t-* 'dupl.'

638. ?otyæ:?táhkɔh 'it uses it', here 'shown toward'

Iden. with **90** except for obj. pref. *?o-* 'neut.'

639. kɛtyóhkwani:yɔ:t 'the dependent group', lit. 'hanging group'

Vb. base: vb. rt. *-niyɔ(:)t-* 'hang'; incorp. nn. rt. *-ityóhkwa-* 'group'
Asp. suff.: *-∅* 'desc.'
Subj. pref.: *kɛ-* 'neut.'

640. ta?ákwistɛ? 'nothing'

641 te?kaiɔ́tahkɔh 'it is not an assigned responsibility'

Vb. base: vb. rt. *-ɔta-* 'attach, assign'; rt. suff. *-'hkw-* 'inst.'; incorp'
nn. rt.-*(C)i-* 'matter, responsibility' (cf. **101**)
Asp. suff.: *-ɔ́h* 'desc.'
Subj. pref.: *-ka-* 'neut.'
Other pref.: *te?-* 'neg.'

See also **1, 6, 7, 10, 11, 30, 233, 531, 532.**

(256)

642. ha?ta:tiyenɔ́wɔ?khɔ? 'they (masc. pl.) all work together'

Coll. for *ha?teatiyenɔ́wɔ?khɔ?*
Vb. rt.: *-yenɔwɔ?khɔ-* 'hold onto' (cf. **610**)
Asp. suff.: *-'?* 'desc.'
Subj. pref.: *-'ati-* 'they (masc. pl.)'
Other pref.: *-te-* 'dupl.'; *ha?-* 'transloc.'

643. tɛɔtiyá?to:we:t 'they (masc. pl.) will deliberate'

Vb. base iden. with **547.**
Asp. suff.: *-∅* 'punc.'
Subj. pref.: *-'ati-* 'they (masc. pl.)'
Mod. pref.: *-ɛ-* 'fut.'
Other pref.: *t-* 'dupl.'

644. hɛ:ne:h 'they (masc. pl.) think'

Iden. with **96** except for subj. pref. *hɛn-* 'they (masc. pl.)'

645. ho?ká:e? 'the time arrives'

Vb. rt.: *-'(h)e-* 'arrive (of time)'
Asp. suff.: *-?* 'punc.'
Subj. pref.: *-ka-* 'neut.'
Mod. pref.: *-o?-* 'indic.'
Other pref.: *h-* 'transloc.'

See also **2, 10, 11, 35, 84, 159, 569.**

(257)

646. tayohtɛtyɔ́:tye? 'it is operating'

Vb. rt.: *-ahtɛty-* 'travel, operate'
Asp. suff.: *-ɔ́-* 'desc.'; *-atye-* 'prog.'; *-'?* 'punc.'
Obj. pref.: *-yo-* 'neut.'
Mod. pref.: *-a-* 'indic.'
Prim. pref.: *t-* 'cisloc.'

See also **1, 6, 7, 10, 11, 47, 89.**

(258)

See 10, 11, 36, 100, 436, 627.

(259)

See 6, 30, 36, 118, 176, 436.

(260)

See 1, 6, 7, 36, 61, 62, 198, 226–228.

(261)

647. tɛ:nɔtɛ́nɔ:ɔnyɔh 'they (masc. pl.) give thanks'

     Coll. for *teɛnɔtɛ́nɔ:ɔnyɔh*
     Vb. base: vb. rt. *-nɔ́ɔnyɔ-* 'thank'; *-atɛ-* 'refl.'
     Asp. suff.: *-'h* 'iter.'
     Subj. pref.: *-'ɛn-* 'they (masc. pl.)'
     Other pref.: *te-* 'dupl.'

648. hekɛ́tyohkwakwe:kɔh 'the entire group'

     Vb. base: vb. rt. *-kwek-* 'be all of'; incorp. nn. rt. *-ityóhkwa-* 'group'
     Asp. suff.: *-ɔ́h* 'desc.'
     Subj. pref.: *-kɛ-* 'neut.'
     Other pref.: *he-* 'transloc.'

See also 1, 3, 11.

(262)

See 6, 30, 36, 153, 198, 221, 226, 233, 531, 532, 598, 627.

(263)

See 1, 3, 10, 11, 191, 584.

(264)

See 11, 30, 36, 42, 109, 159, 263, 316, 585.

(265)

See 1, 2, 7, 40, 90, 512, 621.

(266)

See 1, 2, 7, 11, 35–38.

(267)

649. ʔɛkhéyatkaʔ 'I shall leave them'

  Vb. rt.: -atka- 'leave, provide'
  Asp. suff.: -ʔʔ 'punc.'
  Trans. pref.: -khey- 'I . . . them'
  Mod. pref.: ʔɛ- 'fut.'

See also **3, 10, 11, 30, 176, 226, 233, 373, 640, 641.**

(268)

See **6, 16, 81, 93, 459.**

(269)

650. tsaʔtetwayɛte:ih 'we (incl. pl.) all know at the same time'

  Vb. rt.: -yɛtei- 'know'
  Asp. suff.: -h 'desc.'
  Subj. pref.: -twa- 'we (incl. pl.)'
  Sec. pref.: tsaʔ- 'coin.'
  Other pref.: -te- 'dupl.'

651. nikawɛnóʔtɛ:h 'what kind of word it is'

  Vb. base: vb. rt. -óʔtɛ- 'be of a certain kind'; incorp. nn. rt. -wɛn- 'word'
  Asp. suff.: -h 'desc.'
  Subj. pref.: -ka- 'neut.'
  Sec. pref.: ni- 'part.'

See also **1, 6, 7, 27, 36, 59, 89, 191.**

(270)

652. haʔtetwayenɔwóʔkhɔʔ 'we (incl. pl.) all work together'

  Iden. with **642** except for subj. pref. -twa- 'we (incl. pl.)'

653. heyoti:wáhtɛtyɔ:h 'the ceremony goes on'

  Vb. base: vb. rt. -ahtɛty- 'travel, go on'; incorp. nn. rt. -(C)i:w- 'matter,
    ceremony'; -at- 'refl.'
  Asp. suff.: -ɔh 'desc.'
  Obj. pref.: -yo- 'neut.'
  Other pref.: he- 'transloc.'

See also **7, 10, 11, 30, 159, 233, 422, 481, 640, 641.**

(271)

654. kɛtyóhkota:tyeʔs 'the group is standing about'

  Vb. base: vb. rt. -ot- 'stand upright'; incorp. nn. rt. -ityóhkw- 'group'
  Asp. suff.: -Ø- 'desc.'; -atye- 'prog.'; -ʔʔs 'iter.'
  Subj. pref.: kɛ- 'neut.'

See also **1, 10, 11, 57, 89, 176, 198.**

(272)

655. ʔonɔ́thɔwi:sɛh 'the women'

> Vb. rt.: *-athɔwis-* 'sing *thɔwi:sas* (a women's dance), be a woman'
> Asp. suff.: *-ɛ́h* 'desc.'
> Obj. pref.: *ʔon-* 'they (nonmasc.)'

See also **11, 30, 46, 226, 233, 234, 640, 641.**

(273)

See **1, 10, 11, 57, 89, 96, 97, 176, 227.**

(274)

See **11, 30, 35, 36, 228.**

(275)

See **1, 3, 30, 89, 198, 226, 233, 275, 619, 640, 641.**

(276)

656. tɔtayakwáɛʔ 'we (excl. pl.) say it here again'

> Iden. with **583** except for subj. pref. *-yakwa-* 'we (excl. pl.)'

See also **1, 3, 10, 11, 36, 40, 159, 263, 584, 585.**

(277)

See **1, 7, 40, 512, 621.**

(278)

See **11, 30, 35–37, 117.**

(279)

657. hatiksaʔshɔ́ʔɔh 'the children'

> Iden. with **602** except for subj. pref. *hati-* 'they (masc. pl.)'

658. ʔɛɔtitakhenɔ́tyeʔse:k 'they (masc. pl.) will always be running about'

> Iden. with **242** except for addition of *-ek* 'cont.' and of mod. pref. *ʔɛ-* 'fut.'

659. tetwayaʔtókɛshɔʔ 'among us (incl. pl.)'

> Vb. base: vb. rt. *-okɛ-* 'be between, among'; incorp. nn. rt. *-yáʔt-* 'body'
> Asp. suff.: *-Ø-* 'desc.'
> Subj. pref.: *-twa-* 'us (incl. pl.)'
> Other pref.: *te-* 'dupl.' (usual with this vb. rt.)
> Attr. suff.: *-shɔ́ʔ* 'plur.'

See also **3, 7, 10, 11, 38.**

(280)

660. ʔɛyɔtaʔkɛiʔsenɔtyéʔse:k 'they will always be crawling about', lit. 'dragging the dust'

    Vb. base: vb. rt. *-iʔse-* 'drag'; rt. suff. *-nɔ-* 'dist.'; incorp. nn. rt. *-aʔkɛ́-* 'dust, ashes'; *-at-* 'refl.'
    Asp. suff.: *-Ø-* 'desc.'; *-tye-* 'prog.'; *-ʔs* 'iter.'; *-ek* 'cont.'
    Subj. pref.: *-y[ɔ]-* 'fem.'
    Mod. pref.: *ʔɛ-* 'fut.'

See also **3, 10, 11, 659.**

(281)

See **1, 7, 10, 11, 89, 198.**

(282)

661. teyethiká:ne:ʔ 'we (incl.) see them'

    Iden. with **240** except for trans. pref. *-yethi-* 'we (incl.) . . . them'

662. ʔɔkwáksaʔtaʔ 'our (pl.) children'

    Nn. rt.: *-ksáʔta-* 'child'
    Nn. suff.: *-ʔ* 'spl. nn. suff.'
    Obj. pref.: *ʔɔkwa-* 'our (pl.)'

See also **30, 36, 118, 242, 659.**

(283)

663. yɔtaʔkɛiʔsenɔ:tyeʔs 'they are crawling about'

    Iden. with **660** except for lack of *-ek* 'cont.' and of mod. pref. *ʔɛ-* 'fut.'

See also **10, 11, 89.**

(284)

See **1, 3, 7, 11, 20, 35, 36, 38, 79, 80, 82, 182, 183.**

(285)

664. ʔo:níyehkɔh 'it is strong, firm, solid'

    Vb. base: vb. rt. *-ʔ:niye-* 'be strong, etc.'; rt. suff. *-ʔhkw* 'inst.'
    Asp. suff.: *-ɔh* 'desc.'
    Obj. pref.: *ʔo-* 'neut.'

See also **1, 6, 7, 10, 47.**

(286)

See **30, 36, 88, 93, 99.**

(287)

See **30, 36, 198, 417–419.**

(288)

See **1, 6, 7, 61, 62.**

(289)

665. ?ethiyatkáthwɛ:ɔtye? 'we (incl.) are seeing them'

Vb. rt.: -atkathw- 'see, look at'
Asp. suff.: -ɛ́- 'desc.'; -atye-; -'? 'desc.'
Trans. pref.: ?ethiy- 'we (incl.) . . . them'

666. hotíyɔ:ɔtye? 'they (masc.) are coming along'

Vb. rt.: -yɔ- 'come, arrive'
Asp. suff.: -'Ø- 'desc.'; -atye- 'prog.'; -'? 'desc.'
Obj. pref.: hoti- 'they (masc.)'

See also 36, 79, 226, 418, 419.

(290)

See 1, 3, 10, 11, 647.

(291)

667. teyakhiká:ne:? 'we (excl.) see them'

Iden. with 240 except for trans. pref. -yakhi- 'we (excl.) . . . them'
(cf. 661)

668. hɛnɔta?kɛ́i?senɔ:tye?s 'they (masc. pl.) are crawling about'

Iden. with 663 except for subj. pref. hɛn- 'they (masc. pl.)'

669. teyakwayá?tokɛ:shɔ? 'among us (excl. pl.)'

Iden. with 659 except for subj. pref. -yakwa- 'we (excl. pl.)'

See also 11, 36, 198, 242, 662.

(292)

See 1, 3, 10, 11, 191, 584.

(293)

See 10, 11, 30, 36, 42, 71, 109, 159, 263, 316, 585.

(294)

See 1, 3, 11, 647, 648.

(295)

670. sa?níkɔɛ? 'your mind'

Iden. with 75 except for obj. pref. sa- '2d pers.'

See also 7, 11, 36, 42, 536.

(296)

671. se?ɔh 'you decided'

Iden. with 38 except for obj. pref. s- '2d pers.'

672. ?ehta?ké:kwa:h 'below'

Nn. rt.: ?éhta- 'dirt' [26.6]
Nn. suff.: -'?ke- 'ext. loc.'
Enclitic: -kwah 'toward'

See also 3, 7, 10, 11, 82, 508.

(297)

See **3, 6, 11, 20, 78, 649.**

(298)

673. ʔɛki:wakháhsɔ:koʔ 'I shall divide their responsibilities'

> Vb. base: vb. rt. *-kháhs-* 'divide, separate'; *-ɔkw-* 'oppos.I'; incorp. nn. rt.
> *-(C)ȼ:wa-* 'matter, responsibility'
> Asp. suff.: *-óʔ* 'punc.'
> Subj. pref.: *-k-* '1st pers.'
> Mod. pref.: *ʔɛ-* 'fut.'

674. ʔɛyohtɛtyɔ́:ɔk 'it will always continue'

> Iden. with **227** except for addition of *-ak* 'cont.' and of mod. pref. *ʔɛ-* 'fut.'

See also **1, 7, 10, 11, 36, 74, 82, 671.**

(299)

See **1, 3, 7, 10, 11, 36, 81, 82, 89, 105, 109–112, 671.**

(300)

See **3, 10, 11, 36, 105–108.**

(301)

See **7, 10, 36, 84, 93, 145, 213.**

(302)

675. nisaʔnikɔɛwɛ́ʔɔh 'what you intended'

> Iden. with **117** except for obj. pref. *-sa-* '2d pers.'

See also **1, 3, 6, 7, 10, 112, 113.**

(303)

See **1, 3, 7, 10, 11, 46, 106, 107, 671.**

(304)

676. nisaye:ɛh 'what you did'

> Iden. with **8** except for obj. pref. *-sa-* '2d pers.' (cf. **34**)

See also **7, 11, 15, 36, 41, 59, 89, 122, 123.**

(305)

677. satkáʔwɛh 'you left'

> Iden. with **127** except for obj. pref. *s-* '2d pers.'

See also **7, 10, 11, 81, 89, 93, 190.**

(306)

678. watíhsi:aʔ 'they (nonmasc. pl.) are standing in array, distributed'

Iden. with **598** except for subj. pref. *wati-* 'they (nonmasc. pl.)'

See also **1, 7, 10, 11, 42, 81, 93, 114, 129.**

(307)

679. hoʔwɛ́:nishætenyɔ:tyeʔ 'days are present there all along'

Iden. with **336** except for addition of *h-* 'transloc.'

See also **7, 10, 11, 190, 498, 671.**

(308)

680. kaʔéohtato:kɛ:h 'a certain plant'

Iden. with **130** except for lack of *-ak* 'cont.' and of *ʔɛ-* 'fut.'

681. sæ:kwɛh 'you chose it'

Vb. base: vb. rt. *-(C)æ-* 'put in'; rt. suff. *-kw-* 'oppos.I' (together meaning 'take out, choose')
Asp. suff.: *-ɛ́h* 'desc.'
Obj. pref.: *sæ* '2d pers.'

See also **1, 6, 10, 11, 46, 676.**

(309)

See **3, 6, 7, 10, 11, 30, 132, 671.**

(310)

See **7, 10, 11, 15, 20, 30, 41, 203, 208.**

(311)

682. ʔoʔka:tkaʔ 'I provide'

Iden. with **282** except for mod. pref. *ʔoʔ-* 'indic.'

See also **11, 15, 20, 36, 40, 42, 483, 587.**

(312)

See **3, 10, 84, 136–138.**

(313)

683. tɛyɔ́kasha:aʔt 'people will remember me'

Vb. base: vb. rt. *-ashaæ-* 'take cognizance of'; rt. suff. *-ʔ-* 'inch. I' (cf. 207)
Asp. suff.: *-t* 'indic.'
Trans. pref.: *-yɔk-* 'people . . . me'
Mod. pref.: *-ɛ-* 'fut.'
Other pref.: *t-* 'dupl.'

See also **7, 10, 11, 20, 41, 67, 671.**

(314)

See **7, 9, 10, 11, 30, 139, 140.**

(315)

See **1, 7, 11, 12, 15, 16.**

(316)

684. ʔɛyakwatɔ́:ɔk 'we (excl. pl.) will continue to say'

     Iden. with **86** except for subj. pref. *-yakw-* 'we (excl. pl.)'

See also **3, 10, 11, 141.**

(317)

685. tsɔsayoʔtáiɛh 'when it becomes warm again'

     Vb. stem iden. with **213.**
     Obj. pref.: *-yo-* 'neut.'
     Mod. pref.: *-ɔ-a-* 'indic.'
     Prim. pref.: *-s-* 'repet.'
     Sec. pref.: *ts-* 'coin.'

See also **1, 7, 145, 155.**

(318)

686. waʔákwatka:thoʔ 'we (excl. pl.) see'

     Iden. with **143** except for subj. pref. *-ʔakw-* 'we (excl. pl.)'

See also **10, 11, 89, 138, 140, 141, 146.**

(319)

See **1, 7, 10, 30, 46, 536, 670.**

(320)

687. ʔɛyé:ek 'people will gather them'

     Vb. rt.: *-(C)eέek-* 'gather'
     Asp. suff.: *-Ø* 'punc.'
     Subj. pref.: *-ye-* 'fem.'
     Mod. pref.: *ʔɛ-* 'fut.'

See also **3, 10, 42, 134.**

(321)

See **6, 10, 81, 149, 150.**

(322)

688. ʔɛtyewɛni:tkɛʔt 'people will speak there'

     Vb. base iden. with **621.**
     Asp. suff.: *-t* 'indic.'
     Subj. pref.: *-ye-* 'fem.'
     Mod. pref.: *ʔɛ-* 'fut.'
     Prim. pref.: *-t-* 'cisloc.'

689. tɛyɔtɛnɔ́:nyɔ:k 'people will continue to give thanks'

    Iden. with **515** except for asp. suff. -∅- 'desc.'

See also **3, 6, 7, 10, 11, 42, 159, 536, 670.**

(323)

690. wa:tí:waye:is 'they (masc. pl.) do as they should'

    Vb. base iden. with **98.**
    Asp. suff.: -∅ 'punc.'
    Subj. pref.: -'ati- 'they (masc. pl.)'
    Mod. pref.: wa- 'indic.'

691. tsáɛnɔtka:tho? 'when they (masc. pl.) see it'

    Vb. stem iden. with **136.**
    Subj. pref.: -'ɛn- 'they (masc. pl.)'
    Mod. pref.: -a- 'indic.'
    Sec. pref.: ts- 'coin.'

See also **1, 7, 10, 11, 84, 140, 141, 146.**

(324)

692. wa?akoyá?taye:ih 'people gather'

    Iden. with **5** except for obj. pref. -?ako- 'fem.'

693. ?ɔkwaya?tayéistha? 'our (pl.) meeting place'

    Iden. with **150** except for obj. pref. ?ɔkwa- 'our (pl.)'

See also **10, 11, 81.**

(325)

694. tayewɛni:tkɛ?t 'people speak there'

    Iden. with **688** except for mod. pref. -a- 'indic.'

See also **7, 10, 11, 36, 106, 108, 153, 159.**

(326)

695. ?o?tyesanɔ́:nyɔ:? 'people thank you'

    Iden. with **506** except for trans. pref. -yesa- 'people . . . you

696. sayɔ́tkatho? 'people see it again'

    Iden. with **136** except for mod. pref. -a- 'indic.' and addition of prim.
    pref. s- 'repet.'

697. nisáiwa:ɔ? 'how you spaced the ceremonies'

    Iden. with **569** except for obj. pref. -sa- '2nd pers.'

See also **2, 10, 11, 27, 28, 30, 36, 89, 205.**

(327)

See **1, 7, 30, 36, 97, 118, 198, 227, 675.**

(328)

See **1, 3, 40, 647.**

(329)

698. tɔta:tíɛ^ʔ 'they (masc. pl.) say it here again'

     Iden. with **583** except for subj. pref. -ʼ*ati*- 'they (masc. pl.)'

See also **1–3, 10, 40.**

(330)

See **10, 11, 30, 36, 109, 159, 263, 316, 584, 585.**

(331)

See **1, 3, 11, 647, 648.**

(332)

See **7, 30, 36, 81, 93, 676.**

(333)

See **7, 10, 11, 81, 82, 89, 162, 671.**

(334)

See **3, 10, 11, 30, 46, 163, 164.**

(335)

699. kye:h 'some, some of them'

See also **10, 11, 30, 46, 165, 166.**

(336)

See **3, 10, 11, 42, 46, 167, 168.**

(337)

See **3, 6, 7, 10, 30, 36, 169–171, 205, 675.**

(338)

See **1, 7, 10, 11, 30, 36, 89, 118.**

(339)

700. nɛyo:nekítkɛshɔ:k 'what springs there will continue to be'

     Iden. with **162** except for addition of sec. pref. *n*- 'part.'

701. hɛyɔ́ɛja:te:k 'there the earth will continue to be present'

    Iden. with **82** except for addition of *h-* 'transloc.'

See also **10, 11, 20, 30, 36, 116, 190, 671.**

(340)

702. kotyæ:ʔtáhkɔh 'people use it'

    Iden. with **90** except for obj. pref. *ko-* 'fem.'

See also **7, 10, 11, 20, 41, 198.**

(341)

703. ʔɛyɔtyaʔtákeskoʔ 'people will arise'

    Iden. with **179** except for subj. pref. *-y[ɔ]-* 'fem.'

704. tɔsayawɛtɔ:tiʔ 'morning dawns again'

    Iden. with **180** except for mod. pref. *-ɔ-a-* 'indic.'

See also **2, 7, 10, 11, 79.**

(342)

705. ʔɛyɔtyǽ:ʔtak 'people will use it'

    Iden. with **178** except for subj. pref. *-y[ɔ]-* 'fem.'

See also **10, 11, 24, 181.**

(343)

See **1, 7, 30, 36, 198, 298, 675.**

(344)

See **1, 6, 7, 61, 62.**

(345)

See **3, 10, 30, 36, 169–171, 671.**

(346)

706. ʔɛyɔhiyostahkɔ́:ɔk 'it will be good for them', lit. 'make their lives good'

    Vb. base: vb. rt. *-iyo-* 'be good'; rt. suff. *-ʼsta-* 'caus. I', *-ʼhkw-* 'inst.'; incorp. nn. rt. *-ɔh-* 'life'
    Asp. suff.: *-ɔ́-* 'desc.'; *-ak* 'cont.'
    Subj. pref.: *-y-* 'neut.'
    Mod. pref.: *ʔɛ-* 'fut.'

707. ʔoʔkhéyaʔtakwɛni:yos 'I did it for their benefit'

    Vb. base: vb. rt. *-kwɛniyo-* 'be the main one'; rt. suff. *-ʼst-* 'caus. I'; incorp. nn. rt. *-yáʔta-* 'body' (the entire base meaning 'benefit')
    Asp. suff.: *-Ø* 'punc.'
    Trans. pref.: *-khe-* 'I . . . them'
    Mod. pref.: *ʔoʔ-* 'indic.'

See also **1–3, 10, 11, 20, 27, 36, 81, 93, 108, 116, 394, 682.**

(347)

708. heyo:to⁷k 'up to that point', here 'in addition'

Vb. base: vb. rt. -*ó*⁷*kt*- 'extend to the limit'; -*at*- 'refl.'
Asp. suff.: -∅ 'desc.'
Obj. pref.: -*yo*- 'neut.'
Other pref.: *he*- 'transloc.'

709. ⁷onɔtyǽ:⁷tahkɔh 'they (nonmasc.) use it'

Iden. with **90** except for obj. pref. *ʔon*- 'they (nonmasc.)'

See also **10, 30, 81, 93, 176, 230, 237, 677.**

(348)

See **1, 3, 89, 97, 198, 226, 227, 298, 333, 619.**

(349)

See **1, 3, 10, 11, 36, 42, 109, 159, 191, 263, 316, 584, 585.**

(350)

See **1, 3, 11, 647, 648.**

(351)

See **7, 11, 30, 36, 536, 670.**

(352)

See **3, 7, 10, 11, 81, 171, 189, 671.**

(353)

710. ⁷ɛyothɔtɔ́ni:ak 'brush will continue to grow'

Iden. with **105** except for incorp. nn. rt. -⁷(*h*)*ɔt*- 'brush'

711. nɛtyóhsawa⁷k 'it will continue to begin there'

Iden. with **257** except for addition of prim. pref. -*t*- 'cisloc'

See also **10, 11.**

(354)

See **3, 10, 11, 15, 20, 116, 190, 205.**

(355)

712. tekhni:h 'two'
713. na⁷tesaye:ɛh 'how you did it (twice)'

Iden. with **676** except for addition of -*te*- 'dupl.'

See also **30, 36, 81, 93, 145.**

(356)

See **7, 10, 11, 36, 109, 191, 192, 194, 671.**

(357)

See **1, 2, 11, 109, 176, 193, 196, 263.**

(358)

714. ʔɛyakoyaʔtataiaʔtahkɔ́:ɔk 'it will continue to be used to make people warm'

Iden. with **197** except for obj. pref. *-yako-* 'fem.'

See also **1, 3, 6, 7, 10, 11, 42, 81, 84, 93, 145, 196, 671, 675.**

(359)

See **1, 7, 10, 11, 89, 671.**

(360)

See **3, 10, 11, 30, 89, 107, 176, 209.**

(361)

See **189, 701.**

(362)

See **1, 6, 10, 11, 176, 676, 681.**

(363)

715. ʔonɔ́hkwaʔshæʔ 'medicine'

Iden. with **114** except for lack of attr. suff. *-shɔ́ʔɔ́h* 'plur.'

See also **3, 10, 11, 15, 20, 30, 116, 203, 204, 671.**

(364)

See **30, 81, 202, 448.**

(365)

716. ʔotíhsɛnɔyɛ:tɔʔ 'they (nonmasc.) have names'

Iden. with **107** except for lack of *-k* 'cont.' and of mod pref. *ʔɛ-* 'fut.'

See also **1, 7, 10, 11, 89, 106.**

(366)

717. yeyɛtéihko:wa:h 'people know well'

Vb. rt.: *-yɛtei-* 'know'
Asp. suff.: *-h* 'desc.'
Subj. pref.: *ye-* 'fem.'
Attr. suff.: *-kowah* 'augment.'
Cf. **544.**

718. nɔʔɔɔtóʔtɛʔ 'what kind of tree it is'

>Vb. base: vb. rt. -óʔlɛ- 'be of a certain kind'; incorp. nn. rt. -(y)ɔt- 'tree'
>Asp. suff.: -'ʔ 'punc.'
>Obj. pref.: -ʔo- 'neut.'
>Mod. pref.: -a- 'indic.'
>Sec. pref.: n- 'part.'

719. waʔéihsa:khaʔ 'people go and look for it'

>Vb. base: vb. rt. -(C)ihsak- 'look for'; rt. suff. -h- 'trans.'
>Asp. suff.: -áʔ 'punc.'
>Subj. pref.: -ʔe- 'fem.'
>Mod. pref.: wa- 'indic.'

720. kahatakɔ:h 'within the forest'

>Iden. with **244** except for lack of attr. suff. -shɔʔ 'plur.'

721. hɛyɔ́tkɔ:tak 'people will go directly there'

>Iden. with **433** except for lack of prim. pref. -[j]- 'repet.' and addition of
>h- 'transloc.'

See also **10, 11, 613.**

(367)

722. sheya:wi:h 'you gave to them'

>Vb. rt.: -awi- 'give'
>Asp. suff.: -h 'desc.'
>Trans. pref.: shey- 'you . . . them'

723. ʔoyaʔtowéhtashæʔ 'the power of thought'

>Nn. base: vb. base iden. with **643**; -shæ- 'nom.'
>Nn. suff.: -'ʔ 'spl. nn. suff.'
>Obj. pref.: ʔo- 'neut.'

724. ʔɛyeyɛtéia:k 'people will continue to know'

>Vb. rt.: -yɛtei- 'know'
>Asp. suff.: -'Ø- 'desc.'; -ak 'cont.'
>Subj. pref.: -ye- 'fem.'
>Mod. pref.: ʔɛ- 'fut.'
>Cf. **717.**

725. ʔɛtkáiwatiyɔ:tɛʔ 'it will cause distress'

>Vb. base: vb. rt. -atiyɔ(:)t- 'stretch'; incorp. nn. rt. -(C)i:w 'matter'
>(together meaning 'cause distress')
>Asp. suff.: -éʔ 'punc.'
>Subj. pref.: -ka- 'neut.'
>Mod. pref.: ʔɛ- 'fut.'
>Prim. pref.: -t- 'cisloc.'

See also **3, 10, 11, 52, 61, 89, 125, 484.**

(368)

726. honɔtyǽ:ʔtahkɔh 'they (masc.) use it'

    Iden. with **90** except for obj. pref. *hon-* 'they (masc.)'

See also **1, 7, 10, 11, 36, 89, 118, 198.**

(369)

See **1, 10, 36, 46, 676.**

(370)

727. ʔɛkæ:koʔ 'I shall choose'

    Vb. base iden. with **681.**
    Asp. suff.: *-óʔ* 'punc.'
    Subj. pref.: *-k-* '1st pers.'
    Mod. pref.: *ʔɛ-* 'fut.'

See also **6, 7, 10, 11, 20, 41, 89, 132, 205, 208, 671.**

(371)

728. kɛɔtato:kɛ:h 'a certain tree'

    Iden. with **206** except for lack of *-ak* 'cont.' and of *ʔɛ-* 'fut.' Cf. **680.**

See also **7, 10, 11, 30, 36, 676, 681.**

(372)

See **10, 30, 36, 84, 109, 110, 135, 136, 205, 214.**

(373)

729. ʔakwa:tɔh 'we (excl. pl.) say'

    Iden. with **233** except for subj. pref. *ʔakw-* 'we (incl. pl.)' Cf. **625.**

See also **1, 7, 10, 11, 30, 210.**

(374)

See **6, 30, 198, 220, 244.**

(375)

730. yeiwastéisthaʔ 'people notice them'

    Iden. with **222** except for asp. suff. *-háʔ* 'iter.' and subj. pref. *ye-* 'fem.'

See also **1, 10, 11, 176, 198, 221.**

(376)

731. waʔóhke:otɔ:ʔ 'people tap them'

    Vb. base: vb. rt. *-ot-* 'stand upright'; rt. suff. *-ɔ-* 'dist.'; incorp. nn. rt.
    -ahke- 'chip' (cf. **223**)
    Asp. suff.: *-ʔ* 'punc.'
    Subj. pref.: *-ʔ[ɔ]-* 'fem.'
    Mod. pref.: *wa-* 'indic.'

732. sayo?táish 'it becomes warm again'

    Vb. stem iden. with **213.**
    Obj. pref.: -*yo*- 'neut.'
    Mod. pref.: -*a*- 'indic.'
    Prim. pref.: *s*- 'repet.'

733. tɔsakæ:wɛnye:? 'the wind stirs again'

    Vb. stem inden. with **193.**
    Subj. pref.: -*kæ*- 'neut.'
    Mod. pref.: -*ɔ-a*- 'indic.'
    Prim. pref.: -*s*- 'repet.'
    Other pref.: *t*- 'dupl.'

See also **10, 11, 36, 79, 84, 93, 134, 351.**

(377)

See **1, 7, 10, 36, 676.**

(378)

734. ?i:sɛ:h 'you said'

    Vb. rt.: -*ɛ*- 'say'
    Asp. suff.: -*h* 'desc.'
    Obj. pref.: *?is*- '2d pers.' [6.11]

735. ?ɛyéhsɛnɔ:ni? 'people will store it'

    Vb. stem iden. with **224.**
    Subj. pref.: -*ye*- 'fem.'
    Mod. pref.: *?ɛ*- 'fut.'

736. ?ɛtwatyéshtak 'it will be done first'

    Vb. stem iden. with **554.**
    Subj. pref.: -*w*- 'neut.'
    Mod. pref.: *?ɛ*- 'fut.'
    Prim. pref.: -*t*- 'cisloc.'

737. ?ɛyɔ:ste?t 'people will boil it down'

    Vb. base: -*aste*- 'be evaporated'; rt. suff. -'*?t*- 'caus. I'
    Asp. suff.: -*∅* 'punc.'
    Subj. pref.: -*y[ɔ]*- 'fem.'
    Mod. pref.: *?ɛ*- 'fut.'

See also **3, 7, 10, 11, 134.**

(379)

738. ?akwas 'that specifically'
739. hɛwɔ:tɔ? 'it will become'

    Vb. rt.: -*atɔ?*- 'become'
    Asp. suff.: -*∅* 'punc.'
    Subj. pref.: -*w*- 'neut.'
    Mod. pref.: -*ɛ*- 'fut.'
    Other pref.: *h*- 'transloc.'

See also **7, 10, 11, 225, 734.**

(380)

740. ʔɛyɔ́te:wa:tɛʔ 'people will store it away'

Vb. rt.: *-atéːwat-* 'put away, store'
Asp. suff.: *-ɛ́ʔ* 'punc.'
Subj. pref.: *-y[ɔ]-* 'fem.'
Mod. pref.: *ʔɛ-* 'fut.'

See also **10, 11, 30, 735, 736.**

(381)

741. ʔɛyékɛ:ya:tɛʔ 'people will put it on top, get it out'

Vb. rt.: *-kɛ́ːyat-* 'put up on top'
Asp. suff.: *-ɛ́ʔ* 'punc.'
Subj. pref.: *-ye-* 'fem.'
Mod. pref.: *ʔɛ-* 'fut.'

742. ʔɛwɔ:yawéthæ:h 'the berries will be between'

Vb. base: vb. rt. *-awethaæh-* 'put between'; incorp. nn. rt. *-áːy-* 'berry'
Asp. suff.: *-Ø* 'punc.'
Subj. pref.: *-w-* 'neut.'
Mod. pref.: *ʔɛ-* 'fut.'

See also **3, 6, 7, 10, 42, 59, 84, 140, 141, 676.**

(382)

743. ʔɛka:nekakaʔɔstahkɔ́:ɔk 'it will continue to be used for flavoring the drink'

Vb. base: vb. rt. *-káʔɔ-* 'be good, taste good'; rt. suff. *-ʼsta-* 'caus.-inst.',
-ʼhkw- 'inst.'; incorp. nn. rt. *-ʼːneka-* 'drink'
Asp. suff.: *-ɔ́-* 'desc.'; *-ak* 'cont.'
Subj. pref.: *-ka-* 'neut.'
Mod. pref.: *ʔɛ-* 'fut.'

744. ʔɛɔtí:ek 'they (masc. pl.) will gather it'

Iden. with **687** except for subj. pref. *-ʼati-* 'they (masc. pl.)'

745. ʔeotiyaʔtayéistak 'they (masc.) will use it for their gatherings'

Vb. base iden. with **150** except for addition of rt. suff. *-ʼhkw-* 'inst.'
Obj. pref.: *-ʼoti-* 'they (masc.)'
Mod. pref.: *ʔɛ-* 'fut.'

746. tɛ:nɔténɔ:ɔnyɔ:ʔ 'they (masc. pl.) will give thanks'

Iden. with **154** except for subj. pref. *-ʼɛn-* 'they (masc. pl.)'

See also **1, 7, 10, 30, 42, 84, 140.**

(383)

See **1, 6, 7, 11, 30, 536, 670.**

(384)

747. hɛyé:nekɔ:nɛt 'people will swallow the drink'

Vb. stem iden. with **148.**
Subj. pref.: -ye- 'fem.'
Mod. pref.: -ɛ- 'fut.'
Other pref.: h- 'transloc.'

See also **1, 7, 10, 11, 30, 210, 671, 736.**

(385)

See **7, 10, 11, 40, 135, 671.**

(386)

See **2, 30, 36, 89, 110, 153, 205, 696, 697.**

(387)

748. ʔɛyako:tɔ:ʔs 'it will be available to people'

Vb. rt.: -atɔʔs- 'be available'
Asp. suff.: -∅ 'punc.'
Obj. pref.: -yako- 'fem.'
Mod. pref.: ʔɛ- 'fut.'

See also **3, 6, 7, 10, 11, 41, 89, 536, 670, 715.**

(388)

749. hɛnɔtyǽ:ʔtahkwaʔ 'they (masc. pl.) use it'

Iden. with **726** except for asp. suff. -áʔ 'iter.' and subj. pref. *hɛn-* 'they (masc. pl.)'

See also **1, 7, 10, 11, 20, 36, 41, 89, 118, 198.**

(389)

See **1, 10, 11, 57, 97, 198, 226, 298, 333.**

(390)

See **1, 3, 36, 89, 97, 226, 227, 619, 675.**

(391)

See **1, 3, 10, 11, 40, 656.**

(392)

See **3, 10, 11, 30, 36, 109, 159, 263, 316, 584, 585.**

(393)

750. ʔɔkwáhsawa:tyeʔ 'we (pl.) are beginning'

Vb. rt.: -ahsaw- 'begin'
Asp. suff.: -∅- 'desc.'; -atye- 'prog.'; -ʔ ʔ 'desc.'
Obj. pref.: ʔɔkw- 'we (pl.)'

751. teyɔkwaténɔ:nyɔtyeʔ 'we (pl.) are giving thanks'

Vb. base iden. with **154**.
Asp. suff.: -∅- 'desc.'; -tye- 'prog.'; -ʔ ʔ 'desc.'
Obj. pref.: -yɔkw- 'we (pl.)'
Other pref.: te- 'dupl.'

See also **1, 2, 7, 11, 35, 36, 183.**

(394)

See **3, 10, 11, 647, 649.**

(395)

See **7, 30, 36, 81, 93, 676.**

(396)

See **3, 7, 10, 11, 30, 229–231, 671.**

(397)

See **6, 30, 231, 244.**

(398)

See **3, 10, 11, 20, 41, 204, 239.**

(399)

See **3, 10, 11, 241, 711.**

(400)

752. ʔotehatóʔktatyeʔ 'along the edge of the forest'

Iden. with **243** except for final -ʔ ʔ 'desc.' and lack of sec. pref. ni- 'part.'

753. ʔɛwɔtitakhenɔ́tyeʔse:k 'they (nonmasc. pl.) will always be running about'

Iden. with **231** except for subj. pref. -wati- 'they (nonmasc. pl.)'

See also **6, 30.**

(401)

754. tejakwaká:neʔ 'we (excl. pl.) see them again'

Iden. with **245** except for subj. pref. -yakwa- 'we (excl. pl.)'

See also **2, 30, 36, 118, 246.**

(402)

755. ʔɛska:tkaʔ 'you will provide them again'

Iden. with **282** except for addition of prim. pref. -s- 'repet.'

756. ?ɛkanyo?towanɛ́?se:k 'there will always be large animals'

> Iden. with **246** except for addition of -*ek* 'cont.' and of mod. pref.*?ɛ-* 'fut.'

See also **3, 10, 11, 30, 36, 671, 676.**

(403)

See **10, 115, 203, 239.**

(404)

757. teyakwaká:ne:? 'we (excl. pl.) see'

> Iden. with **240** except for subj. pref. -*yakwa-* 'we (excl. pl.)'

See also **1, 2, 36, 89, 237, 246, 251.**

(405)

See **1, 3, 7, 10, 11, 59, 106, 107, 176, 671.**

(406)

See **6, 7, 11, 20, 41, 47.**

(407)

758. ta?a:yokwe:ni? 'it might be impossible'

> Coll. for *te?a:yokwe:ni?*
> Vb. rt.: -*kweny-* 'be possible'
> Asp. suff.: -*i?* 'punc.'
> Obj. pref.: -*yo-* 'neut.'
> Mod. pref.: -*?aa-* 'opt.'
> Other pref.: *te-* 'neg.'

759. na:yakɛ? 'people might say'

> Vb. rt.: -*ɛ-* 'say'
> Asp. suff.: -'*?* 'punc.'
> Subj. pref.: -*yak-* 'fem.'
> Mod. pref.: -*aa-* 'opt.'
> Sec. pref.: *n-* 'part.'

760. hó:ɔweh 'there, over there'

761. twakékɛ:nɔ? 'I saw it there'

> Vb. rt.: -*kɛ-* 'see'
> Asp. suff.: -*∅-* 'desc.'; -':*nɔ?* 'part.'
> Obj. pref.: -*wake-* '1st pers.'
> Prim. pref.: *t-* 'cisloc.'

762. sha?tewatiya?tó?tɛ:h 'they (nonmasc. pl.) have the same kind of form, look alike'

> Vb. base: vb. rt. -*ó?tɛ-* 'be of a certain kind'; incorp. nn. rt. -*yá?t-* 'body, form'
> Asp. suff.: -*h* 'desc.'
> Subj. pref.: -*wati-* 'they (nonmasc. pl.)'
> Sec. pref.: *sha?-* 'coin.'
> Other pref.: -*te-* 'dupl.'

See also **7, 10, 11, 30, 49, 217, 230, 237, 464.**

(408)

763. ʔɛyéyashɔːʔ 'people will call them'

> Vb. base: vb. rt. -yas- 'call'; rt. suff. -hɔ- 'dist.'
> Asp. suff.: -ʔ 'punc.'
> Subj. pref.: -ye- 'fem.'
> Mod. pref.: ʔɛ- 'fut.'

764. nɔʔkayaʔtóʔtɛʔ 'what kind of form it has'

> Vb. base iden. with **762.**
> Asp. suff.: -ʔ 'punc.'
> Subj. pref.: -ka- 'neut.'
> Mod. pref.: -aʔ- 'indic.'
> Sec. pref.: n- 'part.'

765. koːkɛːh 'people see'

> Vb. rt.: -kɛ- 'see'
> Asp. suff.: -h 'desc.'
> Obj. pref.: ko- 'fem.'

See also **1, 2, 7, 10, 11, 36, 40, 191.**

(409)

See **1, 30, 36, 118, 174, 198, 239.**

(410)

766. ʔɛkaːnekakaʔɔ́stak 'it will be used for flavoring the water'

> Iden. with **743** except for asp. suff. -∅ 'punc.'

767. ʔis 'you (sg. or nonsg.)'

768. ʔoʔsyaʔtakwɛniyóʔheʔt 'it is for your benefit'

> Vb. base: vb. rt. -kwɛniyo- 'be the main one'; rt. suff. -ʔhɛʔ- 'inch I';
> incorp. nn. rt. -yáʔta- 'body'
> Asp. suff.: -t 'punc.'
> Subj. pref.: -s- '2d pers.'
> Mod. pref.: ʔoʔ- 'indic.'
> Cf. **707.**

See also **10, 11, 42, 84, 89, 343, 504.**

(411)

See **1, 36, 97, 118, 226, 227, 333.**

(412)

See **3, 10, 30, 234–6, 238, 671.**

(413)

769. ʔɛkanɔʔnóstha꞉k 'whenever it becomes cold'

    Iden. with **196** except for asp. suff. *-h-* 'iter'; *-ak* 'cont.'

See also **3, 10, 30, 36, 42, 59, 232, 402, 671, 676, 701.**

(414)

770. hɛ꞉nɔtsistaké꞉ɔʔ 'they (masc. pl.) will lay down their fire there'

    Vb. base: vb. rt. *-kéɔ-* 'lay down'; incorp. nn. rt. *-sista-* 'fire'; *-at-* 'refl.'
    Asp. suff.: *-ʔ* 'punc.'
    Subj. pref.: *-'ɛn-* 'they (masc. pl.)'
    Mod. pref.: *-ɛ-* 'fut.'
    Other pref.: *h-* 'transloc.'

See also **6, 30, 606, 720.**

(415)

See **1, 10, 30, 36, 57, 118, 198.**

(416)

See **233–235, 277.**

(417)

771. tɛ꞉nɛʔnikɔɛwɛnyáʔtha ʔ 'they (masc. pl.) use it as a source of amusement'

    Coll. for *teɛnɛʔnikɔɛwɛnyáʔthaʔ*
    Iden. with **238** except for lack of *-ak* 'cont.' and of mod. pref. *-ɛ-* 'fut.'

See also **10, 30, 81, 93, 230, 237.**

(418)

772. saiwihsáʔɔh 'you planned it'

    Vb. base: *-ihsáʔ-* 'complete'; incorp. nn. rt. *-(C)i꞉w-* 'matter' (together meaning 'plan')
    Asp. suff.: *-ɔh* 'desc.'
    Obj. pref.: *sa-* '2d pers.'
    Cf. **228.**

See also **1, 3, 36, 97, 108, 226, 227, 333.**

(419)

See **1, 3, 36, 89, 97, 226, 227, 619, 675.**

(420)

See **1, 3, 10, 11, 30, 36, 40, 109, 159, 263, 316, 584, 585.**

(421)

See **1, 10, 11, 647, 648.**

(422)

See 3, 7, 10, 11, 30, 36, 138, 253, 260, 671, 676.

(423)

773. hɛyawenɔ́:ɔk 'it will continue to go there'

> Iden. with 539 except for addition of -ak 'cont.' and of mod. pref. -ɛ-
> 'fut.'

See also 3, 6, 36, 59, 254, 258, 377.

(424)

See 2, 6, 10, 11, 36, 109, 110, 176, 264, 671.

(425)

774. ʔɛyoʔtáiɛɔk 'it will continue to be warm'

> Vb. rt.; -aʔtaiɛ- 'be warm'
> Asp. suff.: -'Ø- 'desc.'; -ak 'cont.'
> Obj. pref.: -yo- 'neut.'
> Mod. pref.: ʔɛ- 'fut.'

See also 1, 6, 7, 10, 11, 84, 145, 264, 675.

(426)

See 1, 10, 11, 36, 89, 118, 176, 277.

(427)

775. sih 'elsewhere, other', here 'larger'
776. nikáji ʔta ʔs 'the size of the birds'

> Vb. base: vb. rt. -a- 'be of a certain size'; incorp. nn. rt. -jiʔt- 'bird'
> Asp. suff.: -'ʔs 'iter.'
> Subj. pref.: -ka- 'neut.'
> Sec. pref.: ni- 'part.'

777. niyo:toʔk 'as far as, up to'

> Iden. with 118 except for lack of -atye- 'prog.' and -'ʔ 'desc.'

778. sasyɔ:ni:h 'you made it'

> Iden. with 322 except for obj. pref. sa- '2d pers.'

See also 10, 11, 176, 276.

(428)

779. ʔɛyɔkwatɔʔseʔɔ́:ɔk 'it will continue to be available to us (pl.)'

> Iden. with 115 except for obj. pref. -yɔkw- 'us (pl.)'

See also 10, 11, 89, 176, 239, 671.

(429)

See **1, 3, 7, 10, 11, 89, 671.**

(430)

See **30, 36, 47, 81, 93, 145.**

(431)

780. ?ɛskánɔ?nos 'it will become cold again'

> Iden. with **196** except for addition of prim. pref. *-s-* 'repet.'

781. tyo?táiɛ:h 'it is warm there'

> Vb. rt.: *-a?taiɛ-* 'be warm'
> Asp. suff.: *-h* 'desc.'
> Obj. pref.: *-yo-* 'neut.'
> Prim. pref.: *t-* 'cisloc.'

782. ?ɛshénɔtkɔ:tak 'they (masc. pl.) will head back there'

> Iden. with **433** except for subj. pref. *-hɛn-* 'they (masc. pl.)'

See also **1, 7, 10, 36, 81, 84, 145.**

(432)

783. tsiyakokwɛ́:ɔ? 'people stay in the same spots'

> Vb. base: vb. rt. *-kwɛ́-* 'be in a particular spot'; rt. suff. *-ɔ-* 'dist.'
> Asp. suff.: *-'?* 'desc.'
> Obj. pref.: *-yako-* 'fem.'
> Sec. pref.: *tsi-* 'coin.'

See also **1, 2, 11, 20, 59, 89.**

(433)

784. tɔtayo?táiɛh 'it becomes warm there again'

> Vb. stem iden. with **213.**
> Obj. pref.: *-yo-* 'neut.'
> Mod. pref.: *-ɔ-a-* 'indic.'
> Prim. pref.: *-t-* 'cisloc.'
> Other pref.: *t-* 'dupl.'

785. sa:tiyá?ta?ti:he?t 'they (masc. pl.) come around again'

> Iden. with **269** except for mod. pref. *-a-* 'indic.'

786. ha?tá:tiwɛnɔ:ke:h 'all their (masc. pl.) voices'

> Coll. for *ha?tɛ́atiwɛnɔ:ke:h*
> Vb. base: vb. rt. *-ake-* 'be separate entities'; incorp. nn. rt. *-wɛn-* 'voice'
> Asp. suff.: *-h* 'desc.'
> Subj. pref.: *-'ati-* 'their (masc. pl.)'
> Sec. pref.: *ha?-* 'transloc.'
> Other pref.: *-te-* 'dupl.'

787. saɛnɔtíʔstaɛʔ 'they (masc. pl.) chatter again'

> Vb. stem iden. with **271**.
> Subj. pref.: -ʹɛn- 'they (masc. pl.)'
> Mod. pref.: -a- 'indic.'
> Prim. pref.: s- 'repet.'

788. hatiwɛni:yo:h 'their (masc. pl.) beautiful voices'

> Vb. base iden. with **272**.
> Asp. suff.: -h 'desc.'
> Subj. pref.: hati- 'their (masc. pl.)'

See also **1, 2, 7, 10, 36, 84, 145**.

(434)

See **1, 2, 7, 11, 20, 36, 108, 153**.

(435)

789. sayewɛnɔ́:ɔk 'people hear the voices again'

> Vb. base: vb. rt. -áɔ(:)k- 'hear'; incorp. nn. rt. -wɛn- 'voice'
> Asp. suff.: -∅ 'punc.'
> Subj. pref.: -ye- 'fem.'
> Mod. pref.: -a- 'indic.'
> Prim. pref.: s- 'repet.'

790. sawati:yɔʔ 'they (nonmasc. pl.) come again'

> Vb. rt.: -yɔ- 'come, arrive'
> Asp. suff.: -ʹʔ 'punc.'
> Subj. pref.: -wati- 'they (nonmasc. pl.)'
> Mod. pref.: -a- 'indic.'
> Prim. pref.: s- 'repet.'

791. watiwɛni:yo:h 'their (nonmasc. pl.) beautiful voices'

> Iden. with **788** except for subj. pref. wati- 'their (nonmasc. pl.)'

See also **2, 260**.

(436)

792. wáɔsasha:aʔt 'they remember you'

> Vb. base: vb. rt. -ashaæ- 'take cognizance of'; rt. suff. -ʹʔ- 'inch. I' (cf.
> **133**)
> Asp. suff.: -t 'punc.'
> Trans. pref.: -ʹɔs- 'they . . . you'
> Mod. pref.: wa- 'indic.'

See also **1, 2, 6, 7, 11, 89, 153, 696, 767**.

(437)

793. ʔoʔtyɔtɛnɔ́:nyɔ:ʔ 'people are thankful'

> Iden. with **154** except for mod. pref. ʔoʔ- 'indic.'

See also **7, 10, 11, 27, 28, 40**.

(438)

See **1, 3, 7, 10, 11, 106, 107, 176, 671.**

(439)

794. waʔe:kɛʔ 'people see it'

> Vb. rt.: -kɛ- 'see'
> Asp. suff.: -'ʔ 'punc.'
> Subj. pref.: -ʔe- 'fem.'
> Mod. pref.: wa- 'indic.'

See also **3, 10, 11, 36, 84, 89, 717, 764.**

(440)

795. teʔsaiwakɔ:tɔh 'it does not escape you'

> Vb. base: vb. rt. -kɔ(:)t- 'perform an irrevocable act'; rt. suff. -ɔ- 'dist.';
>   incorp. nn. rt. -(C)i:wa- 'matter'
> Asp. suff.: -'h 'iter.'
> Obj. pref.: -sa- 'you'
> Other pref.: teʔ- 'neg.'

796. tɔʔɔ́sa:tikwe:niʔ 'they (masc. pl.) are no longer able'

> Coll. for teʔɔ́sa:tikwe:niʔ
> Vb. rt.: -kweny- 'be able'
> Asp. suff.: -iʔ 'punc.'
> Subj. pref.: -'ati- 'they (masc. pl.)'
> Mod. pref.: -ʔɔ-a- 'indic.'
> Prim. pref.: -s- 'repet.'
> Other pref.: te- 'neg.'

797. ʔɔ́:sa:tiya:shɔ:ʔ 'they (masc. pl.) might still name them'

> Vb. stem iden. with **763.**
> Subj. pref.: -'ati- 'they (masc. pl.)'
> Mod. pref.: ʔɔɔ-a- 'opt.'
> Prim. pref.: -s- 'repet.'

798. niyotihsɛ́noʔtɛ:h 'what kind of names they (nonmasc.) have'

> Vb. base: -óʔtɛ- 'be of a certain kind'; incorp. nn. rt. -hsɛn- 'name'
> Asp. suff.: -h 'desc.'
> Obj. pref.: -yoti- 'they (nonmasc.)'
> Sec. pref.: ni- 'part.'

799. ʔɔkwéʔɔwe:kha:ʔ 'characterized by Indianness', here 'the Indian language'

> Vb. base: vb. rt. -ʔɔwe- 'be native, genuine'; incorp. nn. rt. -ɔkwe- 'person'
>   (together meaning 'Indian')
> Asp. suff.: -∅- 'desc.'
> Subj. pref.: ʔ- 'indef.'
> Attr. suff.: -khaʔ 'charact.'

See also **1, 11, 30, 36, 49, 89, 106, 275.**

(441)

See　1, 10, 11, 36, 57, 89, 97, 226, 298, 333, 675.

(442)

See 1, 3, 6, 7, 11, 36, 74, 89, 97, 226, 227, 619, 670, 675.

(443)

See 1, 3, 11, 647, 648.

(444)

See 3, 6, 7, 11, 27, 36, 42, 81, 82, 282, 288, 671, 676.

(445)

See 3, 6, 7, 97, 287, 675.

(446)

See 1, 7, 10, 11, 84, 89, 294, 295.

(447)

800. satɛ́hɔʔshɛʔ 'your helpers'

> Iden. with **456** except for obj. pref. *sa-* '2d pers.'

801. ʔɛyákwathyo꞉wiʔ 'we (excl. pl.) shall tell about it'

> Vb. base: *-hyowi-* 'tell'; *-at-* 'refl.' (cf. **85**)
> Asp. suff.: *-ʔ* 'punc.'
> Subj. pref.: *-yakwa-* 'we (excl. pl.)'
> Mod. pref.: *ʔɛ-* 'fut.'

See also 2, 7, 10, 12, 36, 42, 74, 84, 296.

(448)

See 6, 7, 10, 11, 84, 308, 314, 685, 801.

(449)

See 1, 7, 42, 81, 89, 93, 677.

(450)

See 2, 10, 11, 20, 41, 283, 284, 671.

(451)

See 3, 6, 7, 10, 11, 112, 113, 285, 286, 675.

(452)

See 1, 30, 36, 118, 312, 757.

(453)

See **30, 91, 293.**

(454)

See **10, 90, 92.**

(455)

802. ʔɔkwayaʔtá:ni:yɔh 'our (pl.) bodies are strong'

     Iden. with **235** except for obj. pref. *ʔɔkwa-* 'our (pl.)'

See also **1, 2, 11, 15, 16, 89, 226.**

(456)

See **1, 6, 7, 61, 62.**

(457)

803. saye:ɛh 'you did it'

     Iden. with **676** except for lack of sec. pref. *ni-* 'part.'

804. tesaʔsɛhtɔ́:tyeʔ 'you are dropping it'

     Vb. base: vb. rt. *-áʔsɛ-* 'fall'; rt. suff. *-ʹht-* 'caus. I'
     Asp. suff.: *-ɔ́-* 'desc.'; *-atye-* 'prog.'; *-ʹʔ* 'desc.'
     Obj. pref.: *-s-* '2d pers.'
     Other pref.: *te-* 'dupl.'

805. ʔa:yakwɛnɔhtɔ́nyɔ:ɔk 'we (excl. pl.) might always think'

     Vb. stem iden. with **288.**
     Subj. pref.: *-yakw-* 'we (excl. pl.)'
     Mod. pref.: *ʔaa-* 'opt.'

806. ʔɔkwæ:hkɔ́:tyeʔ 'we (pl.) are along in it'

     Vb. base: vb. rt. *-(C)æ-* 'put in'; rt. suff. *-ʹhkw-* 'inst.'
     Asp. suff.: *-ɔ́-* 'desc.'; *-atye-* 'prog.'; *-ʹʔ* 'desc.'
     Obj. pref.: *ʔɔkwæ-* 'we (pl.)'

See also **3, 11, 27, 30, 42, 95, 109.**

(458)

See **1, 3, 10, 11, 40, 81, 93, 512, 677.**

(459)

See **1, 3, 36, 89, 97, 108, 226, 227, 619, 772.**

(460)

See **1, 3, 10, 11, 191, 584.**

(461)

See **3, 10, 11, 30, 36, 42, 109, 159, 263, 316, 585.**

(462)

807. ʔɔkwátɔʔe:sɛh 'we (pl.) are grateful'

Vb. base: vb. rt. -ɔʔes- 'gratify'; -at- 'refl.'
Asp. suff.: -ɛ́h 'desc.'
Obj. pref.: ʔɔkw- 'we (pl.)'

808. nioyɛnoʔtɛʔhéʔɔh 'what he fashioned'

Vb. base iden. with **170.**
Asp. suff.: -ɔ́h 'desc.'
Obj. pref.: -ʹo- 'masc.'
Other pref.: ni- 'part.'

See also **1, 2, 7, 10, 11, 35–37, 40, 750.**

(463)

See **1, 7, 38, 81, 82, 124, 299, 300.**

(464)

809. tɛyɔkhnɔ:nyɔʔtáhkwa:k 'people will always use it for thanking
me'

Vb. base: vb. rt. -nɔ́ɔnyɔ- 'thank'; rt. suff. -ʹʔta- 'caus. I', -ʹhkw- 'inst.'
Asp. suff.: -∅- 'iter.'; -ak 'cont.'
Trans. pref.: -yɔk- 'people . . . me'
Mod. pref.: -ɛ- 'fut.'
Other pref.: t- 'dupl.'

See also **3, 10, 11, 15, 20, 42, 116.**

(465)

810. ʔostówæʔko:wa:h 'Great Feather Dance'

Nn. rt.: -stowæ- 'headdress'
Nn. suff.: -ʹʔ- 'spl. nn. suff.'
Obj. pref.: ʔo- 'neut.'
Attr. pref.: -kowah 'augment.'

811. konéoɔʔ 'Thanksgiving Dance', lit. 'people are covered with hide'
(p. 2)

Vb. base: vb. rt. -o- 'cover'; incorp. nn. rt. -né- 'hide, skin (?)'
Asp. suff.: -ɔ́- 'desc.'
Nn. suff.: -ʹʔ 'spl. nn. suff.' [26.4]
Obj. pref.: ko- 'fem.'

812. kanɛ:hwɛ́ʔko:wa:h 'Great Bowl Game'

Nn. rt.: -nɛɛhwɛ- (occurs only in this word)
Nn. suff.: -ʹʔ- 'spl. nn. suff.'
Subj. pref.: ka- 'neut.'
Attr. suff.: -kowah 'augment.'

813. ?atɔ:wɛ? 'Personal Chant'
See also **1, 7, 10, 11, 89, 127, 299, 300.**

(466)

See **10, 11, 35, 38, 809.**

(467)

See **1, 7, 10, 298, 563.**

(468)

See **11, 36, 40, 807, 808.**

(469)

814. tekaɛnókɛhkeh 'it is between the songs'

> Vb. base: vb. rt. -okɛ- 'be between'; incorp. nn. rt. -(C)ɛn- 'song'
> Nn. suff.: -'hkɛ́h 'ext. loc.' [26.4]
> Subj. pref.: -ka- 'neut.'
> Other pref.: te- 'dupl.'

See also **3, 10, 11, 38, 811.**

(470)

815. ?ɛwɔ:tɔ? 'it will become'

> Iden. with **529** except for mod. pref. ?ɛ- 'fut.'

See also **6, 153, 221, 688.**

(471)

816. ?ɔkwatyæ:?tahkɔ́:tye? 'we (pl.) are using it'

> Iden. with **90** except for addition of -atye- 'prog.' and -'? 'desc.'

817. ?ɔkwathyowíatye? 'we (pl.) are telling about it'

> Vb. base: vb. rt. -'(hy)owi- 'tell'; -at- 'refl.'
> Asp. suff.: -'Ø- 'desc.'; -atye- 'prog.'; -'? 'desc.'
> Obj. pref.: ?ɔkw- 'we (pl.)'

See also **1, 7, 10.**

(472)

See **1, 7, 10, 11, 35–37, 117.**

(473)

See **1, 3, 36, 89, 97, 226–228, 619.**

(474)

See **1, 3, 11, 30, 36, 40, 109, 159, 263, 316, 584, 585.**

(475)

See **1, 10, 11, 647, 648.**

(476)

818. wa:e⁷ 'he thought'

> Vb. rt.: -e- 'think'
> Asp. suff.: -⁷ 'punc.'
> Subj. pref.: -'∅- 'masc.'
> Mod. pref.: wa- 'indic.'

819. ⁷o⁷kyɛnɛ:ta⁷t 'I finished the creation'

> Vb. stem iden. with **622.**
> Subj. pref.: -k- '1st pers.'
> Mod. pref.: ⁷o⁷- 'indic.'

See also **2, 7, 171.**

(477)

See **1, 3, 10, 11, 38, 89, 355.**

(478)

See **6, 10, 11, 322, 324, 325.**

(479)

820. ⁷ɛyota⁷éɔɔ:k 'it will continually be covered by a veil'

> Iden. with **323** except for addition of -ak 'cont.' and of mod. pref. ⁷ɛ- 'fut.'

821. nɛtyoyé:ɔk 'how it will continually go, move'

> Iden. with **327** except for addition of -ak 'cont.' and of mod. pref. -ɛ- 'fut.'

822. ⁷ɛyotkahatɔ́:ɔk 'it will continue to revolve'

> Iden. with **328** except for addition of -ak 'cont.' and of mod. pref. ⁷ɛ- 'fut.'

See also **3, 10, 59, 326.**

(480)

823. ⁷ɛtyawehtɔ́:tye⁷ 'it will be coming from there'

> Vb. rt.: -eht- 'come from'
> Asp. suff.: -ɔ́- 'desc.'; -atye- 'prog.'; -'⁷ 'punc.'
> Obj. pref.: -yaw- 'neut.'
> Mod. pref.: ⁷ɛ- 'fut.'
> Prim. pref.: -t- 'cisloc.'
> Cf. **416.**

824. ⁷ɛyɛnɔhtɔ́:nyɔ:⁷ 'people will think'

> Iden. with **28** except for asp. suff. -⁷ 'punc.' and mod. pref. ⁷ɛ- 'fut.'

See also **3, 6, 11, 20, 27, 59, 116, 193.**

(481)

See **1, 7, 10, 11, 36, 89, 118, 145, 175, 354.**

(482)

825. te?ó?tɛ:h 'it is not that way'

Iden. with 47 except for *te-* 'neg.' in place of *ni-* 'part.'

826. ná:yo?ha:ste:k 'how strong it might continue to be'

Iden. with 369 except for mod. pref. *-aa-* 'opt.'

827. ta:kæ:wɛnye:? 'the wind might stir'

Iden. with 193 except for mod. pref. *-aa-* 'opt.'

828. ni:wa? 'how big it is'

Vb. rt.: *-a-* 'be of a certain size'
Asp. suff.: *-'?* 'desc.'
Subj. pref.: *-w-* 'neut.'
Sec. pref.: *ni-* 'part.'

829. twanɔkenyɔ? 'our (incl. pl.) abodes'

Vb. base: vb. rt. *-nɔke-* 'dwell together'; rt. suff. *-nyɔ-* 'dist.'
Asp. suff.: *-'?* 'desc.'
Subj. pref.: *twa-* 'our (incl. pl.)'

830. ?ɔkwé?ɔ:weh 'Indian(s)'

Iden. with 799 except for lack of attr. suff. *-kha?* 'charact.'

See also **6, 49, 81, 233.**

(483)

See **1, 6, 9, 12, 30, 47.**

(484)

See **3, 7, 10, 11, 136, 332–334.**

(485)

831. tsiɔwó:wi:atye? 'when they were telling him'

Vb. rt.: *-'(hy)owi-* 'tell'
Asp. suff.: *-'Ø-* 'desc.'; *-atye-* 'prog.'; *-'?* 'desc.'
Trans. pref.: *-'ɔwɔ-* [3.17] 'they . . . him'
Sec. pref.: *tsi-* 'coin.'

See also **84, 492, 494.**

(486)

832. hɔwéɔhse:h 'they said to him'

Vb. base: vb. rt. *-ɛɔ-* 'say'; rt. suff. *-'hse-* 'dat.'
Asp. suff.: *-h* 'desc.'
Trans. pref.: *hɔw-* 'they . . . him'

See also **7, 10, 11, 136, 333, 334, 498.**

(487)

See **6, 11, 42, 337.**

(488)

833. ʔɛyóʔhastɛh 'it will become strong'

Iden. with **352** except for mod. pref. *ʔɛ-* 'fut.'

See also **10, 11, 193, 203.**

(489)

See **3, 10, 11, 46, 81, 93, 333, 343, 344.**

(490)

See **1, 30, 36, 118, 567.**

(491)

834. twaɾka:thwas 'we (incl. pl.) see'

Iden. with **143** except for asp. suff. *-ás* 'iter.' and lack of mod. pref. *ʔe-* 'indic.'

835. ʔɔkwátæʔswi:yo:h 'our (pl.) good luck.

Vb. base: vb. rt. *-iyo-* 'be good'; incorp. nn. rt. *-atæʔsw-* 'luck'
Asp. suff.: *-h* 'desc.'
Obj. pref.: *ʔɔkw-* 'our (pl.)'

836. teʔa:wɛs 'it doesn't happen'

Iden. with **348** except for *te-* 'neg.' in place of *ni-* 'part.'

837. ʔɔkwákwɛ:ɔʔ 'our (pl.) spots, we are scattered here and there'

Vb. base: vb. rt. *-kwɛ́-* 'be in a particular spot'; rt. suff. *-ɔ-* 'dist.'
Asp. suff.: *-ʔ* 'desc.'
Obj. pref.: *ʔɔkwa-* 'our (pl.)'

See also **2, 6, 7, 10, 11, 49, 67, 81, 191, 348.**

(492)

838. ʔɛhni:wakwáihsiʔ 'we (incl. du.) shall attest to it'

Iden. with **347** except for subj. pref. *-hni-* 'we (incl. du.)'

Sec. also **6, 10, 11, 57, 89, 348.**

(493)

839. káiwakwɛni:yoʔ 'it is true'

Vb. rt.: *-kwɛniyo-* 'be the main one'; incorp. nn. rt. *-(C)i:wa-* 'matter' (together meaning 'be true')
Asp. suff.: *-ʔ* 'desc.'
Subj. pref.: *ka-* 'neut.'

See also **1, 7, 9, 36, 346.**

(494)

See **7, 10, 11, 332, 339, 340.**

(495)

840. sí:kwa:h 'in the direction away, too much'

    sih 'elsewhere' **(775)**
    Enclitic: *-kwah* 'toward'

841. thá:yoʔha:stɛh 'it wouldn't become strong'

    Vb. stem iden. with **833.**
    Obj. pref.: *-yo-* 'neut.'
    Mod. pref.: *-aa-* 'opt.'
    Sec. pref.: *th-* 'contr.'

842. ʔa:watkáhatɔh 'it would revolve'

    Iden. with **342** except for mod. pref. *ʔaa-* 'opt.'

See also **10, 49.**

(496)

See **1, 3, 6, 11, 175, 191, 331.**

(497)

See **1, 40, 62.**

(498)

See **1, 3, 11, 35, 36, 89, 226, 227, 228, 619.**

(499)

See **1, 3, 10, 11, 30, 36, 109, 159, 263, 316, 584, 585.**

(500)

See **1, 10, 11, 647, 648.**

(501)

843. ʔɛ́:niʔtyɔ:taʔk 'they (masc. pl.) will continue to dwell'

    Iden. with **356** except for lack of prim. pref. *-t-* 'cisloc.'

See also **7, 30, 36, 324, 325, 355, 671, 676.**

(502)

See **3, 6, 10, 59, 81, 358, 359.**

(503)

See **3, 6, 7, 10, 11, 30, 59, 173, 360, 675.**

(504)

See **1, 7, 10, 11, 89, 205, 296.**

(505)

844. ʔɛyakwathyónya:neʔ 'we (excl. pl.) are going to tell about it'

Iden. with **85** except for subj. pref. -*yakw*- 'we (excl. pl.)'

See also **7, 10, 11, 83, 84, 588, 671.**

(506)

845. ʔakhíhsɔ:t 'we (excl.) have them as grandparents'

Iden. with **364** except for trans. pref. *ʔakhi*- 'we (excl.) . . . them'

See also **1, 10, 11, 30, 365, 366, 729.**

(507)

See **7, 10, 11, 30, 36, 108, 112, 173, 360–362, 671, 677.**

(508)

846. ʔo:nɔnya:nɔtyéʔse:k 'they (nonmasc.) will always be making them'

Coll. for *ʔeonɔnya:nɔtyéʔse:k*
Vb. base: vb. rt. -*ɔnya*- 'make'; rt. suff. -*ʔ:nɔ*- 'dist.'
Asp. suff.: -*Ø*- 'desc.'; -*tye*- 'prog.'; -*ʔs*- 'iter.'; -*ek* 'cont.'
Obj. pref.: -*ʔon*- 'they (nonmasc.)'
Mod. pref.: *ʔɛ*- 'fut.'

See also **3, 10, 11, 46, 173, 671.**

(509)

See **30, 46, 186–188.**

(510)

847. ʔɛyonɔtɔʔseʔó:ɔk 'it will continue to be available to them (nonmasc.)'

Iden. with **115** except for obj. pref. -*yon*- 'they (nonmasc.)'

See also **3, 10, 46, 173, 184, 671.**

(511)

848. sheiwakéistani:h 'you gave them the responsibility'

Iden. with **392** except for trans. pref. *she*- 'you . . . them'

See also **1, 10, 30, 46, 176, 365, 366, 845.**

(512)

849. hesá:ah 'you took them there'

> Vb. rt.: -ʾ(h)a- 'take'
> Asp. suff.: -h 'desc.'
> Obj. pref.: -sa- '2d pers.'
> Other pref.: he- 'transloc.'

See also **7, 10, 11, 30, 36, 246, 285, 676.**

(513)

850. ʔa:kakwe:niʔ 'it might be possible'

> Iden. with **203** except for mod. pref. *ʔaa-* 'opt.'

851. ʔɔ:sayákohtɛ:tye:t 'it might kill people'

> Vb. base: vb. rt. *-ahtɛty-* 'travel'; rt. suff. *-et-* 'caus. II' (together, with
> repet., meaning 'kill')
> Asp. suff.: -Ø 'punc.'
> Obj. pref.: -yako- 'fem.'
> Mod. pref.: *ʔɔɔ-a-* 'opt.'
> Prim. pref.: -s- 'repet.'

See also **10, 11, 20, 41, 191.**

(514)

852. ʔá:yɔtka:thoʔ 'people might see'

> Iden. with **136** except for mod. pref. *ʔaa-* 'opt.'

853. niyoyaʔtánæ:ækwat 'how frightening it is'

> Vb. base: vb. rt. *-næækwáht-* 'be frightening, awe-inspiring'; incorp. nn.
> rt. *-yáʔta-* 'body'
> Asp. suff.: -Ø 'desc.'
> Obj. pref.: -yo- 'neut.'
> Sec. pref.: ni- 'part.'

See also **11, 30, 36.**

(515)

854. hotíto:ækɔh 'they (masc.) are holding it down'

> Vb. rt.: -lóæk- 'hold down'
> Asp. suff.: -óh 'desc.'
> Obj. pref.: hoti- 'they (masc.)'

See also **1, 6, 7, 10, 285, 848.**

(516)

See **1, 36, 100, 176, 277, 333, 436.**

(517)

See **1, 3, 36, 89, 226, 227, 619, 675.**

(518)

See **1, 3, 10, 11, 30, 36, 109, 159, 263, 316, 584, 585.**

(519)

See **1, 10, 11, 647, 648.**

(520)

855. no:tinɔ́ʔɛ:ɛtih 'on which side of their (masc.) heads'

Iden. with **378** except for obj. pref. -'*oti*- 'their (masc.)'

See also **3, 7, 10, 11, 20, 30, 36, 41, 376, 377, 671, 676.**

(521)

See **3, 7, 10, 11, 81, 355, 376, 671.**

(522)

See **3, 6, 10, 59, 81, 376, 382.**

(523)

856. to:hathéʔtɔ:ɔk 'he will continue to make it light'

Coll. for *teohathéʔtɔ:ɔk*
Vb. base: vb. rt. -*hathe*- 'be light'; rt. suff. -'*ʔt*- 'caus. I'
Asp. suff.: -ɔ́- 'desc.'; -*ak* 'cont.'
Obj. pref.: -'*o*- 'masc.'
Mod. pref.: -ɛ- 'fut.'
Other pref.: *t*- 'dupl.'

See also **3, 10, 36, 59, 81, 93, 170, 590.**

(524)

857. ʔethéhtahkwa:k 'he will always use it for coming from'

Vb. base: vb. rt. -*ehta*- 'come from'; rt. suff. -'*hkw*- 'inst.'
Asp. suff.: -Ø- 'iter.'; -*ak* 'cont.'
Subj. pref.: -*h*- 'masc.'
Mod. pref.: ʔɛ- 'fut.'
Prim. pref.: -*t*- 'cisloc.'
Cf. **384.**

See also **10, 11, 46, 109, 266, 385.**

(525)

858. ʔɛkayasɔ́:ɔk 'it will always be called'

>Vb. rt.: *-yas-* 'call'
>Asp. suff.: *-ɔ́-* 'desc.'; *-ak* 'cont.'
>Subj. pref.: *-ka-* 'neut.'
>Mod. pref.: *ʔɛ-* 'fut.'

See also **1, 3, 7, 10, 11, 398, 671.**

(526)

859. wáiwaye:is 'he does what he is supposed to'

>Vb. base iden. with **98.**
>Asp. suff.: *-Ø* 'punc.'
>Subj. pref.: *-ʹa-* 'masc.'
>Mod. pref.: *wa-* 'indic.'

See also **1, 6, 7, 30, 81, 89, 380, 381, 574.**

(527)

See **1, 10, 11, 20, 41, 57, 83–85, 671.**

(528)

See **1, 7, 10, 30, 386, 388, 396.**

(529)

860. hehsi:wakéistani:h 'you gave him the responsibility'

>Iden. with **392** except for trans. pref. *hehs-* 'you . . . him' (cf. **420**)

861. thaʔakwáiwayɛte:ih 'if we (excl. pl.) were only aware of it'

>Vb. base: vb. rt. *-yɛtei-* 'know'; incorp. nn. rt. *-(C)i:wa-* 'matter'
>Asp. suff.: *-h* 'desc.'
>Subj. pref.: *-ʔakwa-* 'we (excl. pl.)'
>Mod. pref.: *-a-* 'indic.' (anomalous before desc. [8.1])
>Sec. pref.: *th-* 'contr.'

See also **1, 7, 10, 11, 59, 97, 562, 578.**

(530)

862. ʔɔkwénɔhtɔʔ 'we (pl.) know'

>Vb. rt.: *-(ɛ)nɔ́htɔ-* 'know'
>Asp. suff.: *-ʹʔ* 'desc.'
>Obj. pref.: *ʔɔkw-* 'we (pl.)'

See also **1, 59, 97, 100, 191, 333, 379.**

(531)

863. ʔoʔtyakwatawɛnye:ʔ 'we (excl. pl.) move about'

> Iden. with **116** except for subj. pref. *-yakw-* 'we (excl. pl.)'

See also **2, 6, 10, 11, 81, 89, 93, 390.**

(532)

864. ʔoʔtáiɛ:h 'it is warm'

> Vb. rt.: *-aʔtaiɛ-* 'be warm'
> Asp. suff.: *-h* 'desc.'
> Obj. pref.: *ʔo-* 'neut.'

865. haiwayɛ́tahkɔh 'his responsibility'

> Iden. with **60** except for subj. pref. *ha-* 'masc.' (cf. **580**)

See also **10, 11, 46, 89, 145.**

(533)

866. ʔoʔwɛnɔtʃ́hɔhtɛ:tiʔ 'they (nonmasc. pl.) flourish'

> Vb. base iden. with **391.**
> Asp. suff.: *-tʔ* 'punc.'
> Subj. pref.: *-wɛn-* 'they (nonmasc. pl.)'
> Mod. pref.: *ʔoʔ-* 'indic.'

See also **10, 11, 36, 81, 89, 93, 108, 112, 362, 677, 767.**

(534)

See **1, 3, 10, 59, 97, 333, 389.**

(535)

867. hoiwayeistɔ́:tyeʔs 'he is doing what he should'

> Vb. base iden. with **98.**
> Asp. suff.: *-ɔ́-* 'desc.'; *-atye-* 'prog.'; *-ʔs* 'iter.'
> Obj. pref.: *ho-* 'masc.'

868. hehsíota:sʔɔh 'you gave him an assignment'

> Iden. with **101** except for trans. pref. *hehs-* 'you . . . him' (cf. **423**)

See also **1, 3, 36, 89, 97, 100, 226, 619.**

(536)

See **1, 3, 10, 11, 40, 584.**

(537)

See **3, 10, 11, 30, 36, 42, 109, 159, 263, 316, 585.**

(538)

See **1, 10, 11, 647, 648.**

(539)

See **7, 30, 36, 81, 381, 676.**

(540)

See **7, 10, 11, 36, 109, 279, 676.**

(541)

869. tɛyohathéhse:k 'it will always be light'

> Vb. rt.: -*hathe*- 'be light'
> Asp. suff.: -'*hs*- 'iter.'; -*ek* 'cont.'
> Obj. pref.: -*yo*- 'neut.'
> Mod. pref.: -*ɛ*- 'fut.'
> Other pref.: *t*- 'dupl.' (usual with this rt.)

870. ʔɛswɔ́tɛ:ɔnos 'it will make shade again'

> Vb. base: vb. rt. -*atɛ́ɔno*- 'be shady'; rt. suff. -'*st*- 'caus. I'
> Asp. suff.: -Ø 'punc.'
> Subj. pref.: -*w*- 'neut.'
> Mod. pref.: *ʔɛ*- 'fut.'
> Prim. pref.: -*s*- 'repet.'

See also **1, 2, 10, 11, 36, 81, 82, 109, 263.**

(542)

871. ʔɛyakoyaʔtáɛʔheʔse:k 'people will always rest', lit. 'their bodies will stop'

> Vb. base: vb. rt. -'(*h*)ɛ́ʔhe- 'stop'; rt. suff. -'ʔ- 'inch. I'; incorp. nn. rt. -*yáʔta*- 'body'
> Asp. suff.: -*s*- 'iter.'; -*ek* 'cont.'
> Obj. pref.: -*yako*- 'fem.'
> Mod. pref.: *ʔɛ*- 'fut.'

872. ʔɛwɔ́tɛ:ɔnos 'it will make shade'

> Iden. with **870** except for lack of -*s*- 'repet.'

See also **3, 7, 10, 11, 20, 41, 84, 671.**

(543)

873. haʔtɛskayɛ́taʔseʔ 'it will return to normal'

> Vb. base: vb. rt. -*yɛta*- 'put down, establish'; rt. suff. -'ʔs- 'trans.'
> Asp. suff.: -*ɛ́ʔ* 'purp.'
> Subj. pref.: -*ka*- 'neut.'
> Mod. pref.: -*ɛ*- 'fut.'
> Prim. pref.: -*s*- 'repet.'
> Other pref.: -*t*- 'dupl.'; *haʔ*- 'transloc.'

874. yeyá'tayɛtatye' 'people's bodies put down all along'

> Vb. base: vb. rt. *-yɛt-* 'put down'; incorp. nn. rt. *-yá'ta-* 'body'
> Asp. suff.: *-Ø-* 'desc.'; *-atye-* 'prog.'; *-'?* 'desc.'
> Subj. pref.: *ye-* 'fem.'

See also **3, 6, 7, 10, 11, 36, 675.**

(544)

See **1, 6, 10, 11, 52, 57, 337, 671.**

(545)

875. tayakohsóta'is 'people run into darkness there'

> Iden. with **404** except for mod. pref. *-a-* 'indic.'

See also **10, 11, 304, 403.**

(546)

876. 'ɛskǽːhkwaːa'k 'there will continue to be another orb'

> Vb. base: vb. rt. *-(C)æ-* [5.4]; incorp. nn. rt. *-(C)æhkwa-* 'sun, moon, orb'
> Asp. suff.: *-'?-* 'desc.'; *-k* 'cont.'
> Subj. pref.: *-kæ-* 'neut.'
> Mod. pref.: *'ɛ-* 'fut.'
> Prim. pref.: *-s-* 'repet.'

See also **1, 3, 7, 10, 11, 81, 376, 405, 671.**

(547)

See **3, 10, 11, 59, 176, 408, 409.**

(548)

877. tyakoyakɛ'ɔh 'people emerged from there'

> Vb. base: vb. rt. *-yakɛ-* 'emerge'; rt. suff. *-'?-* 'inch. I'
> Asp. suff.: *-ɔh* 'desc.'
> Obj. pref.: *-yako-* 'fem.'
> Prim. pref.: *t-* 'cisloc.'

See also **11, 20, 41, 81, 203, 432, 433.**

(549)

878. 'oiwayeistóːtye's 'it is performing its obligation'

> Vb. base iden. with **98.**
> Asp. suff.: *-ɔ-* 'desc.'; *-atye-* 'prog.'; *-'?s* 'iter.'
> Obj. pref.: *'o-* 'neut.'

See also **1, 6, 7, 11, 36, 89, 118.**

(550)

879. sɔ:ni:h 'you made it'

> Vb. rt.: -ɔ(:)ni- 'make'
> Asp. suff.: -h 'desc.'
> Subj. pref.: s- '2d pers.'

880. yeyá'tate' 'she is there'

> Iden. with **306** except for subj. pref. ye- 'fem.' (cf. **474**)

See also **1, 7, 10, 11, 81, 83, 176.**

(551)

881. nɛyakwaye:ha:k 'how we (excl. pl.) will always do it'

> Iden. with **367** except for subj. pref. -yakwa- 'we (excl. pl.)'

See also **6, 7, 10, 11, 30, 84, 388, 407, 671, 801, 845.**

(552)

882. koiwayeistó:tye's 'she is performing her obligation'

> Iden. with **878** except for obj. pref. ko- 'fem.'

See also **1, 7, 10, 11, 36, 89, 118.**

(553)

See **10, 11, 30, 36, 47, 59, 412, 413, 676.**

(554)

See **3, 6, 7, 10, 11, 59, 414, 676.**

(555)

883. nɛyakotkɛistó:tye' 'as people will be moving along'

> Iden. with **411** except for obj. pref. -yako- 'fem.'

See also **3, 6, 7, 10, 11, 20, 36, 59, 427, 675.**

(556)

See **1, 10, 30, 46, 176, 580.**

(557)

884. wɛnóthɔwi:sas 'the women'

> Vb. rt.: -athɔwis- 'be a woman' (cf. **655**)
> Asp. suff.: -ás 'iter.'
> Subj. pref.: wɛn- 'they (nonmasc. pl.)'

See also **6, 11, 30, 36, 79, 417, 657, 676, 823, 880.**

(558)

885. koti:wahtɛ́tya'tɔh 'she has carried out her responsibility'

> Vb. base: vb. rt. -*ahtɛtya*- 'travel, operate'; rt. suff. -'*ʔt*- 'caus. I'; incorp.
> nn. rt. -(C)*i:w*- 'matter, responsibility'; -*at*- 'refl.'
> Asp. suff.: -*ɔ́h* 'desc.'
> Obj. pref.: *ko*- 'fem.'

886. shéiɔta:sʔɔh 'you have given her an assignment'

> Iden. with **101** except for trans. pref. *she*- 'you . . . her'

See also **1, 36, 89, 98, 100, 118, 176.**

(559)

See **1, 7, 10, 11, 36, 40, 97, 98, 100, 333, 886.**

(560)

See **1, 3, 36, 89, 226, 227, 578, 619, 675.**

(561)

See **1, 3, 11, 30, 36, 40, 109, 159, 263, 316, 584, 585.**

(562)

See **1, 10, 35–37, 751, 808, 817.**

(563)

See **1, 7, 11, 35, 38, 81, 376.**

(564)

887. ʔɛkajistánohkwa:ɔʔ 'there will be speckles, stars in it'

> Vb. base: vb. rt. -(C)- 'put in'; rt. suff. -*ɔ*- 'dist.'; incorp. nn. rt. -*jista-
> nóhkwa*- 'speckles'
> Asp. suff.: -'*ʔ* 'punc.'
> Subj. pref.: -*ka*- 'neut.'
> Mod. pref.: *ʔɛ*- 'fut.'

See also **7, 10, 11, 84, 89, 782.**

(565)

See **3, 10, 11, 81, 376, 421.**

(566)

888. **ʔɛyakotyaʔtasyɔnyaʔtáhkɔ:ɔk** 'she will continually be clothed in it'

> Vb. base: vb. rt. *-ɔnya-* 'make'; rt. suff. *-ʔta-* 'caus. I', *-ʹhkw-* 'inst.'; incorp. nn. rt. *-asy-* 'clothing'; second incorp. nn. rt. *-yáʔt-* 'body'; *-at-* 'refl.'
> Asp. suff.: *-ɔ́-* 'desc.'; *-ak* 'cont.'
> Obj. pref.: *-yako-* 'fem.'
> Mod. pref.: *ʔɛ-* 'fut.'

889. **ʔɛyɔtotáhsiʔ** 'she will appear'

> Vb. base: vb. rt. *-otáhs-* 'bring to light'; *-at-* 'refl.' (together meaning 'appear')
> Asp. suff.: *-iʔ* 'punc.'
> Subj. pref.: *-y[ɔ]-* 'fem.'
> Mod. pref.: *ʔɛ-* 'fut.'

See also **3, 10, 30, 84, 365, 388, 407.**

(567)

890. **ʔoiwakɛ́istɔh** 'it is an obligation'

> Vb. base iden. with **392** except for lack of *-ni-* 'dat.'
> Asp. suff.: *-ɔ́h* 'desc.'
> Obj. pref.: *ʔo-* 'neut.'

See also **1, 176, 436.**

(568)

891. **hoiwayɛɔnyá:nɔʔ** 'he pointed them out'

> Vb. base: vb. rt. *-yɛɔnya-* 'point out'; rt. suff. *-ʹ:nɔ-* 'dist.'; incorp. nn. rt. *-(C)í:wa-* 'matter'
> Asp. suff.: *-ʹʔ* 'desc.'
> Obj. pref.: *ho-* 'masc.'

See also **11, 20, 41, 89, 427.**

(569)

892. **ʔɛyóhsɛnɔyɛ:tɔ:k** 'they will continue to have names'

> Iden. with **107** except for obj. pref. *-yo-* 'neut.'

893. **ʔɛyojihsɔ́ʔtæ:ʔk** 'the stars will continue to be in it'

> Vb. base: vb. rt. *-(C)æ-* 'put in'; incorp. nn. rt. *-jihsɔ́ʔta-* [5.4] 'star'
> Asp. suff.: *-ʹʔ-* 'desc.'; *-k* 'cont.'
> Obj. pref.: *-yo-* 'neut.'
> Mod. pref.: *ʔɛ-* 'fut.'

See also **10, 11, 30, 36, 38, 76, 106, 108.**

(570)

See **3, 10, 11, 20, 41, 724.**

(571)

See **6, 7, 10, 117, 176, 203, 428, 432.**

(572)

See **1, 10, 11, 36, 57, 59, 89, 100, 277, 423.**

(573)

See **1, 6, 7, 59, 416.**

(574)

894. ?ɛyoti:nekahsɔ́nye?se:k 'they (nonmasc.) will always savor the water'

    Iden. with **439** except for addition of *-ek* 'cont.' and of mod. pref. *?ɛ-* 'fut.'

See also **30, 36, 38, 108, 112, 127, 362.**

(575)

895. ?ɛwɔti:nékeha:k 'they (nonmasc. pl.) will always drink'

    Vb. rt. -': *neke-* 'drink'
    Asp. suff.: *-h-* 'iter.'; *-ak* 'cont.'
    Subj. pref.: *-wati-* 'they (nonmasc. pl.)'
    Mod. pref.: *?ɛ-* 'fut.'

See also **10, 11, 30, 36, 38, 89, 440.**

(576)

896. setéhjiah 'early in the morning'

897. ?etwatya?tákesko? 'we (incl. pl.) arise'

    Iden. with **179** except for mod. pref. *?e-* 'indic.'

898. teyaɔko:h 'it is wet'

    Vb. rt.: *-ɔko-* 'be wet'
    Asp. suff.: *-h* 'desc.'
    Obj. pref.: *-ya-* 'neut.'
    Other pref.: *te-* 'dupl.'

899. ?asté:kwa:h 'outside, outdoors'

    ?asteh 'outside'
    Enclitic: *-kwah* 'toward'

See also **1, 7, 10, 11, 89.**

(577)

900. ʔoʔa:yeʔ 'dew'

>   Nn. rt.: -ʔaye- 'dew'
>   Nn. suff.: -´ʔ 'spl. nn. suff.'
>   Obj. pref.: ʔo- 'neut.'

See also **10, 11, 89, 899.**

(578)

901. watí:neke:haʔ 'they (nonmasc. pl.) drink'

>   Iden. with **895** except for lack of -ak 'cont.' and of mod. pref. ʔɛ- 'fut.'

902. kajihsɔʔtáhsi:aʔ 'the stars are standing in array'

>   Iden. with **421** except for lack of -k 'cont.' and of mod. pref. ʔɛ- 'fut.'

See also **6, 10, 30, 89, 416, 436.**

(579)

See **1, 7, 36, 96, 100, 176, 277, 436.**

(580)

903. kɛɔnyɔʔ 'they are in it'

>   Vb. base: vb. rt. -(y)- 'put in'; rt. suff. -ɔ- 'dist.', -nyɔ- 'double dist.'
>   Asp. suff.: -´ʔ 'desc.'
>   Subj. pref.: kɛ- 'neut.'

904. kotɛnɔʔkæ:htashɛtáhkɔh 'people use it for measuring'

>   Iden. with **427** except for lack of -ak 'cont.' and of mod. pref. ʔɛ- 'fut.'

See also **11, 20, 41, 89, 153, 176, 226.**

(581)

See **1, 7, 10, 11, 30, 36, 38, 62, 89, 100, 427.**

(582)

See **1, 3, 30, 36, 89, 100, 118, 226, 277, 436, 619.**

(583)

See **1, 3, 10, 11, 40, 584.**

(584)

See **10, 11, 36, 42, 109, 159, 263, 316, 585.**

(585)

See **1, 2, 7, 30, 43, 586.**

(586)

905. ʔɔkwatɔʔeshɔnyɔ́:tyeʔ 'we (pl.) are being grateful'

>Vb. base: vb. rt. -ɔʔes- 'gratify'; rt. suff. -hɔ- 'dist.'; -nyɔ- 'double dist.';
>-at- 'refl.'
>Asp. suff.: -ʹØ- 'desc.'; -atye- 'prog.'; -ʹʔ 'desc.'
>Obj. pref.: ʔɔkw- 'we (pl.)'

See also **6, 7, 10, 35, 621, 808.**

(587)

See **1, 7, 10, 11, 20, 59, 89, 464, 465.**

(588)

See **7, 10, 11, 56, 466.**

(589)

See **7, 10, 11, 467–469.**

(590)

See **1, 6, 7, 10, 11, 47, 281, 317, 473, 474.**

(591)

See **10, 36, 42, 47, 322, 479.**

(592)

906. hotɔ́hɔhtɛ:tyɔ:h 'his life went on'

>Vb. base: vb. rt. -ahtɛty- 'travel, move on'; incorp. nn. rt. -ɔh- 'life';
>-at- 'refl.'
>Asp. suff.: -ɔh 'desc.'
>Obj. pref.: ho- 'masc.'

See also **30, 36, 46, 47.**

(593)

See **30, 36, 46, 47, 81, 93, 475.**

(594)

907. hatɔisyɔ́hkwaʔ 'he asks, prays, hopes'

>Vb. base: vb. rt. -ɔisyɔ́hkw- 'persist'; -at- 'refl.' (cf. **530**)
>Asp. suff.: -áʔ 'iter.'
>Subj. pref.: h- 'masc.'

See also **1, 7, 10, 11, 89.**

(595)

See **10, 11, 46, 477.**

(596)

908. hoʔníkɔɛʔ 'his mind'

>Iden. with **75** except for obj. pref. ho- 'masc.'

See also **1, 2, 6, 7, 35, 42, 47.**

(597)

909. shakótka⁷wɛh 'he left people'

> Iden. with **127** except for trans. pref. *shako-* 'he . . . people'

See also **11, 20, 41, 89, 399, 485.**

(598)

See **10, 11, 49, 274, 486–488.**

(599)

910. thiyotye:ɛh with **kwa⁷** 'it was not as it should be'

> Vb. base: vb. rt. *-ye-* 'do'; *-at-* 'refl.'
> Asp. suff.: *-ɛ́h* 'desc.'
> Obj. pref.: *-yo-* 'neut.'
> Sec. pref.: *thi-* 'contr.'

See also **191, 542.**

(600)

911. to⁷óiwato:kɛ:h 'it's not a straight matter, it might be better'

> Coll. for *te⁷óiwato:kɛ:h*
> Vb. base: vb. rt. *-tokɛ-* 'be straight'; incorp. nn. rt. *-(C)i:wa-* 'matter'
> Asp. suff.: *-h* 'desc.'
> Obj. pref.: *-⁷o-* 'neut.'
> Other pref.: *te-* 'neg.'

912. ⁷ɔ:takyɔ́⁷tak 'I might use it for entering'

> Vb. base: vb. rt. *-yɔ-* 'enter'; rt. suff. *-⁷⁷ta-* 'caus. I', *-⁷hkw-* 'inst.'
> Asp. suff.: *-∅* 'punc.'
> Subj. pref.: *-k-* '1st pers.'
> Mod. pref.: *⁷ɔɔ-a-* 'opt.'
> Prim. pref.: *-t-* 'cisloc.'

913. ⁷ɔ:sakhé:owi⁷ 'I might repeat it to them'

> Vb. rt.: *-⁷(hy)owi-* 'tell'
> Asp. suff.: *-⁷⁷* 'punc.'
> Trans. pref.: *-khe-* 'I . . . them'
> Mod. pref.: *⁷ɔɔ-a-* 'opt.'
> Prim. pref.: *-s-* 'repet.'

914. kheyátka⁷wɛh 'I left them'

> Iden. with **127** except for trans. pref. *khey-* 'I . . . them' (cf. **910**)

See also **1–3, 6, 10, 11, 20, 42, 818.**

(601)

915. hɔkweh 'man, male person'

> Nn. rt.: *-ɔkwe-* 'person'
> Nn. suff.: *-⁷h* 'spl. nn. suff.'
> Subj. pref.: *h-* 'masc.'

916. thakí:wayɛ:ni:h 'he is concentrating on me'

Vb. base: vb. rt. *-yɛ-* 'put down, establish'; rt. suff. *-ni-* 'dat.'; incorp. nn. rt. *-(C)i̜:wa-* 'matter'
Asp. suff.: *-h* 'desc.'
Trans. pref.: *-hak-* 'he . . . me'
Prim. pref.: *t-* 'cisloc.'

See also **30, 91, 92.**

(602)

See **1, 2, 6, 7, 30, 299, 456, 461, 490.**

(603)

917. hɔwɔowíatye:ʔ 'they were telling him'

Vb. rt.: *-ʾ(hy)owi-* 'tell'
Asp. suff.: *-ʾØ-* 'desc.'; *-atye-* 'prog.'; *-Ø-* 'desc.'; *-ʔ* 'past'
Trans. pref.: *hɔwɔ-* 'they . . . him'

See also **7, 10, 492–494.**

(604)

918. tyonɔ́hsate:kɛh 'Cornplanter village', lit. 'burnt house there'

Vb. base: vb. rt. *-atek-* 'burn'; incorp. nn. rt. *-nɔ́hs-* 'house'
Asp. suff.: *-ɛ́h* 'desc.'
Obj. pref.: *-yo-* 'neut.'
Prim. pref.: *t-* 'cisloc.'

919. tá:hsawɛʔ 'he began there'

Vb. rt.: *-ahsaw-* 'begin'
Asp. suff.: *-ɛ́ʔ* 'punc.'
Subj. pref.: *-ʾØ-* 'masc.'
Mod. pref.: *-a-* 'indic.'
Prim. pref.: *t-* 'cisloc.'

920. naʔoʔt 'such, such things'
See also **7, 10, 36, 42, 499, 917.**

(605)

See **11, 36, 497, 498.**

(606)

921. taohtɛtyɔ́:tyeʔ 'he traveled on (in this direction)'

Vb. rt.: *-ahtɛty-* 'travel'
Asp. suff.: *-ɔ́-* 'desc.'; *-atye-* 'prog.'; *-ʾʔ* 'desc.'
Obj. pref.: *-ʾo-* 'masc.'
Mod. pref.: *-a-* 'indic.'
Prim. pref.: *t-* 'cisloc.'

922. ka:oʔ 'this way'

923. nithawe:nɔ:h 'how he came'

> Vb. base: vb. rt. *-e-* 'go'; rt. suff. *-n-* 'direct.'
> Asp. suff.: *-ɔh* 'desc.'
> Obj. pref.: *-haw-* 'masc.'
> Prim. pref.: *-t-* 'cisloc.'
> Sec. pref.: *ni-* 'part.'

See also **1, 7, 10, 11, 89.**

(607)

924. nɔkhoh 'here'

925. héohtɛtyɔ:h 'he went, came from'

> Vb. rt. *-ahtɛty-* 'travel, go'
> Asp. suff.: *-ɔh* 'desc.'
> Obj. pref.: *-'o-* 'masc.'
> Other pref.: *he-* 'transloc.'

See also **6, 7, 59, 89, 565.**

(608)

See **1, 10, 11, 57, 89, 96, 389.**

(609)

926. ye:i? 'six'

927. ska:e? 'in the ten series'

See also **6, 7, 11, 249.**

(610)

928. waɛɔyákɛ?tak 'he labored'

> Vb. base: vb. rt. *-(y)ɔ́:yakɛ́?ta-* 'force to labor'; rt. suff.: *-'hkw-* 'inst.'
> Asp. suff.: *-Ø* 'punc.'
> Subj. pref.: *-'ɛ-* 'masc.'
> Mod. pref.: *wa-* 'indic.'

929. shako:wíatye?s 'he is telling people'

> Vb. rt.: *-'(hy)owi-* 'tell'
> Asp. suff.: *-'Ø-* 'desc.'; *-atye-* 'prog.'; *-'?s* 'iter.'
> Trans. pref.: *shako-* 'he . . . people'

930. shakónɔkshɔ? 'his kinsmen'

> Vb. rt.: *-nɔk-* 'be related'
> Asp. suff.: *-Ø-* 'desc.'
> Trans. pref.: *shako-* 'he . . . people'
> Attr. suff.: *-shɔ́?* 'plur.'

See also **10, 11, 35, 36, 42, 463.**

(611)

931. kanɔktiyóʔkeh 'at the good place, Onondaga Reservation'

> Vb. rt.: -*iyo*- 'be good'; incorp. nn. rt. -*nɔkt*- 'place, area, bed'
> Nn. suff.: -ʹ*ʔkéh* 'ext. loc.' [26.4]
> Subj. pref.: *ka*- 'neut.'

932. heoyaʔtyénɛʔɔh 'he collapsed there'

> Vb. base: vb. rt. -*yenɛ*- 'fall'; rt. suff. -ʹ*ʔ*- 'inch. I'; incorp. nn. rt. -*yáʔt*- 'body'
> Asp. suff.: -*ɔ́h* 'desc.'
> Obj. pref.: -ʹ*Ø*- 'masc.'
> Other pref.: *he*- 'transloc.'

See also **1, 6, 7, 10, 11.**

(612)

See **1, 7, 96, 97, 389.**

(613)

933. jɔkwatyǽːʔtahkɔh 'we (pl.) still use it'

> Iden. with **90** except for addition of prim. pref. [*j*]- 'repet.'

934. tethotwɛnéhtɔh 'he caused his words to fall here'

> Vb. base: vb. rt. -*ɛ*- 'fall'; rt. suff. -ʹ*ht*- 'caus. I'; incorp. nn. rt. -*wɛn*- 'word'; -*at*- 'refl.'
> Asp. suff.: -*ɔ́h* 'desc.'
> Obj. pref.: -*ho*- 'masc.'
> Prim. pref.: -*t*- 'cisloc.'
> Other pref.: *te*- 'dupl.'

See also **7, 10, 11, 35.**

(614)

See **1, 3, 6, 7, 10, 11, 30, 70, 74, 75, 102, 103, 494, 506, 507.**

(615)

See **1, 7, 35–38.**

(616)

See **3, 10, 11, 221, 299, 355.**

(617)

See **7, 10, 11, 15, 20, 30, 442.**

(618)

935. ʔoʔtyɔ́tɔɛjine:hsɔ:ʔ 'people cross the earth (at various times)'

 Vb. base: vb. rt. *-ine-* 'go, proceed', here 'cross'; rt. suff. *-hsɔ-* 'dist.';
  incorp. nn. rt. *-ɔɛj-* 'earth'; *-at-* 'refl.' (usual with this vb. rt.)
 Asp. suff.: *-ʔ* 'punc.'
 Subj. pref.: *-y[ɔ]-* 'fem.'
 Mod. pref.: *ʔoʔ-* 'indic.'
 Other pref.: *-t-* 'dupl.'

See also **116.**

(619)

See **7, 10, 11, 81, 446–448.**

(620)

936. taʔa:kakwe:niʔ 'it might be impossible'

 Coll. for *teʔa:kakwe:niʔ*
 Vb. rt.: *-kweny-* 'be possible'
 Asp. suff.: *-iʔ* 'punc.'
 Subj. pref.: *-ka-* 'neut.'
 Mod. pref.: *-ʔaa-* 'opt.'
 Other pref.: *te-* 'neg.'

937. koyaʔtoská?ah 'people alone'

 Iden. with **444** except for obj. pref. *ko-* 'fem.'

938. ta:yakotawɛnyé:ak 'people might continue to move about'

 Iden. with **577** except for mod. pref. *-aa-* 'opt.'

See also **7, 10, 11, 49.**

(621)

See **10, 11, 20, 41, 59, 191, 450, 452.**

(622)

939. ʔɛkatɛhɔ́ʔshɛ:ʔ 'I shall have help'

 Vb. base iden. with **355.**
 Asp. suff.: *-ʔ* 'punc.'
 Subj. pref.: *-k-* '1st pers.'
 Mod. pref.: *ʔɛ-* 'fut.'

See also **1, 7, 10, 11, 38, 221, 299, 442.**

(623)

940. hakɔiwakɛ́istani:h 'he gave them the responsibility'

 Iden. with **392** except for trans. pref. *hakɔ-* 'he . . . them'

941. hɔwɛnɔtkáɛɔʔ 'they watch them'

 Vb. rt.: *-atkáɛɔ-* 'watch'
 Asp. suff.: *-ʔʔ* 'desc.'
 Trans. pref.: *hɔwɛn-* 'they . . . them'

942. tɛyɔ́khisnye:k 'they will continue to look after us'

Iden. with **458** except for trans. pref. *-yɔkhi-* 'they . . . us'

See also **1, 10, 11, 15, 30, 36, 108, 176, 456.**

(624)

See **1, 10, 30, 36, 96, 100, 118, 176, 277, 436.**

(625)

943. ʔɛtwáka ʔɛ:yɔ:ʔ 'we (incl. pl.) shall notice it'

Vb. rt.: *-kaʔɛyɔ-* 'notice'
Asp. suff.: *-ʔ* 'punc.'
Subj. pref.: *-twa-* 'we (incl. pl.)'
Mod. pref.: *ʔɛ-* 'fut.'

944. ʔatyéɔshæ ʔ 'accident'

Nn. base: vb. rt. *ʔatyeɔ-* 'happen accidentally'; *-shæ-* 'nom.'
Nn. suff.: *-ʔɛʔ* 'spl. nn. suff.'

See also **10, 11, 89, 124, 453.**

(626)

945. teyókɛshɔʔ 'it is between (several things)'

Vb. rt.: *-okɛ-* 'be between'
Asp. suff.: *-∅-* 'desc.'
Subj. pref.: *-y-* 'neut.'
Other pref.: *te-* 'dupl.'
Attr. suff.: *-shɔ̃ʔ* 'plur.'

946. hwa ʔɔkhí:atye ʔ 'they are taking us', with **945** 'leading us'

Vb. rt.: *-ʔ(h)a-* 'take'
Asp. suff.: *-ʔ∅-* 'desc.'; *-atye-* 'prog.'; *-ʔɛʔ* 'desc.'
Trans. pref.: *-ʔɔkhi-* 'they . . . us'
Mod. pref.: *-wa-* 'indic.'
Other pref.: *h-* 'transloc.'

947. ʔaetwɛnɔ̃htɔnyɔ:ʔ 'we (incl. pl.) ought to think'

Iden. with **69** except for asp. suff. *-ʔ* 'punc.' and addition of mod. pref.
ʔae- 'opt.'

See also **1, 10, 11, 27, 91, 92, 95.**

(627)

See **1, 6, 7, 36, 61, 62, 100, 277, 423.**

(628)

See **1, 3, 89, 97, 117, 226, 227, 619.**

(629)

See **1, 3, 10, 11, 30, 36, 109, 159, 191, 263, 316, 584, 585.**

(630)

See **1, 10, 11, 20, 38, 40, 116, 118, 515, 751, 817.**

(631)

See **30, 170, 422, 481, 513.**

(632)

948. niká:wiˀs 'where it brings it'

    Vb. rt.: -ʹ(h)awi- 'carry, bring'
    Asp. suff.: -ʹʔs 'iter.'
    Subj. pref.: -ka- 'neut.'
    Sec. pref.: ni- 'part.'

949. hetwa:yɔˀ 'we (incl. pl.) have arrived there'

    Vb. rt.: -yɔ- 'arrive'
    Asp. suff.: -ʹʔ 'desc.'
    Subj. pref.: -twa- 'we (incl. pl.)'
    Other pref.: he- 'transloc.'

See also **1, 2, 6, 7, 10, 36, 103, 183.**

(633)

See **3, 6, 7, 11, 15, 20, 38, 510, 587.**

(634)

See **6, 11, 30, 67, 377, 508, 509.**

(635)

950. ˀɛyɔ́tɔˀe:shɔ:ˀ 'people will repeatedly be grateful'

    Iden. with **135** except for lack of -nyɔ- 'double dist.'

See also **3, 6, 11, 15, 510, 516.**

(636)

951. ˀɛyakothyówi:ak 'people will continue to tell about it'

    Vb. base: -at-hyowi- 'tell about' (cf. **85**)
    Asp. suff.: -ʹØ- 'desc.'; -ak 'cont.'
    Obj. pref.: -yako- 'fem.'
    Mod. pref.: ʔɛ- 'fut.'

See also **10, 11, 36, 170, 191, 587.**

(637)

952. ˀetwáiwaye:is 'we (incl. pl.) do as we should'

    Iden. with **690** except for subj. pref. -twa- 'we (incl. pl.)'

953. sweʔɔh 'you (pl.) decided'

> Iden. with 38 except for obj. pref. *sw-* 'you (pl.)' (cf. **671**)

954. hetwawɛnɔkwe:kɔh 'all our (incl. pl.) words'

> Iden. with 534 except for subj. pref. *-twa-* 'our (incl. pl.)'

See also **1, 7, 11, 30, 67, 533.**

(638)

955. ʔetwáthyo:wiʔ 'we (incl. pl.) told about it'

> Vb. base: *-at-hyowi-* 'tell about' (cf. **85**)
> Asp. suff.: *-ʼʔ* 'punc.'
> Subj. pref.: *-tw-* 'we (incl. pl.)'
> Mod. pref.: *ʔe-* 'indic.'

956. nyo:yɛnoʔtɛʔhéʔɔh 'what he created'

> Coll. for 808.

957. ʔatwɛnɔta:kshæʔ 'hope'

> Nn. base: vb. rt. *-tak-* (occurs only in this word); incorp. nn. rt. *-wɛnɔ-*
> 'voice, word'; *ʔat-* 'refl.'; *-shæ-* 'nom.'
> Nn. suff.: *-ʼʔ* 'spl. nn. suff.'

See also **10, 191, 512, 583.**

(639)

See **1, 43, 66, 191, 217.**

(640)

See **10, 11, 27, 30, 69, 298, 564.**

(641)

See **1, 3, 6, 7, 10, 11, 35, 36, 70, 71, 74, 75, 102, 103, 506, 524.**

(642)

See **1–4, 30, 952.**

(643)

See **11, 30, 67, 533, 953, 954.**

(644)

958. haʔtékyaʔti:h 'I myself'

> Vb. stem iden. with **32.**
> Subj. pref.: *-k-* '1st pers.'
> Other pref.: *-te-* 'dupl.'; *haʔ-* 'transloc.'

959. katɔ́ʔeshɔ:nyɔh 'I am grateful'

Vb. base iden. with **135.**
Asp. suff.: -ʹh 'iter.'
Subj. pref.: k- '1st pers.'

960. kɛnɔ́htɔnyɔh 'I think'

Iden. with **28** except for subj. pref. k- '1st pers.'

See also **1, 10, 11, 27, 30, 36, 67, 738.**

(645)

961. ʔeswe:ʔ 'you (pl.) decided'

Vb. rt.: -e- 'decide'
Asp. suff.: -ʔ 'punc.'
Subj. pref.: -sw- 'you (pl.)'
Mod. pref.: ʔe- 'indic.'

962. tɛktaʔt 'I shall stand up'

Vb. base: vb. rt. -ta- 'stand'; rt. suff. -ʹʔ- 'inch. I'
Asp. suff.: -t 'punc.'
Subj. pref.: -k- '1st pers.'
Mod. pref.: -ɛ- 'fut.'
Other pref.: t- 'dupl.'

See also **6, 30, 36, 67, 590.**

(646)

See **81, 84, 814.**

(647)

See **6, 512, 533, 954.**

(648)

963. tekwánɔ:ɔnyɔh 'I thank you (pl.)'

Vb. rt.: -nɔ́ɔnyɔ- 'thank'
Asp. suff.: -ʹh 'iter.'
Trans. pref.: -kwa- 'I . . . you (pl.)'
Other pref.: te- 'dupl.'

964. swǽ:ʔseshɛʔ 'you (pl.) are in opposite moieties'

Vb. stem iden. with **531** (-æǽʔse- except after n)
Obj. pref.: sw- 'you (pl.)'

965. swatí:ɔt 'you (pl.) Faith Keepers'

Iden. with **532** except for obj. pref. sw- 'you (pl.)'

See also **1, 3, 6, 11, 30, 36, 533–535, 961.**

(649)

966. jǽ:ʔseshɛʔ 'you (du.) are in opposite moieties'

Iden. with **964** except for obj. pref. j- 'you (du.)'

967. kaɛnɔ? 'song'

> Nn. rt.: -(C)ɛnɔ- 'song'
> Nn. suff.: -'ʔ 'spl. nn. suff.'
> Subj. pref.: ka- 'neut.'

See also 1–3, 30, 60.

(650)

See 6, 7, 10, 11, 35, 58, 76.

(651)

968. shɔkwayaʔtæ:kwáɔ? 'he chose several of us (pl.)'

> Vb. base: vb. rt. -(C)æ- 'put in'; rt. suff. -kwa- 'oppos. I', -'ɔ- 'dist. I';
>   incorp. nn. rt. -yáʔta- 'body'
> Asp. suff.: -'ʔ 'desc.'
> Trans. pref.: shɔkwa- 'he . . . us (pl.)'

969. ʔɛyɔkwayɛʔheʔɔ́:ɔk 'we (pl.) shall continue to learn'

> Vb. base: vb. rt. -yɛ(C)- 'know'; rt. suff. -'ʔhêʔ- 'inch. I'
> Asp. suff.: -ɔ́- 'desc.'; -ak 'cont.'
> Obj. pref.: -yɔkwa- 'we (pl.)'
> Mod. pref.: ʔɛ- 'fut.'

See also 11, 15, 42, 67, 422, 481.

(652)

970. jiɛnɔkwe:nyɔ:h 'you (du.) are able to do the songs'

> Vb. base: vb. rt. -kweny- 'be able'; incorp. nn. rt. -(C)ɛnɔ- 'song'
> Asp. suff.: -ɔh 'desc.'
> Subj. pref.: ji- 'you (du.)'

971. nikaɛnóʔtɛ:h 'the kind of songs they are'

> Vb. base: vb. rt. -óʔtɛ- 'be of a certain kind'; incorp. nn. rt. -(C)ɛn- 'song'
> Asp. suff.: -h 'desc.'
> Subj. pref.: -ka- 'neut.'
> Sec. pref.: ni- 'part.'

See also 1, 30, 233, 767, 811, 966.

(653)

972. ʔesní:waye:is 'you (du.) did as you should'

> Iden. with 690 except for subj. pref. -sni- 'you (du.)'

973. teʔkanó:ɔ? 'it is not difficult', here 'you didn't make it difficult'

> Vb. rt.: -noɔ- 'be difficult'
> Asp. suff.: -'ɔ́ʔ 'iter.'
> Subj. pref.: -ka- 'neut.'
> Other pref.: teʔ- 'neg.'

974. wa'etsiyέ'nyata:t 'they extended their hands to you (nonsg.)'

Vb. base: vb. rt. -*t*- 'be in place'; rt. suff. -*at*- 'caus. II'; incorp. nn. rt. -*'nya*- 'hand'; -*ε*- 'refl.'
Asp. suff.: -*∅* 'punc.'
Trans. pref.: -*'etsiy*- 'they . . . you (nonsg.)'
Mod. pref.: *wa*- 'indic.'

See also **1, 10, 11, 49, 84.**

(654)

See **1, 3, 10, 11, 40, 698.**

(655)

975. wa'étsiejεɔnyɔ:' 'they encourage you (nonsg.)'

Vb. base: vb. rt. -*'(h)ejεɔ*- 'encourage'; rt. suff. -*nyɔ*- 'dist.'
Asp. suff.: -*'* 'punc.'
Trans. pref.: -*'etsi*- 'they . . . you (nonsg.)'
Mod. pref.: *wa*- 'indic.'

976. nɔ:yo'tέɔtye' 'how it might be'

Vb. rt.: -*ó'tε*- 'be a certain way'
Asp. suff.: -*'∅*- 'desc.'; -*atye*- 'prog.'; -*'*' 'desc.'
Subj. pref.: -*y*- 'neut.'
Mod. pef.: -*aa*- 'opt.'
Sec. pref.: *n*- 'part.'

977. ji'níkɔε' 'your (du.) minds'

Iden. with **75** except for obj. pref. *ji*- 'your (du.)'

978. nεsháti'nyatatye' 'how they will be extending their hands'

Vb. base: -*t*- 'be in place'; incorp. nn. rt. -*'nya*- 'hand'
Asp. suff.: -*∅*- 'desc.'; -*atye*- 'prog.'; -*'*' 'desc.'
Subj. pref.: -*hati*- 'they (masc. pl.)'
Mod. pref.: -*ε*- 'fut.'
Prim. pref.: -*s*- 'repet.'
Sec. pref.: *n*- 'part.'

979. jiyá'tate' 'your (du.) bodies are present'

Iden. with **306** except for subj. pref. *ji*- 'your (du.)'

See also **6, 10, 11, 30, 36, 40, 52, 336, 498, 557, 973.**

(656)

980. hoiwihsá'hɔ' 'the things he completed'

Vb. base: vb. rt. -*ihsá'*- 'complete'; rt. suff. -*hɔ*- 'dist.'; incorp. nn. rt. -(*C*)*i:w*- 'matter'
Asp. suff.: -*'*' 'desc.'
Obj. pref.: *ho*- 'masc.'

981. sakáiwayɛta:theʔt 'it becomes your responsibility again'

> Vb. base: vb. rt. *-yɛta-* 'establish'; rt. suff. *-t-* 'caus. II', *-héʔ-* 'inch. I';
> incorp. nn. rt. *-(C)i:wa-* 'matter'
> Subj. pref.: *-ka-* 'neut.'
> Mod. pref.: *-a-* 'indic.'
> Prim. pref.: *s-* 'repet.'

982. tó:tiʔkwah 'however many'

983. nɛskaɛnókeʔheʔt 'how many songs there will still be'

> Vb. base: *-ake-* 'be separate entities'; rt. suff. *-ʔhéʔ-* 'inch. I'; incorp·
> nn. rt. *-(C)ɛn-* 'song'
> Asp. suff.: *-t* 'punc.'
> Subj. pref.: *-ka-* 'neut.'
> Mod. pref.: *-ɛ-* 'fut.'
> Prim. pref.: *-s-* 'repet.'
> Sec. pref.: *n-* 'part.'

984. netwátkwe:niʔ 'as much as we (incl. pl.) are able'

> Vb. base: vb. rt. *-kweny-* 'be able'; *-at-* 'refl.'
> Asp. suff.: *-iʔ* 'punc.'
> Subj. pref.: *-tw-* 'we (incl. pl.)'
> Mod. pref.: *-e-* 'indic.'
> Sec. pref.: *n-* 'part.'

985. tetwawɛni:tkɛʔt 'we (incl. pl.) speak'

> Vb. base iden. with **621.**
> Asp. suff.: *-t* 'punc.'
> Subj. pref.: *-twa-* 'we (incl. pl.)'
> Mod. pref.: *-e-* 'indic.'
> Prim. pref.: *t-* 'cisloc.'

See also 1–3, 6, 7, 10, 11, 35, 36, 74, 75, 108, 198, 751, 767.

Excerpts

(657)

986. ʔoyéʔkwaʔɔ:weh 'native tobacco, Indian tobacco'

> Vb. base: vb. rt. *-ʔɔ(:)we-* 'be native'; incorp. nn. rt. *-yéʔkwa-* 'tobacco'
> Asp. suff.: *-ʼh* 'desc.'
> Obj. pref.: *ʔo-* 'neut.'

987. waʔakwatyǽ:ʔtak 'we (excl. pl.) use it'

> Vb. base iden. with **90.**
> Asp. suff.: *-Ø* 'punc.'
> Subj. pref.: *-ʔakw-* 'we (excl. pl.)'
> Mod. pref.: *wa-* 'indic.'

See also 1, 3, 10, 11, 205.

(658)

See 1, 6, 7, 10, 11, 30, 74, 81, 104, 145, 323, 329, 670.

(659)

988. ʔoʔkáyɛʔkweotɛʔ 'the smoke rises'

Vb. base: vb. rt. -ot- 'stand upright'; incorp. nn. rt. -yɛ́ʔkwa(æ)- [14.4] 'smoke'
Asp. suff.: -ɛ́ʔ 'punc.'
Subj. pref.: -ka- 'neut.'
Mod. pref.: ʔoʔ- 'indic.'

See also **1, 3, 10, 11, 205, 986.**

(660)

See **10, 11, 30, 109, 191, 316, 584.**

(661)

989. nɔ:taka:te:k 'it might continue to be at such a level'

Vb. rt.: -te- 'be in place'
Asp. suff.: -∅- 'desc.'; -k 'cont.'
Subj. pref.: -ka- 'neut.'
Mod. pref.: -ɔɔ-a- 'opt.'
Prim. pref.: -t- 'cisloc.'
Sec. pref.: n- 'part.'

990. nɔ:yɔkwaʔnikɔiyostahkɔ́:ɔk 'we (pl.) might be content'

Vb. base iden. with **175.**
Asp. suff.: -ɔ́- 'desc.'; -ak 'cont.'
Obj. pref.: -yɔkwa- 'we (pl.)'
Mod. pref.: -aa- 'opt.'
Sec. pref.: n- 'part.'

See also **6, 11, 42, 145, 191.**

(662)

991. ʔakwɛ́nɔhtɔ:nyɔh 'we (excl. pl.) think'

Iden. with **28** except for subj. pref. ʔakw- 'we (excl. pl.)'

See also **6, 11, 27, 30, 36, 95, 145, 191, 354.**

(663)

See **1, 3, 6, 7, 11, 59, 74, 109, 191, 316, 336, 498, 584, 670.**

(664)

See **1, 2, 7, 10, 35–38, 76, 82, 89, 819.**

(665)

See **1–3, 6, 7, 10, 11, 49, 191, 316, 317, 443.**

(666)

992. ʔɛkésyɔ:niʔ 'I shall make it'

    Vb. rt.: -ʹsyɔ(:)ni- 'make, fix, prepare'
    Asp. suff.: -iʔ 'punc.'
    Subj. pref.: -ke- '1st pers.'
    Mod. pref.: ʔɛ- 'fut.'

See also **1, 7, 10, 11, 81, 82, 193, 317.**

(667)

See **1, 6, 7, 10, 11, 322–328.**

(668)

993. ʔotatɔ:ni:h 'it forms'

    Iden. with **329** except for lack of prim. pref. t- 'cisloc.'

See also **1, 2, 6, 11, 15, 16, 27, 69, 145.**

(669)

See **6, 11, 15, 38, 46, 74, 145, 175, 191, 330, 331, 459.**

(670)

See **1, 2, 9, 12, 205, 296.**

(671)

See **7, 10, 11, 42, 136, 332–334, 498.**

(672)

See **6, 10, 52, 81, 193, 337, 341, 448.**

(673)

994. ʔɛkaiwáhtɔʔt 'it will destroy'

    Iden. with **349** except for mod. pref. ʔɛ- 'fut.'

995. koʔníkɔ:iyo:h 'people are content'

    Iden. with **350** except for obj. pref. ko- 'fem.'

996. kokwɛ́:ɔnyɔʔ 'people's property, the spots where people are'

    Vb. base: vb. rt. -kwɛ́- 'be in a particular spot'; rt. suff. -ɔ- 'dist.'; -nyɔ-
    'double dist.'
    Asp. suff.: -ʹʔ 'desc.'
    Obj. pref.: ko- 'fem.'
    Cf. **837.**

997. niyɔkwaʔníkoʔtɛ:h 'the way our (pl.) minds are'

    Iden. with **463** except for obj. pref. -yɔkwa- 'our (pl.)'

See also **1, 6, 7, 10, 11, 42, 46, 81, 93, 333, 343, 344.**

(674)

998. ʔɛtwátkathoʔ 'we (incl. pl.) will see it'

> Vb. rt.: *-atkathw-* 'see'
> Asp. suff.: *-óʔ* 'punc.'
> Subj. pref.: *-tw-* 'we (incl. pl.)'
> Mod. pref.: *ʔɛ-* 'fut.'

999. nɔʔtkakɛːseːʔ 'how it scrapes'

> Vb. rt.: *-kɛse-* 'scrape'
> Asp. suff.: *-ʔ* 'punc.'
> Subj. pref.: *-ka-* 'neut.'
> Mod. pref.: *-aʔ-* 'indic.'
> Sec. pref.: *n-* 'part.'
> Other pref.: *-t-* 'dupl.'

See also **1, 2, 6, 7, 9–12, 89, 343, 346, 348, 454, 472, 996.**

(675)

1000. taʔaetwakweːniʔ 'we (incl. pl.) might not be able'

> Coll. for *teʔaetwakweːniʔ*
> Vb. rt.: *-kweny-* 'be able'
> Asp. suff.: *-iʔ* 'punc.'
> Subj. pref.: *-twa-* 'we (incl. pl.)'
> Mod. pref.: *-ʔae-* 'opt.'
> Other pref.: *te-* 'neg.'

1001. ʔáetwatkaːthoʔ 'we (incl. pl.) might see it'

> Iden. with **998** except for mod. pref. *ʔae-* 'opt.'

1002. nɔ́ːyoʔhaːstɛh 'how strong it might become'

> Iden. with **341** except for mod. pref. *-aa-* 'opt.'

1003. takæːwɛːnyeːʔ 'the wind stirs there'

> Iden. with **353** except for lack of *-t-* 'dupl.' and addition of *t-* 'cisloc.'

1004. naːyɔkwatoweːhtak 'how it might harm us (pl.)'

> Vb. stem iden. with **345.**
> Obj. pref.: *-yɔkwa-* 'us (pl.)'
> Mod. pref.: *-aa-* 'opt.'
> Sec. pref.: *n-* 'part.'

See also **1, 7, 11, 36, 42, 49, 67, 118, 226, 835.**

(676)

1005. ʔɛtwatɔʔéshɔnyɔːk 'we (incl. pl.) shall continue to be grateful'

> Vb. base: vb. rt. *-ɔʔes-* 'gratify'; rt. suff. *-hɔ-* 'dist.', *-nyɔ-* 'double dist.';
> *-at-* 'refl.'
> Asp. suff.: *-Ø-* 'desc.'; *-k* 'cont.'
> Subj. pref.: *-tw-* 'we (incl. pl.)'
> Mod. pref.: *ʔɛ-* 'fut.'

See also **1, 6, 7, 11, 27, 42, 61, 62, 67, 69, 191.**

(677)

1006. tyotá'eoɔh 'it is covered with a veil there'

    Iden. with **323** except for addition of prim. pref. *t-* 'cisloc.'

See also **1, 3, 6, 7, 11, 30, 70, 74, 75, 192, 104, 145.**

(678)

See **1, 2, 7, 38.**

(679)

See **10, 11, 30, 36, 93, 318.**

(680)

1007. nɛtka:te:k 'how much will continue to be present there, how strong it will be'

    Iden. with **331** except for addition of *-k* 'cont.' and of mod. pref. *-ε-* 'fut.'

See also **6, 46, 191.**

(681)

1008. tha:yakótowe:htak 'it won't harm people'

    Vb. base iden. with **345.**
    Asp. suff.: *-Ø* 'impv.' [25.4]
    Obj. pref.: *-yako-* 'fem.'
    Mod. pref.: *-aa-* 'opt.'
    Sec. pref.: *th-* 'contr.'

See also **42, 95, 473.**

(682)

See **1, 6, 47, 59.**

(683)

1009. tewáktatye' 'it is near all along', here 'surrounding us'

    Vb. rt.: *-akt-* 'be near'
    Asp. suff.: *-Ø-* 'desc.'; *-atye-* 'prog.'; *-'?* 'desc.'
    Subj. pref.: *-w-* 'neut.'
    Other pref.: *te-* 'dupl.'

See also **30.**

(684)

1010. nitwáte'ha:stɔ' 'how strong things are there'

    Vb. base: vb. rt. *-'hast-* 'be strong'; rt. suff. *-ɔ-* 'dist.'; *-ate-* 'refl.'
    Asp. suff.: *-'?* 'desc.'
    Subj. pref.: *-w-* 'neut.'
    Prim. pref.: *-t-* 'cisloc.'
    Sec. pref.: *ni-* 'part.'

See also **1, 6, 59, 840.**

(685)

See **6, 11, 20, 42, 345.**

(686)

See **601, 602.**

(687)

1011. ʔɔkwákwɛ:ɛʔ 'our (pl.) spots' (cf. **837**)

    Vb. rt.: -*kwɛ́ɛ*- 'be in a particular spot'
    Asp. suff.: -*ʔ* 'desc.'
    Obj. pref.: *ʔɔkwa*- 'our (pl.)'

1012. tyɔkwéʔɔ:weh 'we (incl. pl.) Indians'

    Iden. with **830** except for subj. pref. *ty*- 'we (incl. pl.)'

See also **6, 30, 57, 81.**

(688)

1013. thikɛɔh 'less'

1014. ʔaikɛ:h with **1013** 'to a lesser degree'

1015. nikáyɛthaʔ 'how it strikes'

    Vb. rt.: -*yɛ́ht*- 'strike'
    Asp. suff.: -*háʔ* 'iter.'
    Subj. prof.: -*ka*- 'neut.'
    Sec. pref.: *ni*- 'part.'

See also **1, 6, 11, 36, 42, 145, 354, 840.**

(689)

1016. ʔóiwaʔ 'thing, matter'

    Nn. rt.: -*(C)i:wa*- 'matter'
    Nn. suff.: -*ʔ* 'spl. nn. suff.'
    Obj. pref.: *ʔo*- 'neut.'

See also **1, 3, 10, 205.**

(690)

See **7, 10–12, 46, 89.**

(691)

1017. twatatɔ:nih 'it forms there'

    Iden. with **329** except for subj. pref. -*w*- 'neut.'

See also **30, 36, 42, 81, 145.**

(692)

See **7, 10, 11, 233, 323.**

(693)

See **1, 6, 36, 42, 145, 329, 448.**

(694)

1018. ʔɛtwatyɛ:nɔ:niʔ 'we (incl. pl.) shall do it properly'

    Vb. stem iden. with **102.**
    Subj. pref.: -*tw*- 'we (incl. pl.)'
    Mod. pref.: *ʔɛ*- 'fut.'

See also **1, 10, 11, 75.**

(695)

1019. ʔoʔtitwanɔ́:nyɔ:ʔ 'we (incl. pl.) thank'

    Iden. with **104** except for subj. pref. -*twa*- 'we (incl. pl.)'

See also **1, 2, 10, 30, 36, 74, 75, 81, 145, 448, 997.**

BIBLIOGRAPHY

CASWELL, H. S.
1892. Our life among the Iroquois Indians. Boston.
CHAFE, W. L.
1960–61. Seneca morphology. Internat. Journ. Amer. Linguistics, vols. 26–27.
CONKLIN, H. C., and STURTEVANT, W. C.
1953. Seneca Indian singing tools at Coldspring longhouse. Proc. Amer. Philos. Soc., vol. 97, pp. 262–290.
CONVERSE, H. M.
1930. The Seneca New Year and other customs. Indian Notes, vol. 7, pp. 69–83.
FENTON, W. N.
1936. An outline of Seneca ceremonies at Coldspring longhouse. Yale Univ. Publs. Anthrop. No. 9. New Haven.
1941. Tonawanda longhouse ceremonies: Ninety years after Lewis Henry Morgan. Bur. Amer. Ethnol. Bull. 128, Anthrop. Pap. No. 15, pp. 139–166.
1947. Seneca songs from Coldspring longhouse. Program notes to Album 17, Folk music of the United States, Libr. Cong. Collect. Archives Amer. Folk Song.
1951. Introduction: The concept of locality and the program of Iroquois research. In Symposium on local diversity in Iroquois culture, ed. by W. N. Fenton. Bur. Amer. Ethnol. Bull. 149, pp. 1–12.
1953. The Iroquois Eagle Dance, an offshoot of the Calumet Dance. Bur. Amer. Ethnol. Bull. 156.
FENTON, W. N., and KURATH, G. P.
1951. The Feast of the Dead, or Ghost Dance, at Six Nations Reserve, Canada. In Symposium on local diversity in Iroquois culture, ed. by W. N. Fenton. Bur. Amer. Ethnol. Bull. 149, pp. 139–165.
HALE, H.
1885. The Iroquois sacrifice of the white dog. Amer. Antiq. and Or. Journ., vol. 7, pp. 7–14.
HEWITT, J. N. B.
1928. Iroquoian cosmology, second part, with introduction and notes. Bur. Amer. Ethnol. Ann. Rep., 1925–26, vol. 43, pp. 449–819.
KURATH, G. P.
1951. Local diversity in Iroquois music and dance. In Symposium on local diversity in Iroquois culture, ed. by W. N. Fenton. Bur. Amer. Ethnol. Bull. 149, pp. 109–137.
MORGAN. L. H.
1901. League of the Ho-dé-no-sau-nee or Iroquois. Ed. by H. M. Lloyd. 2 vols. New York.
PARKER, A. C.
1913. The Code of Handsome Lake, the Seneca prophet. New York State Mus. Bull. 163.
SHIMONY, A. A.
———. Conservatism at Six Nations Reserve. MS., Ph. D. dissertation, Yale Univ., 1958.
SPECK, F. G.
1949. Midwinter rites of the Cayuga longhouse. Philadelphia.

RECORDED VERSIONS OF THE THANKSGIVING RITUALS

The following is an attempt to cite all published, manuscript, and tape recorded versions of the Thanksgiving Speech, Thanksgiving Dance, and Tobacco Invocation. Reasonably complete summaries of the items in the Thanksgiving sequence are included. The dates refer to the year of performance, not of publication. The collector is given in parentheses. All tapes will ultimately be deposited in the New York State Museum, Albany, with copies in the Bureau of American Ethnology.

ALLEGANY RESERVATION.

1940. Thanksgiving speech by Sherman Redeye. MS., Seneca and English (Fenton).

1945. Thanksgiving speech by Albert Jones. Disc recording in Library of Congress, Archives of American Folk Song, No. 8080 (Fenton).

1947. Thanksgiving dance by Chauncey Johnny John and Albert Jones. Seneca and English (abbreviated). Published disc recording. In Fenton, 1947, pp. 6–10.

1948. Thanksgiving speech by Sherman Redeye. Tape (Fenton).

1949 a. Tobacco invocation from Green Corn Ceremony by Sherman Redeye. Tape (Fenton).

1949 b. Tobacco invocation from New Year's Ceremony by Sherman Redeye. Tape (Fenton).

CATTARAUGUS RESERVATION.

Ca. 1860. Tobacco invocation by Silverheels. English summary. In Caswell, 1892, pp. 219–220.

1896. Thanksgiving dance. MS., Seneca and English (Hewitt). Bur. Amer. Ethnol. Archives No. 2315.

1906 a. Thanksgiving dance. English. In Parker, 1913, pp. 94–100.

1906 b. Tobacco invocation. English. In Parker, 1913, pp. 85–94.

1956. Thanksgiving speech by Solon Jones. Tape (Chafe). See pp. 142–145.

TONAWANDA RESERVATION.

Before 1851. Tobacco invocation. English. In Morgan, 1901, vol. 1, pp. 210–1133. Copied in Converse, 1930, vol. 7, pp. 78–80.

1959 a. Thanksgiving dance by Corbett Sundown. Tape (Chafe). Transcribed in full in this work.

1959 b. Thanksgiving speech by Corbett Sundown. Tape (Chafe). Transcribed in full in this work.

1959 c. Thanksgiving speech by Corbett Sundown. Tape (Chafe). See pp. 140–143.

1960. Tobacco invocation by Corbett Sundown. Tape (Chafe). See pp. 140–141.

GRAND RIVER RESERVE.

Before 1885. Tobacco invocation by George Buck, Onondaga. English summary. In Hale, 1885, pp. 10–12.

1900. Thanksgiving speech by John Arthur Gibson. Onondaga and English. In Hewitt, 1928, pp. 568–570.

1930's. Thanksgiving sequence used by Alexander General, Sour Springs Cayuga. Terminology in Cayuga and English. In Speck, 1949, p. 30.

1948. Thanksgiving speech by Alexander General. MS., Cayuga and English (Lounsbury).

Mid–1950's. Thanksgiving speech by Alexander General, Sour Springs Cayuga. English with interpolated commentary. In Shimony, MS., pp. 254–267.